Decolonising Science, Technology, Engineering and Mathematics (STEM) in an Age of Technocolonialism:
Recentring African Indigenous Knowledge and Belief Systems

Edited by
Artwell Nhemachena, Nokuthula Hlabangane & Joseph Z. Z. Matowanyika

Langaa Research & Publishing CIG
Mankon, Bamenda

Publisher
Langaa RPCIG
Langaa Research & Publishing Common Initiative Group
P.O. Box 902 Mankon
Bamenda
North West Region
Cameroon
Langaagrp@gmail.com
www.langaa-rpcig.net

Distributed in and outside N. America by African Books Collective
orders@africanbookscollective.com
www.africanbookscollective.com

ISBN-10: 9956-551-86-4

ISBN-13: 978-9956-551-86-6

About the Authors

Artwell Nhemachena holds a PhD in Social Anthropology. In addition to having a good mix of social science and law courses in his undergraduate studies, he also has a Certificate in Law and a Diploma in Education. He has lectured in Zimbabwe before pursuing his PhD studies in South Africa. His current areas of research interest are Knowledge Studies; Development Studies; Environment; Resilience; Food Security and Food Sovereignty; Industrial Sociology; Agnotology, Sociology and Social Anthropology of Conflict and Peace; Transformation; Sociology and Social Anthropology of Science and Technology Studies, Democracy and Governance; Relational Ontologies; Decoloniality and Anthropological /Sociological Jurisprudence. He has published over 80 book chapters and journal articles in accredited and peer-reviewed platforms. He has also published over eighteen books in accredited and peer reviewed platforms. At the University of Namibia, he lectures, and chairs the Faculty of Humanities and Social Sciences Seminar Series on Researching, Writing and Publishing. Artwell Nhemachena is also a Research Fellow in the College of Humanities of the University of South Africa. He is also an active member of the Council for the Development of Social Science Research in Africa (CODESRIA).

Joseph Z. Z. Matowanyika is a Professor at the Chinhoyi University of Technology where he is the Director of the Institute of Lifelong Learning and Development Studies. He holds a PhD in Geography from the University of Waterloo, Canada; MA in Environmental Planning for Developing Countries, University of Nottingham, UK; BA Honours Degree in Geography from Reading University UK; and a Postgraduate Diploma in Planning Management & Evaluation of Rural Development Projects from the Pan-African Institute for Development, Eastern & Southern Africa, in Kabwe, Zambia.

Olúwọlé Tẹ́wọ́gboyè Òkéwándé has been lecturing in the Department of Linguistics and Nigerian Languages, University of Ilorin, Ilọrin, Nigeria since 1998. His research interests include the fields of African religions, semiotics, stylistics and culture. His Doctoral Thesis, "A semiotic investigation of links between *Ifá, Ìbejì* and *Ayò Ọlọpọn*" is a study that establishes *Ifá's* relationship with *Ayò Ọlọpọn* and *Ìbejì* around codes, symbols, icons and indices. He has published in reputable local, national and international journals.

David O. Akombo (dakombo@hotmail.com) is Faculty Fellow in the College of Liberal Arts at Jackson State University (Jackson, MS). Having engaged in cultural research in Kenya, Southeast Asia, and the United States, his research interests include: cultural identity and Afrocentricity issues in choral and instrumental music; multicultural music education; ethnomusicology; community music; teaching and learning theory; music technology; psychology of music; and quantitative research in music and biomedical sciences. Some of his publications include: *The Unity of Music and Dance in World Cultures* (2016), *Music and Medicine: Connections Found* (2009), *Music and Healing Across Cultures* (2006), and *Uwenzi: The Pan-African Factor, A 21st-Century View* (2015). Dr. Akombo's academic background includes a BA – Education from Kenyatta University, an MA – Ethnomusicology from Bowling Green State University and a PhD - Music Education from the University of Florida.

Pearl S. Gray (psgray@aol.com) is an independent scholar. She formerly served as an Associate Professor and the Chair of Education at Edward Waters College (Jacksonville, FL), where she was a member of the Ujuzi Group, the College think tank, and its component lecture series, the Wakaguzi Forum. Dr. Gray's academic background includes an undergraduate degree (BA) in Sociology (Wilberforce University), a Master's degree (MAT) in Teaching (Antioch-Putney University), and a Doctorate (PhD) in Social Foundations of Education & Cultural Anthropology (Oregon State University). She has participated in numerous seminars, conferences, and panel discussions. Her scholarship efforts include numerous papers (e.g., *Africa, Jatropha Seeds, and Biofuel* 2007). Her research interests include West African oral tradition, women's issues, teacher education, affirmative action, and applications of multicultural education to school curricula.

George O. Griffin (georgegriffin2003@yahoo.com) is currently the Communications Professor at Keiser University (Orlando, FL) as well as an Adjunct Professor of Communications at Stetson University (Deland, FL). He formerly served as an Assistant Professor and Interim Chair of Communications at Edward Waters College (Jacksonville, FL), where he was also a member of the College think tank, Ujuzi Group. Prof. Griffin's academic background includes a BA - Speech/English/Education from the University of West Florida and an MA - Communication Arts from Auburn University. He authored *STAGE FRIGHT! A Student-Friendly Guide to Managing the Jitters* (2008) and was lead author and editor of *Effective Public Speaking: A Top Hat Interactive Text* (2016).

Baruti I. Katembo (ufundi320@yahoo.com) is a mathematics faculty member in the Departments of Adult Education and Mathematics at Florida State College at Jacksonville (Jacksonville, FL). He is the author of several article and book publications, including "Africa, Seeds, and Biofuel" (2007) and *UWENZI: The Pan-African Factor, a 21st Century View* (2015). Prof. Katembo's academic background includes undergraduate and graduate degrees from North Carolina A & T State University (BSIE; MS – Applied Mathematics) and North Carolina State University (MLArch). His primary research interests are numeracy, resource usage and sociotechnology.

Martin Mujinga (PhD) is a Research Fellow in the Department of Systematic Theology and Ecclesiology of the University of Stellenbosch. He has published in peer-reviewed journals and presented papers at regional and international platforms. Currently he is a lecturer of Christian Theology and Christian History and Thought at United Theological College, Harare, Zimbabwe. He can be contacted at martrinmujinga@gmail.com, martinmujinga@icloud.com, +263 772 207 033, +236 716 402 119.

Okewande Esther Oyeniwe holds Degrees of Bachelor and Master of Science Education in Chemistry. She is currently a PhD student in the Department of Science Education, University of Ilorin, Nigeria. Her teaching career in both secondary and post-secondary schools spans over seventeen years. She has several local, national and international publications.

Maria B. Kaundjua teaches Sociology at the University of Namibia. She holds a Masters Degree in Population and Development Studies. She is involved in research on sexual and reproductive health, demographic studies, climate change, environmental health and development. She has published a number of journal articles.

Robert Matikiti holds a PhD in Systematic Theology, a Masters Degree in Systematic Theology (1992), Honours Degree in Religious Studies (1990) and a Graduate Certificate in Education (1994), all with the University of Zimbabwe. He also holds a National Diploma in Computer Studies with Masvingo Polytechnic. The title of his PhD thesis is *Christian Theological Perspectives on Political Violence in Zimbabwe: The Case of The United Church of Christ in Zimbabwe.* His PhD thesis addresses the challenges of political violence in Zimbabwe. The thesis explores the political dimensions affecting humanity. He previously taught Political Theology and African Theology at Masvingo State University, Zimbabwe Open University and University of Zimbabwe for many years. He is the author of a number of articles and the recent books *Christian Faith and Cultural Justice* and *Theology and Political Violence: The Church at The Devil's Throne in Zimbabwe?* Dr Matikiti's research interests include transitional justice, ecology, human rights and social development. He is a board member of the Zimbabwe Combined Residents and Rate Payers Association (ZICORRA). He is an active member in community development issues in Zimbabwe. He is currently a lecturer in Systematic Theology at Christ College of Zimbabwe.

Nokuthula Hlabangane was awarded a PhD in Anthropology in 2012 by the University of the Witwatersrand, South Africa. Her Doctoral thesis is entitled: "The Political Economy of Teenage Sexuality in the Time of HIV/AIDS: The Case of Soweto, South Africa". Her research interests include knowledge and power. So far, her research interests have directed her towards home – she chooses to be a student in her own community – the reasons have been both ideological and practical. Her ethics are about redress and restoration and as such she has vested interest in decolonising Anthropology (and the academy at large) by painting pictures of strength and resilience where others have left bleak images of savagery and inferiority. Her research practices shy away from delving into descriptions of the mundane-made-exotic. Rather, she attempts to interpret micro-practices through macro-systems. Her thinking is informed by decolonial meditations that place a responsibility for African(ist) intellectuals to see Africa from within. She also gravitates towards transdisciplinarity in her work. Hlabangane teaches at the University of South Africa.

Collins Nhengu is a lecturer in Religion and Ethics at Goshen Bible Institute in Harare, Zimbabwe. He is a PhD student at the University of KwaZulu Natal, in South Africa. The title of his thesis is 'A Theological Exposition of the Interface Between the Ministry of The Zimbabwe Council of Churches and the Experience of Civil Rights in Murewa District in Zimbabwe (2000-2018). The thesis interrogates the interaction between Faith-Based Organisations and political players in Zimbabwe. It focuses on issues that relate to the Ministry of The Zimbabwe Council of Churches (ZCC) in human rights issues in Zimbabwe. His line of research is mainly about church state relations in Zimbabwe. He is deeply committed to the idea of the church being involved in the political arena in Zimbabwe. The church has been taking a backstage and there is need for the church to be the light of the world. Nhengu is a holder of a Diploma in Theology from Goshen Bible Institute, Post Graduate Diploma in Education from the Zimbabwe Open University (ZOU). He holds a Bachelor of Arts General Degree in Religious Studies, Bachelor of Arts Special Honours Degree in Political Theology, Master's Degree in Political Theology, all from the University of Zimbabwe. He lectured at Goshen Bible Institute, Living Waters Theological Seminary. Collins Nhengu was Registrar at National Education College, a teacher of Old Testament Studies as well as New Testament survey. Nhengu is also an associate pastor of a fast-growing church, in the city of Harare, that teaches the authority of the Word of God.

Babarinsa Olayiwola Isaac is a full-time mathematics lecturer at Federal University Lokoja, Nigeria, and he was a part-time mathematics lecturer at University of London (international programme) – Centre for Law and Business. He obtained his Doctor of Philosophy (PhD.) in Linear Algebra at University Sains Malaysia (USM), Postgraduate Diploma in Education (P.G.D.E.) at National Open University of Nigeria (NOUN), Master of Science (M.Sc.) and Bachelor of Science (B.Sc.) degree in Mathematics and Statistics respectively at University of Lagos (UNILAG), and National Diploma (N.D.) in Textile Technology at Yaba College of Technology (YABATECH). During his doctoral program at USM, he was a USM's ambassador and a Graduate Assistant for two years where he tutored undergraduate students of diverse cultures and backgrounds (Malays, Chinese and Indians) in Linear Algebra and Calculus. He is an enthusiastic, confident presenter and passionate lover of mathematics with nine years of quality teaching experience. He can impart complex information to learners of different levels. He has several publications in Scopus and ISI WoS, and he has attended many conferences (local and international), receiving awards for the presentations. He has professional qualifications in Nigerian Institute of Management, Teachers Registration Council of Nigeria, Institute for Operations Research of Nigeria, and Nigerian Institute of Industrial Statisticians.

Siqabukile Ndlovu is a lecturer in the Department of Computer Science at the National University of Science and Technology, Bulawayo in Zimbabwe. She holds a Master's Degree in Computer Science. Her research interests are in the fields of Data Science/Big Data, Software Engineering and Machine Learning. She is a registered Technovation mentor and coach who teaches and motivates young girls to solve problems in their communities using modern ICTs technology. Siqabukile has published work in various journals and she has attended several conferences.

Sindiso M. Nleya received a BSc degree in Applied Physics and the MSc degree in Computer Science from the National University of Science and Technology (NUST), Bulawayo in Zimbabwe - in 2003 and 2007 respectively. He completed his PhD in 2016 at the

University of Cape Town in South Africa. He is currently a lecturer in the Department of Computer Science at the National University of Science and Technology. His research interests focus on ICTs for Development, on Dynamic spectrum, access, game theory, and optimization techniques.

Email: sindiso.nleya@nust.ac.zw

Sibongile Nyoni is a senior mathematics lecturer at Mkoba teachers' College in Gweru, Midlands Province in Zimbabwe. She holds Bachelor and Masters degrees in mathematics education. She is currently studying for a PhD with the Central University of Technology (CUT), South Africa. Nyoni's thesis topic is on the preparation of teachers in handling mathematically gifted learners. Her research interests are on teacher education, improving the teaching and learning of mathematics and motivating learners in the learning of mathematics.

Munyonga Alex is a Philosophy of Science senior lecturer at Mkoba Teachers College in Gweru, Zimbabwe. He holds a Master of Arts Degree in Philosophy and is working on a PhD in Environmental Ethics. He also assists the Catholic University of Zimbabwe in lecturing ethics and applied ethics courses. Alex has contributed a book chapter entitled, 'The Death Penalty Law in the Context of Xenophobic Attacks in South Africa, 2008 and 2018'. The book was edited by Fainos Mangena and Jonathan Okeke –Mpi Chimakonam and published by Venom Press, 2018. Munyonga has also contributed a chapter entitled, 'Land (Dis) Possession and Environmental Destruction in Zimbabwe: A Critical Reflection of Events Since the Beginning of the 21st Century', in a book edited by Artwell Nhemachena and Munyaradzi Mawere and published by Langaa (2019). Munyonga has research interests in Environmental Ethics, Social Ethics, Neo-Colonial issues and African Indigenous Knowledge Systems. He also enjoys academic debates and presentations.

Table of Contents

Chapter One: Centuries-old Colonial/
Imperial Denialism of African Originality:
An Introduction to Decolonising
STEM in Africa 1
Artwell Nhemachena & Joseph Z. Z. Matowanyika

Chapter Two: Relationality or
Hospitality in Indigenous
Knowledge Systems? Big Data, Internet
of Things and Technocolonialism in Africa 63
*Artwell Nhemachena, Nokuthula Hlabangane
& Maria Kaundjua*

Chapter Three: Global Coloniality
Through Science and Technology:
The Theft of African Traditional Medicine 99
Alex Munyonga

Chapter Four: Audit of Mathematical
Concepts in Pre-colonial Africa 125
Sindiso M. Nleya & Siqabukile Ndlovu

Chapter Five: African Indigenous
Knowledge Systems of Mathematics
and Science: Insights from the Faculties
of Ifá among the Yorùbá of Nigeria................................ 151
Olúwọlé Tẹ̀wọ́gboyè Òkèwándé

Chapter Six: 'We Know Our Africans':
Missionaries as Torchbearers of the
Colonisation in Zimbabwe... 175
Robert Matikiti

Chapter Seven: Algebra in African
Indigenous History 199
Babarinsa Olayiwola

Chapter Eight: Circularity in Msonge
and Music: African Genius or Just
"Primitivism"?.. 213
David O. Akombo; Pearl S. Gray;
George O. Griffin & Baruti I. Katembo

Chapter Nine: Liberating African Theology
from Misfooted Eurocentric Theologisation 237
Martin Mujinga

Chapter Ten: Pentecostalism and the
Suppression of African Indigenous Religion:
The Rejection of African Spiritism in the
Apostolic Faith Mission (AFM) in Zimbabwe 257
Collins Nhengu

Chapter Eleven: Mathematics, Circularity
and the Msonge as African Heritages................................. 283
Baruti I. Katembo

Chapter Twelve: African Indigenous Science
as a Solution for Students' Underachievement
in Science Education: Insights from Nigeria 297
Okewande Esther Oyeniwe

Chapter Thirteen: Decolonising
Mathematics in Africa.. 311
Sibongile Nyoni

Chapter One

Centuries-old Colonial/Imperial Denialism of African Originality: An Introduction to Decolonising STEM in Africa

Artwell Nhemachena & Joseph Z. Z. Matowanyika

The consequences of policies based on views such as these can be fatal. Thabo Mbeki's denial that HIV caused AIDS prevented thousands of HIV positive mothers in South Africa receiving anti-retrovirals so that they, unnecessarily transmitted the disease to their children (Diethelm & Mckee, 2009).

...but colonialism denial is real and useful because it serves colonialism present; it serves the primary purpose of the Conservative government today, which is to push through resource extraction projects – many of which are in direct contradiction with Indigenous peoples – at all costs (O'Keefe, 23 October 2013).

Introduction

Although there is a lot of literature condemning denialism of AIDs (Acquired Immuno-deficiency Syndrome) and castigating climate change denialism (Jylhan, 2016; Washington, 2011; Lewandowsky *et al.*, 2015; Diethelm & Mckee, 2009; Smith & Novella, 2007; Moore, 2009; Kalichman *et al.*, 2010; Kalichman, 2014; Nattrass, 2011; Mckee, 2010; Chigwedere & Essex, 2010), there is virtually no literature condemning colonialism/imperialism denialists. For instance, AIDs denialists have been condemned as denying the existence of AIDs; as claiming that HIV is harmless; as undermining HIV prevention; as associated with poor health outcomes; as causing unnecessary deaths by undermining HIV testing, prevention, and treatment; and as offering false hope to people living with HIV/AIDS (Diethelm & McKee, 2009; Smith & Novella, 2007; Moore, 2009; Kalichman *et al.*, 2010; Kalichman, 2014; Nattrass, 2011). On the other hand, there is barely any literature condemning colonialism/imperialism denialism and genocide denialism that have been perpetrated against indigenous people of Africa and other continents. Typical of other forms of denialism, colonialists/imperialists and their lackeys have denied responsibility for colonialism, they deny that colonialism has continued beyond the notional independence granted to Africans/indigenous people; they deny that colonialism/imperialism has injured indigenous people; they deny that colonialism/imperialism has any victims and they have condemned their condemners (Wyatt & Brisman, 2017). In this regard, if denialism is bad in climate change and in HIV and AIDs matters, it is also bad to engage in colonialism/imperialism denialism. Wyatt & Brisman (2017: 330) write about colonial denialism of biopiracy thus:

> While intellectual property regimes are necessary for technological growth, Western institutions perpetuate and legitimate the exploitation of indigenous knowledge through a biased global patent system…The existence of globalised legal patent systems is a key part of how corporations construct their denial of any wrongdoing in cases where uncompensated and unrecognised indigenous knowledge has resulted in patented profitable products. The power of corporations also enables them to deny biopiracy…Part of this denial is enabled by the global governance system that allows the patenting of this knowledge and thus legitimises theft. Denying that indigenous communities have some intellectual property over their centuries of practices is a human right violation that has cultural, financial and environmental impacts.

Redefined as oppression and domination, colonisation becomes naturalised in the sense of assuming the veil of nature wherein some animals are more dominant than others. If places can be described as colonised by bacteria or pathogens, and if plant-growth can be described as colonising particular places; and if even ants can be described as colonising their habitat, colonisation becomes naturalised and human colonists become harder to separate from nature and hence to apprehend. Conversely, defining colonisation in terms of dispossession, plunder, looting and biopiracy (theft of indigenous knowledge), this book shies away from definitions of colonisation that would, via naturalisation, ironically serve to dissipate the possibilities of decolonisation. Thus, defining decolonisation in terms of reversals of processes of dispossession, plunder, looting and biopiracy, the book conceives colonisation as the anthropogenic process of cursing the colonised with absence/deficits, rather than generating presence or positivity in the same. Because colonisation is about dispossession, plunder, looting and biopiracy, it should be understood as the process of cursing with negativity. Since decolonisation is about reversing the colonial dispossession, plunder, looting and biopiracy, it should be understood as the process of generating/re-calling presence and positivity in the sense of seizing and regenerating that which has been made absent. Thus, defining colonisation in terms of domination, hierarchy and oppression erroneously presupposes that it is essentially about presence. The point here is that redefining colonisation in terms of presence and constructivism follows logics of underhand plea bargaining wherein someone who has actually stolen or robbed another person pleads that he/she has brought something constructive to the victim of the crime. It is a form of denialism wherein the perpetrator denies harm to the victim of colonialism/imperialism by pleading that the victim has benefited, *albeit* from crumps off the crimes.

Africans who are the original owners of land and other resources, including indigenous knowledge, were dispossessed, robbed and exploited by colonialists who also engaged in biopiracy of indigenous knowledge. Put differently, Africans are the original owners that had ownership, mastery, authority and dominion over African patrimony, including tangible and intangible heritages. Colonialists negated and subverted African mastery; they subverted African ownership, order, hierarchy, authority/authorship and dominion over African heritages/patrimonies. In this regard, postcolonial theorists who critique and deconstruct African mastery, domination, patrimony, authority, ownership and hierarchies are effectively replicating colonial subversions and thus deepening the (re)colonisation of Africans. The point here is that one cannot decolonise by deconstructing African mastery, ownership, dominion, authority/authorship and hierarchies. One can only decolonise by enhancing and promoting African ownership, mastery and dominion over patrimonies, and by enhancing African authority and the attendant authorship (Nhemachena, 2018; Nhemachena *et al.,* 2018). The point here is that decolonial projects that decentre Africans in the guise of opposing African hierarchy, domination and authority constitute neocolonial sleights of hand. To decolonise Africa entails recentring Africans as the owners or masters of African material resources and of indigenous knowledge, including indigenous science, technology and engineering. To decolonise Africa entails recentring Africans as owners and masters or as having dominion and domination over African patrimony or heritages for which they should be compensated by those that are looting and plundering them. To argue that Africans do not have rights to dominion (control/rule) or domination (mastery) amounts to denying Africans autonomy and sovereignty over their resources, including land, minerals, indigenous science, technology, mathematics and engineering. Put succinctly, African opposition to African domination and authority constitutes opposition to African mastery and authorship more broadly. For Africans to be decentred from mastery, dominion, authority and authorship over their heritages is not *ipso facto* to be decolonised; in fact, to be decentred and deconstructed is to be colonised such that one then loses authorship, dominion and mastery over one's patrimony.

Thus, in biopiracy African authorship, authority and mastery are denied by Euro-American institutions, individuals and corporations that steal African indigenous knowledge; in biopiracy African dominion and domination or mastery over their heritages is negated (Wyatt & Brisman, 2017). In fact, Africans are unfortunately made to believe that having indigenous hierarchies, dominions, domination, authority, authorship and mastery is bad. To goad Africans to deconstruct their own authorship, mastery, domination and authority, Eurocentric scholars and institution, often writing in the guise of postcolonialism, misdefine colonialism in terms of authority, domination, hierarchy and mastery. For this reason, Africans are gradually losing sight of the fact that colonisation is essentially about dispossession, looting, plunder, biopiracy, robbery, theft of African tangible and intangible resources. Instead of fighting against neocolonial dispossession, plunder, looting, robbery and biopiracy that are going on in relation to African resources, Africans are increasingly erroneously fighting their own domination, mastery, authority and authorship over their heritages. To become an author, one needs to have authority, dominion, domination (mastery), hierarchy, order and structure yet these are the very things or aspects that postcolonial Africans are slyly goaded to deconstruct in the erroneous belief that they are fighting or deconstructing colonialism. The point here is that colonialism did not necessarily bring about domination (mastery), dominion, hierarchy, authority and authorship – rather colonialism brought about colonial plunder, disorder, looting, robbery, dispossession and biopiracy which negate African originality. Postcolonialists who have erroneously defined colonialism in terms of imposition of domination, hierarchy, binaries, dichotomies, order, purity, structure and authority have effectively missed the constitutive essence of colonialism at the centre of which are colonial robbery, dispossession, looting, plunder and biopiracy. To put it in other words, Africa is not originally colonised through the imposition of order, structure, hierarchy, mastery, authority, binaries and dichotomies – rather, Africa is colonised through imperial dispossession, robbery, plunder and biopiracy which continue in this twenty-first century. Indigenous domination, mastery, authority, authorship, binaries/dichotomies and hierarchies have been imperially constituted as effigies that indigenous people can protest and destroy in lieu of struggles against neocolonial dispossession, robbery, plunder, looting and biopiracy.

The upshot of the foregoing is that instead of fighting for restitution of their indigenous epistemologies and artefacts subjected to biopiracy, indigenous people are subtly hailed by imperial ideologists to waste time deconstructing and decentring their own mastery, authority, authorship, dominion, domination and hierarchies over their patrimonies or heritages. Indigenous people are made to mistakenly believe that colonisation was essentially about mastery. But then, if colonialists failed to master the humanity of the enslaved and colonised, how can they claim to have mastery over nature, science and technology? If colonisers failed to master the fact that Africans were the owners of African resources, how can the same colonialists claim to have mastery over nature and knowledge? If colonialists failed to master the fact that Africans were human beings, with human essence contrary to animals, how can the same colonialists claim mastery over nature and knowledge? If colonialists failed to master the fact that Africans had indigenous knowledge including science, technology, mathematics and engineering, how can the same colonialists claim to have mastery over nature and knowledge? If colonialists failed to notice that precolonial Africans had notions of God, religion, saints, laws and philosophy, how can the same colonialists claim to possess mastery over nature and knowledge? If colonialists failed to acknowledge great precolonial African states, industries, commerce and civilisations, how then can they be described as masters of knowledge? Similarly, if the colonialists failed to see and acknowledge great African juristic systems, how can they be described as masters of knowledge? In other words, if Euro-American colonisers could not see and acknowledge precolonial African modernity, how then can we describe them as modern and as masters of knowledge? The point here is that colonisation was less about bringing mastery, domination, authority and authorship than it was about colonial dispossession, plunder, looting and biopiracy on indigenous heritages.

Colonialism was also about the destruction of everything that testified to indigenous authority, authorship, domination, order and structure. There was destruction of indigenous artefacts, of manuscripts in precolonial indigenous libraries, destruction of indigenous precolonial universities, plunder of indigenous belief systems and destruction of indigenous science, mathematics, engineering and technology – it was about rendering indigenous people *tabula rasa* so that they would not be able to reclaim their authorship, authority, dominion, domination and mastery over their heritages. The upshot of the foregoing is that colonialism was not about creating structures, order, hierarchies, domination, mastery, dominions, authority and authorship: rather it was about creating emptiness in various ways – it was about creating emptiness by destroying and denying African authorship and authority, it was about destroying African structures that were necessary for authorship and authority, it was about destroying precolonial African technologies, science, knowledge systems and belief systems, it was about destroying African dominion and domination over African patrimonies; indeed it was also about destroying the lives and livelihoods of the Africans themselves. The imperial assumptions of *terra nullius* (empty land), *tabula rasa* (blank minds) and *res nullius* (unowned things) describe less what existed in precolonial Africa than they describe what the colonialists were doing – colonialists created *tabula rasa, res nullius* and *terra nullius* by emptying Africa through dispossession, destruction and biopiracy (Nhemachena *et al.*, 2019). The terms savagery, backwardness and barbarism described less what existed in precolonial Africa than they described what the colonialists were doing – colonialists created backwardness, savagery and barbarism even as they claimed to be on a mission to civilise and modernise indigenous people. Savagery, barbarism and backwardness were not necessarily features of Africans' past, rather they have become features of Africans' present and future wherein their historical achievements, mastery, authorship and civilisations have been imperially erased and plundered.

In the light of the foregoing, coloniality has to be understood not necessarily in terms of coloniality of knowledge (Dastile & Ndlovu-Gatsheni, 2013) but in terms of what we call **coloniality of ignorance** – colonialists/imperialists colonised indigenous people by erasing/looting indigenous knowledges and thus by producing ignorance among the colonised. Similarly, coloniality must be understood in terms of what we call **geopolitics of ignorance** rather than in terms of geopolitics of knowledge – colonialists created regions of ignorance by destroying indigenous artefacts, sciences, technology, and knowledges in a broader sense. Besides, coloniality should be understood in terms of **coloniality of biopiracy** and **coloniality of dispossession** so that the theft of indigenous knowledge and material resources is foregrounded. Thus, instead of foregrounding coloniality of power, we need to foreground coloniality of biopiracy and coloniality of dispossession which accurately capture the activities by which colonialism was instantiated and is being replicated. Coloniality is replicated not necessarily because of the exercise of power (in the sense of coloniality of power), rather it is replicated because of continued dispossession and biopiracy in respect of indigenous people's properties and heritages. In this sense, instead of focusing on epistemic disobedience, decolonial scholars would need to notice that decolonisation will be achievable through epistemic restitution which addresses biopiracy and the restitution of indigenous artefacts.

The problem with some contemporary scholars and thinkers is that they believe that colonial epistemologies were premised on correspondence theories of truth, yet the epistemologies described more the processes that colonialists engaged in than they did the reality on the African indigenous ground. Colonial anthropologists often described indigenous people as primitive, as incapable of abstract thought, unable to think in terms of causal laws and categories, unable to distinguish between supernatural and physical reality, as incapable of addressing contradictions, as childish, clumsy and unable to use logic and speculation (Levy-Bruhl, 1926; 1979; 2018). This book contends that such anthropological attributions of indigenous illiteracy, inability to use logic and to speculate, inability to think in terms of causal laws and categories were meant to disinhibit colonialists at a time when they were expected by their colleagues to steal from indigenous people. If a group of would-be victims of theft or robbery are described as illiterate, unable to count and to think, the effect is to encourage the robbery or theft on the supposition that the group of victims would not be able to take stock of what has been stolen. The point here is that, if anthropologists and other colonial scholars had described indigenous people as rational, literate, scientific, and technologically advanced and so on, colonialists would have known that precolonial Africans could count and quantify their property including livestock and land, and therefore that they would know or find out that their property was being stolen by colonialists. Put differently, to describe the victim of robbery, theft and dispossession as illiterate, irrational, mythical, mystical and supernaturally inclined amounts to saying that they cannot count and quantify and therefore that they cannot notice when robbery, theft and dispossession happen. Considering indigenous people as comparable to psychotic patients, as irrational, animistic, magical, and so on (Heinz, 1998) effectively meant that indigenous people could not own and control resources/property.

Irrational and insane people cannot legally own and control property. Similarly, by deconstructing binaries/dichotomies between sanity and insanity, the sane and the insane, postcolonial theorists are replicating colonial epistemologies that denied sanity and rationality to indigenous people. Similarly, contemporary decolonial theorists should not be preoccupied with describing indigenous people as mystical, magical, animistic and irrational because these epithets imply that indigenous people are insane, incapable of distinguishing the supernatural from the physical, and cannot therefore own and control their resources and their own lives. An insane person cannot own and control his/her life – he cannot have autonomy and sovereignty. It was on the pretext that indigenous people were comparable to psychotic patients that colonialists denied autonomy and sovereignty to the indigenous people. On the other hand, colonial/imperial science and technology were ironically depicted as rational, objective and positivistic even as they were used to poison indigenous people's water wells, food, clothes, blankets and so on in the colonial/apartheid genocidal context (Gould & Folb, 2002) – colonialists/imperialists did not want to see this for what it was - as witchcraft and sorcery.

Ignoring the presence of indigenous knowledge, that is, the cumulative body of strategies, practices, techniques, tools, intellectual resources, explanations, beliefs and values accumulated over time in a particular locality (Emeagwali, 2014), Eurocentric scholars like Hegel portrayed Africans as uncivilised, as unhistorical, underdeveloped, devoid of morality, lacking reason, religions, and political constitutions (Adegbindin, 2015; Oladipo, 1995). We argue in this book that these were not merely erroneous or mistaken descriptions of Africans, rather the descriptions were deliberately meant to aid colonial dispossession because describing colonial victims as devoid of morality, as lacking reason, as irrational, as mystical and prelogical is effectively writing them off from the realm of humanity and from possibilities of ownership and control of resources that were targeted by colonialists. Put in other words, such colonial and Eurocentric scholarship was not merely racist but criminal in the sense of producing ideologies meant to aid and abet colonisation. Ironically, colonialists ideologically mystified colonisation by describing their African victims as mystical, prelogical, unable to think of the physical as physical, lacking cognitive representations, lacking apprehension of material phenomena in the physical and causal fashion (Kebede, 2004). Kebede (2004: 2) states thus:

> The mixture of intellectual elements with affective reactions postulate occult forces, which hinder the apprehension of material phenomena in the physical and causal fashion… The social and technological retardation of native peoples is wholly due to this inability to think physically and logically. Some such turn of mind is adamantly opposed to scientific thinking and technological orientation…

This book argues that depictions such as the above were meant to caricature indigenous people who were mischievously assumed to be ignorant of the physical laws of gravity. If indigenous people were hunter-gatherers, one would ordinarily expect them to have been aware of the force of gravity that caused fruits to fall to the ground. Indigenous people who trapped animals by digging pits must have known about the physical force of gravity that caused animals to collapse into the pits. Similarly, indigenous people who threw arrows and spears at animals and birds must have had knowledge about the physical laws of gravity. They also knew about the mathematical angles and velocity at which they could successfully shoot a sprinting animal or a flying bird. Similarly, indigenous people who constructed houses knew about the physical forces that affected their building. Some indigenous people who caught fish knew about physical weights as they pulled fish out of water. Indigenous people also knew about the biological parts of animals and birds which they eviscerated arguably daily. Indigenous people chose high ground in building their settlements because they knew about the physical aspects of flooding – it was colonialists who displaced indigenous people from highveld areas to infertile and poorly watered lowveld areas susceptible to flooding and infestation with mosquitos and tsetse flies. In the light of these observations, it is strange that Eurocentric scholars and thinkers depict indigenous people as ignorant of the existence of physical forces.

In the light of the above, we argue that colonialists/imperialists did not represent Africans, but they misrepresented them; they did not invent or socially construct Africans, but they destroyed Africans' institutions. Colonial/imperial scholars had to generate ideological foils to justify the colonial project. Arguments that Africans were devoid of morality, ethics and religion were meant to disinhibit colonialists/imperialists at a moral level as they would otherwise have felt guilty of colonising moral, rational and religious indigenous human beings. Equally, arguments that Africans did not have notions of God, Heaven and Hell were meant to disinhibit colonialists/imperialists who would otherwise fear God's punishment for colonising other [African] human beings. Therefore, colonial arguments that precolonial Africans were mere animists, believing in earthly "natural" spirits, were also meant to disinhibit colonialists/imperialists who would otherwise fear punishment from the Supreme Being in Heaven. Colonial/imperial arguments to the effect that Africans lacked cognitive representations, reasonableness and laws were also meant to disinhibit colonialists/imperialists who would otherwise have feared legal reprisals from indigenous people targeted for colonial robbery. Equally colonial/imperial arguments that Africans did not have social organisations including polities, families and states were meant to disinhibit colonialists/imperialists who would otherwise have feared reprisals from organised Africans. Arguments that Africans did not have proper families were meant to preempt questions about African heritages and genealogies. Similarly, arguments that Africans did not have knowledge and capacity to objectively represent knowledge were meant to disinhibit colonialists/imperialists who would have otherwise been inhibited by fears that their crimes of dispossession, robbery and exploitation would be known/seen by the Africans targeted for colonisation. Besides, arguments that Africans did not have technology and science were meant to disinhibit colonialists/imperialists who would otherwise have been inhibited or deterred by fear of the technological/moral rectitude/superiority of Africans who were being targeted for colonisation. Put succinctly, the colonial/imperial scholars were as much on a mission as were the colonial missionaries who went about looking for demons among Africans but failed to see the chief demons driving the colonial project to which they were complicity.

Thus, colonial/imperial scholars devised theories of evolution that assumed that victims of colonial savagery and barbarity were themselves savage and barbaric. The colonial/imperial theories of evolution presumed that the victims of colonial/imperial immorality were themselves immoral/devoid of morality. Besides, the colonial/imperial theories of evolution assumed that victims of colonial/imperial irrationality were themselves irrational. The theories of evolution presumed that victims of colonial/imperial mystification were themselves mystical and mythical. The evolutionary theories assumed that victims of colonial/imperial violence/atavism were themselves violent/atavistic. Similarly, colonial/imperial technologies of surveillance – including prisons - assume that victims of colonial/imperial crimes are the criminals *par excellence*. Furthermore, the theories of evolution presumed that victims of colonial/imperial animism were themselves animistic. Victims of colonial/imperial ignorance were assumed to be ignorant in the evolutionary theories. The evolutionary theories assumed that the colonial/imperial victims of theft of knowledge/biopiracy were themselves devoid of knowledge. Similarly, colonialists/imperialists destroyed indigenous people's states, families, economies and then ironically, they depicted the indigenous people as lacking organisation, structure and order. Put otherwise, the evolutionary theories postulated by colonial/imperial scholars erroneously assume that the victims of colonisation have progressed from bad (in the past) to better (in the present and future) when in fact they have been consistently subjected to the presence of dispossession, looting, plunder, biopiracy, genocide, destruction, irrationalities, colonial illiteracy, invasions, mystifications, exploitation, enslavement and colonisation. It does not constitute progress or evolution to be subjected to colonial/imperial dispossession, robbery, looting, plunder, biopiracy, genocide, enslavement and colonisation: decolonisation has to be defined in terms of reversing these processes so that real progress and evolution can start among the victims of enslavement and colonisation. Curricula in African universities must focus on these issues rather than on deconstructing authority/authorship, mastery, dominion and domination – evolution and progress are about indigenous mastery, having dominion, authority and authorship over their heritages including indigenous knowledge.

The question arising from the foregoing is that if humankind originated from Africa, why did evolution not originate or begin from Africa such that African people were ahead of everyone else – technologically, epistemically, socially, religiously, politically and economically? If Africa is the cradle of humankind, why then is it associated in Eurocentric discourses with darkness, savagery, barbarism and backwardness? If cradles must be associated with darkness, savagery, barbarism and backwardness, must the supposed European origins or cradles of technology, science and development be associated with darkness, savagery, barbarism, irrationality and backwardness? In other words, if Africa is the cradle of humankind and Europe claims to be the cradle of science and technology, why must one cradle be demonised as constitutive of darkness while the other is glorified as constitutive of progress and evolution? The point here is that the demonisation of Africa as a heart of darkness was not necessarily because Africa was dark or backward, rather Africa was demonised because it was targeted for colonial/imperial cannibalisation, including dispossession, biopiracy, iconoclasm, looting, plunder and robbery. Africa was depicted as darkness because the colonialist/imperialists had set out on a colonial/imperial project to create and produce darkness on the continent of Africa. In other words, the thesis about the darkness of Africa was less about describing the condition in precolonial Africa than it was about describing the state of Africa following subjection to colonisation and imperialism. The thesis we are making here is that precolonial Africans were much more inventive, innovative, literate, intelligent, skilled, technologically wise, scientific, rational and logical than Africans since subjection to colonial and imperial darkness that has generated mimetic scholarship among indigenous people. From humanities, social sciences to science and technology African scholarship has sadly become largely mimetic without chances of inventing anything of note.

13

Science, technology and the questions of origins: Wither African originality

Misled by evolutionary theories, Eurocentric scholars often portrayed precolonial Africans as illiterate and so they did not notice the existence of precolonial universities in Africa. The University of Timbuktu in precolonial Mali housed 25 000 students and had one of the largest libraries in the world – with between 40 000 and 700 000 manuscripts; it was the first university in the world; it taught subjects including medicine, literature, maths, philosophy, religion, jurisprudence, theology, sufism, psychology, biology, geometry, logic, rhetoric, grammar, geography, history, politics, arithmetic, astronomy, astrology, chemistry, physics, meteorology and botany (Olajide, 2013; Sidi, 2016; Haidara, 2008; Takawira, 2016; Selin, 1997). Precolonial Africa also had written languages including hieroglyphics and alphabet for instance in ancient Egypt; there were great libraries in precolonial Africa particularly in Timbuktu (Mali) and at Alexandria in Egypt but these libraries were destroyed by Europeans that also looted the African manuscripts/books (Abdi, 2007; Warrior, n.d). Whereas Eurocentric scholars argue that Africans got knowledge from Euro-America, it is in fact Euro-America that stole knowledge from Africans – and Isocrates, Pythagoras, Anaxagoras, Plato, Democritus, Thales and other Europeans first studied, for many years, in precolonial Africa where they learnt science, mathematics, philosophy and other fields (Asante, 2015; Duchesne, 2011; Netshitenzhe, 4 March 2015; Rambane & Mashige, 2007; Nhemachena *et al.*, 2018). In this regard, precolonial Africans not only experimented/innovated based on trial and error at sites of work/homesteads (Chirikure, 2017), they also had precolonial universities, libraries and laboratories some of which were subsequently destroyed and or looted by marauding colonialists. The point here is that indigenous scholars must begin to seriously question the provenance of so-called modernist epistemologies and universities – have these not in fact been stolen from indigenous peoples? If so, what are the implications for decoloniality and decolonisation?

Thus, science, philosophy, religion, architecture, civilisation, universities and mathematics originated from Africans; chemistry began in Africa with the use of fire; mathematics was also connected to the counting of cowry shells used as money in precolonial Africa; the flourishing precolonial trade necessitated the development of mathematics and number systems including weights, bases, taxation and commercial practices relying on indigenous science and mathematics; there were precolonial accountants and scribes who calculated food rations, land allocations, grain distributions, land surveying, architecture etc (Lumpkin, 1987; Rambane & Mashige, 2007; Joseph, 2011; Kienon-Kabore, 2017). Although some scholars like Gerdes (1994) and Huylebrouck (2006) argue that indigenous mathematical ideas are only implicit in precolonial art, craft, riddles, games, graphic systems and woven fabrics, it is also important to note that mathematics was taught as a subject in precolonial African universities. Eurocentric scholars and thinkers have an interest in depicting Africa as intellectually, socially, politically, legally and economically indebted to the West and so they erase or ignore the seminal presence and impact of African civilisations (Rambane and Mashige, 2007).

After destroying precolonial African universities and libraries, Europeans have consistently portrayed themselves as the originators of university education, of literacy, numeracy, technology and science. With the Latin root, *scientia,* meaning knowledge in the broadest possible sense (Snively and Corsiglia, 2000), the colonial denial of science to Africans presupposes that precolonial Africans had no knowledge at all. Notwithstanding the presupposition of absence of knowledge in precolonial Africa, it has been noted that indigenous people were capable of scientific abstractions, had astronomy, mathematics, agriculture, navigation, mathematics, astronomy, medical practices, engineering, pharmacology, military science, architecture and ecology; indigenous people made rational observations of natural events, did classifications and problem solving (Snively and Corsiglia, 2000; Shizha and Emeangwali, 2016). Indigenous people had knowledge of central nervous system, blood circulation, brain pulsations, cardio-vascular system, animal husbandry, fish and wildlife management; indigenous people developed thousands of varieties of potatoes, grain, oilseed, squashes, hot peppers, corn, pumpkins, sunflowers and beans; they first discovered rubber, vulcanizing and metallurgy (Shizha and Emeangwali, 2016). Precolonial indigenous people also had knowledge about the physics of musical instruments/science of sound systems (Nzewi and Nzewi, 2007; Ellert, 1984).

While Eurocentric diffusionist theories erroneously assume that precolonial Africans had no inventions and innovations of their own, Shizha and Emeangwali (2016) observe that indigenous people had scientific knowledge; they had building technologies, they had physics and mathematical principles that were used in constructing indigenous structures such as Great Zimbabwe; indigenous people had medical sciences; they developed capacity to mix paint in containers and they coated their ornaments with iron oxide pigment as early as 100 000 years ago. For Shizha and Emeangwali (2016), the unfortunate thing is that African inventions and innovations were, subsequent to colonialism, named after adventurers, merchants and others rather than the African owners themselves. It is necessary to take cognisance of this fact in decolonising science, technology, engineering and mathematics. If colonialists stole African knowledge and then renamed the inventions/innovations after European adventurers and merchants, what it means is that decolonial scholars do not have to assume that universities are Eurocentric in the sense of originating or belonging to Europeans because Europeans have in fact plundered and looted African knowledge. Besides, decolonial scholars should not assume that it is the curricula that is Eurocentric because subjects that are taught in universities have been taught in precolonial Africa.

What decolonial scholars must do is to ensure that Africans are compensated and paid for their knowledge that has been and is being stolen in biopiracy. Africans must repossess their knowledge and institutions. The problem is that colonialists/imperialists wrote their names on institutions, artefacts, continents, epistemologies and even on human bodies that do not belong to them – colonised Africans as well as enslaved Africans have been forced to adopt European names. In fact, the names of slave "masters" have been etched, often using red hot iron, onto the bodies of enslaved Africans to prevent them from running away; also, some mountains, rivers and waterfalls in Africa were renamed after some Europeans. The question then is do these assume European origins simply because European names are etched on them? What are the implications for decolonisation/decoloniality?

Dismissing the precolonial African past as prehistory was part of colonial/imperial efforts to erase African innovations, inventions and knowledge systems as a prelude to postulating diffusionist paradigms that would explain whatever good thing is found in Africa as originating from Euro-America. Thus, colonial historians dismissed precolonial African history even as they propagated diffusionist theories. Similarly, colonial anthropologists were not keen on the African precolonial past (Prior n.d). The colonial anthropologists were not keen to research and write about precolonial African industries, civilisations, science, technology and material culture because doing so would undermine the colonial ideology of civilising Africans (Prior n.d). The colonial anthropologists argued that studying indigenous techniques, artefacts and material culture would deflect them from their proper professional role of studying culture (Pfaffenberger, 1992). The irony in the colonial scholarship was that colonialists were stealing African artefacts, pieces of technology, science and so on even as they claimed that Africans had no science and technology. Popularising magic, animism, fetishes, mysticism and superstitions that supposedly preoccupied the indigenous minds, colonial anthropologists paid blind eyes to indigenous inventions, innovations, science and technology. By ignoring these aspects, colonial anthropologists misrepresented indigenous people such that their ethnographies have come to be described as works of fiction and as distorted accounts (Matthews, 2017; Franco, 2016; Marcus, Fischer and Fischer, 1998; Clifford, 1986; Stewart-Harawira, 2013).

However, we argue that because colonialists/imperialists have already destroyed precolonial indigenous universities and libraries and stolen indigenous artefacts, technology and scientific knowledge for centuries, it is not easy for contemporary indigenous people to rewrite their stories. Indigenous artefacts and material culture are still lodged in Euro-American museums such that indigenous people (with no access to the museums) cannot witness and celebrate the inventiveness and creativity of their own ancestors. All that the contemporary indigenous people are forced to believe is that they were primitive, backward, irrational, underdeveloped, savage, unscientific and without technology (Ngozi, 2014). There has been colonial/imperial destruction of the inventiveness and creativity of indigenous people who had precolonial industries, science and technology including black-smithing, wood-carving, textile-weaving and dyeing, leather works, beadworks, pottery making, architecture, agricultural breeding, metal-working, salt production, gold-smithing, copper-smithing, leather-crafting, soap-making, bronze-casting, canoe-building, brewing, indigenous glass-making, agriculture and production of flint guns (Ngozi, 2014; Killick, 2016; Osuala, 2012; Adamu & Bello, 2015; Gerdes, 1994; Olaoye, 1989; Shizha, 2016; Kienon-Kabore, 2017; Ekeh, 2010). To efface the precolonial history of inventions and innovations, including textile industries, colonialists stripped Africans and other indigenous people before photographing them – indigenous people were photographed naked as a colonial way of negating the existence of textile industries in precolonial Africa. The erroneous impression left is that precolonial Africans could not produce clothes: the existence of thriving textile industries with cotton growing and weaving in various parts of Africa, including west Africa and southern Africa (Oyebade 2007; Dickson 1977; Adamu & Bello 2015; Olaoye 1989; Adu *et al.,* 2018; Killick, 2015; 2016; Kriger, 2006) has been forgotten by many contemporary indigenous people who now erroneously believe that textile industries are western in origin.

The point in the foregoing is that despite the existence of textile manufacturing, local and long-distance trade in precolonial Africa (Okoduwa, 2007), Africans have been portrayed by colonialists as having lived in primitive nakedness. Despite the existence of precolonial trade/commerce, precolonial Africans are often depicted as subsistence based – with the erroneous impression that trade and commerce are Western inventions and innovations. In textile manufacturing, cotton lint was used for cloth weaving, cottonseeds were edible and were used for cooking soup; cotton cultivation, yarn making, dyeing and weaving were all specific industries for both indigenous men and women (Okoduwa, 2007). In the light of the foregoing, it is necessary to note that the colonialists' depictions of precolonial Africans as naked were mere ideological attempts to paint indigenous people as backward, savage, barbaric and underdeveloped. Of course slave drivers and colonialists/imperialists enjoyed seeing the naked bodies of the enslaved and colonised – the enslaved were for instance stripped naked just before the Middle Passage; the enslaved were not even allowed to wear loin cloths lest they hanged themselves; slave buyers wanted the enslaved to be naked as they lined the pens and auction houses (Gruber, 2018; Johnson, 1999; Mays, 2004). Slave drivers and colonialists redefined the enslaved and colonised's physical and social spaces including by stripping the enslaved's body and denying his or her natal name – to take off the enslaved and colonised's clothes was to reduce him/her to cultural *tabula rasa*; the undressing was used to justify claims of barbarism, cultural lack, symbolic debasement (Gikandi, 2014). Thus, it is noted that undressing the enslaved and colonised was a precondition for enslavement; it was reduction of the enslaved to beastliness depriving them of memory and social connection – the body was stripped of all its accoutrements and reduced to a state of cultural nakedness (Gikandi, 2014; Likuwa, 2014).

Contrary to colonial/imperial assumptions, precolonial Africans had irrigation schemes with furrows, dams and contours that demonstrate presence of scientific and technological knowledge. Furrows cascaded down hill valleys onto the fields showing possession of sophisticated irrigation technology in precolonial Africa, including in the 16th century Nyanga District in Zimbabwe; colonialists who settled in Africa destroyed precolonial African irrigation schemes (Davies, 2008; Templehoff, 2006). At Nyanga District, precolonial terraces were built and the irrigation works show considerable skill in hydraulic engineering – sadly colonial scholars attributed the irrigation schemes at Nyanga District to Arabs, as they did to the Great Zimbabwe ruins which they also attributed to Arabs instead of the real African originators/builders (Templehoff, 2006). The fact that precolonial Africa had irrigation schemes in various areas, including east, west and southern Africa, underscores the reality that precolonial Africans had sophisticated knowledge about engineering and agriculture. There were extensive and complex

19

irrigation projects in east Africa with canals and furrow systems traversing tens of kilometres of country and irrigating thousands of hectares in contiguous blocks – these furrows and canals demonstrate considerable engineering skill and represent the most extensive and complex indigenous water management in Africa south of the Sahara (Adam & Anderson, 2016).

In the light of the foregoing, it is shocking that some contemporary Africans believe that agriculture was invented by Euro-American colonialists/imperialists. One may consider arguments by some scholars, including African ones, associating Zimbabwean agriculture with White farmers to the point of implying that without White farmers Zimbabwean agriculture is doomed (Nhemachena *et al.*, 2017). Such arguments are oblivious of the African origin of agricultural techniques/inventions. Instead of noticing the colonial/imperial destruction of African ingenuity/inventions, the scholars consider colonialists/imperialists as inventors/innovators *par excellence*. The question here is, if colonialists/imperialists were/are great inventors/innovators, then why did they fail to invent solutions to the enclosure system within the bounds of their own states. In other words, if they were/are really great inventors/innovators, why did they have to colonise, dispossess, rob, and steal from Africans? Enslaving and colonising others is not a sign of great inventiveness or innovation, rather, it is a sign of great failure to handle one's own problems. Great inventors and innovators did not enslave and colonise other human beings and so Africans must begin to [historically] see themselves as great inventors and innovators who managed to innovatively solve their own problems without having to enslave and colonise other people. Inventions and innovations did not and do not come from Euro-Americans, they come from Africans who have sadly been made to believe that they are savage and barbaric.

Thus, colonialists/imperialists have not only given their own names to African children, but also great African architecture has been attributed to Europeans instead of to the real indigenous originators/inventors. In this regard, while there are popular misconceptions that precolonial Africans lived in mud huts and thatched dwellings, historical research shows that square, circular and rectangular forms are of great antiquity and have existed in diverse geographical regions of Africa (Odeyale and Adekunle, 2008). There were huts with conical roofs resting on square walls, roofs around walls would be conical and roofs above rectangular walls could be saddle back heaped on pyramid; some villages were built on steep sides of the cliffs (Odeyale and Adekunle, 2008). Demostrating their architectural sophistication, precolonial Africans built precolonial towns on sound town planning, design and architectural principles with plazas, passage ways or streets, walls and dwellings – in this sense, several great precolonial cities existed including Great Zimbabwe, Gao, Timbuktu, Djenne, Bosiu, Umgungundlovu, Kumasi, Ife and Kilwa (Amankwah-Ayeh, 1996). Many precolonial cities had circularity of dwellings, roads/passages, walls, plazas and settlement patterns; some precolonial African settlement patterns were curved, non-rectangular with a strong sense of enclosure; in the plazas of precolonial cities, people traded, public celebrations took place, plays were staged, state proceedings were carried out, laws were proclaimed; plazas also served as meeting places between the rulers and the ruled, taxation of goods entering and leaving the Kingdoms happened in the plazas (Amankwah-Ayeh, 1996; Blier, 2012).

In the light of the above, it is cause for wonder why some contemporary Africans believe that architectural development originates from Euro-American institutions and individuals who they worship, treat as inviolable and sacred. Having had the capacity to construct roads, avenues and streets some of which they used when travelling to trading or marketplaces and to the palaces (Charney, 2016), precolonial Africans also invented the wheel, which was initially wooden (Charney, 2016). In Africa there were great road systems in the precolonial empires that also engaged in trade; some roads led to sacred places lined with trees, surfaced with stone, regularly levelled, with bridges across rivers – this is an indication of great engineering capacity (Charney, 2016). On the road, precolonial indigenous cartwheels consisting of slab wheels, not hollowed and rimmed or spoked, were used: the wheels were constructed out of wood cut in the shape of circles (Charney, 2016). Because the precolonial indigenous heavy and jagged slab wheels were disliked by colonial officials, traditional indigenous owners of carts were forced

21

into oblivion through taxation (Charney, 2016). In precolonial Africa, wheels were made by cutting a circle from timbers, glued and nailed into position – such wheels were strong and would not puncture (Conroy, 2003).

Pre-colonial Burmese cart with one type of slab wheel cited in Charney (2016: 30)

Wheels were developed long before history was recorded and they were indigenous people's handiwork (Kleinschmidt, 1944). Wood was one of the important means of artistic representation which the Africans used and are still making use of – wood is the African's most favourite material or medium for sculpture and so it was wood that they used to make wheels (Azeez, 2011). In Egypt and elsewhere in the world, there were also chariots with spoked wheels (Choudros *et al.*, 2016).

Because some of the chariots and carts were used in war and trade, precolonial Africans also invented guns and bullets to protect themselves. It is noted that precolonial Africans produced handguns and muskets; they made powder for use in the barrels of the guns, bullets were manufactured locally in Africa; some west Africans also invented and used rockets – bullets were carried in leather bags (Smith, 1989; Olaoye, 1989; Pilossof, 2010). Thus, carts and chariots were used to carry arms as well as in trade of such items as gold, ivory, soap, iron tools and weapons, salt, cloth, dried fish and animal skins and cowrie shells (Morris, 2006).

Underscored in the foregoing is the importance of inventiveness and innovation among precolonial Africans. It also underlines the shortfalls of contemporary Africans who arguably cannot invent and innovate as much as precolonial Africans did. Furthermore, the foregoing indicates the direction African universities must take: currently African universities are graduating hundreds of thousands of people who unfortunately cannot match the inventiveness and innovativeness of precolonial Africans. Decolonisation must not be simplistically about fighting the university hierarchies, structures, domination and mastery – it must be *a fortiori* about inventiveness and innovation among African graduates and scholars. In other words, the problem is not essentially with hierarchies, domination, mastery and structures: the problem is with absence of mastery, innovativeness and inventiveness. Put differently, the problem is with absence of mastery and, by extension, absence of dominion and domination by African graduates and scholars. Inventiveness and innovation are functions of mastery, domination and dominion – decolonisation must therefore ensure mastery and domination by Africans. When precolonial Africans had dominion over African heritages, they could invent and innovate; when colonised Africans lost dominion, domination and mastery over African heritages, they ceased to be inventive and innovative – they became mimetic. To decolonise, it is imperative to exercise mastery, dominion and domination over African heritages so that they do not get cannibalised by biopiratic predatory forces in the world.

Predatory epistemologies and the imperatives of decolonisation

Colonial/imperial epistemologies should not be theorised in terms of constructivism or constructionism because they are designed and used for biopiracy which is destructive to the indigenous epistemologies that are thereby cannibalised. By colonial/imperial or Eurocentric epistemologies, we do not mean to say the epistemologies originate in Europe or in the centres of empire because the epistemologies are themselves biopirated. Much as colonialists/imperialists captured some indigenous people and then used them against their fellows, colonialists/imperialists capture indigenous knowledges and then use them against their source. This is what we mean by Eurocentric epistemologies – they often constitute indigenous epistemologies that have been captured and turned against their source. Thus, history attests to the fact that colonialists/imperialists captured and turned indigenous people against their fellows – the captured became Eurocentric without necessarily originating from Europe. Colonialists/imperialists have captured and turned some African states and used them against African citizens – the captured states become Eurocentric without necessarily originating in Europe. They are Eurocentric because they have been captured and turned against their own indigenous others. Similarly, indigenous children/offsprings have been captured and turned (in a Eurocentric way) against their own ancestors who are sadly depicted as demons. In this regard, the remedy is not to reject them, but it is to turn them again so that they become of good service in favour of indigenous people. Eurocentrism for our purposes does not mean having an origin in Europe or America – it means being turned against one's fellow indigenous people. In this regard, what is Eurocentric is not necessarily constructionistic or constructivistic in relation to indigenous people – rather, it is destructivistic and destructionistic in the sense of having been inverted in order to depredate against the indigenous origin.

When Africans protest Eurocentric epistemologies, they should not be understood as protesting against domination, mastery, dominion, hierarchy, hegemony and so on; rather they are protesting depredations or the destruction that is inherent in Eurocentrism, including being turned against oneself. When someone has destroyed one's house or institutions, the proper charge is not that the criminal has dominated, or exercised mastery or dominion or hegemony or that they have hierarchies – the charge is simply that they have destroyed the institutions or house. Colonialists and their epistemologies have plundered and destroyed African institutions, including African epistemologies, for which decolonial scholars and thinkers must propose a remedy.

Like predatory states, predatory epistemologies are epistemologies of capture: they do not merely oppress, dominate or hegemonise but they destroy and annihilate and incorporate/assimilate or efface. Predatory epistemologies corrupt indigenous epistemologies in the same way predatory states are believed to corrupt the societies within which they find location. Much like predatory states, predatory epistemologies are purveyed by individuals and institutions that have been captured and turned against their own indigenous people or origin. Predatory epistemologies rely on what we call predatory researchers who wittingly and unwittingly facilitate biopiracy and depredations against indigenous epistemologies. Predatory epistemologies rely on predatory theories that regard indigenous epistemologies as mere raw data to be interpreted and incorporated using the lenses of the data-prospectors. The point here is that scholars must not only take into cognisance discourses on predatory states and predatory journals, they must also take into cognisance the existence of what we call **predatory epistemologies, predatory academies and predatory researchers/researches** that promote coloniality. Predatory researches/researchers have seen Euro-American institutions and individuals sponsoring researches and flocking to Africa to do research even as Africans are disallowed to flock to Euro-America to similarly do research (Nhemachena *et al.*, 2016). Decolonisation is a function of abating the predation and biopiracy [and pursuing restitution], which is not synonymous with jettisoning mastery, authority and domination.

Predatory research/researchers are witnessed when Africa is bioprospected and then subjected to biopiracy wherein the foreign researchers and their institutions often patent African indigenous knowledge. It is not in every case that researches are done to facilitate cultural appropriation or biopiracy but there is a lot of potentially predatory researches on African indigenous knowledge systems and rituals (Young, 2000; Kunene, 21 December 1997; Khoza, 1 December 2016; Mthethwa, 29 March 2017; Hackett and Soares, 2015; Teppo, 2011).

A South African traditional healer initiating some white people into healing (Source Khosa, 1 December 2016)

In order to dismiss African epistemologies, colonialists/imperialists devised several strategies which decolonial scholars need to tackle. One of the strategies was to depict indigenous knowledge as unscientific, devoid of truth, devoid of certitudes, as ambiguous and uncertain. As noted earlier, the strategy was also to depict indigenous knowledge as irrational, pre/illogical. Indigenous people were also depicted as incapable of distinguishing between spirit and matter or the physical and the spiritual, their knowledge systems were deemed to lack objectivity, rationality and clarity (Campbel, 29 April 2010; Tannert *et al.*, 2007). The point is that colonialists dismissed indigenous knowledge on the basis that it had no binaries between truth and falsehood, between the certain and uncertain, between the objective and subjective, between the scientific and unscientific, the physical and the spiritual and so on. Whereas the remedy to these colonial assumptions would have been to show that indigenous knowledge has certitudes, has distinctions between truth and falsehood, between belief and knowledge, between the subjective and objective, between the scientific and the unscientific and so, we witness the preemptive proliferation of Eurocentric theories condemning binaries or distinctions. Instead of decolonisation being defined in terms of indigenous knowledge reasserting distinctions between these aspects, Eurocentric scholars are craftly redefining decolonisation in terms of retaining absence of distinctions/binaries – in effect decolonisation, for Eurocentric scholars, means retaining the colonial status quo that condemned indigenous knowledge systems as incapable of making distinctions/binaries between truth and falsehood, the subjective and objective, the human and nonhuman.

The point in the foregoing is that when one is described as incapable of making distinctions/binaries between truth and falsehood, between knowledge and belief, between the objective and subjective, between humans and nonhumans and so on – one is effectively being said to be ignorant, as without knowledge, that is as foolish, savage, illiterate, barbaric; in short one is being depicted again as *tabula rasa*. To portray indigenous knowledge systems as incapable of making distinctions or binaries is a surreptitious way to effectively dismiss it as nothing and as useless because it is supposedly incapable of distinguishing truth from falsehood, the subjective from the objective – in other words to be incapable of making distinctions or binaries is to subsists or to reinhabit in the realm of darkness or ambiguity. Similarly, it is not an accolade to be described as hybrid in the postcolonial theoretical sense because to be hybrid also amounts to failure to distinguish between the pure and the dirty, truth and falsehood, belief and knowledge, the subjective and objective. What indigenous knowledge needs in order to decolonise is not absence/deconstruction of binaries, rather indigenous knowledge systems need to reassert distinctions in order to count as knowledge, science and technology. Once indigenous knowledge demonstrates and reasserts its scientific and technological feat, African people will be able to resist technological colonialism or technocolonialism that is creeping into the continent. The continent is in the grip of technological and scientific solutionism being purveyed by the new missionaries of Eurocentric science and technology (Goss, 2009; Petitjean, 2005; Seth, 2009: Gilmartin, 1994; Bridle, 2018; Fuchs, 2013; Scott, 2016). To put it in other words, Western technology may transform Africa, but it will not decolonise the continent which is increasingly subjected to imperial/colonial biopiracy, dispossession, surveillance and sousveillance.

Decolonisation will be achieved through changing mindsets, redefining African institutions from an African perspective, through indigenisation and Africanisation (Matola *et al.,* 2019; Makhubela, 2018) but there is more that needs to be done and or avoided. Decolonisation will neither be achieved through deconstructing binaries nor through diversity, multiculturalism and inclusivist projects couched in the logic of neoliberalism. Decolonisation will be achievable by recentring indigenous knowledge systems, enhancing indigenous mastery, ownership and control; abating biopiracy, strengthening indigenous people's identity, abating plunder, looting and destruction of indigenous knowledge systems (Makhubela, 2018; Porsanger, 2004). Decolonisation will be achievable by teaching courses on sociology/anthropology of science and technology studies which bring to the fore indigenous science, technology, engineering and mathematics and ways in which indigenous knowledge can be protected from biopiracy. So far courses on sociology/anthropology of science and technology studies have focused on the shaping of scientific culture, on innovations and inventions, material culture, technological determinism and technological possibilism (Borup *et al.,* 2006; Star, 2014; Pinch and Bijker, 1984; Zuckerman, 2018; Coyler, 2011; Collins and Restivo, 1984; Ingold, 1997; Fischer, 2007; Pfaffenberger, 1988). A sociology/anthropology of science and technology studies must examine the interface between, on the one hand, Western science and technology and, on the other hand, indigenous science and technology – in the process it must interrogate coloniality at this interface.

If Western science developed from Rene Descartes' dreams of the 10th of November 1619; from Western scholars some of whom were mystics; from freemasonry which has/had connections with the Enlightenment, universities and some scientists – including Francis Bacon, Isaac Newton (Whithers, 2008; Davies and Hersh, 2005; Browne, 1977; Ellyatt, 21 November 2013; Calance, 2014), why should African mystics and thinkers be dismissed as irrational and unscientific? If Western mystics were deemed to be enlightened, rational and scientific mathematicians and physicists, why must African mystics be dismissed as darkness, unscientific and irrational? The argument is that Francis Bacon, Isaac Newton, Pythagoras and Rene Descartes – deemed to be rational and champions of science - were connected to freemasonry and to gods/religion including Lucifer (considered to be the rebellious angel of light in the Enlightenment) (Calance, 2014; Whithers, 2008; Davies and Hersh, 2005; Karamanides, 2005). In fact, Rene Descartes's dream on 10 November 1619 was interpreted to mean the unification and illumination of the whole of science, the whole knowledge by one and the same method: the method of reason –and the dream was interpreted as a positive source of knowledge and truth (Davies and Hersh, 2005; Jones, 1979; Mcgushin, 2018). Thus, freemasons and their European lodges became centres of mathematics, medical and physiological subjects, astronomy, microscopy, magnetism, chemistry, metalwork, architecture and magnetism.

The upshot of the foregoing is that whereas Europeans' dreams are interpreted in Eurocentric scholarship as rational, scientific, truthful, objective and so on, indigenous people's dreams are interpreted as irrational, mystical, subjective, falsehood and unscientific. If Rene Descartes, Francis Bacon, Pythagoras, Isaac Newton and so on developed their scientific, mathematical and technological ideas based on their dreams, religions and gods, why must indigenous people not be allowed to do the same? Is it not possible that an idea originates from a dream or mystical source and then materialises as scientific or technological, overtime? Why must such an idea continue to be interpreted as irrational, mystical, unscientific, subjective and so on? Is it not possible that an idea is born/conceived in a dream, but it gradually becomes reality, scientific, objective and rational? Is it not because of the instincts of gatekeeping that Eurocentric scholars dismiss African dreams as sources of science and technology while ironically celebrating European dreams as sources of scientific, rational and technical ideas? Why must Africans be interpreted as benefiting from diffusion of scientific and technological ideas from European dreams? Is it not possible that Africans benefited from diffusion of scientific and technological ideas from their own dreams and experiences on the continent of Africa? Why must Europe be considered as the sole source of both valuable, truthful and reasonable dreams, religions and technological and scientific ideas? The point here is that Euro-America has sadly come to be understood as the origin of technology and ideas including those that it did not invent and innovate. No longer dreaming scientific and technical ideas, indigenous people have been forced to believe that scientific and technological ideas should necessarily have one source, which is Euro-America.

Apart from relying on their dreams, gods and religions for sources of scientific and technological ideas, Europeans and Americans also engaged in biopiracy – looting and plundering indigenous knowledge systems of the colonised peoples. Much as Euro-Americans do not acknowledge that they industrialised and developed as a result of enslaving and colonising Africans and other peoples, they also do not acknowledge the fact that indigenous people are the original sources of biopirated knowledge central to science, technology and development. Much as Euro-Americans do not acknowledge the looting, plunder and stealing of material wealth from indigenous peoples of the world, they also do not acknowledge the science and technology that they are looting from indigenous peoples (Amusan, 2017; James, 2009; Yeshitela, 1983; West, 2016; Tanaka, 2011). While Euro-Americans got knowledge, from the enslaved Africans, of agricultural techniques, corn planting, corn harvesting, advanced methods of refining sugar and sugar beets, lubricating process for machinery and rail road airbrakes (Yeshitela, 1983), there is no acknowledgement of the African origins of these inventions and innovations. In the light of the foregoing, we argue that antiplagiarism software being developed by Euro-America are useless in preventing biopiracy and they cannot force Euro-Americans to acknowledge the African origins of science, mathematics, engineering and technology. The point is that the antiplagiarism software is not useful in decolonising science, technology, engineering and mathematics because the software is not designed to apprehend Euro-Americans engaged in biopiracy and looting of indigenous knowledge.

In order to preempt charges of biopiracy and theft of indigenous knowledge, Eurocentric scholars and thinkers are redefining indigenous knowledge as embodied knowledge where the body, and not the mind, is the knowing subject (Tanaka, 2011). Because intellectual property rights protect intellectual work, which is the work of the mind, such intellectual property rights laws would not protect embodied knowledge which originates from the body and not the mind. In this sense, defining indigenous knowledge as embodied knowledge denies it protection under intellectual property rights laws. To preempt charges of biopiracy and theft of indigenous knowledge systems, Eurocentric scholars are also defining indigenous knowledge as place-based knowledge, as local knowledge and as knowledge and science written onto landscapes (Hecht, 2011; Johnson, 2010). Depicting indigenous knowledge systems as place-based knowledge also excludes it from intellectual property rights laws: if it is place-based and not mind-based, then it follows that it is not included as intellectual property of the indigenous people because it is not based on the intellect but on place. Similarly, defining indigenous knowledge as local knowledge excludes it from intellectual property rights laws because it is not defined as the work of the mind or the intellect – to be local is not necessarily to be based on the mind or intellect. Defining indigenous knowledge as local knowledge merely indicates the place where it is located but it does not categorically say that it is the work of the indigenous intellect.

Depicting indigenous knowledge as written on the landscape is also a sleight of hand to preempt charges of biopiracy and theft of indigenous knowledge. If indigenous knowledge is written on landscapes, it effectively means that it is not a product of the intellect and therefore it cannot be protected by intellectual property rights laws. Intellectual property rights laws protect works of the mind or intellect, they do not protect knowledge written on landscapes. Portraying indigenous knowledge as written on the landscape presupposes that indigenous minds are themselves empty in the

31

sense of *tabula rasa*. If techne, as Heidegger (1977) notes, is the name of activities and skills of the craftsman's mind, then it follows that indigenous people will not be able to claim to have technology if their indigenous knowledge is not written in their minds but onto the landscape.

Underscored in the foregoing is the fact that Eurocentric scholars and thinkers would be happy to empty indigenous minds, to depict indigenous minds as empty, or to consider indigenous people as having no minds at all - to validate the assumptions of *tabula rasa*. Technologies are being developed to delete and edit memories and genes; the justification is partly the need to create spaces for new knowledges (Griffin 19 May 2016; Gregory, 19 February 2019). Indigenous archives and memories have been subject to destruction, deletion and editing or at least vilifications by Eurocentric scholars and thinkers (Okere, 2005). The deletion and editing of memories have a long history in Western culture where for instance there was a decree called *"damnatio memoriae"* meaning the name and memory of the damned were scratched from inscriptions so that they would be forgotten (Bond, 14 May 2011). *Damnatio memoriae* was an institutional decree by way of an attempt at conscious forgetting analogous to wiping a tablet clean (Petersen, 2011). *Damnatio memoriae* involved the formal or informal erasure of records and sometimes tangible works of an individual. Also, the tombs of those declared *damnatio memoriae* were destroyed or carefully reattributed through replacement of the individual's names, titles and images (Robey, 2013; Wilkinson, 2016).

Although some scholars argue that "modernist" epistemologies are occularcentric privileging vision or the sense of sight (Townsend-Gault, 2009; Classen and Howes, n.d; Keblowska-Lawniczak, 2005), we argue here that *damnatio memoriae* negates this claim to occularcentrism. In a context where colonialists/imperialists destroyed indigenous shrines, looted and plundered indigenous tombs and artefacts, and perpetrated genocide erasing indigenous people, it would be incorrect to claim that European epistemologies are occularcentric or privilege the sense of sight. Colonialists/imperialists destroyed what they did not want to see, they erased and rendered indigenous knowledges invisible, indigenous artefacts that were visible and subject to the sense of sight in Africa have become invisible as a result of colonial looting and plunder. In this sense, colonial or European epistemologies privileged invisibility because they rendered artefacts and indigenous people invisible in the colonial/imperial context.

Claims that colonial epistemologies were/are rational are inconsistent with the irrational looting, plunder, biopiracy and destruction perpetrated on indigenous knowledges, including artefacts and skulls that were looted. Similarly, claims that colonial epistemologies were/are objective and truthful are inconsistent with the theft, plunder, biopiracy and looting that were perpetrated in relation to indigenous people/epistemologies. An objective person would not loot, plunder and colonise others – he/she would be able to tell the difference between his own property and property belonging to others. In this sense, colonial epistemologies ignored the binaries between property belonging to Europeans and property belonging to indigenous people that were colonised – colonialists/imperialists were confused as to which property belonged to them and which one belonged to indigenous people – western epistemologies were not necessarily premised on certitudes, or on binaries between knowledge and belief or truth and falsehood, or the subjective and objective or subject-object dichotomies. Epistemologies that legitimise dispossessing and robbing other people, plundering and looting resources and property belonging to others cannot be described as premised on certitudes, truthfulness, positivism, objectivity and rationality. Colonisation was not necessarily about setting up dichotomies or binaries or distinctions – it was about creating confusion, disorder, uncertainty and collapsing distinctions in the colonial frontiers. Decolonial scholarship would benefit by taking this into cognisance. For there to be meaningful decolonisation, there must be distinctions, dichotomies or binaries between decolonisation and colonisation. Post-colonial epistemologies would want hybridity and confusion between colonisation and decolonisation, between the colonisers and the colonised.

While some scholars and thinkers have argued that indigenous epistemologies do not privilege the sense of sight/occularcentrism/visibility (Nhemachena, 2017), we argue here that it is necessary to appreciate the context of indigenous people before making definitive pronouncements about their epistemologies. Subjected to colonial/imperial raids, wars, robbery and exploitation, indigenous people could not have privileged sight or visibility in the sense of wanting to be seen by colonisers and their agents. Naturally, indigenous people would hide away in the bushes, mountains and other places so that colonialists would not raid their livestock, kidnap them and their wives and children, destroy their granaries and other property. The point here is that indigenous people that were colonised were anxious to avoid the colonial/imperial evil eye (Abu-Rabia, 2005; Gersham, 2014) that would result in raids, looting, plunder, kidnapping, robbery and dispossession. It is not that indigenous epistemologies rely on lower senses (Classen and Howes, n.d); rather the fact is that indigenous people knew that if they were seen or if they became visible to colonialists, they would suffer dispossession, raids, looting and plunder as a result of the colonial/imperial evil eyes associated with bad luck, strange gazes, admiration without blessings and so on.

It would be inaccurate to simply associate occularcentrism or the predominance of the sense of sight with Western science and technology: occularcentrism or the predominance of the sense of sight is also associated with the evil eye, with colonial/imperial plunder, robbery and dispossession which must also be addressed by decolonial scholars. This book contends that indigenous science and technology depended as much on the senses of vision, visibility and occularcentrism as did Western science and technology – the big problem is that Westerners also relied on occularcentrism or primacy of the sense of sight to colonise other people. Both indigenous knowledge and Eurocentric epistemologies privilege the sense of sight/occularcentrism, depending on the contexts. One may for instance consider the science of digging trenches, in the World Wars, wherein European combatants would hide or take refuge – the idea behind the science of digging trenches, was to become invisible to the enemies. Similarly, indigenous people hid from the colonialists/imperialists, but this does not mean that their indigenous epistemologies do not generally privilege the sense of sight or occularcentrism; or binaries between being visible and being invisible, being at peace and being at war.

Decolonisation must be distinguished from mere transformation which can be neocolonial. Decolonisation and decoloniality must include Africanisation and Afrocentricity; decolonial epistemic perspective must constitute a combative discourse, a redemptive methodology and survival kit for pan-Africanists during the present moment (Mbele, 7 September 2019; Ndlovu-Gatsheni, 2013; Modiba, 2019). Decolonisation includes rethinking and redesigning the curriculum to suit indigenous people; it includes epistemic disobedience and resisting the reproduction of colonial taxonomies (Le Grange, 2016; Aikens *et al.*, 2015; Quijano, 2007). Decolonisation also involves resisting biopiracy and looting of indigenous knowledge; it involves restitution and compensation by those that have plundered and looted indigenous knowledge. In other words, the problem is not simply between having Western and indigenous worldview rather the problem concerns compensation for epistemologies subjected to biopiracy, theft and looting. The challenge is not simplistically in the question about whether Western epistemologies are universal, but the problem is in biopiracy and theft of indigenous knowledge systems which biopiracy must be abated and compensated for. Thus, decolonisation does not have to focus on felling statues or on demanding for fees to fall or the falling of European languages (Modiba, 2019); the idea is also to ensure that Western institutions that hold indigenous scientific collections repatriate and return what they looted from indigenous people (Roy, 13 April 2018).

Global support for "decolonising" universities and epistemologies should be understood in the context of indigenous people's demands for repatriation of their artefacts and scientific collections looted, by colonialists/imperialists, over centuries. There is a contestation in which Westerners are resisting repatriation of the artefacts, scientific collections and even skulls and skeletons of indigenous people that are lodged in Western museums. As they are resisting such repatriation of indigenous artefacts, skulls, skeletons and scientific collections, Westerners are pushing a competing agenda for the "decolonisation" of universities and epistemologies in former colonies. The "decolonisation" of universities and epistemologies in former colonies involves indigenous people rejecting and "repatriating" Western epistemologies and institutions ironically even as Westerners are refusing to repatriate indigenous artefacts, skulls, skeletons and scientific collections. The point here is that Westerners could sponsor the project of decolonising the mind, "decolonising" universities and epistemologies in lieu of returning indigenous artefacts, scientific collections and skulls as demanded for by indigenous people since independence. The question here is, if indigenous people agree to reject and "repatriate" Western epistemologies and institutions, will Westerners eventually also agree to "repatriate" and return indigenous artefacts, scientific collections, skulls and skeletons that are lodged in Western museums and private collections? If epistemologies and institutions that are Western are deemed to be colonising in Africa, why is it that indigenous artefacts, scientific collections, skulls and skeletons are not similarly considered to be colonising Euro-Americans who are keeping them in their museums and private collections in spite of demands by indigenous people? Might Euro-America be sponsoring and supporting the projects of decolonising African universities and epistemologies as a diversionary tactic to evade indigenous demands for repatriation of artefacts, scientific collections, skulls and skeletons currently lodged in Western museums? The question is it the colonised who owe debts to the colonisers or it is the colonisers who owe debts to the colonised – who must return and "repatriate" to who and why? Must decolonisation or decoloniality be defined in terms of indigenous people returning anything to the colonisers or it must be defined in terms of indigenous people getting compensation for colonial/imperial plunder, biopiracy, looting and dispossession? Might Westerners have infiltrated and hijacked the agenda of African academies by inverting the definition of decolonisation so that it would appear as if it is indigenous people that owe the colonisers "repatriation" and return (which are being defined as decolonisation) of epistemologies and institutions?

If indigenous people are collectively guilt of benefiting from "modernist" epistemologies which are "colonising" them, the question is why must Euro-Americans not be also collectively guilty of colonial/imperial dispossession, robbery, plunder and looting in respect of indigenous people. If present-day indigenous people are deemed to be collectively guilt of benefiting from centuries-old "modernist" epistemologies, it follows that Euro-Americans must also be collectively guilt of centuries-old enslavement and colonial crimes. In any case, given the history of colonial looting, plunder, dispossession and biopiracy, the provenance of the so-called modernist epistemologies is contestable. For this reason, some scholars like Taiwo (2010) note that indigenous people have had their precolonial modernities stolen along with the precolonial civilisations.

Indigenous people are demanding repatriation and return of their artefacts, scientific collections, skulls and skeletons lodged in Western museums and private collections (Hunt, 29 June 2019). In this regard, Egypt demanded the return of the Louvre, wall painting from tombs; Nigeria demanded the return of artefacts looted by the British from the Royal Palace of Benin City in 1897; Ethiopia has demanded back its wood and stone tablets, its Christian plaques which belong to the Ethiopian Orthodox Church (Trilling, 9 July 2019). Opposing the repatriation and return of the artefacts, Westerners have argued that the artefacts have become part of the property of the Western museums that have "cared" for them; they have argued that empire is neither good nor bad but that it is cosmopolitan and hybrid in the sense of creating universal museums; it has also been argued that museums are institutes of knowledge production, conservation and distribution (Hunt, 29 June 2019; Tlostanova, 2015). Thus, while indigenous people argue that decolonisation involves the return and repatriation of their artefacts (Bruchac, 2014), these demands for repatriation have sparked nervous reactions from Western museum officials and politicians who fear that their museums will be emptied – they therefore view restitution not as decolonisation but as "a symptom of destructive identity politics" (Trilling, 9 July 2019). In opposing repatriation, restitution and return of the indigenous artefacts, Westerners also argue that their museums are cosmopolitan and not merely European museums; they have argued that decolonisation and return or repatriation are not identical (Van Beurden, 2018; Higgins, 13 April

2018; International Council of Museums, 11 July 2019; Drieenhuizen, 2018). Some Westerners have argued that the artefacts reflected and exercised agency; that the artefacts if returned may be used in nationalist politics; they have argued that the question should not be about who the rightful owner is but it should be about the meaning of the objects or artefacts (Drieenhuizen, 2018).

The problem with shifting from the question about ownership to the question about meanings of artefacts or objects also underpins the biopiracy of indigenous knowledges – colonialists/imperialists have long depicted indigenous people as incapable of ownership and control of resources. In fact, indigenous people in the contemporary era are being taught that patrimony (heritages) are bad, that indigenous domination (having mastery) and dominion over indigenous heritages is also bad – the logic is to negate and subvert indigenous ownership and control of heritages. Heritages are reduced to the question of meanings and they are sadly shifted from questions of indigenous ownership, mastery and control. The provenance of indigenous artefacts is subjected to contestation including by scholars and thinkers who cannot fathom the contestability of the so-called modernist epistemologies (Irving, 2013; Jones, 2019). To subvert indigenous people's demands for restitution, it is often argued that the artefacts have independent agency, are relational in the sense of being subject to polyvocality, uncertainty and subject to multiple truths – these relational principles subvert indigenous claims to ownership, autonomy, mastery, control and sovereignty.

From the foregoing, we argue that given the Western history of looting, plunder and dispossession of resources including artefacts belonging to indigenous people, it is contestable that the universities in Africa are Western in origin; it is also contestable that the epistemologies in African universities are Western in origin. Colonialists/imperialists have a tendency to capture African "generals" and then invert them such that they kill their own kind; similarly, colonialists/imperialists have tended to appropriate indigenous gods and goddesses/ancestors and then invert them so that they torment, trouble and kill their own kind. In the colonial era, colonialists assimilated some indigenous Chiefs and Kings and inverted them so that they would work against their own people but in favour of colonialists. Now the argument here is that colonialists/imperialists captured and assimilated precolonial African universities, institutions and epistemologies which they inverted and turned against their original owners, but into service for colonialists. A good example is when Euro-American slave drivers noticed that precolonial Africans wore bangles and necklaces as part of their identity. The slave drivers and owners then designed and forced enslaved Africans to wear slave collars and slave badges as well as slave tattoos as part of their identity as slaves (Stephen, 1824; Blockson & Fry, 1991; Fuhrmann and Fuhrmann, 2012). Slave drivers noticed that Africans were collectivist and communalist in their relations and so the slave drivers and slave owners devised slave chains and yokes to tie the enslaved Africans together regardless of the imperatives of binaries between innocence and culpability.

In the contemporary era, imperial powers are sponsoring indigenous knowledges systems, particularly aspects like the wearing of bangles, necklaces, tattoos, amulets and so on: the reason, we argue, is to appropriate and invert these aspects so that indigenous people buy into contemporary discourses on digital humanities wherein they are expected to wear enhancement devices, wearable computers, "smart" textiles, "smart" watches, nanobots and so on that enhance imperial surveillance on indigenous people across the world. The point is that what are often addressed as Western or Eurocentric epistemologies are in fact indigenous knowledges that have been inverted and turned against indigenous people, as they serve imperialism/colonialism. To put it succinctly, the states that are in Africa are indigenous African states that have been inverted and turned against indigenous Africans; the economies in Africa are African economies that have been inverted and turned against Africans, the epistemologies in Africa are also African epistemologies that have been inverted and turned against indigenous people; the families of Africans are African but they have been inverted and turned against Africans. They are not necessarily "modernist" or new epistemologies or institutions, but they are the same old institutions and epistemologies that are simply inverted and turned against the original owners. Coloniality is about inversions, dispossession, plunder and looting which is what decoloniality and decolonisation must address.

Chapter outlines

In chapter two, Artwell Nhemachena, Nokuthula Hlabangane & Maria Kaundjua argue that indigenous knowledge should be theorised in terms of hospitality and not in terms of relationality. Noting that empire relied on networks, connections and relationality, this chapter argues that the Internet of Things and Big Data are not necessarily decolonial: they are used to mine data from indigenous people who are often denied data sovereignty, autonomy and human integrity. The chapter further contends that it is more appropriate to theorise indigeneity in terms of hospitality than it is to do so through relationality and relational research methods. It is argued that relationality sadly assumes that there is absolute openness, that there are no distinctions between indigenous human beings and animals; that indigenous people do not have or even deserve sovereignty and autonomy – the same assumptions were made by colonialists. On the other hand, it is noted that theorising indigeneity in terms of hospitality does not take away indigenous human essence, autonomy and sovereignty; it affirms distinctions between indigenous human beings and animals. It is noted that relational ontologies would discount humanism and humanist ethics, whereas theorising indigeneity in terms of hospitality would reaffirm the humanism and humanist ethics that indigenous people are known for since the precolonial era. Whereas hospitality theories would affirm indigenous sovereignty, autonomy, human essence, ownership and control over their material resources, epistemologies and data, relationality theories would deny the same to indigenous peoples.

Chapter three is authored by Alex Munyonga who argues that global coloniality through science and technology is real and not just a drill. For Munyonga, Western pharmaceutical corporations are capitalising on African desperation, low confidence and porous looting routes which are usually oiled through corruption. Such are permitting environments for the West to coerce Africans to dance according to the imperialist oppressive tunes. He further argues that sound pharmaceutical development for Africa is not a solo journey. Instead, it calls for African governments, communities and individuals to synchronise their energies towards arresting corruption to pave way for meaningful ownership, control and development of African herbal and medicinal lore. Clamouring for access and benefit sharing with giant Western pharmaceutical corporations which loot Africa is not a lasting solution. Without firm indigenous ownership, control and development policies in place, the progress path for herbal and medicinal knowledge development for Africa will remain a mirage. Predatory Western researches on African traditional herbs and medicines must be closely monitored and guarded against to seal medicinal-knowledge-leaking points.

Sindiso M. Nleya & Siqabukile Ndlovu's chapter four focuses on indigenous mathematics. They argue that the markings on the Ishango and Lebombo bones point to the existence and use of mathematical concepts and principles such as counting and mathematical modelling in the case of the lunar calendar. Furthermore, numerical systems such as those found in ancient Egypt and Mali are important shreds of evidence that dispel the Eurocentric view that mathematics was non-existent in pre-colonial Africa. Nleya and Ndlovu further argue that from a geometric point of view, the existence of a Rind papyrus instruction manual, for students in arithmetic and geometry, contains evidence of other mathematical knowledge, including composite and prime numbers and arithmetic. It also shows how to solve first order linear equations as well as arithmetic and geometric series. Also, recreational mathematics was an important aspect of life to the extent that puzzles and games such as Mancala and Morabaraba have been found to encompass important "modern" day mathematical concepts such as geometrical shapes, algebra, ratio and proportion, symmetry, logical reasoning, counting, combinatorial game theory, search algorithms, empirical and mental calculation. The authors argue that the family of Mancala games offers opportunities for new research in both mathematics and Artificial Intelligence. It is noted that prior work in "ethnomathematics" and "ethnocomputing" found in traditional practices (e.g., weaving, beading, sculpture, tattoo, drumming, and graffiti) show mathematical concepts such as Cartesian and polar coordinates and transformational geometry, and computational practices such as iteration and conditionals. Just like computer science is nowadays considered to be a field of research distinct from mathematics, "ethnocomputing" is considered to be a research topic distinct from "ethnomathematics". Some aspects of "ethnocomputing" that have their roots in "ethnomathematics" include: counting and sorting, locating, measuring, designing, playing and explaining.

In chapter five, Olúwolé Téwógboyè Òkéwándé focuses on *Ifá* that is believed to be the foundation of Yorùbá culture. *Ifá's* scope of knowledge can broadly be categorised into religion and science. However, till today, within and outside the Yorùbá communities, *Ifá* is generally believed to be associated more with one of the major divinities than with any other human aspects of life. As a result, many people are uninformed, uneducated and ignorant about the faculties of *Ifá's* mathematical and scientific knowledge. Therefore, this study attempts to critically review available works on *Ifá* mathematics and science and then relate these to contemporary mathematics, computer science and biology. The aim in this study is to promote the development and sustainability of African mathematical and scientific knowledge systems: this is done through an evaluation of the African indigenous knowledge systems before the incursions of colonialism. It is hoped that this chapter will go a long way to bring African indigenous knowledge systems of mathematics and science into limelight. The chapter demonstrates that colonial mathematics, science and technology were preceded by African indigenous science, mathematics and technology. The chapter urges Africanist researchers, authors and scholars - particularly, mathematicians and scientists - to delve more into African indigenous knowledge systems such as *Ifá's* mathematics and science. It concludes that, *Ifá* is more than a religion: it encapsulates indigenous knowledge systems of mathematics and science that can be equated to contemporary mathematics, science and technology in other places of the world.

Robert Matikiti's chapter six dwells on the incursions of Christianity on indigenous Zimbabweans. He argues that the spread of Christianity was a threat to African culture, and it explains why some Africans are no longer practising their indigenous customs, epistemologies and other practices. The missionaries saw themselves as people created in a very superior and special way. The early missionaries were inclined to think that most African practices and customs were unchristian. When missionaries introduced Christianity into Zimbabwe it brought with it an alien culture, which inevitably affected the psychological, sociological, cultural and religious aspects of the natives. There is clear evidence that the missionaries viewed Africans as strange people whom the European readers would easily consider subhuman, or at most would regard as worse than themselves. The Westerners that came to Africa saw the extraordinary everywhere on the continent. Their psyche misled them into seeing the opposite of the reality. Many early missionaries held that indigenous African religions were totally without merit. Colonialists, including missionaries commonly held that indigenous Africans are devoid of any culture and epistemology. Such a prejudice on its own is uncalled for because Africans had a strong culture to reckon with as a people. Moreover, in the context of prejudices about Africans, we should bear in mind that the concept of Black inferiority reached its high point when the philosophers of the Enlightenment era internationalised it. The description of the African by the colonialists and missionaries paints a gloomy picture of what an African was in the socio-cultural and religious outlook. The initial perception of Africans by colonialists and missionaries alike negates the possibility of tolerance towards their religion and culture. Matikiti also argues that it is very important for Africans to guard their culture and epistemology jealously as failure to do so creates an identity crisis since culture is the basis of African identity.

In chapter seven, Babarinsa Olayiwola focuses on algebra. He argues that the history of algebra in Africa got relatively little awareness unlike other regions of the world. There are remarkable pre-colonial African achievements in mathematics. It is forgotten, all too often, that Africa was the first continent to know literacy and to institute a school system. Thousands of years before the Greek letters or Arabic numerals were invented, and before the use of the Latin word "schola" school; the scribes of ancient Egypt wrote, read, administered and philosophised using papyrus. Although Mesopotamian mathematics is known from a great number of cuneiform texts, the Egyptian mathematics is known from only a small number of papyrus texts. Since, the Egyptian and Babylonian mathematical texts display great similarities, it is evident that algebra originated from Africa. Egypt existed long before Babylon and, anatomically, "modern" Homo sapiens and early civilisations (90,000 to 60,000 years ago) are traceable to the Great Rift Valley in Africa.

David O. Akombo; Pearl S. Gray; George O. Griffin & Baruti I. Katembo's chapter eight critically analyses circularity in msonge (round hut) and music. They argue that the Eurocentric disdain for the supposed primitivism of Afrocentric culture can be detected and examined at many levels; however, this supposed European superiority may well be based on ignorance of cultural history. The authors argue that the inherently genius design of the msonge – mathematically, structurally and spatially – was also known to early Europeans. The central hypothesis here is that Europeans abandoned the natural advantages of circularity in favour of rectilinearity only as a pragmatic necessity due to the dense populations of emerging cities; the architectural shift was therefore an essential adaptation rather than an intellectual advancement. Similarly, the circularity of African music and dance is in direct reflection of the native cultural philosophy on life – not dissimilar from the European attempt to synchronise musical compositions rectilinearly with the emerging philosophies of reason. Precolonial African architecture and music hold no false pretence of sophistication; rather, they reflect a culture fully accepting and incorporative of their natural innate beauty, intelligence and genius.

In chapter nine, Martin Mujinga focuses on the liberation of African theology from Eurocentric theology. Mujinga argues that Jesus addressed issues of oppression of his day. He further argues that African theologians and Christians should address issues of colonial/imperial dispossession, biopiracy, looting, plunder, robbery, exploitation and impoverishment on the continent of Africa. African theology is also challenged to expose the dehumanisation of Africans, oppression and land grabbing and all that which is haunting African peoples. He contends that in the light of the fact that colonialism and imperialism destroyed African cultures and epistemologies, it is imperative for decolonial scholars and thinkers to ensure that African cultures and epistemologies are revived and recentred.

Collins Nhengu's chapter ten focuses on the rejection of African spirituality by the Apostolic Faith Mission in Zimbabwe (AFM). Nhengu notes that there was no attempt to accommodate positive aspects of African indigenous religion and epistemologies. The AFM shared similarities with the colonialists in that they regarded the Africans as inferior and their religion as demonic, primitive, fetishistic, magic, barbaric and witchcraft. These terms were used to justify the colonial enterprise, to pave way for the colonisers. The author contends that this was the same attitude that the early missionaries portrayed as they facilitated the entrance for the colonisers. The suppression of African spiritism is a confirmation that the AFM remains cast in Western mould of worship. Any attempts to respect African ancestors and to uphold culture in the church was seen as sinful. AFM is a church whose principles rest squarely on exclusivism and colonial attitudes.

In chapter eleven, Baruti I. Katembo discusses msonge in relation to mathematics and architecture. The msonge as discussed in this chapter is much more than a shape or dwelling. It encapsulates heritage aspects of Africans' art, technology and nature-based worldview through a geometric aesthetic – circularity. For Baruti, round dwelling structures are iconically African, but they are found in the ancestral architecture of most global societies; it is something that most human cultures share – a connector. He contends that ancient treasures should be preserved in the present, i.e., "modernity" can be enriched with the past. In the case of Africa, msonge-inspired applications should be incorporated into societal architecture – schools; hospitals; office buildings; churches; residences and other structures.

Okewande Esther Oyeniwe's chapter twelve contends that indigenous science, when recentred, can support the teaching of science in Africa, and Nigeria in particular. She argues that Western science does not have a monopoly on experimentation, positivism and truth: indigenous people in Africa also had their own sciences which were positivistic, and which were realised through experimentation in the field and not necessarily always in enclosed laboratories. Indigenous science is not necessarily about the supernatural, the irrational, the mystical, magical or esoteric. Indigenous knowledge includes the esoteric and supernatural, but it is irreducible to such mysticism and esotericism. In much the same way Westerners have their science as well as their esoteric and mystical religions, indigenous Africans have their own science as well as religions including the esoteric and mystical. Oyeniwe further posits that African indigenous knowledge is not all about the mystical, esoteric and spiritual – there is more to these aspects.

In chapter thirteen, Sibongile Nyoni argues that schools are supposed to be viewed as privileged centres for transmission and perpetuation of cultural heritage of all learners rather than hero worshipping the supremacy of a particular race. The mathematical heritage of the Africans must be valued, and African cultures must be embedded into the mathematics teacher education curriculum. For Nyoni, mathematics education easily promotes the learners' understanding of their lives if there is connection with their everyday experiences. Teacher education is linked with the preparation of future citizens therefore it should reflect what is currently important to the nations which they serve. The author argues that Africa presently needs youths that are creative and innovative. Therefore, teacher education programs for training mathematics teachers should equip the teachers with skills and knowledge of teaching mathematics for synthesis and connecting it with the learners' environment so that mathematics can be used to solve problems faced in Africa.

References

Abdi, A. A. (2007). Oral societies and colonial experiences: SubSaharan Africa and the de facto power of the written word. *International Education* vol 37 (1): 42-59.

Abu-Rabia, A. (2005). The evil eye and cultural beliefs among the Bedouin tribes of the Negev, Middle East. *Folklore* vol 116: 241-254.

Acemoglu, D. & Robinson, J. A. (2010). Why is Africa poor? In *Economic History of Developing Regions* vol 25 (1): 21

Adams, W. M. & Anderson, D. M. (2016). Irrigation before development: Indigenous and induced change in agricultural water management in East Africa. *African Affairs*. Vol 87 (349): 519 – 535.

Adamu, J. & Bello, N. (2015). Rethinking on the pre-colonial traditional industries: A means for the transformation of the Nigerian economy in the 21st century, in *ASPROAEDU* vol 1 (1): 1-10.

Adegbindin, O. (2015). Critical Notes on Hegel's Treatment of Africa, in *Ogirisi: A New Journal of African Studies* vol 11: 19 – 43.

Adu, F. M., Ajayi, A. T. & Aremu, J. O. (2018). Textile industry in Yorubaland: Indigenous knowledge and modernity in the era of globalisation. *Advances in Social Sciences Research Journal* vol 5 (4): 282-292.

Ahlin, J. (2018). What justifies judgments of inauthenticity? *HEC Forum* vol 30 (4): 361-377

Aikens, N. *et al.* (2015). *Decolonising museums*. L'Internationale Books

Amankwah-Ayeh, K. (1996). Traditional planning elements of pre-colonial African towns. *New Contree* vol 39

Amusan, L. (2017). Politics of biopiracy: An adventure into Hoodia/Xhoba patenting in southern Africa. *Afr J Tradit Complement Altern Med* vol 14 (1): 103-109.

Asante, M. K. (2015). Engaging Nkrumah's consciencism: An Afrocentric close reading, in Asante, M. K. & Ledbetter, C. (eds) *Contemporary Critical Thought in Africology and Africana Studies*. Rowman and Littlefield.

Azeez, O. A. (2011). Indigenous art of West Africa in wood, in *Global Journal of Human Social Science* vol 11 (2): 62-

Babalola, A. B. (2017). Ancient history of technology in West Africa: The indigenous glass/glass bead industry and the society in early Ile-Ife, South Nigeria. *Journal of Black Studies* vol 48 (5): 501-527.

Blier, S. P. (2012). The African urban past: Historical perspective on the metropolis, in Adjaye, D. (ed) *African Metropolitan Architecture*. New York: Rizzoli

Blockson, C. L. & Fry, R. (1991). *Black genealogy*. Baltimore: Black Classic Press.

Boiselle, L. N. (2016). Decolonising science and science education in a postcolonial space (Trinidad, a Developing Caribbean Nation, Illustrates) in *SAGE Open* vol 1: 1-11

Bond, S. E. (14 May 2011). Erasing the Face of History, in *The New York Times*
https://www.nytimes.com/2011/05/15/opinion/15bond.html

Borup, M. *et al.,* (2006). The sociology of expectations in science and technology. *Technology Analysis and Strategic Management* vol 18 (3/4): 285 – 298.

Bridle, J. (2018). *New dark age technology and the end of the future.* Verson Books.

Browne, A. (1977). Descartes's dreams. *Journal of the Arburg and Courtauld Institutes* vol 40: 256 – 273.

Bruchac, M. (2014). Decolonization in archaeological theory, in Smith, C. (ed) *Encyclopedia of Global Archaeology: 2069 – 2077.* New York: Springer.

Calance, M. (2014). Reason, liberty and science: The contribution of freemasonry to the enlightenment. *HSS* vol 3 (2): 111-136

Campbell, H. (29 April 2010). Particle physics opens up new sense of purpose for Africa. *Pambazuka News*
https://www.pamabazuka.org/pan-africanism/particle-physics-opens-up-new-sense-purpose-africa

Charney, M. W. (2016). Before and after the wheel: Precolonial and colonial states and transportation in mainland Southeast Asia and West Africa. *HumanNetten* vol 37: 10 – 38.

Chigwedere, P & Essex, M. (2010). AIDS denialism and public health practice. *AIDS and Behavior* vol 14: 237 – 247.

Chirikure, S. (2017). The metalworker, the potter, and the pre-European African "laboratory", in Mavhunga, C. C. (ed) *What Do Science Technology, and Innovation Mean from Africa?* MIT Press.

Choudros, T. G. *et al.* (2016). The evolution of the double-horse chariots from the bronze age to the Hellenistic times. *FME Transactions* vol 44 (2): 229 – 236.

Classen, C. & Howes, D. (n.d) The Museum as Sensescape: Western Sensibilities and Indigenous Artifacts.
WebclassenTheMuseumsasSen

Clifford, J. (1986). Introduction: Partial truths, in Clifford, J. & Marcus, G. E. (eds) *Writing Culture: The Poetics and Politics of Ethnography*. Berkeley & Los Angeles: University of California Press.

Cockell, C. (2010). Ethics and extraterrestial life, in Landfester, U. *et al.* (eds) *Humans in Outer Space – Interdisciplinary Perspectives*. Springer Science and Business Media.

Collins, R. & Restivo, S. (1983). Development, diversity, and conflict in the Sociology of Science. *The Sociological Quarterly* vol 24(2): 185 – 200.

Collyer, F. (2011). Reflexivity and the sociology of science and technology: The invention of "Eryc" the antibiotic. *The Qualitative Report* vol 16 (2): 316 – 340.

Conroy, D. (2003). Using oxen for farm work and transportation, in Hazeltine, B. & Bull, D (eds) *Field Guide to Appropriate Technology*. Academic Press.

Dastile, N. P. & Ndlovu-Gatsheni, S. J. (2013). Power, knowledge and being: Decolonial combative discourse as a survival kit for pan Africanists in the 21st century. *Alternation* vol 20 (1): 105-134.

Davies, M. (2008). The irrigation system of the Poot, Northwest Kenya. Azania XLIII: 50-76.

Davis, P. J. & Hersh, R. (2005). *Descartes' dream: The world according to mathematics*. Courier Corporation.

De Leeuw, S. & Hunt, S. (2018). Unsettling decolonizing geographies. *Geography Compass* vol 12: 1 – 14.

Diakanyo, S. (28 December 2010). We are not all Africans, black people are! in *Mail and Guardian* https://thoughtleader.co.za/sentletsediakanyo/2010/12/28/we-are-not-all

Dickson, K. B. (1977). Trade patterns in Ghana at the beginning of the eighteenth century, in Konczacki, Z. A. & Konczacki, J. M. (eds) *An Economic History of Tropical Africa: The Precolonial Period*. Psychology Press.

Diethelm, P. & Mckee, M. (2009). Denialism: What is it and how should scientists respond? *European Journal of Public Health* vol 19 (1): 2- 4.

Drieenhuizen, C. (2018). Mirrors of time and agents of action: Indonesia's claimed cultural objects and decolonisation, 1947 – 1978. *BMGN – Low Countries Historical Review* vol 133 (2): 91-104.

Duchesne, R. (2011). *The uniqueness of Western civilization.* Leiden: BRILL.

Ekeh, L. U. (2010). *Industrialization and national prosperity (lessons for the Developing Countries)* Luzek Publishers.

Ellert, H. (1984). *Material culture of Zimbabwe.* Longman.

Ellyatt, H. (21 November 2013). Freemasons see young blood as key to survival, in CNBC Business News https://www.cnbc.com/2013/11/19/see-young-blood-as-key-to-survival.html

Emeagwali, G. (2014). Intersections between Africa's indigenous knowledge systems and history, in Emeagwali, G. & Dei, G. J. S. (eds) *African Indigenous Knowledge and the Disciplines.* Rotterdam/Boston: Sensepublishers.

Esquivel, R. M. (2018). Global gistory and freemasonry: 300 years of modernity, sociability and imperialism. *REHMLACT* vol 9 (2): 1 – 18.

Fischer, M. M. J. (2007). Four genealogies for a recombinant anthropology of science and technology. *Cultural Anthropology* vol 22 (4): 539 – 615.

Franco, M (2016). *Entrepreneurship: Practice-oriented perspectives.* BOD-Book on Demand.

Fuchs, C. (2013). *Social media: A critical introduction.* SAGE.

Fuhrmann, C. J. & Fuhrman, C. (2012). *Policing the Roman empire: Soldiers, administration, and public order.* Oxford University Press.

Gerdes, P. (1994). On mathematics in the history of sub-Saharan Africa. *Historia Mathematica* vol 21: 345 – 376.

Gersham, B. (2014). The economic origins of the evil eye belief https://papers.ssrn.com/sol3/papers.cfm?abstract_id=2308137

Gikandi, S. (2014). *Slavery and the culture of taste.* Princeton University Press.

Gilmartin, D. (1994). Scientific empire and imperial science: colonialism and irrigation technology in the Indus basin. *The Journal of Asian Studies* vol 53 (4): 1127 -1149.

Goss, A. (2009). Decent colonialism? Pure science and colonial ideology in the Netherlands East Indies 1910-1929. *Journal of Southeast Asian Studies* vol 40 (1): 187-214.

Gould, C & Folb, P. (2002). *Project Coast: Apartheid's chemical and biological warfare programme.* Geneva & Cape Town: United nations Institute for Disarmament Research & Centre for Conflict Resolution.

Gregory, A. (19 February 2019). Scientists have discovered how to find your bad memories and delete them from your mind for good. *Mirror* https://www.mirror.co.uk/science/scientisst-discovered-how-find-your

Griffin, A. (19 May 2016). How to make yourself forget things and delete your memories, according to science. *Independent* https://www.independent.co.uk/news/science/how-to-make-yourself-forget

Gruber, K. E. (2018). Slave clothing and adornment in Virginia. *Encylopedia Virginia* https://www.enclopediavirginia.org/slave_clothing_and_adorn ment_in_virginia

Hackett, R. I. J. & Soares, B. F. (eds) (2015). *New media and religions transformations in Africa.* Indiana University Press.

Haidara, A. K. (2008). The state of manuscripts in Mali and efforts to preserve them, in Jeppie, A. & Diagne, S. B. (eds) *The Meanings of Timbuktu.* Cape Town and Dakar: HSRC and CODESRIA.

Hecht, G. (ed) (2011). *Entangled geographies: Empire and technopolitics in the global cold war.* MIT Press

Heidegger, M. (1977). *The question concerning technology and other essays.* New York: Karper Torchbooks.

Heinz, A. (1998). Colonial perspectives in the construction of the psychotic patient as primitive man. *Critique of Anthropology* vol 18 (4): 421-444.

Heleta, S. (2016). Decolonisation of higher education: Dismantling epistemic violence and eurocentrism in South Africa. *Transformation in Higher Education* vol 1 (1): 1 – 8.

Higgins, C. (13 April 2018). British Museum Director Hartwig Fischer: 'There are no foreigners here – the museum is a world country'. *The Guardian* https://www.theguardian.com/culture/2018/apri/13/british-museum-director-hartwig-fischer-there-are-no-foreigners-here-the

Hunt, T. (29 June 2019). Should museums return their colonial artefacts. *The Guardian* https://www.theguardian.com/culture/2019/jun/29/should-museums-return-their-colonial-artefacts

Huylebrouck, D. (2006). Mathematics in (Central) Africa before colonization. *Anthropologica et Praehistorica* vol 117: 135 – 162.

Ingold, T. (1997). Eight themes in the Anthropology of technology. *Social Analysis: The International Journal of Anthropology* vol 41 (1): 106 – 138.

International Council of Museum, (11 July 2019). Panel/discussion an drestitution: Moving towards a more holistic perspective and relational approach htps://com.museum/en/news/panel-decolonisation-and-restitution-moving-towards-a-and-restitution-moving-towards-a-more-holistic-perspecive-and-relational

Irving, S. (2013) The restitution of ancient artefacts. Reinvention: *An international Journal of UndergraduateResearch* https://warwick.ac.uk/fac/cross_fac/iat//reinvention/rchive/b cur2013speicl

James, G. G. M. (2009). *Stolen legacy: Greek philosophy is stolen Egyptian philosophy.* The Journal of Pan African Studies eBook.

Johnson, D. & Davis, C. (2015). Introduction, in Davis, C. & Johnson, D. (eds) *The Book in Africa: Critical Debates.* Springer

Johnson, J. T. (2010). Place-based learning and knowing: Critical pedagogies grounded in indigeneity, in *Springer Science and Business Media* https://www.jstor.org/stable/23325391?seq=1#page.scan

Johnson, W. (1999). *Soul by soul: Life inside the Antebellum slave market.* Harvard University Press.

Jones, M. (2019). Collections in the expanded field: Relationality and the provenance of artefacts and archives. *Heritage* vol 2: 884 – 897.

Jones, W. T. (1979). Somnio ergo sum: Descartes' three dream. Division of the Humanities and Social Sciences, California Institute of Technology, Humanities Working Paper 40: 1 -41

Joseph, G. G. (2011). *The crest of the peacock: Non-European roots of mathematics*. Princeton and Oxford: Princeton University Press.

Jylha, K. M. (2016). Refusing to acknowledge the problem of climate change. *E-International Relations*
https://www.e.ir.info/2016/06/13/refusing-to-acknowledge

Kalichman, S. C. (2014). The Psychology of AIDS denialism: Pseudoscience, conspiracy thinking, medical mistrust. *European Psychologist* vol 19 (1): 13 – 22.

Kalichman, S. C. Eaton, L. & Cherry, C. (2010). There is no proof that HIV causes AIDS: AIDS denialism beliefs among people living with HIV/AIDS. *J Behav Med* vol 33: 432 – 440.

Kao, V. (2017). Science, technology, and the human: Integrating STEM and the introductory Humanities Course. *Interdisciplinary Humanities* vol 34 (3): 7 – 21.

Karamanides, D. (2005). *Pythagoras: Pioneering mathematician and musical theorist of ancient Greece*. The Rosen Publishing Group, inc

Kaya, H. O. and Seleti, Y. N. (2013). African indigenous knowledge systems and relevance of higher education in South Africa. *The International Educational Journal: Comparative Perspectives* vol 12 (1): 30 -44.

Kebede, M. (2004). Africa's quest for a philosophy of decolonization, Philosophy Faculty Publications Paper 109
http://ecomons.udayton.edu/phl_fac_pub/109

Keblowska-Lawniczak, E. (2005). Seeing things and being seen: Distorted scopic regimes in some modern plays, in Vernon, P. (ed) *Seeing Things: Literature and the Visual Presses* Universitaires Francois-Rabelais

Khoza, A. (1 December 2016). US nurse comes to SA to graduate as sangoma. *News24*
https://www.news24.com/SouthAfrica/News/us-nurse-comes-to-sa-to-graduate

Kienon-Kabore, T. H. (2017). History of traditional science and technology in sub-Saharan Africa: Problematic and methodology of approach. *International Journal of Academic Research and Reflection* vol 5 (5): 47 – 59.

Killick, D. (2015). Invention and innovation in African iron-smelting technologies. *Cambridge Archaeological Journal* vol 25(1): 307-319.

Killick, D. (2016). A global perspective on the pyrotechnologies of sub-Saharan Africa. *Azania: Archaeological Research in Africa*, vol 51 (1): 62-87.

Kleinschmidt, H. E. (1944). Evolution of the wheel. *The Scientific Monthly* vol 59 (4): 273-282.

Kriger, C. E. (2006). Mapping the history of cotton textile production in precolonial West Africa. *African Economic History* vol 33: 87-116.

Kunene, T. (21 December 1997). Zimbabwe: White sangoma claims to be high. *Standard* https://allafrica.com/stories/1997/22/0035.html

Le Grange, L. (2016). Decolonising the university curriculum. *South African Journal of Higher Education* vol 30 (2): 1-12.

Legates, D. R. *et al.* (2015). Climate consensus and 'misinformation': A rejoinder to agnotology, scientific consensus and the teaching and learning of climate change. *Science and Education* vol 24: 299 – 318.

Levy-Bruhl, L. (1926). *Revival: How natives think.* London: Routledge.

Levy-Bruhl, L. (1979). *How natives think.* Ravenio Books.

Levy-Bruhl, L. (2018). *Revival: Primitives and the supernatural.* Taylor and Francis.

Lewandowsky, S. *et al.,* (2015) Seepage: Climate change denial and its effects on the scientific community. *Global Environmental Change* vol 33: 1 – 13.

Likuwa, K. M. (2014). Contract labourers from Kavango on farms in Namibia 1925-1972. *Journal of Namibian Studies* vol 16: 47-60.

Lissovoy, N. D. (2019). Decoloniality as inversion: Decentring the west in emancipatory theory and pedagogy. *Globalisation, Societies and Education* vol 17 (4): 419-431.

Lomas, R., (8 February 2018). I'm a freemason and the discrimination against us has to stop, in Independent https://www.independent.co.uk/voices/fremasons-discrimination-hand-shake-secret

Ludwig, D. & Poliseli, L. (2018). Relating traditional and academic ecological knowledge: Mechanistic and holistic epistemologies across cultures. *Biology and Philosophy* vol 33 (43): 1-19.

Lumpkin, B. (1987). African and African-American contributions to mathematics, in Portland Public Schools. Geocultural Baseline Essay Series

Lutkehaus, N. & Cool, J. (1999). Paradigms lost and found: The "crisis of representation" and visual Anthropology, in Gaines, J. M. & Renov, M. (eds) *Collecting Visible Evidence*. Minneapolis: University of Minnesota Press.

Makgubela, M. (2018). Decolonise, don't diversify: Discounting diversity in the South African academe as a tool for ideological pacification. *Education as Change* vol 22 (1): 1 -21.

Maranda, L. & Soares, B. B. (2017). The predatory museum, in ICOFOM Study Series vol 45 http://journals.opnedition.org/iss/290

Marcus, G. E., Fischer, M. M. J. and Fischer, M. (1998). *Anthropology as cultural critique: An experimental moment in the human sciences.* University of Chicago Press.

Matola, N. *et al.* (2019). Contextual decolonisation of higher education in South Africa, in Fomunyam, K. G. (ed) *Decolonising Higher Education in the Era of Globalisation and Internationalisation.* Africa Sun media

Matthews, J. R. (2017). Understanding indigenous innovation in rural West Africa: Challenges to diffusion of innovations theory and current social innovation practice. *Journal of Human Development and Capabilities* vol 18 (2): 223-238.

Mays, D. A. (2004). *Women in early America: Struggle, survival and freedom in a new world.* ABC-CLIO.

Mbele, V. (7 September 2019). The Africanisation and Decolonisation of Higher Education: Progress and Challenges, in *Pambazuka News* https://www.pambazuka.org/pan-africanism/africanisation-and-decolonisation

Mcgushin, E. (2018). The role of Descartes's dream in the Meditations and in the historical ontology of ourselves. *Foucault Studies* vol 25: 84 – 102.

McKee, M. (2010). How the growth of denialism undermines public health. *BMJ* vol 341 http://doi.org/10.1136/bmj.c6950

Mehos, D. C. & Moon, S. M. (2011). The uses of portability, in Hecht, G. (ed) *Entangled Geographies: Empire and Technopolitics in the Global Cold War.* MIT Press.

Modiba, N. S. (2019). Decolonising the curriculum in higher education, in Fomunyam, K. G. (ed) *Decolonising Higher Education in the Era of Globalisation and Internationalisation.* African Sun Media.

Moore, J. (2009). The dangers of denying HIV. *Nature* vol 459 (168) doi:10.1038/459/68a

Morris, B. (2006). The ivory trade and chiefdoms in pre-colonial Malawi. *The Society of Malawi Journal* vol 59 (2): 6-23.

Mthethwa, B. (29 March 2017). White sangoma to jet off to the US. *Sowetan Live* https://www.sowetanlive.co.za/news/2017-03-29-white-sangoma-to-jet

Muldoon, J. (20 March 2019). Academics: It's time to get behind decolonising the curriculum. *The Guardian* https://www.theguradian.com/education/2019/mar/20/academics-its-time-to-go

Nattrass, N. (2011) Defending the boundaries of science: AIDS denialism, peer review and the medical hypotheses saga. *Sociology of Health and Illness* vol 33 (4): 507 - 521

Ndlovu-Gatsheni, S. J. (2015). Africa, in *History Campass* vol 13 (10): 485-496.

Netshitenzhe, J. (4 March 2015). Theorising the South African renaissance ideal, panel discussion: roundtable: Role of intellectuals in the state-society nexus.

Ngozi, E. (2014). The blight of African indigenous technology in the 21st century: The way forward. *Journal of Tourism and Heritage Studies* vol 3 (1): 59 – 73.

Nhemachena, A. (2017). *Relationality and resilience in a not so relational world? Knowledge, chivanhu and (de)coloniality in 21st century conflict-torn Zimbabwe.* Bamenda: Langaa RPCIG.

Nhemachena, A. *et al.,* (2017). Transnational corporations' land grabs and the on-going second mad scramble for Africa: An introduction, in Warikandwa, T. V., Nhemachena, A. & Mtapuri, O. (eds) *Transnational Land Grabs and Restitution in an Age of the (De-)Militarised New Scramble for Africa: A Pan African Socio-Legal Perspective.* Bamenda: Langaa RPCIG.

Nhemachena, A. (2018). Decolonisation, Africanisation and the cannibalistic figure of the posthuman. Presentation at the University of South Africa's Africa Speaks Occasional Lecture Series, 20 September 2018

Nhemachena, A. *et al.*, (2018). Transitology as cannibalism/cannibalism as transitology: An examination of (neo)imperial processes of consuming African people. *Africology: The Journal of Pan African Studies* vol 12 (6)

Nhemachena, A., Kangira, J. & Mlambo, N. (2019). Theorising displacement, elimination and replacement of indigenous people: An introduction to decolonising land issues, in Kangira, J. *et al.*, (eds) *Displacement, Elimination and Replacement of Indigenous People: Putting into Perspective Land Ownership and Ancestry in Decolonising Contemporary Zimbabwe*. Bamenda: Langaa RPCIG

Nuraan, D. (2018). On the problematique of decolonisation as a post-colonial endeavour. *Educational Philosophy and Theory* vol 50 (14) 1434; doi:10.1080/001311857.2018.1462518

Nzewi, M. & Nzewi, O. (2007). *A contemporary study of musical Arts: Illuminations, reflections and explorations*. African Minds.

Odeyale, T. O. & Adekunle, T. O. (2008). Innovative and sustainable local material in traditional African architecture – Socio-cultural dimension, in D'Ayala, D. & Fodde, E. (eds) *Structural Analysis of Historic Construction*. London: Taylor and Francis Group

Okere, T. (2005). *African philosophy and the hermeneutics of culture: Essays in honour of Thephilus Okere*. LIT Verlag Munster.

O'Keefe, D. (23 October 2013). The colonialism denialists. SocialWorker.org https://socialworker.org/2013/10/23/the-colonialism-denialists

Okoduwa, A. I. (2007). Where bottom dropped off manufacturing innovation in Nigeria: An example of the Esan people in Edo State. *Stud. Tribes Tribals* vol 5 (1): 29-34.

Oladipo, O. (1995). Reason, identity, and the African quest: The problems of self-definition in African philosophy. *Africa Today* vol 42 (3): 26 – 38.

Olajide, O. (2013). *The complete concise history of the slave trade*. Authorhouse.

Olaoye, R. A. (1989). A study of twentieth century weaving in Ilorin, Nigeria. *Africa Study Monographs* vol 10 (2): 83-92.

Onipede, K. J. (2010). Technology development in Nigeria: The Nigerian machine tools industry experience. *J Economics* vol 1 (2): 85 – 90.

Oshewolo, R. M. (2018). Reconsidering the Owe woven cloth of Nigeria from a gendered perspective. *Africology: The Journal of Pan African Studies* vol 12 (6): 110-121.

Osuala, U. S. (2012). Colonialism and the disintegration of indigenous technology in Igboland: A case study of blacksmithing in Nkwere. *Historical Research Letter* vol 3: 11 – 20.

Oyebade, A. (2007). *Culture and customs of Angola.* Greenwood Publishing.

Petersen, L. H. (2011). The presence of "damnatio memoriae" in Roman art. *Notes in the History of Art* vol 30 (2): 1-8.

Petitjean, P. (2005). Science and the Civilising Mission: France and the Colonial Enterprise, in Benediky, S. (ed) Science Across European Empires – 1800 – 1950. Oxford University Press.

Pfaffenberger, B. (1988). Fetished objects and humanised nature: Toward an anthropology of technology. *Man, New Series* vol 23 (2): 236 -252.

Pfaffenberger, B. (1992). Social Anthropology of technology. *Annu Rev Anthropol* vol 21: 491-516.

Pilossof, R. (2010). 'Guns don't colonise people…': The role and use of firearms in pre-colonial and colonial Africa. *Kronos* vol 36(1): 266-277.

Pinch, T. J. & Bijker, W. E. (1984). The social construction of facts and artefact or how the sociology of science and the sociology of technology might benefit each other. *Social Studies of Science* vol 14 (3): 399 – 441.

Pinto, M. F. (2014). PhD thesis summary: Learning from ignorance: Agnotology's challenge to philosophy of science. *Erasmus Journal for Philosophy and Economics* vol 7 (2): 181-184.

Pojman, L. P. (2003). Philosophy of religion: An anthology. Wadsworth/Thomson Learning.

Porsanger, J. (2004). An essay about indigenous methodology https://septentrio. Uit.no

Prior, C. (n.d). Writing another continent's history: The British and pre-colonial Africa, 1880-1939. *Historical Perspectives* https: www.gla.ac: 1- 16.

Quijano, A. (2007). Coloniality and modernity/rationality. *Cultural Studies* vol 21 (2-3): 168-178.

Rambane, D. T. & Mashige, M. C. (2007). The role of mathematics and scientific thought in Africa: A renaissance perspective. *International Journal of African Renaissance Studies – Multi-Inter-and Transdisciplinarity* vol 2 (2): 183-199.

Robey, T. E. (2013). Damantio memoriae: Rebirth of condemnation of memory in renaissance.

Roy, R. D. (13 April 2018). It's time to decolonise science and end another imperial era, in *Independent* https://www.independent.co.uk/news/long-reads/decolonise-science

Scott, B. (2016). How can cryptocurrencies and blockchain technology play a role in building social and solidarity finance? UNRISD working paper 2016-1 www.unrisd.org

Selin, H. (1997). *Encyclopedia of the history of science, technology, and medicine in Non-Western cultures.* Springer Science and Business Media.

Seths, S. (2009). Putting knowledge in its place: Science, colonialism and the postcolonial. *Postcolonial Studies* vol 12 (4): 373-388.

Shizha, E. & Emeagwali, G. (2016). Introduction, in Emeagwali, G. & Shizha, E. (eds) *African Indigenous Knowledge and the Sciences: Journeys into the Past and Present.* Rotterdam: Sensepublishers.

Shizha, E. (2016). African indigenous perspectives on technology, in Emeagwali, G. & Shizha, E. (eds) *African Indigenous Knowledge and the Sciences. Anticolonial Educational Perspectives for Transformative Change.* Rotterdam: Sensepublishers.

Sidi, A. O. (2016). Maintaining Timbuktu's unique tangible and intangible heritage, in Ekern, S. *et al.* (eds) *World Heritage Management and Human Rights.* Routledge.

Singh, A. K. (2012), Alternative systems of knowledge: A study in process and paradigms. *Indian Literature* vol 56 (2): 216-242.

Sithole, M. (2016). Indigenous physics and the academy, in Emeagwali, G. & Shizha, E. (eds) *African Indigenous Knowledge and* the Sciences. *Anticolonial Educational Perspectives for Transformational Change*. Rotterdam: Sensepublishers.

Smith, R. S. (1989). *Warfare and diplomacy in precolonial West Africa*. Madison: University of Wisconsin Press.

Smith, T. C. & Novella, S. P. (2007). HIV denialism in the Internet era. *PLOS Med* vol 4 (8) e256https://doi.org/10.1371/journal.pmed.0040256

Snively, G. & Corsiglia, J. (2000). *Discovering indigenous science: Implications for science education*. John Wiley & Sons, Inc.

Star, S. L. (2014). Introduction: The sociology of science and technology. *Social Problems* vol 35 (3): 197-205.

Stephen, J. (1824). *The slavery of the British West India colonies delineated: Being a delineation of the state in point of law*. J Butterworth & Son.

Stewart-Harawira, M. (2013). Challenging knowledge capitalism indigenous research in the 21st Century. *Socialist Studies* vol 9 (1): 39 – 51.

Takawira, L. (2016). *Imagine Africa*. Lulu.Com.

Tanaka, S. (2011). The notion of embodied knowledge, in Stenner, P. *et al.* (eds) *Theoretical Psychology: Global Transformations and Challenges*. Captus Press: Concord.

Tannert, C. *et al.*, (2007). The Ethics of uncertainty. *Embo report* vol 8 (10): 892-896.

Taiwo, O. (2010). *How colonialism preemptied modernity in Africa*. Indiana University Press.

Tempelhoff, J. (2006). The hidden power of water in the southern African irrigation furrow. www.anthonyturton.com

Tempelhoff, J. W. N. (2009). Historical perspectives on precolonial irrigation in southern Africa. *African Historical Review* vol 40 (1): 121- 160.

Teppo, A. (2011). "Our spirit has no boundary": White sangomas and mediation in Cape Town. *Anthropology and Humanism* vol 36 (2): 225-247.

Tlostanova, M. (2015). A salt box and a bracelet conversing with a painting: Decolonising a post-Soviet Museum in the Caucasus, in Aikens, N. *et al.*, (eds) *Decolonising Museums*. L'Internationale Books

Townsend-Gault, C. (1997). Kinds of knowing, in Morphy, H. & Perkins, M. (eds) *The Anthropology of Art: A Reader.* John Wiley and Sons.

Trilling, D. (9 July 2019). Britain hoarding a treasure no one is allowed to see in *The Atlantic* https://www.theatlantic.com/international/archive/2019/07/why-britain-wont-return-ethiopias-sacred-treausres/593281/

Van Beurden, J. (2018). Decolonisaton and colonial collections: An unresolved conflict BMGN – Low Countries. *Historical Review* vol 133 (2): 66-78.

Warrior, M. (n.d). *Mandigo warrior: The ancient African secret to male enhancement.* Lulu.com

Washington, H. (2011). *Climate change denial: Heads in the sand.* Routledge.

West, R. M. (2016). Academic bondage: A look at the history of slavery on University Campuses in America and how these schools are addressing their past, MA Thesis, The University of Georgia

Wilkinson, R. H. (2016). Damantio memoriae in the valley of the kings, in Wilkinson, R. H. & Weeks, K. R. (eds) *The Oxford Handbook of the Valley of the Kings.* Oxford Handbooks.

Withers, R. (2008). Descartes' dreams. *J Anal Psych* vol 53 (5): 691-709.

Wrefrod, J. O. (2008). *Working with spirit: Experiencing izangoma healing in contemporary South Africa.* Berghanh Books.

Wright, W. D. (1997). *Black intellectuals, black cognition, and a black aesthetic.* Greenwood Publishing group.

Wyatt, T. & Brisman, A. (2017). The role of denial in the theft of nature: Comparing biopiracy and climate change. *Critical Criminology* vol 25: 325 – 341.

Yeshitela, O. (1983). *Stolen black labour: Economy of domestic colonialism.* California: Burning Sper Publications.

Young, J. O. (2000). The ethics of cultural appropriation. *Dalhouse Review* vol 80 (3): 301-316.

Zembylas, M. (2018). Decolonial possibilities in South African higher education: Reconfiguring humanising pedagogies as/with decolonising pedagogies. *South African Journal of Education* vol 38 (4): 1-11.

Zieherl, V. (2015). Interview: Forced closures in Aikens, N. *et al.* (eds) *Decolonising museums.* L'Internationale Books

Zuckerman, H. (2018). The sociology of science and the Garfield effect: Happy accidents, unanticipated developments and unexploited potentials. *Front. Res. Metr.Anal* vol 3 (2): 1-19.

Chapter Two

Relationality or Hospitality in Indigenous Knowledge Systems? Big Data, Internet of Things and Technocolonialism in Africa

Artwell Nhemachena, Nokuthula Hlabangane &
Maria Kaundjua

Introduction

The Big Data transformations, that are reconfiguring research in the 21st century, efface African indigenous data sovereignty, national sovereignty, epistemological sovereignty and DNA/gene sovereignty in ways that are reminiscent of the colonial epoch. Theorised in terms of relationality rather than hospitality, indigenous people are ambiguated, they are deemed in the relational theories to be indistinct and indiscernible from nonhuman animals. Effacing various forms of indigenous sovereignties, relationality theories deny indigenous human essence, identity and autonomy – the relational theories presume absence of distinctions between the human and nonhuman, between knowledge and ignorance, ethical and unethical, inside and outside, consent and dissent, between the colonial and decolonial. Emphasising connections, relations and networks between otherwise distinct objects and subjects, relationality defies distinctions/binaries/dichotomies and thus it generates ambiguities, uncertainties and ignorance – which are central in the growing academic field of Anthropology/Sociology of Scientific Ignorance. On the other hand, hospitality assumes the existence of distinctions between insiders and outsiders, it assumes the existence of distinctions between humans and nonhumans; it recognises the existence of indigenous human essence, identity, autonomy and sovereignty. Thus, relational assumptions of openness, borderlessness and unboundedness sadly legitimise the contemporary imperial projects to implant or insert "smart" electronic chips and intelligent nanobots (microscopic autonomous robots) into the bodies and brains of indigenous [African] people who then become subject to remote control and mind manipulation through the emergent cerebral internet and via the Internet of Things (an emergent tapestry of internet that connects various environmental objects and subjects imbued with sentience) and Big Data (huge volumes of data transmitted at high velocity from objects and subjects connected in the Internet of Things). The technologies are part of imperial apparatuses for remotely monitoring and controlling indigenous people at a distance.

Assuming that indigenous people were open, borderless, unbounded, without distinctions between insiders and outsiders, without sovereigns, without autonomy, without human essence and ownership rights (Parekh, 1995), colonialists managed to trivialise and even disregard the hospitality that was extended to them by indigenous people. For this reason, if researchers theorise indigenous people in terms of relationality (openness), they risk ingratitude for the hospitality that is extended to them by such indigenous African people. Because one can only exercise hospitality in a defined and delimited space and place which they own and control, this chapter argues that theorising indigenous people relationally in terms of openness, borderlessness and unboundedness was meant by colonialists to pre-empt indigenous claims to hospitality, autonomy and sovereignty. For this reason, acknowledging the hospitality of indigenous people would have negated and contradicted colonial assumptions of indigenous people as savage, barbaric, backward, uncivilised, stateless, and heteronomous and without sovereignty. Further, it is argued in this chapter that admitting the existence of indigenous hospitality would have made it illogical to colonise them, to invade them, to dispossess them – colonisation was legitimised by theorising indigenous people as relational, open, without borders, boundaries, without laws, without human essence, without states, without sovereignty, autonomy and without ownership rights/property rights. In other words, assumptions of relationality undergirded colonisation wherein indigenous people were deemed to be 'relational Bushmen', living in the open and therefore incapable of exercising humanistic hospitality: they were erroneously deemed to live in networks of animalistic relationality rather than networks of humanistic hospitality. Arguing that decolonial researchers need to carefully think through the distinctions between relationality and hospitality, this chapter prefers theorising indigenous people in terms of humanistic hospitality rather than in terms of animalistic/animistic relationality.

With digital colonialism materialising in the contemporary era (Coleman, 2019), indigenous people's humanity must be recognised and so relational theories that deny distinctions between indigenous humans and nonhumans are not in the service of indigenous people. If indigenous people are theorised in terms of relationality entailing absence of distinctions between humans and animals, the implication is that indigenous people will lose their human right to privacy, right to dignity and protection from slavery. In this regard, it is not ethical to theorise indigenous people in terms of relationality because it legitimises the erosion of their rights as human beings. While the European Union has enacted the General Data Protection Regulation (GDPR) which stringently protects data from EU citizens (Hawkins (25 May 2018; Chassang, 2017), indigenous people in Africa and other places continue to be exposed to digital colonialism wherein transnational corporations bully developing countries in their efforts to extract profitable data from indigenous people. Coleman (2019: 417-439) writes thus:

> Digital colonialism refers to a modern day "Scramble for Africa" where large-scale tech companies extract, analyze, and own user data for profit and market influence with nominal benefit to the data source. Under the guise of altruism, large scale tech companies can use their power and resources to access untapped data on the continent…Much like the colonialists of the nineteenth century, who built infrastructure like railroads for the sole purpose of continuing to economically exploit the natural resources of Africa, giant tech companies like Facebook and Alphabet are building network connectivity infrastructure for the benefit of profiting from the use of their online services…Large tech companies, typically owned and primarily operated by White men, are extracting data from uninformed users and controlling that data to profit via predictive analytics.

Relationality or hospitality: Colonisation and the embodiment of the other

Presumed to be colonised by their own ignorance, beastly sexual desires, backwardness, cultures and bodily deformities, polities, social hierarchies and illnesses, indigenous people were subjected to the savagery of colonial research that also served to conceal the ugliness of imperialism (Nhemachena, Mlambo and Kaundjua, 2016). Thus, depicted as internally colonised by biological, cognitive and social-cultural deformities or to be suffering internal colonialism, indigenous people were assumed to need the aid of colonialists who then portrayed themselves as civilisers, liberators and messiahs. Although colonialists assumed that indigenous people were open, they also presupposed that they were internally colonised; this was meant to legitimise imperial invasions supposedly to free indigenous people from internal colonisation/colonialism. Thus, indigenous polities, societies, communities and bodies were supposed to open up to the imperial Other assumed to be on a mission to decolonise the indigenous people conceived as suffering internal colonisation/colonialism. Opening up and embodying the imperial Other was an antidote to the supposed indigenous self-colonisation. For this reason, indigenous minds, thought systems, social-cultural institutions, political and religious institutions and bodies have been subjected to colonial experiments and researches some of which involved opening up indigenous people's bodies and skulls - similar to the contemporary efforts to insert electronic chips and nanobots into bodies and brains of indigenous peoples of the world. Like colonial logics wherein the indigenous people were supposed to embody the imperial Other as a supposed antidote to internal or self-colonisation, contemporary implantations or insertions of technological devices into indigenous brains and bodies speak to biotechnological and information-technological experimentations that will be discussed in this chapter. There is notable resilience of colonial suppositions that indigenous people constitute realms of internally colonising dark matter – that they are still internally colonised by self-ignorance which supposedly necessitates embodying the imperial Other that is incarnate in the technological "smart" devices.

Connected in the Internet of Things wherein subjects and objects, humans and nonhumans in the environments are all inserted with intelligent devices to sense and transmit Big Data at high velocity in real time, indigenous people become colonised by the systems or networks of the Internet of Things even as it is often ironically assumed that the technological devices are liberating. Similar to the colonial era, empire would emphasise indigenous challenges such as illness, [imagined] bodily deformities, social-cultural and political deformities and [imagined] indigenous economic deformities as apparatuses with which to cajole indigenous people to agree to embodying the imperial Other lodging in the technological devices. We argue that whenever empire wants to portray and present itself as a liberator, rather than a coloniser, it increasingly depicts indigenous people as self-colonised by internal colonisation/deformities that supposedly necessitate embodying the imperial Other assumed to be possessed with superior powers to **exorcise** indigenous people's internal deformities. However, as historical evidence from colonialism shows (Nhemachena and Warikandwa, 2019), embodying the imperial Other does not necessarily entail exorcism of indigenous challenges – indeed indigenous people often lose their cultures, identities, indigenous entitlements and human essence; embodying the imperial Other legitimises invasions, loss of indigenous autonomy, sovereignty and ownership and control of material and nonmaterial resources, including data sovereignty. The point here is that contemporary implantations and insertions with brain nanobots and microchips, that are remotely controlled, are fundamental forms of invasions not merely into indigenous societies and polities but into the brains of indigenous people who then risk losing autonomy, sanity, sovereignty and control over their faculties.

The issue in the foregoing is that theories about relationality, entanglements, posthumanism and embodiment are hardly adequately teased out in relation to decolonisation. We argue that discourses on embodiment should be teased out in relation to logics of assimilation and incorporation that undergirded colonisation.

Discourses about relationality, connections, networks and entanglements should be teased out in relation to the exigencies of decolonisation, including what Ndlovu-Gatsheni (2013) calls deimperialisation. For instance, whereas decolonial scholars advocate for deimperialisation, other scholars note that the internet, technologies of surveillance, dataveillance (the monitoring of electronic data relating to personal details or online activities) and sousveillance (monitoring of activities by way of wearable or portable personal technologies), smart technologies and Geographical Positioning Systems are connected to or originated from the imperial militaries, secret intelligence agencies, imperial academies and governments – this results in digital colonialism, techno-colonialism and data colonialism (Couldry, *et al.* 2018; Kwet, 2019; Fejerskov, 2017; Helbing, 2017). In a world context where binaries, including between consenting and nonconsenting, are being effaced, it would be preposterous to simply impute indigenous consent to the implantations and insertions with technological devices. Consenting necessarily presupposes binaries with nonconsenting, between human and nonhuman yet such binaries are being assaulted in favour of relationality that effaces them. The contemporary effacement of binaries dangerously presupposes the immateriality of dichotomies between consent and dissent, agreement and disagreement, safe and unsafe, humans and technology. This is particularly dangerous in a context where the global elites and their transnational corporations and institutions are anxious to implant and insert chips, nanobots and biometric sensors into indigenous brains and bodies, homes and cities for purposes of global surveillance, dataveillance and sousveillance in the emergent One World Government that globalisation processes are ultimately leading to.

The upshot of the foregoing is that in a context where binaries or dichotomies between safe and unsafe, smart and dirty, food and poison, human and animal, colonisation and decolonisation are effaced, it would be unwise for indigenous people to consider smart devices to be simply smart as opposed to dangerous and dirty; it would be unwise to assume that there are material distinctions between "smart" homes, "smart" cities, "smart" chips, "smart" minds, "smart" power and "smart" bombs (Dargiel, 2009; Miller,

2015). In other words, there is in a relational world cause for wonder whether by embodying a "smart" mind, by adopting "smart" homes, "smart" cities, "smart" structures, "smart" chips, "smart" transport, "smart" cars and so on, one is not also embodying or connecting to a "smart" bomb. The question is, in a context where binaries are being effaced, would implanting one "smart" device (like a "smart" chip or nanobot) be distinct from implanting a "smart" bomb in the mind/brain? In a context where there are renewed calls for recolonisation and for new imperialism - of which Africa is already being invaded and land is being grabbed by transnational corporations (Gilley, 2017; Mheta, 23 January 2019; Mbalawu, 23 January 2019) -, the networks, connections, implantations, insertions, relations, embodiments and entanglements can as well be colonial and neoimperial.

Thus, in a global context where binaries between agreement and disagreement, consenting and nonconsenting are being effaced, transnational corporations are noted as allowing intelligence agencies to conduct mass surveillance in the Global South using the digital ecosystem. Surveillance capitalism extracts data from the Global South thereby perpetrating digital colonialism and data colonialism which is a predatory form of capitalist 'accumulation by dispossession' that colonises and commodifies everyday life in ways previously impossible (Kwet, 2019; Couldry *et al.*, 2018). In this sense, the Global South is subjected to technological experimentations (Fejerskov, 2017) wherein they are expected to embody the imperial Other that is immanent in the nanobots, brain/memory chips, Internet of Things, "smart" homes, "smart" cities, "smart" environments, "smart" minds, "smart" structures and so on. The exigencies of embodying the imperial Other are being theorised in terms of animistic relationality as opposed to indigenous humanistic hospitality.

Having abused and mangled indigenous humanistic hospitality provided at the inception of colonialism (Genger, 2018; Bragg, 2015), empire needs another tool or theory with which to cajole indigenous people to re-embody imperial reincarnations in the twenty-first century and beyond. Colonialists that sought to be embodied and offered indigenous hospitality have historically come in the guise of friendships networks, but they did not hesitate to subsequently violate the bodies and domiciles of the hosts. The issue here is whether embodying the contemporary imperial Other, lodged in "smart" technological devices, does not pose risks of violence, reenslavement and recolonisation for the hosts. Noting Derrida's warnings that hospitality poses dangers in the sense that the visitor can become an invader or colonist that then abuses the hospitality by conquering the host (Caze, 2006), we contend that embodying imperial "smart" technological devices is a form of hospitality that poses dangers to the indigenous people. Via implantations and insertions with remotely controlled brain/memory chips and nanobots, indigenous people can be easily recolonised. Because recolonisation relies on the politics of forgetting (Verovsek, 2015; Morefield, 2014), we argue that the revitalisation of empire depends on manipulating indigenous memories such that indigenous autonomy and sovereignty are cancelled out. Having lost autonomy and sovereignty on Africa, indigenous people will cease to be hosts [that would exercise hospitality on the continent] – they will become indiscernible from beasts exercising animalistic relationality in place of precolonial humanistic Ubuntu-informed hospitality.

Although some thinkers and scholars credit Western countries as the origins and champions of humanism and humanistic research (Kutac et al., 2016; Summit, 2012), other scholars from Africa have pointed out that precolonial African societies were functional human communities with ethical values, principles, rules, dignity of human beings, equality of human beings, moral behaviour, human welfare, interests and needs (Gyekye, 2010). On the other hand, Eurocentric posthumanism assumes absence of distinctions between humans and nonhumans (Hoppe, 2019); it presupposes identity crises for indigenous people who have been regarded as indistinct from animals since the enslavement and colonial eras. Deemed to lack human essence, human dignity, integrity, identities and other human entitlements, indigenous people have had their privacy, human dignity, autonomy, sovereignty and right to life violated since the enslavement and colonial eras.

In the contemporary era, posthumanists argue that adding technological implants, like brain nanobots, and inserting DNA will

70

improve the human beings – they ignore the fact that human beings are being experimented on; that the implants with brain nanobots may cause loss of autonomy/mind control such that the carriers are controlled by the global elites; that the subjects lose privacy, memory, identities and can be permanently and remotely spied on by the global elites who own and control the technologies implanted into the human brains/minds/bodies (Flores, 2018). While transhumanists and posthumanists are encouraging human beings to embrace the technological devices, it is necessary to note that those that "accept" the devices risk becoming slaves of the emerging global digital fascist movements by which the global elites seek to govern world citizens/netizens with technological implants and insertions (Flores, 2018). In this vein, Flores (2018: 385 - 390) notes that:

> This mafia of the transnational technology companies and the corrupt governments involve administrators of hospitals, corrupt health unions rectors, professors, librarians and university students, mafia police, prosecutors' offices, judges, intelligence services and especially press media and its extensive network of journalists who develop an insolent campaign to promote the use of technological implants…The transhumanist mega-project "Safe Neighbourhood" that is also applied in other Latin American countries like Chile, to convince citizens of the obligatory use of the cerebral internet under the argument of being a weapon against crime. The "Safe neighbourhoods" are the anteroom of the smart neighbourhoods and the "Smart City", where the objective is for all citizens to be "smart", use brain chips and voluntarily accept the cerebral internet, as a weapon of the government against crime…Thus, there would be a secret global medical network that would be executing, together with engineers, these transhumanist projects involving Schools of Human Medicine and hospitals that would be working secretly in this global transhumanist project camouflaged as telemedicine…The new slavery will be the human robotisation promoted by the transhumanism, and the brain nanobots and chips will be the new chains and shackles.

The brain or cerebral internet is part of the Internet of Things designed to harvest massive amounts of data, from the connected

71

[indigenous] individuals, to be transmitted, processed and analysed by transnational corporations, in real time. Relying on embedded sensors and actuators in machines and other physical objects like cars, buildings, TVs, game consoles, "smart" meters, home appliances, medical instruments, animals, people, toys and traffic control (GSMA, July 2014; Patel *et al.*, 2016), the Internet of Things entails a global distributed network of physical objects. The objects are capable of sensing or acting on their environment and to communicate with each other, other machines and computers that capture vast quantities of data (European Parliament, May 2015). In this regard, human brains will be inserted with chips such that people will be able to buy, edit and delete memories; there will be direct uploading of encyclopaedias, databases or dictionaries into the brain and the brains will be wirelessly connected to the internet; already neuroscientists have built a technology called Braingate that wirelessly connects the human brain/mind to computers and they are now seeking to get computer chips/electronic chips to be embedded in everyone's brain (Schermer, 2009; Mark, 2010; Stibel, 2017; Ajemian, 2017). With these "smart" technological insertions, implants and injections, human beings will become walking robots, talking robots and fighting robots (Mark, 2010) – in short, they will become posthumans. The technologies will defy binaries between the human and nonhuman, human and technology, human and animal, nature and culture; they will also unhinge indigenous autonomy and sovereignty; they will also undo indigenous people's claims to intellectual property rights; and because there will be huge capacity to move large data seamlessly across borders, the "smart" technologies will also undo indigenous nation states' claims to sovereignty over natural resources and data within their jurisdictions (Meltzer *et al.*, 2018; Third World Network, 2017). The point here is that, with the Internet of Things and Big Data, we are witnessing a new scramble for African indigenous data – Africans are losing sovereignty over natural resources as well as sovereignty over their bodies, brains and data.

The new scramble for African data: Cannibalising indigenous bodies and minds

Thus, via the Internet of Things and associated Big Data including from smartphones, wearable technologies, "smart" textiles and other wearable clothing, there is availability of passively emitted data about human actions, generated and collected digitally (Hammett *et al.*, 2014). Big Data or data science/data revolution is machine data gathered from machines or sensors; Big Data is exhaust data such as web log or mobile phone traces; Big Data is also social data mined from the traces that people are leaving behind on large scale social media platforms like Facebook and Twitter or data actively sent and contributed such as emails, free-form text images, audio and video; Big Data also assumes the form of transactional data in the form of logs of processes, emails, stores or documents; also, Big Data is secured through electronic sensors concealed in hats, helmets and neurogadgets in iPhones (Hammett *et al.*, 2014; Tana *et al.*, 2017). While the EU has strict laws about the ownership, use and dissemination of personal data, there are not as strict laws in developing countries (Hammett *et al.*, 2014). In this sense, developing countries have more vulnerability to data piracy and to loss of data sovereignty which explain global coloniality (Oppermann, 2016).

Although some academic disciplines have been handy in decolonisation, coloniality is also enhanced by contemporary anthropological depictions of indigenous bodies and personhood as permeable, partible, porous, heteronomous and heterarchic dividuals. While Western people are depicted in some scholarship as bounded, individuals, autonomous, whole, constant, fixed selves, unitary, totalised, complete, capable of expression as whole numbers, self-enclosed, sovereign, impermeable, and so on (Niehaus, 2002; Patino *et al.*, 2018; Duncan *et al.*, 2014; Geller, 2014; Fowler, 2004;), indigenous people are sadly portrayed as porous, partible, permeable, composite mosaics, desecrated, fragmented bodywise, constituted and deconstituted, configured and reconfigured, maintained and altered, in constant change, fractual, incapable of expression as whole numbers, composite, unbounded, heteronomous and chaotic. During the enslavement and colonial eras, the colonised people were similarly regarded as three quarter humans, as less than human and as unwholesome. Depicted as permeable and partible, indigenous people are assumed to be violable, penetrable, decomposable, dismantle-able, open, lacking human essence, integrity and identity – they are assumed to be so imperfect/incomplete that they require enhancement devices, chips, nanobots, biometrics and so on (Behun, 2010). Thus, indigenous people will more easily be cajoled and coxed into implantations and insertions with the remotely controlled 'enhancement' devices.

Just as the enslavers and colonisers assumed the bodies of the enslaved and colonised to be open, violable, penetrable, dividual, unwholesome, partible and permeable; there are some contemporary theories which depict enslaved and colonised bodies as distributed, as shared embodiment, as unfolded bodies that do not end at one's skin and as inter-corporeal bodies that do not warrant individual integrity and liberty (Schick et al., 2010). In the posthumanistic and postanthropocentric theories, the bodies are depicted as unfolding into "pervasive" and "ubiquitous" technosphere; they are deemed to be "inseparable" from the environments and from the technologies humans live through; the bodies are depicted as "inseparable" from the clothing worn close to the skin and from the technologies embedded in the interactive clothing/textiles (Schick et al., 2010). Theorising bodies and personhood as dividuals, permeable, partible, and so on legitimises the insertions or implantations, into or onto the bodies, with small biometric sensors such as pulse sensors, nanobots, radio frequency sensors, galvanic skin-response sensors, thermos-measuring sensors and tilt sensors that facilitate global surveillance, sousveillance and dataveillance. As a way to normalise implantations and insertions with "smart" devices, indigenous bodies are sadly depicted as hybrid and impure; the posthuman bodies are celebrated by some scholars as contaminated bodies, technobodies, queer bodies, partible, permeable and as already infected bodies that do not belong to the human family but to the 'zoo of posthumanities' (Halberstam et al., 1995). Such posthuman bodies meet transnational capitalism's needs for flexible bodies that allow for flexible accumulation, of Big Data (Hancock et al., 2000).

Regarded as belonging not to the family of human beings but to the zoo of posthumanities and other-than-humans, indigenous people have historically been denied data sovereignty since the enslavement and colonial eras. In the contemporary Internet of Things and Big Data, the indigenous people are similarly denied their data sovereignty. Just as animals or nonhumans would be deemed to be undeserving of data sovereignty, enslavers and colonisers have denied indigenous Africans' data sovereignty for centuries. While the demand by indigenous people for data sovereignty is growing in the face of Big Data and the Internet of Things, we note that the Internet of Things and Big Data are mechanisms for siphoning indigenous peoples' data. Just like the enslavers and colonisers who stripped data from indigenous jurisdictions, contemporary Big Data, the Internet of Things and cloud computing siphon or extract data from indigenous jurisdictions and from indigenous physical bodies (Oguamanam, 2018). Indigenous data are stolen and monopolised by data-based giants such as Google, Facebook, Twitter, Instagram, e-Bay, Amazon and Wikipedia, which constitute global data merchants (Oguamanam, 2018).

The contemporary Internet of Things and Big Data do not require the data merchants to travel. Instead, data is mined directly from the bodies and brains of the indigenous people, from "smart" homes, "smart" cities and so on and then they are sent in real time directly to the global data merchants. Because the Big Data are regarded as messy, fuzzy and elusive (Law, 2004), indigenous people would find it difficult, if not impossible, to effectively decolonise the data, that is, to ensure that data reflect indigenous values, to avoid misrepresentation, to collect, own, control and apply own indigenous data (Kitchin, 2014; Marley, 2018; Jennings *et al.*, 2018). In other words, the hugeness and velocity of Big Data make it difficult to decolonise the data and to make the data to speak to the autonomy, integrity, identity, dignity and sovereignty of indigenous people and their states.

Thus, the knowledge economy and information society have turned human bodies, including brains, into mines for data – mining is no longer being done in traditional geophysical mines alone but the binaries/distinctions between the geophysical mine and the human body/mind have been effaced. With the effacement of binaries/distinctions between children and adults, the able bodied and disabled, the healthy and the sick, humans and animals, the "smart" devices will be inserted/implanted in all and sundry so as to generate the Big Data that is necessary for global governance including surveillance, sousveillance and dataveillance. Datafied without class and status distinctions, indigenous people will have wearable devices, nanobots, chip insertions, wearable "smart" textiles or wearable clothing, "smart" homes with intelligent tracking devices, datafied spaces including "smart" cities all of which siphon indigenous data (Lupton *et al.,* 2017; Smith *et al.,* 2017). Also, defying binaries between the human and nonhuman, human beings will, just like livestock, be inserted with tracking devices in ways that negate privacy, individual integrity, dignity, and human rights – indigenous people will increasingly be subjected to surveillance capitalism; they will be monitored, categorised, sorted and profiled, including in ways that defy conventional humanistic ethics (Hintz *et al.,* 2018).

Constantly sending or emitting data through Facebook, Twitter, and Instagram and so on, indigenous people are increasingly becoming digital slaves sending data to the corporations that own the global media technology (Fuchs, 2014; Gokten *et al.,* 2019). The indigenous human beings/subjects become witting or unwitting digital labourers working to supply data to the global corporations that receive the data, but without paying the human beings from whom the data is constantly emitted. With the binary between work and play effaced, indigenous people would not readily know that they are operating in terms of playboy or quasi-labour (Couldry *et al.,* 2018; Gokten *et al.,* 2019; Ghayavat *et al.,* 2019; Marques *et al.,* 2016) while on the digital platforms where they emit data in real time and at high velocity to the transnational corporations. In other words, those from whom the data is mined via biometric devices become workers who are not paid by corporations that benefit from the data constantly mined and emitted from the indigenous people. If humans do not cooperate, their brains, memories or minds get hacked while on the Internet of Things (Nugent *et al.,* 2011; Marques *et al.,* 2016). The point we are making here is that the Internet of Things and Big Data, including the technological devices inserted into human brains and bodies would make it possible for some people to hack the human mind and the human bodies can also get infected by viruses in the assemblages, beyond the distinctions between human and nonhuman.

Making substantial inroads into all aspects of contemporary life, the Internet of Things ecosystems covers e-health, "smart" cities, "smart" grids, transportations, crowdsensing, ambient assisted living, "smart" homes and automation (Minoli *et al.*, 2017). In this regard, huge volumes and varieties of Big Data are being collected at high velocity from "smart"-living environments, "smart" cities and bodily sensors and pervasive sensing facilitated by Wireless Sensor Networks (WSNs) technologies which integrate modern technology into daily routine (Diraco *et al.*, 2019; Ghayvat *et al.*, 2015; Dlodlo *et al.*, 2016). Although these assemblages and ensembles of "smart" cities, "smart" homes and body sensors are depicted as instrumental in crime prevention, in managing city life, as increasing efficiency, reducing expenses, improving the quality of life and improving health (Dlodlo *et al.*, 2016; Buschauer, 2016), they have got some serious limitations.

The devices can reverse engineer the human brain/mind, scan it, model it, insert nanobots into it and upload it into technological substrates (Kurzweil, 2005; Barfield, 2015), but the technology turns human beings into slaves with rewired brains. The technology, while touted to offer security against crime in the homes and cities and other spaces, has got a limitation in the sense that it cannot deal with colonial historical crimes. Put in other words, "smart" homes, "smart" cities and "smart" spaces in the world would become "smart" not necessarily because they have been emptied of colonial historical crimes but simply because they have had "smart" technologies installed in them. In this sense, while "smart" technologies may be marketed on the basis of crime prevention, the "smartness" is not about absence of criminality, but it is in terms of concealing colonial historical crimes. Put in other words, "smart" technologies cannot track colonial/imperial historical crimes that have resulted in dispossession, plunder, looting, robbery, biopiracy and exploitation. In this sense, the "smart" technologies cannot help indigenous people to decolonise and deimperialise.

Furthermore, the scientists' celebrations of their abilities to reverse engineer the human brain and to insert nanobots and chips into it may be premature if looked at in the context of the challenges of global warming caused by earlier technological innovations that have obviously been historically celebrated as well. The rewiring of the human brains, the insertion of chips and nanobots into the human brains may backfire in the same way earlier technologies have backfired in terms of generating global warming. As Harari (2018) argues, the biotechnology and information technology may generate breakdown of the complex human minds/brains that are being manipulated by scientists who redesign brains, extend lives, kill some human thoughts, desires, opinions and decisions. For Harari (2018), some humans will be manipulated; lose freedom and autonomy; they will be inserted with chips; subjected to constant surveillance; democracy will vanish resulting in digital dictatorships; nanobots will identify human fears, hatreds, cravings and manipulate human emotions; meanwhile, the global corporations capture human attention by providing free information services/entertainment and then they hack the deepest secrets of human life. Also, ordinary humans will find it very difficult to resist the process of datafication because they are already giving away their personal information – they will have come to rely heavily on the network for all their decisions; so, Harari (2018) likens biotechnology and information technology revolutions to imperialism and colonisation wherein the global elite monopolise godlike powers over the rest of humanity.

The invasive biotechnologies and information technologies that are used in the Internet of Things and Big Data imply that individual human beings cease to have ownership and control over their brains and minds; they also lose control over the data that is mined from them. In fact, the transnational corporations will have leverages to edit and delete individuals' human memories (Pereira *et al.,* 2014; Burkell, 2016; Lavazza, 2015). Keen to ensure that the enslaved and colonised indigenous people forgot the wrongs of imperialism, there are high possibilities that the global elite will increasingly delete and edit some indigenous people's memories connected to contemporary indigenous struggles for restitution, repossession and reparations. In this sense, world peace will supposedly be achieved by deleting and editing memories of enslaved and colonised indigenous people – erasing their epistemologies and memories. Already, there are arguments that forgetfulness and erasure of data are necessary for people to grow and change (Pereira *et al.,* 2014; Burkell, 2016). Also, neuroscientific research on the removal of 'unpleasant' and 'traumatic' memories is already making strides even though such removal of memories threatens core identities, authenticity and human essences (Lavazza, 2015). Editing, deleting and changing the memories of indigenous people is one possible political function of the "smart" technologies inserted or implanted into the brain/mind. Such editing and deleting of the memories will depoliticise indigenous people by depriving them of epistemologies and memories based on which they are launching indigenous struggles for restitution and reparations for enslavement and colonisation. The point is that the "smart" technologies will not help indigenous people to decolonise, they will in fact deepen colonialism and imperialism, ironically in an age where scholars are increasingly agitating for decolonisation and decoloniality.

It is useful to point out that once indigenous knowledge is uploaded onto the Internet of Things it becomes deterritorialised – it ceases to be indigenous in the original sense because it stops recognising rubrics of locality and of being internal to a group of people. In a context where people increasingly rely on the Internet of Things indigenous knowledge vanishes because information and knowledge will flow seamlessly across territories and geographical scales. Besides, when human beings become posthumans or half technology and half biology cyborgs, indigenous people, in their original state and identity, will disappear. In the same way, when indigenous people are afflicted with foreign spirits (Behrend, 1999; Nhemachena, 2016; 2017; Nhemachena *et al.,* 2019), they lose their original indigenous identities and they even start to speak in foreign languages or glossolalia. The question here is what happens when indigenous knowledge is uploaded onto the internet and then it is technologically deleted or edited out of the minds of indigenous people? Will the world still have indigenous people when indigenous knowledge is deleted from indigenous minds? Was this not the reason why colonialists allowed foreign spirits to afflict indigenous people – do possessions by foreign spirits not transform indigenous people into something other than themselves? When colonialists/imperialists dissuaded and forced indigenous people to stop respecting their ancestors, was this not a colonial sleight of hand to open up space for possession by foreign spirits that were hoped to transform indigenous people so that they would lose their original identities and hence original claims to indigenous heritages? Was the colonial promotion of possession by foreign spirits not designed to spiritually edit and deterritorialise indigenous people so possessed?

Similarly, the insertions of the technological devices should not necessarily be narrowly understood as revitalisation of indigenous people's bodies or as restoring connections, relations, networks, vitality, animism and sacredness (Young *et al.*, 2005; Va'ai *et al.*, 2017; Chilisa *et al.*, 2016; Gerlach, 2018). On the contrary, the devices erode indigenous people's individual integrity, human dignity, privacy and human essence. Decolonisation is not simplistically a matter of restoring sacredness, vitality, relations, connections or networks (Young *et al.*, 2005); decolonisation is *a fortiori* about reasserting indigenous autonomy, sovereignty, ownership and control over their tangible and intangible heritages. The point here is that vitality without autonomy and sovereignty is pointless for indigenous people who are keen to decolonise. Similarly, sacredness without autonomy and sovereignty is meaningless. Decolonisation is therefore a function of autonomy and sovereignty.

Sadly, indigenous people are portrayed anthropologically as having relational selves indistinct from animals while Westerners are deemed to be nonrelational selves distinct from animals (Chilisa *et al.*, 2016; Va'ai *et al.*, 2017; Gerlach, 2018). Indigenous people are therefore assumed to be disposable, dispensable, not entitled to ownership of resources including to possession of their data sovereignty. As hinted above, animistic relationality, as opposed to humanistic hospitality presupposes that indigenous people are open, live in the open as assumed by the epithet "bushmen", are unbounded, do not have autonomy, sovereignty and do not have homes that are bounded. On the other hand, hospitality presupposes autonomy, sovereignty, boundedness, human essence, it assumes distinction between foreign and domestic, self and other, relatives and nonrelatives (Genger, 2018; Bragg, 2015; Verdeja, 2014; Chukwu, 2015). If one has no bounded home, territory or domicile, one cannot be a host. One can only relate without being a host to anyone because one cannot be a host to openness, unboundedness or to a bush, as for "bushmen" that are assumed to live in the open. To concede to openness and unboundedness is to concede to be a "bushman" of an indigene. One can only exercise hospitality within a bounded and circumscribed space – hospitality is not exercisable for open, unbounded, and unowned spaces. The underlying assumptions of animistic relational theories negate rubrics of human indigenous hospitality.

In this regard, Fanon (1963: 42-3) observes, referring to colonialists' treatment of the humanistic and hospitable indigenous people, that:

> ...dehumanizes the native and turns him into an animal. In fact, the terms the settler uses when he mentions the native are zoological terms. He speaks of the Yellow man's reptilian motions, of the stink of the native quarter, of breeding swarms, of foulness, of spawn, of gesticulation...The native knows all this, and laughs to himself every time he spots an allusion to the animal world in the Other's words. For he knows that he is not an animal; and it is precisely at the moment he realizes his humanity that he begins to sharpen the weapons with which he will secure its victory.

Records of such denigratory and dehumanising treatment of indigenous people have been deleted and edited at the time independence was granted. Efforts to delete and edit colonial archives have been widely reported for instance with reference to the British empire, Britain has deleted sensitive, shameful and incriminating colonial archives so that they would not fall into the hands of postcolonial states or postindependence governments (Sato, 2017; Cooke et al., 2014). The point here is that the human mind would similarly be technologically subjected to editions and deletions in the same way that national and international archives are deleted and edited to erase histories of enslavement and colonial crimes. The societies that will emerge from such deletions and editions of indigenous memories will be post-truth societies as well as postpolitical societies (Nhemachena & Warikandwa, 2019) that deny both truth and political space to indigenous people whose memories are deleted and edited. Politics of memory and of memorialisation have been evident in Africa where imperialists/colonialists edited and deleted indigenous memorialisations of precolonial indigenous heroes; the colonialists archived and memorialised their own heroes; yet on gaining independence, African nationalist states edited and deleted colonial archives and memorialisations in ways that annoyed colonialists and their descendants (Fisher, 2010).

Noting that posthumanism is occurring in the context of growth of the internet which unfortunately is embedded in the framework of the intelligence, military, academic, government and corporate politics (Marshall, 2006: 14; Maguire *et al.,* 1999; Chossudovsky, 9 March 2018), this chapter critically interrogates the ethics of editing and deleting indigenous memories. We note that the shift from attachments to territorial nation states/spaces to digital/cyberspaces - shifting identities from citizens to netizens - is itself unsettling to the indigenous national archives and memorialisations. Yet, once trapped into netizenry, indigenous people have got their memories deleted and edited as well in ways that further destroy their cognitive archives. In this regard, we concur with Braidotti (2017: 31 -2) who argues that:

> The convergence between different and previously differentiated branches of technology – notably nanotechnology, biotechnology, information technology, and cognitive sciences – has placed traditional understandings of the human under extreme pressure. The biogenetic structure of contemporary capitalism involves investments in "life" as an informational system; stem cell research and biotechnological intervention upon humans; animals, seeds, cells, and plants pave the way for scientific and economic control and the commodification of all that lives…The data- mining techniques employed by "cognitive capitalism" to monitor the capacities of "biomediated" bodies – DNA testing, brain fingerprinting, neural imaging, body heat detection, and

iris or hand recognition – are also operationalized in systems of surveillance....

In the light of the above, studies of the future, futurology, anticipation studies, forecasts of the future, speculative studies - including speculative anthropology, anticipatory anthropology, anthropology of the future and anthropology of expectation (Strzelecka, 2013; Granjou *et al.*, 2017) are imperative. Against the background of enslavement and colonisation, we argue that to commodify human lives requires the effacement of distinctions or binaries between humans and nonhumans, the ethical and nonethical: the posthuman future threatens to do exactly that – erode distinctions/binaries/dichotomies in an era where there is increasing commodification of African human life.

Since transnational mining corporations have scarified the African environment, we wonder whether data mining through the Internet of Things and Big Data would not also scarify the brains and bodies of indigenous people that are implanted with the "smart" devices. Apart from the fact that the networked empire sets the agenda in the world of communicative capitalism (Passavant *et al.*, 2004; Fuchs, 2007), we note that the world has failed to ensure corporate social responsibility that would have assuaged the humans who get subjected to insertions and implantations with electronic chips and nanobots. The issue here is that mining has resulted in scarification of the environment and so data mining from indigenous bodies will also result in scarification of indigenous minds and bodies. The transnational corporations which have already failed to exercise corporate social responsibility in mining indigenous territories will not become more responsible when they start mining the minds and bodies of indigenous people for data – after all indigenous people are being depicted as indistinct from nonhumans.

The point in the foregoing is that oppression and domination in Africa do not happen simply because of states, stasis, statuses or structures – they also happen *a fortiori* because of imperial and neocolonial processes including flows, circulations and connections beyond the nation state, beyond stasis and beyond statuses in Africa. In this regard, there is need to decolonise networks/connections/flows/processes that constitute global coloniality. Because the flows and processes deprive indigenous people of their data sovereignty, the so-called knowledge or information society will in fact be an ignorance society. In such ignorance societies, characterised by absence of indigenous data sovereignty and absence of indigenous state sovereignty, indigenous knowledge systems will be constantly streamed out of [networked] indigenous communities as well as from indigenous bodies to the transnational corporations that own and control the technologies. As indigenous data is constantly siphoned away through Big Data, it will become increasingly difficult to realise pan-Africanism, Afrocentrism and African Renaissance. The indigenous communities, individuals and the continental gatekeepers will be bypassed by the Big Data – Africanisation will thus become a pipe dream because to Africanise and to create African Renaissance requires African state and data sovereignty.

With African indigenous people's minds scanned and uploaded onto technological substrates (Thoren *et al.*, 2018; Kuhn, 2015), it becomes more than difficult to decolonise, Africanise and establish African Renaissance. With indigenous Africans increasingly becoming posthumans, it will become difficult to assert African human identities and human essence which are necessary to resist enslavement and recolonisation. Thus, fitted - like slaves, vehicles and animals - with tracking devices, with identification tattoos, chip insertions, GPS-enabled collars, slave collars and tags in the logics of biometric wearable devices (Weber, 2006; Dawson, 2003; Gasson, 2010), Africans would fail to resist enslavement and colonisation once they accept that they are indistinct from animals/nonhumans. The enslaved were historically forced to wear iron or copper slave collars and tags (Thums *et al.*, 2018; Gasson, 2010) which made it difficult for them to physically run away/escape without being identified and caught by their masters – in the contemporary era, indigenous people are similarly cajoled to wear biometric devices that datafy them and make them easily identifiable and trackable. Thus, indigenous people would find it impossible to cognitively divorce empire or to deimperialise because the remotely controlled smart devices will have been inserted or implanted into their memories/brains/homes.

We argue that decolonisation should not necessarily be interchangeable or synonymous with deconstructing indigeneity, or with antistructure, anarchism, chaos, heteronomy, heterarchy, onticology or flatness of Africa (Gordon, 2017; Knickerbocker, 2015; Grosfoguel, 2011; Tuck *et al.,* 2012). Decolonial research methods must emphasise indigenous data sovereignty, ownership and control of data about themselves and utilisation of the data for the betterment of indigenous societies and communities. Also, decolonial research methods must be about reaffirming indigenous people's autonomy, sovereignty, inviolability, structures of integrity and order. Whereas colonialists historically destroyed the indigenous people's sovereignty, autonomy, order, hierarchies, structures, human identities and essence, contemporary decolonial research must reassert indigenous autonomy, sovereignty, structures, integrity, human essence, identities, memories and so on. Colonisation was not necessarily about setting up structures or order for the colonised, rather colonisation was about destroying indigenous forms of order, structures, autonomy, sovereignty and identities. In this regard, decolonisation should not continue to destroy or impair indigenous order, identity, autonomy, integrity, dignity, sovereignty, structures and so on – decolonisation must reaffirm indigenous structures and forms of order.

In a world marked by the presence of global apartheid, decolonisation should not be simplistically construed in terms of inclusivity. To be included in global apartheid structures does not amount to being decolonised; to be recognised, assimilated, connected, linked, networked and related to such global apartheid does not amount to being decolonised. Even the enslaved and colonised peoples were also included, connected, assimilated, networked and linked to empire (Van Krieken, 2003; Elinghaus, 2009) yet this did not amount to decolonisation. Although the logics of the Internet of Things, networks, relationality and Big Data are embedded in inclusivity, we note that colonial problems that are haunting indigenous people also emanate from their assimilation into the global matrices of power which thrive on mining material resources as well as data/information from the indigenous people. The devices are therefore inserted/implanted to also manipulate the indigenous minds and adjust them to the needs and interests of the global matrices of power.

The structural adjustment of indigenous minds: Bypassing autonomy and sovereignty

Insertions or implantations of invasive pieces of intelligent technologies into human brains, bodies, homes and indigenous spaces are risky particularly when understood in the light of the colonial/imperial destruction of indigenous institutions that they penetrated/invaded first. Recently, the neoliberal shocks, through the economic structural adjustment programs (ESAP), that were administered to African states underscore the possibility that transnational corporations and global elites could implant/insert "smart" devices in indigenous people's brains/minds only to subsequently administer shocks on/in them as ways to create what we call **structural adjustment of indigenous minds (SAIM)**. The point we are making here is that since enslavers and colonisers achieved their goals by terrorising the indigenous people, it would be unimaginable for contemporary indigenous people to be terrorised by an empire that will have assumed immanence in their brains and bodies, via chip and nanobot insertions/implantations. Put in other words, we are arguing that in a world where global elites and their transnational corporations often take pleasure in sanctioning other people, the penalty of shocks and sanctions would be worse for indigenous people that would have chips and nanobots inserted/implanted into their brains/bodies. Once empire is technologically lodged in the indigenous brains, it will become impossible to decolonise and resist the imperial force and voice within. To directly receive mental shocks from an empire that has become technologically immanent in the indigenous brain is arguably worse than the shocks of economic structural adjustment programs. Empire assumes immanence in indigenous spaces in order to subsequently administer shock to indigenes – the question then is empire not becoming technologically immanent in the indigenous brains in order to administer shocks from within them?

In addition to the above, if the global elites and their transnational corporations insert chips into human brains for remote control and surveillance, it would become very easy for them to induce insurgencies and rebellions, simply by pressing remote control buttons, in the indigenous nation states. African states are already loathed and described as weak, failed, corrupt, rogue and so on and some African states are already subjected to anarchist revolutions, insurgencies and coups on the bases of networks of new technologies (Crofford, 2015; Global Policy Forum, 17 October 2007; Bennett *et al.*, 2011; Findlen, 2018). Since Big Data is remotely connected between the individuals emitting the data and the big screens of transnational companies, it would be possible for the global elites to do monitoring and evaluation of the behaviour of those that would have been connected to the Internet of Things and Big Data. In other words, just like in the case of economic structural adjustment programs that retrenched African states from controlling the economies, the structural adjustment of indigenous minds (SAIM) will also retrench African states from governing African citizens/netizens who get connected to the Internet of Things and Big Data, which bypass the African states. Therefore, much as colonialists and imperialists historically bypassed and made precolonial African states irrelevant, contemporary global coloniality is also designing programs to bypass and render the African states irrelevant. Africans are colonised not simplistically by being dominated and oppressed by global matrices of power but by being bypassed and rendered irrelevant in their own communities, nation states, on their own continent and in the wider world. The new form of coloniality is one that does not necessarily oppress, dominate or impose – it is one that increasingly displaces indigenous people from the plane of humanity and renders them irrelevant as human beings with necessary political, family, religious, economic and social institutions.

Conclusion

Noting that empire relied on networks, connections and relationality, this chapter has argued that the Internet of Things and Big Data are not necessarily decolonial: they are used to mine data from indigenous people who are often denied data sovereignty, autonomy and human integrity. The chapter further argued that it is more appropriate to theorise indigeneity in terms of hospitality than it is to do so through relationality and relational research methods. It is argued that relationality assumes that there is openness, that there are no distinctions between indigenous human beings and animals; that indigenous people do not have or even deserve sovereignty and autonomy – the same assumptions were made by colonialists. On the other hand, it is noted that theorising indigeneity in terms of hospitality does not take away indigenous human essence, autonomy and sovereignty; it affirms distinctions between indigenous human beings and animals. It is noted that relational ontologies would discount humanism and humanist ethics, whereas theorising indigeneity in terms of hospitality would reaffirm the humanism and humanist ethics that indigenous people are known for since the precolonial era. Whereas hospitality theories would affirm indigenous sovereignty, autonomy, human essence, ownership and control over their material resources and data, relationality theories would deny the same to indigenous peoples.

References

Adowski, J. *et al.,* (2015). The spectrum of control: A social theory of the smart city. *First Mondays* vol 20 (7)

Ajemian, R. (2017). Gentler alternatives to chips in the brain. *Nature* vol 544 (416)

Barfield, W. (2015). *Cyber-Humans: Our future with machines.* Springer.

Behrend, H. (1999). *Spirit possession, modernity and power in Africa.* University of Wisconsin Press.

Behun, W. (2010). The body of light and the body without organs. *Substance* vol 39 (1): 125-140

Bennett, B. and Hodge, J. (eds). (2011). *Science and empire: Knowledge and networks of science across the British empire, 1800 – 1970.* Palgrave Macmillan.

Bragg, N. (2015). Between belonging and dwelling: The hospitality of David Malouf's remembering Babylon. *Cultural Studies Review* vol 21 (2): 205-222.

Braidotti, R. (2017). Four theses on posthuman feminism, in Grusin, R (ed) *Anthropocene Feminism.* London & Minneapolis: University of Minnesota Press.

Burkell, J. A. (2016). Remembering me: Big Data, individual identity, and the psychological necessity of forgetting. *FIMS Publication* vol 38 https://ir.lib.uwo.ca/fimspub/38

Buschauer, R. (2016). Datavisions – on panoptica, oligoptica, and (Big) Data. *International Review of Information Ethics* vol 24 (5)

Caze, M. L. (2006). Should radical evil be forgiven? In Mason, T. (ed) *Forensic Psychiatry: Influences of Evil.* Totowa, NJ: Humana Press.

Chassang, G. (2017). The impact of the EU general data protection regulation on scientific research, in ecancer vol 11: 709 DOI: 10.3332/ecancer.2017.709

Chilisa, B. *et al.,* (2016). Decolonizing and indigenizing evaluation practice in Africa: Towards African relational evaluation approaches. *Canadian Journal of Program Evaluation* vol 30 (3): 313-328.

Chossudovsky, M. (9 March 2018). Social Media is a Tool of the CIA: "Facebook, Google and other Social Media Used to Spy on People" https://www.globalresearch.ca/social-media-is-a-tool-of-the-cia-facebook-google-and-other-social-media-used-to-spy-on-people/5606170 in Global Research

Coleman, D. (2019). Digital colonialism: The 21st century scramble for Africa through the extraction and control of user data and the limitations of data protection laws. *Michigan Journal of Race and Law* vol 24 (2): 417 – 439.

Couldry, N. *et al.,* (2018). Data colonialism: Rethinking Big Data's relation to the contemporary subject. Television and New Media http://eprints.lse.ac.uk/89511

Chukwu, J. C. (2015). Traditional Igbo humane character: Nature and application. *Journal of Culture, Society and Development* vol 10: 9 – 17.

Cooke, G. *et al.* (2014). Archival memory and dissolution: The After/Image Project. *Convergence: The International Journal of Research into New Media Technologies* vol 21 (1): 8 – 26.

Crofford, B. (2015). Youth, technology, and the Arab Spring: Is Sub-Saharan Africa next? *International Affairs Review: The Elliot School of International Affairs at George Washington University* vol 23 (2): 56-76.

Dargiel, J. (2009). 'Smart power': A change in U.S. diplomacy strategy in e-international relations https://www.e-ir.info/2009/06/21/smart-power-a-change-in-us-diplomacy-strategy/

Dawson, V. (2003). Copper neck tags evoke the experience of American slaves hired out as part-time laborers https://www.smithsonianmag.com/history/copper.neck-tags-evoke-experience-american-slaves-hired-out-part-time-laborers-76039831/

Diraco, G. *et al.* (2019). Big Data analytics in smart living environments for elderly monitoring, in Leone, A. *et al.* (eds) Ambient Assisted Living. ForltAAL 2018: Lecture Notes in Electrical Engineering, vol 544. Springer, Cham

Dlodlo, N. *et al.,* (2016). Internet of Things Technologies in Smart Cities https://researchspace.csir.co.za/dspace/bitstream/handle/10204/8673/Dlodlo_2016.pdf?sequence=1&isAllowed=y

Dodge, M. *et al.,* (2005). The Ethics of Forgetting in an Age of Pervasive Computing http://www.casa.ucl.ac.uk/working-papers/paper92.pdf

Duncan, W. N. *et al.,* (2014). Partible, permeable, and relational bodies in a Maya mass grave, in Osterholtz, J. A. *et al.,* (eds) *Commingled and Disarticulated Human Remains: Working Towards Improved Theory, Methods and Data.* Springer.

Elinghaus, K. (2009). Biological absorption and genocide: A comparison of indigenous assimilation policies in the United States and Australia. *Genocide Studies and Prevention: An International Journal* vol 4 (1) Articles http://scholarcommons.usf.edu/gsp/vol4/iss1/5

European Parliament., (May 2015). The Internet of Things: Opportunities and challenges. Briefing European Parliamentary Research Service http://www.europarl.europa.eu/RegData/etudes/Brie/2015/55 7012/EPRS-BRI (2015) 557012_EN.pdf.

Fanon, F. (1963). *The wretched of the earth.* New York: Grove Wedenfeld.

Fejerskov, A. M. (2017). The new technopolitics of development and the global south as a laboratory of technological experimentation. *Science, Technology and Human Values* vol 42 (5): 947-968.

Findlen, P. (2018). *Empires of knowledge: Scientific networks in the early modern world.* Routledge.

Fisher, J. L. (2010). *Pioneers, settlers, aliens, exiles: The decolonisation of white identity in Zimbabwe.* ANU Press.

Flores, D. S. (2018). Transhumanism: The big fraud-towards digital slavery. *International Physical Medicine and Rehabilitation Journal* vol 3 (5)

Fowler, C. (2004). *The archaeology of personhood: An anthropological approach.* London & New York: Routledge.

Fuchs, C. (2007). *Internet and society: Social theory in the information age.* New York: Routledge.

Fuchs, C. (2014). *Digital labour and Karl Marx.* Routledge.

Gasson, M. N. (2010). Human enhancement: Could you become infected with a computer virus? In IEEE International Symposium on Technology and Society 61-68

Geller, P. L. (2014). Sedimenting social identity: The practice of pre-Columbian Maya body partibility, in Robel G. D. (ed) *The Bioarchaeology of Space and Place.* Springer.

Genger, P. (2018). The British colonization of Australia: An expose of the models, impacts and pertinent questions. *Decolonizing Through a Peace and Conflict Studies Lens* vol 25 (1): 1-28.

Gerlach, A. 2018. Thinking and researching relationality: Enacting decolonizing methodologies with an indigenous early childhood program UN Canada. *International Journal of Qualitative Methods,* vol 17 (1) https://doi.org/10.1177/1609406918776075

Ghayvat, H. *et al.,* (2019). Smart aging system: Uncovering the hidden wellness parameter for well-being monitoring and anomaly detection. in *Sensors* vol 19 (766) Doi: 10.3390/s19040766

Ghayvat, H. *et al.,* (2015). Internet of Things for smart homes and buildings. *Journal of Telecommunications and the Digital Economy* vol 3 (4)

Gilley, B. (2017). The Case for colonialism. *Third World Quarterly* DOI:10.1080/01436597.2017.1369037

Global Policy Forum., (17 October 2007). The geopolitical stakes of Saffron Revolution https://www.globalpolicy.org/security-council/index-of-countries-on-the-security-council-agenda/burmamyanmar/25935.html

Gokten, K. *et al.,* (2019). *Economic & business issues in retrospect and prospect.* IJOPEC Publication

Gordon, U. (2017). Anarchism and nationalism: On the subsidiarity of deconstruction, in Jun, N. (ed) *The Brill Companion to Anarchism and Philosophy.* Leiden: Brill.

Granjou, C. *et al.,* (2017). The Politics of Anticipation: On knowing and governing environmental futures https://halshs.archives-ouvertes.fr/halshs-01540806/document

Grosfoguel, R. 2011). Decolonizing post-colonial studies and paradigms of political economy: transmodernity, decolonial thinking and global coloniality. *Transmodernity: Journal of Peripheral Cultural Production of the Luso-Hispanic World* vol 1 (1): 1-39.

GSMA., (July 2014). *Understanding the Internet of Things (IOT).* GSM Association.

Gyekye, K. (2010). African ethics in Stanford encyclopaedia of philosophy http://plato.stanford.edu/archives/fall2011/entries/african-ethics/

Halberstam, J. M. & Livingstone I. (1995). *Posthuman bodies.* Indiana University Press.

Hammett, D. *et al.,* (2014). *Research and fieldwork in development.* Routledge.

Hancock, P. *et al.* (2000). *The body, culture and society: An introduction.* Buckingham & Philadelphia: Open University Press.

Harari, Y. N. (2018). *21 lessons for the 21ˢᵗ century*. London: Jonathan Cape.

Hawkins, D. (25 May 2018). The cybersecurity 202: Why a privacy law like GDPR would be a tough sell in the US, in The Washington Post https://www.washngtonpost.com

Helbing, D. (2017). Dictatorship 4.0: How the digital revolution threatens our freedom – and what our alternatives are https://www.researcgate.net/publication/317533191

Hintz, A. *et al.* (2018). *Digital citizenship in a datafied society*. Polity.

Hoppe, K. (2019). Responding as composing towards a post-anthropocentric feminist ethic for the Anthropocene. *Distinktion: Journal of Social Theory* DOI: 10.1080/1600910x.2019.161836

Hussain, S. *et al.,* (n.d). A wearable device-based personalized Big Data analysis model http://uclab.khu.a.kr/rsources/publication/c_304.pdf

Jennings, L. L. *et al.,* (2018). *Indigenous data sovereignty: How scientists and researchers can empower indigenous data governance.* American Geographical Union.

Kitchin R. (2014). Big Data, new epistemologies and paradigm shifts. *Big Data & Society* https://doi.org/10.1177/2053951714528481

Knickerbocker, D. (2015). Why zombies matter: The undead as critical posthumanists. *Behemica Litteraria* vol 18 (2): 59-82.

Kuhn, R. L. (2015). The singularity, virtual immortality and the trouble with consciousness (Op-Ed) https://www.livescience.com/52503-is-it-possible-to-transfer-your-mid-into-a-computer.html

Kurzweil, R. (2005). *The singularity is near: When humans transcend biology.* New York: Penguin Books.

Kutac, J. *et al.,* (2016). Innovation through tradition: Rediscovering the "humanist" in the medical humanities. *J Med Humanit* vol 37 (4): 371-387.

Kwet, M. (2019). Digital colonialism: US empire and the new imperialism in the global south. *Race & Class* vol 60 (4) https://ssrm.com/abstract=3232297

Lavazza, A. (2015). Erasing traumatic memories: When context and social interests can outweigh personal autonomy. *Philos Ethics Humanit Med* vol 10 (3): 1-7.

Law, J. (2004). *After method: Mess in social science research.* London: Routledge.

Lupton, D. (2018). How do data come to matter? Living and becoming with personal data. *Big Data and Society* https://doi.org/10.1177/2053951718786314

Lupton, D. *et al.* (2017). The datafied child: The dataveillance of children and implications for their rights. *New Media & Society* vol 19 (5): 780-794.

Maguire, G. O. *et al.* (1999). Implantable brain chips? Time for debate. *The Hastings Centre Report* vol 29 (1): 7 – 13.

Makulilo, A. B. (2016) African data privacy laws DOI: 10.1007/978-3-319-47317-8

Mark, C. W. (2010). *Spiritual intelligence and the neuroplastic brain: A contextual interpretation of modern history.* Authorhouse.

Marley, T. L. (2018). Indigenous data sovereignty university institutional review board policies and guidelines and research with American Indian and Alaska native communities. *American Behavioural Scientists* vol 63 (6): 722-742.

Marques, G. *et al.,* (2016). A survey on IOT: Architectures, elements, applications, QOS, platforms and security concepts, in Mavromoustakis, C. *et al.,* (eds) *Advances in Mobile Cloud Computing and Big Data in the 5G Era.* Springer

Marshall, J. (2006). Negri, Hardt, distributed governance and open source software. *Journal of Multidisciplinary Internal Studies* vol 3 (1): 1-25.

Matthewman, S. (2013). Michel Foucault, technology, and Actor Network Theory https://www.researchgate.net/publication/269955985

Mbalamu, S. (23 January 2019). British Lord suggest recolonizing Zimbabwe to end crisis https://thisisafrica.me/british-lord-suggests-recolonizing-zimbabwe-to-end-crisis/

Meltzer, J. P. *et al.,* (2018). Regulating for a digital economy: Understanding the importance of cross – border data flows in Asia. Global Economy and Development Working paper 113 https://www.brookings.edu/wp-content/uploads/2018/03/digital-economy-meltzer-lovelock-working-paper.pdf.

Mheta, M. B. (23 January 2019). Africa is being recolonised all over again, in Mail & Guardian https://mg.co.za/article/2019-01-23-00-africa-is-being-colonised-all-over-again

Miller, M. (2015). *The Internet of Things: How smart TVs, smart cars, smart homes, and smart cities are changing the world*. Que Publishing.

Minoli, D. *et al.*, (2017). IOT security (IOTsec) mechanisms for e-health and ambient assisted living applications, in IEEE/ACM International Conference on Connected Health: Applications Systems and Engineering Technologies (CHASE) 17 – 19 July 2017Philadelphia, PA, USA

Moravec, H. (1999). *Robot: Mere machines to transcendent mind*. Oxford: Oxford University Press.

Morefield, J. (2014). *Empires without imperialism: Anglo-American decline and the politics of deflection*. Oxford University Press.

Ndlovu-Gatsheni, S. J. (2013). *Coloniality of power in postcolonial Africa*. Dakar: CODESRIA

Nhemachena, A., Mlambo, N. & Kaundjua, M. (2016). The notion of the field and the practices of researching and writing Africa: Towards decolonial praxis, in *Africology: The Journal of Pan African Studies* vol 9 (7): 15-36.

Nhemachena, A. (2016). Double-trouble: Reflections on the violence of absence and the 'culpability' of the present in Africa, in Mawere, M. & Marongwe, N. (eds) *Violence, Politics and Conflict Management in Africa: Envisioning Transformation, Peace and Unity in the Twenty-First Century*. Bamenda: Langaa RPCIG.

Nhemachena, A. (2017). *Relationality and resilience in a not so relational world? Knowledge, chivanhu and (de)coloniality in 21st century conflict-torn Zimbabwe*. Bamenda: Langaa RPCIG.

Nhemachena, A., Kangira, J. & Mlambo, N. (2019). Theorising displacement, elimination and replacement of indigenous people: An introduction to decolonising land issues, in Kangira, J. *et al.*, (eds) *Displacement, Elimination and Replacement of Indigenous People: Putting into Perspective Land Ownership and Ancestry in Decolonising Contemporary Zimbabwe*. Bamenda: Langaa RPCIG

Nhemachena, A. & Warikandwa, T. V. (eds). (2019). *From African peer review mechanisms to African queer review mechanisms? Robert Gabriel*

Mugabe, empire and the decolonisation of African orifices. Bamenda: Langaa RPCIG.

Nugent, C. D. *et al.,* (2011). Managing sensor data in ambient assisted living. *Journal of Computing Science and Engineering* vol 5 (3): 237-245.

Oguamanam, C. (2018). Big Data, data sovereignty and digitalization: A new indigenous research landscape, in Oguamanam, C. (ed) *Genetic Resources, Justice and Reconciliation: Canada and Global Access and Benefit Sharing*. Cambridge University Press.

Oppermann, S. (2016). From posthumanism to posthuman ecocriticism. *Relations* vol 4 (1): 23 – 37.

Parekh, B. (1995). Liberalism and colonialism: A critique of Locke and Mill, in Pieterze, J. and Parekh, B. (eds) *Decolonisation of the Imagination: Culture, Knowledge, Power*. London: Zed Books.

Passavant, P. *et al.,* (2004). *Empire's new clothes: Reading Hardt and Negri*. Routledge.

Patel, K. K. *et al.* (2016). Internet of Things – IOT: Definition, characteristics, architecture, enabling technologies, application and future challenges. *International Journal of Engineering, Science and Computing* vol 6 (5): 6122-6131

Patino, D. C. *et al.* (2018). Body and health: A look from Anthropology. *International Journal of Current Advanced Research* vol 7 (6): 13297 - 13299

Pereira, A. G. *et al.,* (2014). The ethics of forgetting and remembering in the digital world through the eye of the media, in Ghezzi, A. *et al.* (eds) *The Ethics of Memory in a Digital Age*. London: Palgrave Macmillan Studies.

Sato, S. (2017). 'Operation legacy' Britain's 'destruction and concealment of colonial records worldwide. *The Journal of Imperial and Commonwealth History* vol 45 (4): 697-719.

Schermer, M. (2009). The mind and the machine. On the conceptual and moral implications of brain-machine interaction. *Nanoethics* vol 3 (3): 217-230.

Schick, L. *et al.* (2010). Bodies, embodiment and ubiquitous computing. *Digital Creativity* vol 21 (1): 63-69

Smith, D. (2018). What is the body without organs? Machine and organism in Deleuze and Guattari. *Continental Philosophy Review* vol 51 (1): 95-110.

Smith, G. J. D. *et al.*, (2017). Health by numbers? Exploring the practice and experience of datafied health. *Health Sociology Review* vol 26 (1): 6 – 21.

Stibel, J. (2012). Hacking the brain: The future computer chips in your head https://www.forbes.com/sites/jeffstibel/2017/07/10/hacking-the-brain/#e691ffb20090

Strzelecka, C. (2013). Anticipatory Anthropology – Anthropological future study. *Prace Etnograficzne* vol 41 (4): 261-269.

Summit, J. (2012). Renaissance humanism and the future of the humanities. *Literature Compass* vol 9/10: 665-678.

Tana, J. *et al.*, (2017). The use of wearables in healthcare – challenges and opportunities, in Arcaba Working Papers 6/2017

Third World Network., (2017). Digitalisation and the gig economy: Implications for the developing world http://www.twn.my/titlez/resurgence/2017/319-320/cover03.htm

Thoren, C. *et al.* (2018). Digital disconnect and assemblages of power: Exploring technology nonuse in the age of the post-digital. *Communicazioni Sociali* n.1: 68-79.

Tuck, E. *et al.*, (2012). Decolonization is not a metaphor. *Decolonization: Indigeneity, Education & Society* vol 1 (1): 1 – 40.

Va'ai, U. L. *et al.*, (2017). *The relational self: Decolonising personhood.* Pacific University of the South Pacific Press & the Pacific Theological College.

Van Krieken, R. (2003). The barbarism of civilization: Cultural genocide and the 'stolen generations". *The British Journal of Sociology* https://doi.org/10.1111/j.1468-4446.1999.00297.x

Verdeja, E. (2004). Derrida and the impossibility of forgiveness. *Contemporary Political Theory* vol 3: 23-47.

Verovsek, P. J. (2015). Collective memory, politics and the influence of the past: The politics of memory as a research paradigm. *Politics, Groups, and Identities* vol 4 (3): 529-543.

Weber, K. (2006). Privacy invasions: New technology that can identify anyone anywhere challenges how we balance individual privacy against public goals. *Embo Reports* vol 7: 536 – 539.

Young, A. E. *et al.,* (2005). Decolonising the body: Restoring sacred vitality. *Atlantis* vol 29 (2): 1-13.

Chapter Three

Global Coloniality through Science and Technology: The Theft of African Traditional Medicinal Knowledge

Alex Munyonga

Introduction

Wielding financial, legal and cultural ammunition, Western countries scour the globe with the goal of looting indigenous knowledge through biopiracy. They hunt and gather traditional knowledge from the world's impoverished indigenous peoples whose culture is also ironically imperially demonised. Africans have been the major victim of cultural, economic and epistemological terrorism from the West. Cultural and epistemological terrorism entail the demonisation of African culture and epistemologies and all that are associated with them. African religion, herbal lore and diet have been imperially branded as backward and savage even as, ironically, Euro-America itself savagely loots the African indigenous knowledge through biopiracy. The West, thus, maliciously branded Africa as a "Dark Continent", incapable of any scientific discoveries. This chapter argues that such Western descriptions of Africa are misguided and prejudiced since Africans have been scientifically exceptional in the field of biomedicine from time immemorial. Gifted with abundant flora and fauna, Africans developed well-knit bio-medical knowledge that sustained them well before the incursions of the imperialists. It is unfortunate that colonialism and its imperial machinations engaged in centuries-old biopiracy on African indigenous knowledge.

In the 21st century, the West continues to loot and exploit African indigenous knowledge through biopiracy, skewed patenting laws and barbaric intellectual property rights laws. Western initiated and directed herbal and medicinal researches on the African continent have been designed to identify and loot African traditional herbal and medicinal lore (Nhemachena *et al.*, 2016). In this respect, a new cultivar of global coloniality is manifesting through science and technology. However, people's preference for traditional foods and herbs over allopathic and synthetic drugs testifies to the value of traditional medical knowledge in the 21st Century. The fact is not that Africans were and are devoid of scientific discoveries. Instead, the wealth of the African medical lore has and is still being stolen, plundered and cartelized by the giant Western pharmaceutical companies that use their political and financial stamina to rob Africans of their knowledge. Sadly, as the African-discovered drugs do wonders the world over, the African source of the knowledge is marginalised and impoverished. Even though royalty payments are proposed, they would not be enough: also, the transnational corporations operating in Africa are known to evade paying taxes and royalties to African states. To decolonise indigenous epistemologies, Africans must own and protect their medical knowledge. This chapter therefore argues that Africa must work on ownership and control mechanisms for their traditional medical lore.

Pre-colonial African herbal lore ownership, control and preservation

The mention of traditional medicine attracts varying feelings across the globe depending on the metaphysical orientation of the persons concerned. Westerners usually demonise traditional herbal knowledge and the capacity of Africans to pioneer any scientific discovery or development. Such undermining of African scientific capabilities, especially in the medicinal field, dates to the colonial period and has persisted in the 21st century even as the same Westerners are busy looting the indigenous medicinal knowledge. This section therefore has the task of revealing how pre-colonial Africans owned, controlled and preserved their traditional herbal and medicinal knowledge.

The World Health Organisation (WHO) has defined African traditional medicine as the knowledge and practices, explicable or not, used in the diagnosis, prevention and elimination of physical, mental or societal imbalances for a particular indigenous people (Ritcher, 2003). In this respect every group of people had its understanding and ways of interacting with nature for the benefit of humanity. Science and technology bridged the gap between nature and human needs in traditional Africa. African indigenous people were therefore the innovators and inventors of science and technologies in their localities, especially in the field of biomedicine. Africa enjoyed climatic and environmental advantages in this regard. Madagascar for example is said to have 70% of the unique species of fauna and flora life in the world (Makunga, 2015). Such an advantage gave Africa ample ground to experiment and discover herbal and medicinal qualities of fauna and flora that surrounded them. The herbal and medicinal knowledge was influenced by internal creativity and experimentation over long periods of time (Warren, 1991). Traditional medical lore was owned and controlled by Africans whose metaphysics informed the use and preservation of the medicines.

African metaphysics is understood to reflect the African universe of experience and the reality of such experience (Etim, 2013). This was corroborated by Ozumba (2004) who remarked that African metaphysics entails the African worldview concerning the existential issues they face in life. Existence from an African metaphysical point of view is onto-triadic in profile. It comprises of three hierarchies namely the Supreme Being at the top, followed by other spiritual beings like ancestors in their descending order of seniority, while the material beings, including human beings, constitute the lower section of the ladder (Mbiti, 1969). What is important here is the fact that there was a very active interaction between the Supreme Being, other spiritual beings and the animate world in traditional African society. The spiritual realm in the face of ancestral spirits and foreign spirits as guided by the Supreme Being endowed the African people with some specialist herbal and other medicinal knowledge. It was common in traditional Africa to have a person with a healing spirit *(mweya wekurapa)* in Shona. Through the guidance of such a spirit, the individual was able to discover herbs and other medicinal materials with curative abilities for the benefit of the society at large. Guided by the spiritual beings, diviners provided diagnosis for health challenges then the herbalist chose and applied relevant remedies. Herbalists, medicine men and midwives were good examples of figures who had specialist herbal and medicinal knowledge in indigenous African societies (Chavunduka, 1994).

Interestingly the knowledge about plants and medicine was kept a secret and only passed to the next generation of practitioners. The secrecy here needs to be understood as security against theft or misappropriation of the medicinal knowledge. Warren (1991) made it clear that the knowledge was intergenerational and kept in trust for the future generations. It is purely practical experiential knowledge, proven through trial and error, which was handed down. In this respect, herbal and medicinal discoveries were a product of thorough 'experimentation' in natural laboratories. It is important to note at this juncture that what is important is not whether the preservation was through written records or through orature. What is crucial is the fact that traditional African people possessed tried and tested herbal and medicinal knowledge well before the colonisers set foot on African soil. The San people for example are best described as first-class botanists, who can identify over 300 different plants with different properties (New Africa, December 2013). In this regard it is the way a given people interacts with their biological resources that gives rise to a knowledge that is unique to that group since those people are the ones who know their environment better. If ever a payment was made, it was often a token of appreciation especially after the restoration of one's health. Usually a hen was given to the herbalist, medicine man or midwife, as a token of appreciation (Chavunduka, 1994). Such sanity and unity with traditional herbal and medicinal lore was disturbed by the bullying nature of the Western colonisers on Africa. The next section therefore briefly presents Western racial and cultural terrorism on Africa as the basis for the theft of African herbal and medicinal lore.

Western racial and cultural terrorism on Africa: The foundation for theft of African traditional medicine

Western racist machinations against Africans have been in existence from time immemorial. Racist philosophers like Kant, Hegel, Hume and the like described the white race as a 'model race' (Eze, 2009). The Negroes/Africans were relegated to the level of the lower animals. Racial and cultural terrorism is understood here to mean denigration or onslaught on the African people and their customs. The historical account, in this chapter, is not an anthropological treatise, rather, it is just a brief narrative aimed at bringing to light the fact that African scientific capabilities have been crippled through a lengthy history of imperial suppression and theft. The racist narratives testify to the existence of global coloniality through science and technology in the 21st century.

Kant (1764) as cited in (Eze, 2009) described Negro Africans as Black, with an abundance of iron in the body which supposedly made them stink. He added that Africans have no feeling of the beautiful beyond the trifling. Just like Kant, Hume as quoted in (Eze, 2009) also remarked that 'not a single example can be cited in which a Negro has shown any talents'. He added that among all the hundreds of thousands of Negroes transported from Africa to Europe as slaves, not even one was ever found who ever presented anything great in art or science or any other praiseworthy quality. Contrary, Hume presents Whites as people who rose aloft even from the worst rabble. He presents Whites as people who have divinely ordained superior gifts which make them respected across the world. It was claimed that the Negroes, if they do not mix with the Whites, will remain Negroes even amid the most civilised western cities. The above insights present the White people as superhuman beings who are at the steering of all scientific and technological discoveries in the world. Africans are therefore forced to believe that their epistemologies are inferior to those of the White people.

In the 21st century, the Whites still believe that they are the torch bearers in as far as medicinal and scientific knowledge is concerned. Africans on the other hand accept their inferiority. Such an inferiority dilemma provides a very fertile seedbed for the stealing of African traditional lore especially in the field of biomedicine. Viriri and Mungwini (2009) made it clear that Westernism has an arrogant and aggressive gaze on Africa. The theft of African biomedicine therefore starts with the demonisation of African values, metaphysics and epistemology. If African material and mental incarceration persists, African herbal and medicinal discoveries will remain overshadowed by Western scientists who siphon out the indigenous knowledge.

Asante (Mengara, 2001) made it clear that an African invented for European purposes could no longer serve the interests of his/her own people. Cultural and racial onslaught on the Africans by the West was in fact a double-edged sword used to conquer and steal African indigenous medical knowledge. The Africans have thus been described as people living in the abyss of darkness in as far as science and technology are concerned. Such claims are not only fallacious but also dangerous in as far as they expose African epistemologies to incessant imperial plunder.

With the incursion of colonialists on the continent, everything African was designated as 'traditional' and not up-to-date. In 1828, Hegel vowed to forget Africa, for it is no part of human history. African knowledge systems were thus branded as backward and archaic. Hegelian, Kantian, Humean and other racist mentalities proved to have propelled colonialism and post-colonial imperialism (Eze, 2009). It is critical to observe that history and culture are intertwined. Cultural destruction and plunder by imperialist forces was thus an attack on the nervous system of the African herbal and medicinal knowledge. Through 'cultural inoculation' Western imperialists found a very strong anchorage upon which African herbal and medicinal knowledge could be plundered, looted and patented for the benefit of the West. The West attempted to obliterate everything African, replacing it with their own conceptions of life and death (Wiredu, 1996). Western culture and religion were presented as 'universal culture'. In the same vein, colonialists and early missionaries were hasty purveyors of this 'universal Western culture' which branded anything African as devilish and backward. It is within this that indigenous medicine was branded as uncivilised, heathen and 'unholy'. It is paining to note that as Africans despise their own herbal and medicinal lore, the Westerners are ironically grabbing, rebranding, patenting and personalising the African indigenous knowledge.

Traditional medicinal knowledge is described, by some, as such knowledge held by those people who are not regarded as 'developed' in as far as modern science and civilisation are concerned (Herman, 2012). Such a description of traditional knowledge points to some marginality and nativity. Such an understanding of traditional knowledge thus exposes African herbal and medicinal lore to Western bullying. Smith (2008) describes Western scientific researchers as knowledge thieves. He made it clear that these knowledge thieves first dehumanise their subjects, indoctrinate African children with epistemologies that paint their own culture, knowledge and their being as backward (Smith, 2008). Most of the so-called 'civilised' Africans have come to believe that African medicine is a domain of the uneducated and the 'uncivilised'. It is a pity that most materially and 'mentally colonised' Africans do not see the value in their indigenous knowledge. They fail to understand that the Western demonisation of African cultural and medicinal lore is a Western prepared concoction for the plunder of the very indigenous herbal and medicinal lore. In the process such Africans, watch as their knowledge treasure is looted by the West in the pretext of civilisation.

During the colonial era, Western imperialists made concerted efforts towards distancing the African people from their indigenous herbal and medical practices. During this period traditional healers underwent strange mutation as pieces of legislation like the Witchcraft Suppression Act as well as the Witchcraft Suppression Amendment Act were instituted (Mposhi, 2013). Such legal instruments prohibited diviners and other traditional medical practitioners from practicing their trade. Indigenous medicine was deemed unhygienic and a risk to the health and well-being of people. It was also branded as old fashioned, attached to the past and unchanging while "modernity" claimed constant renewal and movement towards the future. Precisely African culture was presented as one that was dying and lying prostrate at the mercy of Western "modernity" and science. Africans were relegated from the equation of reasonableness. They were reduced to consumers of Western brewed medicinal dishes in the form of allopathic drugs which were branded as possessing healing wonders if compared to indigenous medicines. The next section presents how these allopathic drugs further destroyed the African respect for indigenous medicines.

Allopathic drugs and the destruction of African indigenous medicinal knowledge

The arrival of 'Western medicine' in Africa was accompanied by the stigmatisation of ancestral medicine, paving way for allopathic drugs. African medicine is regarded as the preserve of the uneducated, uncivilised and regressive people: this is ironic because the same Westerners also plunder and loot African medicinal knowledge and various *materia medica*. African medicinal knowledge is also mischievously regarded as of poor quality, as inefficient and as ineffective. Western medicine is usually glorified as the most effective even when the so-called Western drugs have synthesised healing components from African traditional *materia medica*. It is the insidious intrusions by the West into African indigenous knowledge systems that signalled disaster for the vibrancy of African medical system. The African traditional medicinal legacy was dislocated by Western supremacist and thieving tendencies.

Although the World Health Organisation (WHO) as quoted in Shetty (2010) reported that up to 80% of the world's population depend on traditional medicine for primary health care, there remains severe criticism against such practices especially from the Western countries which are eager to market their allopathic drugs as superior. The Zimbabwean (11 March 2010) reported that stigma associated with traditional medicine has led many Zimbabweans to shun the use of traditional medicine in favour of allopathic drugs. It is crucial to observe that before colonialism in Africa, some African people viewed the forest as their pharmacy, butchery, granary and the like. This implied effective and sustainable use of the environment for the benefit of the people. Solutions to most health problems, dietary and food issues were in fauna and flora that surrounded the Africans. Health needs of the society were therefore catered for through herbal and medicinal knowledge possessed by African specialists. All this was however rubbished by the Westerners anxious to market their medicine as the only viable one. It needs to be understood that imperialism is a criminocratic oriented endeavour. As such, as the West demonised traditional medicine they were paving the market-way for their pharmaceutical companies. These companies engage in some treacherous researches designed to plunder and loot African traditional herbal and other medicinal knowledge. It is the goal of the next section to bring to light how giant pharmaceutical companies are agents of theft of traditional medicine from Africa.

Giant Western pharmaceuticals and the thievery of African indigenous medicine through research

There is a wide range of the world's renowned drugs that have been discovered from African traditional knowledge. Modern drugs like quinine, salicyclic acid, artemisnin and the like are said to have been discovered from African traditional medicinal knowledge (Mposhi, 2013). What is crucial is to point out the fact that such traditional medicinal knowledge doing wonders in the world and 'possessed' by the Western pharmaceutical corporations have been stolen from the Africans through treacherous researches. Traditional herbs are crucial in providing leads for the development of useful pharmaceutical products. Due to potential benefits, giant Western pharmaceutical companies invade Africa to harvest indigenous medicinal knowledge for the benefit of their companies and countries. Western pharmaceutical companies, with their criminocratic and exploitative orientation, see in Africa a source of wealth realisable through looting African medical knowledge. Western scientists have shifted their interest towards genetic resources in a bid to make super profits through solving global health challenges like HIV and cancers. Whereas the development of new and useful drugs is not bad, it is the stealing of African traditional medical knowledge through bio-piracy that is of concern in this chapter.

The American Heritage Dictionary (2009) defined bio-piracy as biological theft involving the illegal collection of indigenous plants by corporations that patent them for their own use without fair compensation to the indigenous people who originally discovered the plant. Giant Western pharmaceutical corporations have realised that the synthetic route for developing new medicine has relatively lower success rate. As such, these Western pharmaceutical corporations engage Africans in herbal and medicinal researches wherein the Africans constitute informants. Nhemachena *et al.*, (2016) remarked that African people participated in Western designed researches more as 'hunters and gatherers' of 'raw data'. In most cases Africans are engaged by Western researchers as research assistants, translators, informants and the like much to the amusement of the African participants. The African inferiority mentality that was cultivated into the minds of Africans through racial and cultural terrorism by the West becomes a cancer in this instance. Africans feel honoured to be research assistants for the Western researchers without realising that in the process they are nourishing imperial projects across the African continent. In the guise of researches and exchange programs, Africans are 'softly coerced' into surrendering, to the West, African indigenous medicinal knowledge, gathered by the indigenes over years of intergenerational experience, exchange and preservation.

The case of Klara Wajkowska: A 'self-styled' Polish 'spirit medium'

Zimbabwean Kwayedza Newspaper (5-11 October 2018) carried a story entitled, "*Mwana 'waMisisi' In'anga*) translated to mean, 'A child of White parentage is a traditional healer.' The story involves a 31-year-old Polish lady, Klara Wajkowska who is referred to as '*mbuya*', (implying that she is a spirit medium). This lady purported that she was possessed by an ancestral spirit of the Shumba (Lion) totem hence she is referred to as '*mbuya Masibanda*'. Klara claimed that she had visited Zimbabwe for some rituals and exchange of herbal and medicinal knowledge. She stayed in Nharira forests near Norton and was assisted by a group of Zimbabwean traditional healers who toured the forests with Klara, showing her medicinal herbs and explaining the ailments cured by each of the herbs. Interestingly Klara collected the dried and the ground herbal samples which she intended to carry back to Poland. This story is crucial for this chapter as it presents other angles through which African herbal knowledge is looted in broad day light and even in the presence of the traditional healers who are supposed to be guardians of the African traditional herbal lore.

It is the submission of this chapter that Klara claimed to be a spirit medium of the Shumba totem to be easily accommodated by the

Zimbabwean healers. A brief biography of Klara raises suspicion over the intention of her visit to Zimbabwe. While Klara is said to be a holder of three degrees and working towards a fourth degree, her father is said to be a mathematics professor (Kwayedza, 5-11 October 2018). Reading from between the lines there is every reason to believe that Klara is carrying out her postgraduate research, likely PhD Degree in traditional herbal and medicinal lore. The fact that her father is a mathematics professor may give a hint to the scientific orientation of Klara. She praised the preservation of African traditional customs as a way of courting the approval of the Zimbabwean traditional healers who would then graciously avail to her advantage all their herbal knowledge. In the guise of herbal exchange programme with Zimbabwean herbalists, Klara harvested Zimbabwean herbal lore for free and transported herbal samples to Poland, most probably for bioprospecting. The surrendering of Zimbabwean traditional medicinal knowledge by Zimbabwean traditional healers from Nharira forests to Klara, a Polish researcher, is just a practical example of what is happening across Africa. Africans who are used as research assistants are, in the process, used as conduits through whom African indigenous herbal and medicinal knowledge is stolen from Africa by the West. In fact, Elise Thompson, an 87-year-old White lady also claimed that she had been accepted by Shona and Ndebele ancestors to be Mambokadzi Dwala high priest of the African God at Njelele shrine (Kunene, 21 December 1997).

The participation of Africans in scientific researches including herbal and medical researches sounds as an honour for the Africans. However, for just a little allowances African herbal and medicinal lore is "donated" to the Western researchers on a platter. Indigenous herbalists are interviewed and lured into touring herbal fields/ forest and they often unwittingly divulge the medicinal value of the herbs in the belief that it's just a research. The double standard of the Western pharmaceutical companies is manifested when they secretly patent the herbs/drugs submitted for research without the knowledge and consent of the African indigenous people. Indigenous herbal knowledge is thus researched and looted from the African people by the giant pharmaceutical companies (Nhemachena *et al.*, 2016). Such practices cannot be described in any kind words other than looting, stealing and plundering of African traditional herbal knowledge for selfish imperial benefits. The Westerners are clandestinely looting African medicinal knowledge while hiding behind the banner of sponsored scientific researches. When allopathic drugs are developed from the stolen herbal and medicinal knowledge, it is the West who are glorified while the primary source of the medicinal knowledge, Africans, are ignored. The paining reality is that, as the Westerners prospect the breadth and width of Africa for medicinal knowledge, no African can explore the West. Nhemachena *et al.*, (2016) made it clear that Africa is researched upon by Westerners, but Africans are disallowed to research the West in return. Also, Africans can be research assistants, but they cannot lead the researches in Africa. Africans avail herbal knowledge for lab testing, but they are subsequently alienated from the developed drugs that come forth. To use Immanuel Kant's words as translated by Paton, the Africans are used to the West's own end (Kant, 1964). Such are the shocking realities in science and technology in the 21st century, hence global coloniality through science and technology.

The Westerners do not only steal herbal and medicinal knowledge, instead, they steal talented personnel as well. There is robust competition for medical knowledge and talent across the world and the winner is the one with money at the end of the day. Western funded scholarships in the field of medicine are lucrative for African talented scholars. This way, African scholars are made to research on herbal and medicinal knowledge in their home countries. In exchange for the sponsorship, African traditional herbal and medicinal knowledge is leaked into the Western domains. Such brain drain is benefiting the West. In simpler terms, African loss is gain for the Westerners. Mills (2011) revealed from his research that the United Kingdom benefited $2,7 billion and USA $846 million through health professionals' brain-drain from Africa. Of importance here is the fact that countries like UK and USA can use the African health professionals to research on and steal African herbal and medicinal knowledge for the benefit of these Western countries. The Western knowledge thieves are quite cognisant of the need to safeguard their loot. To bolster their security over the stolen herbal and medicinal knowledge, the West relies on patenting the stolen knowledge. The legal instruments for protecting the looted lore make up the next section of the chapter.

Intellectual Property Rights: Western legality-contrivances for the protection of stolen knowledge

Various legal instruments have been put in place by the Western countries to safeguard their pharmaceutical loot. Intellectual Property Rights (IPR) have proved to be the new weapon for global coloniality in the 21st century. IPRs are rights given to persons for the creations of their minds. These rights are derived from what are known as Lockean rights which were proposed by the social and political philosopher, John Locke. These rights enable the owner to enjoy the benefits of his/her creation. The general premise for such rights is to motivate the owner of the innovation and stimulate further discoveries (Warren, 1991). IPRs include patents, copyrights, trademarks, geographic indications, trade secrets and trade designs (Mposhi, 2013). This section is more interested in patents as they are used in the protection of science and technological knowledge. Saha (2005) defines a patent as an exclusive right granted by a country to the owner of an invention. Such rights ward-off competition and promote monopoly in the production and marketing of a particular invention or discovery. Patenting therefore is a form of durawall so that no one else can make, use, manufacture or market the invention without the consent of the 'owner'. In the context of biomedical knowledge, there are complexities in determining and ascertaining the owner given the long history of looting of traditional biomedical knowledge especially from Africa. The other challenge lies in the fact that it is the looters who grant the patents. Such a playing field is obviously uneven, rugged and prejudiced towards the Western looters. Considering such an observation patents are an avenue for scientific and technological bullying of Africa by the West.

Armed with Intellectual Property Rights, the greedy, selfish and cruel Western knowledge predators instantiate global coloniality through scientific and technological knowledge patenting. A snap survey on the Trade Related International Property (TRIPS) of the World Trade Organisation unveils a plethora of articles with a bullying impact on African herbal and medicinal knowledge. Frommer (2003) spelled out that Article 27.3(b) gives space for the 'mighty' in world politico-economic issues to seize and monopolise particular knowledge. Historically the (IPR) only applied to works of art and/or industrial innovations. However, Article 27.3(b) extended exclusive rights of ownership to property and processes derived from biological substances (Frommer, 2003). A telescopic look at the details of the Article proves that the article was designed and lobbied by industrialised nations who developed and profited from biologically related substances and processes, for which the bulk was stolen from the developing world. The specifics of this article testify that there is no justice and fairness whatsoever in the patenting processes on the part of the developing world that is plundered. The worrying issue is the fact that the article is designed in such a way that stolen medical knowledge from Africa is quickly durawalled and electric-fenced through this cruel legal instrument. It is so paining to note that the real owners of some of the 'fenced' knowledge, in this case Africans become aliens to the knowledge they preserved and protected as handed to them by the past generation. Through (IPR) and instruments like patents, the West gained control over African traditional genetic resources. As a result, though Africans live nearer to their herbal resources they are estranged from them via biased and alienating IPR. Western industrial laboratories, academia and patent offices have therefore become slaughterhouses for African herbal and medicinal lore (The Patriot, 26 April 2018). Such deserves no other description other than global coloniality through science and technology.

The coloniality of patenting lies in the fact that the patenting system does not protect herbal lore nurtured in Africa over generations. As the giant pharmaceutical companies scour the globe ripping traditional knowledge from poorest communities, the poverty-stricken owners of that knowledge are never consulted, neither are they recognised or compensated. The patent system also lays claims in the name of research discoveries on plants, foods and other medicinal knowledge that is innately indigenous and have been used and relied on by African people for centuries (Pawledge, 2001). If the IPRs were fair, respecting innovation and knowledge possession irrespective of geographical location of the owner, then herbal and medicinal knowledge of African people should have been the most respected due to its long history of experience, use and preservation. Shockingly African people are made to accept that their herbal and medicinal knowledge is inferior compared to Western allopathic drugs. Western pharmaceutical researchers are thus selfish in orientation. Nhemachena *et al.,* (2016) described such researchers as 'collectors and gatherers' of African traditional knowledge for their advantages and the benefit of their home countries.

A close look shows that; the applauded allopathic drugs are extracted from African herbs. "Aloe vera" for instance is commonly used by 21st century pharmaceuticals, as a recent discovery, yet history has it that the aloe has been used by the Egyptians for fungal and bacterial treatment as far back as 6000 years ago (The Patriot, 26 April 2018). The Patriot also reports of another African herb, the "devil's claw", that was stolen by the West. This herb is found in the Kalahari Desert and the Zambezi valley in Africa and was used by Africans from antiquity to treat cancer of the skin and fevers of all kinds. Interestingly developed countries have bulldozed their way in to develop drugs that are being used to cure several conditions like gastro-intestinal problems, arthritis, diabetes and the like (The Patriot, 26 April 2018). Shockingly a German pharmaceutical firm has already patented the herb for commercialisation and marketing globally without any recognition or benefit sharing with local communities and governments in Africa. The other shocking truth is that the pirated and packaged drug is thrown into the market including Africa. Though Africa has provided raw medicinal knowledge towards the development of the drug, it is nerve stripping to observe that prices for those lifesaving drugs are far higher in Africa than they are in Europe (The New York Times, 17 June 2000). The implication is that medicinal pricing system by Western pharmaceutical companies is deliberately for-profit maximisation, leaving Africans in desperation. This anthropogenic desperation reduces Africans to toys, so that in desperation they cry to the West for aid. The 21st century therefore is the epicentre of historic global coloniality through science and technology.

The World Trade Organisation (WTO) is the watchdog for the observance of the Trade Related International Property Rights (TRIPS). It is saddening that no African nation is part of the decision-making board of this organisation. The WTO and its TRIPS are protective only to the developed world, while exposing African herbal and medicinal knowledge to exploitation by the West. In this respect there seem to be a new scramble for Africa whose main objective is the theft of African herbal and medicinal lore, hence global coloniality through science and technology in the 21st century. WTO also demand compliance to TRIPS from all members including African ones. Sanctions are preferred on all members who violate the Articles of TRIPS. This is a double tragedy for the Africans who are compelled to be members in exchange for aid and other related assistance. When they are members, they are then molested and forced to comply with patenting systems of Western pharmaceuticals, even when it is manifest that African herbal and medicinal knowledge have been pirated. Following such observations, it suffices to affirm that, global coloniality through science and technology is not a myth but a reality. International Intellectual Property Rights legislation is flawed and biased in favour of the West. The piece of legislation acts as a spider's web that traps small insects, (African pharmaceutical companies and personnel) while bigger game (Western pharmaceuticals) just bulldoze through. Global coloniality has thus proved to be a cancerous acid of gut-rot eating the inner intestines of African herbal and medicinal lore. A new cultivar of coloniality in the face of knowledge colonisation by the West has thus surfaced and is being nourished through science and technology and trapping pan type of aid. Aid in all its cultivars has often been used to coerce the Africans to remain silent about the theft of their traditional medicinal knowledge. The coercive nature of Western initiated aid makes up the focus of the next section of this chapter.

Looted knowledge, medicinal developments and post-colonial colonisation of Africa

The very knowledge stolen from Africa is used as a decoy to ensnare the Africans. All this points to global coloniality through science and technology in the 21st century. The Western imperialist machinery has taken the science and technology route in the 21st century. Conditional health-related-aid extended to the developing countries is used to incarcerate the African continent and force it to expose more natural resources for Western plundering. In this vein, drugs developed from the smuggled and stolen African traditional medicinal knowledge are returned to Africa as aid decoys for post-colonial colonisation. Trade agreements and other health agreements are signed all for the benefit of the Western pharmaceutical companies and their home countries. It is the asymmetrical nature of the aid relationship between the West and Africa that is soaring. At the end of the day Africans continue to starve and even die of various ailments while amid abundant resources.

Niyokuru (2016) defined aid as 'assistance' that usually come from former colonial powers to strengthen bilateral ties with the former colony. The corrupt nature of Western aid to Africa is its conditionality and selectivity. In the guise of unlocking "foreign direct investment", African nations are ensnared to an extent that they relinquish their ownership and control of indigenous herbal and medicinal knowledge. For instance, the West may extend aid in exchange for mining or researching rights or on condition that the identified countries become signatories of some oppressive world bodies like WTO. In the process the West munches the best out of Africa. In most cases loans advanced to any state are mandated to be spent on goods and medicines supplied by the donor countries. What is worrying is the fact that much of the so-called Western drugs have their roots in African indigenous knowledge. It is therefore a double tragedy for the Africans whose stolen herbal and medicinal knowledge is used to develop drugs which are used to further cripple the freedom, ownership and control of the African indigenous people. The conditionalities of the aid destool Africans from their epistemological pedestals. Ownership and control of African medicinal knowledge becomes corrupted in the process. Independent policy formulations for Africa are curtailed due to aid restrictions and specifications. African policies regarding ownership, control and protection of indigenous medical knowledge is modelled by the West, for the best benefit of the West (Wade, 2000). In the 21st century, aid needs to be understood as a Western tool to meddle in other states and societies. Also, Non-Governmental Organisations', some of which are involved in medical researches, are usually aligned to geopolitical interests of their home countries (Niyokuru, 2016). Economic bailouts have therefore proven to be a form of exploitation and subjugation for the African people. Aid coupled with mental colonisation of the Africans further pushes the prospects of African herbal – medicinal revival onto murky ground. Despite such a gloomy picture, there is a ray of light for Africa in as far as valuing of traditional health practices is concerned. There is need for a clear decision map by African policy makers if ever Africa is to enjoy benefits of the herbal and medicinal knowledge of its people. The 21st century African leaders must synchronise their energies towards restoring African ownership, control and development of African traditional herbal and medicinal lore. The last section of this chapter presents insights into how Africa can escape 21st century coloniality. Africa can do so by designing 'colonial insulators' through ownership control and development of African herbal and medicinal lore.

African traditional medicinal knowledge ownership, control and development: An insulator against global coloniality in the 21st century

That Africa is already sprawled in a mud of Western plunder is a verity. It is true also that the Europeans have installed a Euro-specific "modernity-tradition" ideology in Africa and Africans are unquestioningly dancing to the alien tune. A closer look at the African people reveals that Africans are nominally Africans because the essentials in Africa, like herbal and *materia medica* within it, are still owned and controlled by the Western imperialist forces. Without benefiting from ownership and control of African resources,

116

Africans should be understood as only **ceremonial or notional citizens** on the continent of Africa. In some instances, African leaders are also just ceremonial leaders without any grip or autonomy when it comes to policy formulation and directing the ship of state towards a harbour of success for the citizens. Precisely they are Western mannequins and captured pleasers. An awareness of such shocking realities prevailing in Africa is the starting point in finding a solution to global coloniality through science and technology. Obbo, (2006) as quoted in Viriri (2009) made a pertinent observation that ownership of the knowledge production system is crucial for Africans. This chapter adds that it is not ownership only, but, ownership, control and development of traditional medicinal knowledge that lead to emancipation from global coloniality.

In this 21ˢᵗ century world order in which 'colonial violence' reverberates even in the silence of arms, there is need for Africa to reform the legal system so that it aligns to the progress path for Africa. Coloniality in the 21ˢᵗ Century is technical and clandestine in profile. Skewed legislative systems and aid traps are the powerful ammunition employed in 'modern colonialism'. Such weapons are sharpened towards protecting the economic interests of the Western imperialists. There is no way by which Africa can grow bio-medically without protecting the economic interests of the indigenous people. It is true that in traditional African society herbal and medicinal knowledge was not necessarily for externalisation in the interest of profit, but for the benefit of the broader indigenous community. However, it needs to be asserted that culture is like a footpath which grows wider as people continue to walk on it. The dynamic nature of culture justifies the need for Africa to develop existing herbal and medicinal knowledge for the economic benefit of the people. Domestic legislation to protect African indigenous herbal and medicinal knowledge is thus crucial for Africa. Africa has to repeal colonial legislative legacies that labelled traditional healers as 'witches' to give room for these practitioners to demonstrate their medicinal feat.

The good in African traditional *materia medica* needs to be retained while the bad is thrown away or refined. An analytical circumspection of traditional thought and culture is thus called for so as to avoid exchanging the good as well as the bad in traditional way of life for dubious cultural imports (Wiredu, 1984). Indigenous knowledge is tried and tested since it is a product of years of trial and error. That trial and error is enough experimentation such that traditional medicine offers quality leads towards the development of drugs for the world market. As such Africans need not demonise their own epistemologies. Such a development allows the Western pharmaceutical companies to feast on such valuable indigenous knowledge. Giant strides towards ownership, control and commercialisation of African traditional herbal and medicinal knowledge is thus of paramount importance in repelling global coloniality that is perpetrated through science and technology.

It is true that the hand of the West is actively involved in the looting of herbal and medicinal lore from Africa. This chapter notes that whereas the West is actively involved in global coloniality, there is a sense in which Africans themselves unwittingly facilitate the coloniality by shunning their own cultural values and epistemologies. Taking pride in being African and in African epistemologies is the foundation for the successful development of traditional medicine and freeing it from Western plunder. The African people need to remember the racist sentiments of Western figures like Hegel who vowed that nothing productive can come from Africa. Figures like Kant also demonised the Africans by stating that the blackness of the African person is indicative of lack of reasoning and any scientific discovery. Africans are not supposed to be put off by Western demonisation. It is a pity to note that thousands of African people are dying of numerous ailments yet much of the world's valuable drugs and plants are in Africa. It is the duty of the Africans to stand aloft and fight for the ownership, control and development of traditional herbal lore to make it valuable and beneficial to the African people.

Africans are presented by the West as providers of 'raw data' for research (Nhemachena et al., 2016). The implication is that Africans do possess 'raw minds' as well that need to be cooked and processed in a Western pot. Such a presentation of African epistemologies is a flawed one. The truth is that African ownership and control of herbal and medicinal knowledge was grabbed by the bully-some Western pharmaceuticals and persons. It is the submission of this chapter therefore that, Africans must fight for full control of their medicinal epistemologies. They must create own space for the transformation and development of their herbal and medicinal lore. Western patenting cages need to be broken for the West cannot be the compass and beneficiaries of African indigenous medicinal knowledge systems. If Africans accept Western epistemologies to be their pacesetter then emancipation of Africa from global coloniality will remain a potentiality that is never actualised. Africans, thus, must rely on their metaphysics and epistemology as they develop their intergenerational herbal lore into globally marketable medicinal products. Ngugi wa Thiongo writes of the cancer of mental colonisation as the ghost that haunts Africans (Thiongo, 1997). Skin bleaching is a clear testimony that some Africans desire to be modelled towards the White people. It reinforces lack of African consciousness and pride. This cancer needs a concentrated concoction of mental decolonisation so that the African mind is scoured of Western impurities of thought and left proud of being African. African educational curricular and religious orientations need to cultivate a sense of African belonging and African pride. Africans must avoid, at all cost, being forced to swim in foreign metaphysical and epistemological waters whose compass they do not have. If a Western compass of action is taken, the destination can never be African but Western in as far as medicinal development is concerned.

It is not the position of this chapter to gloss over Africa in as far as medicinal and technological development is concerned. Ownership and control of the critical epistemologies alone is incomplete in fostering scientific and technological advancement for Africa. Instead, there is need for accountability also on the part of Africa. A thick cloud of scepticism hover around and hamper the possibility of a vibrant African pharmaceutical industry. The scepticism anchors on dishonesty and corruption among some Africans. Traditional African medical practitioners should desist from making false claims about the efficacy and safety of traditional drugs as this reduces the credibility of indigenous drugs. In the same vein African countries must do away with corruption. The scientific and medicinal progress route for a continent like Africa is barricaded by corrupt practices.

As Western coloniality and aggression towards Africa were blamed for African pharmaceutical stagnation, there was deafening silence on the role of corruption and bad governance in lubricating that coloniality. Generally understood, corruption is the abuse of public office through rent seeking activities for private gain, (World Bank, 1997). Extortive corruption for instance entails demanding personal compensation for services or goods, (Alatas, 1990). This form of corruption acts as an "investment" disincentive as those in authorising offices demand huge sums of kick-back for them to fraudulently authorise business contracts (Mauro, 1998). It is on this background that some pharmaceutical companies are corruptly granted space to explore and exploit African herbal and medicinal knowledge for the benefit of a selected few. The worrying fact is that gains obtained through corruption are most unlikely reinvested in the country. Offshore accounts are the main receptors of the looted wealthy. In this vein corruption is parasitic in nature. Like an aphid that suck up the life-giving sap from a plant, so is corruption, as it strangles the economy and developmental possibilities. Capital leakage through corruption paralyses the economy and halts any meaningful scientific and technological development due to lack of funding. At the end of the day most African countries then desperately look up to the West for aid, which then comes with entangling strings attached.

It is a pity that corruption has become a vocation for those who win elections in Africa. Winning elections or ascending to an influential post is synonymous with getting a password to wealth. In such a socio-economically fragile situation solutions are elusive, and this makes it difficult to develop indigenous African *materia medica*. Controversial research permissions and access to African herbal and medicinal resources are clandestinely granted by some African governments for the benefit of those political heavy weights.

Africa must wean itself from dependence on aid. Africa must unite and fight for owning, controlling and developing indigenous epistemologies for the good of the African people. African unity is the panacea for meaningful ownership, control and development of African traditional herbal and medicinal lore.

Conclusion

Global coloniality through science and technology is real and not just a drill. Western pharmaceuticals are capitalising on African desperation, low confidence and porous looting routes which are often oiled through corruption. Such are permitting environments for the West to coerce Africans to dance according to the imperialist plunderous tunes. Sound pharmaceutical development for Africa is not a solo journey. Instead, it calls for African governments, communities and individuals to synchronise their energies towards arresting corruption to pave way for meaningful ownership, control and development of African herbal and medicinal lore. Clamoring for access and benefit sharing with giant Western pharmaceutical corporations that loot Africa, is not a lasting solution. Without firm ownership, control and development policies in place, the progress path for herbal and medicinal knowledge development for Africa will remain a mirage. Predatory researches on African traditional herbs and medicines by the West must be closely monitored and guarded against to seal medicinal-knowledge-leaking points.

References

Alatas, H. (1990). *Corruption: its nature causes and functions'*. Kuala Lumpur: S. Abdul Majeed and Co.

Chavunduka, G. (1994). *Traditional medicine in modern Zimbabwe.* Harare: University of Zimbabwe Publications.

Downs, A. (1966). *Inside bureaucracy.* Boston: Little, Brown and Company.+

Etim, F. (2013). African metaphysics. *Journal of Asian Scientific Research, Asian Economic and Social Society* vol 3 (1): 11-17.

Eze, E. C. (2009). *Race and enlightenment: A reader.* Boston: Blackwell Publishing.

Frommer, C. (2003). *Protecting traditional medical knowledge in Zimbabwe.* Harare: Cultural Survival Quarterly Magazine.

Herman, E. (2012 Sepember 10). *South African online encyclopaedia .* Retrieved from www.myfundi.co.za.

Kant, I. (1964). *Groundwork of the metaphysic of morals as translated by Paton, H,J.* New York : Harper and Row Publishers.

Kunene, T. (21 December 1997) Zimbabwe: White Sangoma Claims to High https://allafrica.com/stories/199712210035.html

Makunga, N. (2015). *How changes in African traditional research can benefit South Africa.* Stellenbosch: University of Stellenbosch.

Mauro, P. (1998). Corruption and the composition of government expenditure. *Journal of Public Economics,* vol 69: 263-279.

Mbiti, J. S. (1969). *African religions and philosophy.* Heinermann Publishing.

Mposhi, A. M. (2013). The importance of patenting traditional medicines in Africa: The case of Zimbabwe. *International Journal of Humanities and Social Science*: 236-246.

Nhemachena, A. *et al.,* (2016). The notion of the "field" and practices of researching and writing Africa: Towards decolonial praxis. *Africology: Journal of Pan African Studies* Vol 9 (7).

Niyokuru, F. (2016). Failure of foreign aid in developing countries : A Quest for alternatives. *Business Economic Journal* vol 7 (231).

Pawledge, F. (2001). Patenting , piracy and the global commons. *Bio-Science* 51(4): 273-277.

Ritcher, M. (2003). *Traditional medicines and traditional healers in South Africa.* Pretoria: Aids Law Project.

Smith, L. (2008). *Decolonising methodologies: Research and indigenous peoples.* London and New York: ZED Books.

The New York Times. (17 June 2000). *Prices for medicines are exorbitant in Africa.* New York: The New York Times.

The Patriot. (26 April 2018). *The value of traditional medicines and herbs.* Harare: The Patriot News.

The Sunday Mail. (25 March 2018). *Unpacking illicit financial flows and capital flight.* Harare: Zimpapers.

Thiongo, N. w. (1997). *Decolonising the mind: The politics of language in African literature. .* Oxford: James Currey.

Viriri, A. (2009). 'Down but not out': Critical insights in traditional Shona metaphysics . *The Journal of Pan- African Studies,* Vol 2, (9): 177-195.

Warren, D. (1991). *Using indeginous knowledge in agricultural development, .* World Bank Discussion Paper 127.

Wiredu, K. (1984). *Philosophy and an African culture.* Cambridge: Cambridge University Press.

Wiredu, K. (1996). *Cultural universals and particulars : An African perspective.* Bloomington: Indiana University Press.

World Bank. (1997). *Helping developing countries combat corruption: The role of the World Bank.* New York,: Oxford.

Chapter Four

Audit of Mathematical Concepts in Pre-colonial Africa

Sindiso M. Nleya & Siqabukile Ndlovu

Introduction

Eurocentrism paints a worldview which, implicitly, posits European history and values as the "norm" and standard for everyone else: this helps to produce and justify the Western world's predatory position within the global system. Contrary to Eurocentric popular claims and beliefs by some colonial scholars that mathematics, science and technology were non-existent in pre-colonial Africa, there is overwhelming evidence that formal and informal educational practices had long been in existence, for example among the Khoi-San and the Bantu-speaking people of southern Africa. Specifically, the community raised an African child and educated them in the culture and traditions of that community. Hence, the curriculum of indigenous education during the pre-colonial period comprised of traditions, legends and tales, which were transferred orally from generation to generation within each community. This process of indigenous education was intimately integrated with the social, cultural, economic, political, religious and recreational life of the indigenous people. Thus, this chapter debunks the pervasive Eurocentric view, which portrays a state of mind that certifies Europe as the cradle of human advancement. Specifically, we focus on mathematics where we subsequently adopt an "ethno-mathematical" approach which concentrates on the importance of African native culture for mathematics. This approach is inspired by the assertion that mathematics is not a culture-free discipline. All cultures are rich in artefacts and other technological products that exhibit mathematical concepts. Examples of mathematical concepts exhibited by traditional African games include geometry, graphs, counting and record keeping. Using this approach, we carry-out an audit of mathematical concepts in pre-colonial African cultural ways of life. To this end, we focus on southern Africa where the oldest mathematical artefact, the Lebombo bone, was discovered and is understood to be the first mathematical model that was used to quantify time. Moreover, we also provide evidence of the existence of early numerical systems, games, puzzles and geometry in north, central, southern and western Africa.

The notion of a 'Cradle of Humankind' relates both to Africa as the birthplace of early human ancestors (early hominids) as well as the birthplace of contemporary humans (Lelliott, 2016). Kama (2018) acknowledges the fact that Africa is the cradle of humanity and opines that it is logical and thus indisputable that Africa is the cradle of the earliest forms of civilisations. Sadly, in the words of Van Sertima (1983) "the nerve of the world has been deadened for centuries to the vibrations of African genius". To this end, a perusal of imperial/colonial era history gives the false impression that Africa has not made any tangible contributions to contemporary mathematics, science and technology. This narrative is made by Joseph (1987) who points to the historical "gaps" concerning the roles of the Arabs, and the Africans, which are fundamental to understanding the history of mathematical development. Most of the discourses on the origins and evolution of contemporary science, technology and mathematics point to works by the Greeks, Romans and other mostly Western nations. To the contrary, there exists strong evidence that most discoveries came thousands of years after similar African developments (Zomahoun, 2017). It is worthy of note that only a few people know, that many modern high-school level concepts in mathematics were first developed in Africa, which was the first to develop methods of counting. More than 35,000 years ago, Egyptians scripted textbooks about mathematics that included division and multiplication of fractions and geometric formulas to calculate the area and volume of shapes (Woods, 1988). Distances and angles were calculated also; algebraic equations were solved, and mathematically based predictions were made about the size of floods of the Nile River. The ancient Egyptians considered a circle to have 360 degrees. Eight thousand years ago, the people in present-day Zaire developed their own numerical system, as did Yoruba people in the country now called Nigeria. The Yoruba system was based on units of 20 instead of 10 and required an impressive amount of subtraction to identify different numbers. Scholars have lauded this system, as it required much abstract reasoning (Peter, 2015).

This chapter is organised as follows: a focus on the genesis of counting systems inspired by the Lebombo and Ishango artefacts and subsequent existence of numerical systems as well as fractions in north Africa exemplified by ancient Egypt; the existence of mathematical concepts in the area of geometry is considered and important concepts identified; a focus on mathematical recreations in the form of games and puzzles. This section practically unearths the existence of several mathematical concepts in recreational mathematics. The final section concludes the chapter by summarising the evidence of existing mathematical concepts in pre-colonial Africa.

Counting systems

The genesis of counting can be traced back from the continuous evolving societies and humankind wherein a simple sense of would prove enough to meet the needs of everyday life. Clearly early communities formed groups and it became important to know how many members were in each group. Moreover, it was important for them to be able to ascertain whether the animals in their care increased or not (Brooks and Smith, 1987).

In order to count items such as animals, it is often conjectured that one of the earliest methods of doing so would be with "tally sticks." These are objects used to track the numbers of items to be counted. With this method, each "stick" (or pebble, or whatever counting device being used) represents one animal or object. This method uses the idea of one to one correspondence, which is to say indigenous people theorised truth in terms of correspondence. In a one to one correspondence, items that are being counted are uniquely linked with some counting tool. This section consists of three subsections namely, the Ishango bone, Lebombo bone, numerical systems and fractions.

Ishango bone

In 1950, Prof J de Heinzeln discovered a bone at Ishango, a Congolese village at the source of the Nile. The 10cm long curved bone which is estimated to be about 20,000 years is now popularly referred to as the Ishango Bone and probably the oldest mathematical tool. One interpretation is that the bone is the earliest known demonstration of sequences of prime numbers and ancient Egyptian multiplication (Scott, 2005). But some scientists have suggested that the groupings of notches indicate that there may be a mathematical understanding that goes beyond counting. (Pletser, n.d) The bone carries notches distributed in three columns along the bone length as shown in table 1. The central column along the most curved side of the bone, is called the M column (French: Milieu), while G and D indicate the Left (Gauche) and Right (Droite) columns. The M column depicts eight groups of respectively 3, 6, 4, 8, 9 or 10, 5, 5 and 7 notches. The G and D columns each show four groups respectively of 11,13,17,19 and 11, 21, 19, 9 notches.

Table 1: Ishango Columns

Column	Notches
M(Milieu)	3,6,4,8,9 or 10,5,5
G(Gauche)	11.13.17,19
D(Droite)	11,21,19,9

Some believe the three columns of asymmetrically grouped notches imply that the implement was used to construct a numeral system (Huylebrouck, 2006). The numbers in Table 1 are not just random; they, in fact, point to an understanding of the principle of multiplication and division by two. Consequently, it suffices to say the bone may have been used as a counting tool for simple mathematical procedures. De Heinzelin (1962) considers the ishango bone as revealing evidence of simple arithmetic. In analysing Table

128

1, the first four groups of the M column look like duplication while the G column shows the prime numbers between 10 and 20. The third column indicates 10 ± 1 and 20 ± 1. The most striking is that all numbers in columns G and D add up to $60 = 5 \times 12$, while the sum of the numbers in the M column is $48 = 4 \times 12$. On the other hand, Marshack (1991) later suggested that the bone was a lunar calendar. Circumstantial evidence supports this alternate interpretation, since present day African civilisations use bones, strings and other devices as calendars (Pletser and Huylebrouck, 1999).

Lebombo bone

A much older artefact in the form of a baboon bone, found in Swaziland, called the Lebombo bone dates from approximately 35,000 BC and is marked by 29 clearly defined notches. This particular bone may have served as a lunar phase counter and ranks with the oldest mathematical artefacts known to exist (Apostolou and Crumbley, 2008). Bhatia (2015) views the Lebombo as the oldest mathematical model ever. It is conjectured that this is the earliest model to quantify time. It has also been suggested that since the Lebombo bone was used as a lunar phase counter, then women may have been the first mathematicians, as keeping track of menstrual cycles requires a lunar calendar (Bangura, 2014).

Numerical systems

The existence of number systems in pre-colonial Africa can be traced back to ancient Egypt. There is evidence of the main Egyptian number system being based on a scale of 10 and other systems based on scales of 5, 12, 20 and 60. Three forms of Egyptian numerals are believed to have existed, namely the hieroglyphic, hieratic and demotic (numerical notation in Africa).

The hieroglyphic system is traced back to the mid-fourth millennium BC (Cajori, 1928:11; Chrisomalis, 2010) about 3300 BC. Hieroglyphic systems have been found mainly on monuments of stone, wood, or metal. The Hieratic is a cursive writing form that was mainly used for recording documents on papyrus. The third form of

Egyptian numerals is the demotic, which is believed to have evolved as a more abbreviated form of cursive writing around the eighth century BC. The three numeral systems are depicted in Figure 1

	Hiero-glyphic	Hieratic	Demotic	Meroitic		Hiero-glyphic	Hieratic	Demotic	Meroitic
1	ı	ı	ı	ı	100	ა	⌐	⌐	⌐
2	ıı	ᄊ	५	ıı	200	ახ	⌐	⌐	⌐
3	ııı	ᄿ	೪	ııı	300	ახა	⌐	⌐	⌐
4	ıııı	ᄼ	ᅥ	ıııı	400	ახახ	⌐	⌐	⌐
5	ııı ıı	ๅ	೪	ᄼ	500	ახახ ა	⌐	⌐	⌐
6	ııı ııı	ꜟ	೬	///ᄼ	600	ახა ახა	⌐	⌐	⌐
7	ıııı ııı	ᆨ	ᅲ	//	700	ახახ ახა	⌐	⌐	//
8	ıııı ıııı	ᄅ	ᅭ	ᅩ	800	ახახ ახახ	⌐	⌐	⌐
9	ııı ııı ııı	ᄾ	ᅵ	ᅵ	900	ახა ახა ახა	⌐	⌐	ᅳ
10	∩	ᄉ	ᅦ	⌐	1000	ı	ꜟ	ꜟ	ꜟ
20	∩∩	ᄊ	ᅩ	⊤	2000	ıı	⌐	ᅥ	ᅥ
30	∩∩∩	ᄉ	ᅭ	×	3000	ııı	ᄆ	ᅨ	
40	∩∩∩∩	ᅩ	ᅩ	ᅩ	4000	ıııı	ᄆ	ᅨ	ᅩ
50	∩∩∩ ∩∩	ꜟ	ᅦ	ᅩ	5000	⊤⊤⊤⊤⊤	ᄆᄆ	ᅥᅨ	
60	∩∩∩ ∩∩∩	ᅢ	ᅩ		6000	⊤⊤⊤	ᄆ	ᅨ	
70	∩∩∩∩ ∩∩∩	ᄽ	ᅲ	⌐	7000	⊤⊤⊤	ᄆ	ᅥᅨ	
80	∩∩∩∩ ∩∩∩∩	ᅢ	ᅨ	ᄼ	8000	⊤⊤⊤⊤	ᄆ	ᅨ	
90	∩∩∩ ∩∩∩ ∩∩∩	ᅢ	ᅵ		9000	⊤⊤⊤⊤	ᄆ	ᅥ	ᅳ
Archaic shapes:					Large Numbers:				
2000	ꜟꜟ				10,000	ı	1		
3000	ꜟꜟꜟ				100,000	⌐ ⌐	⌐		
4000	ꜟꜟꜟꜟ				1,000,000	ᄽ			
					10,000,000	Ω			

Figure 1: Numerical systems (Rovenchak, 2012)

An analysis of Figure 1, with reference to hieroglyphic reveals a series of signs used to represent powers of ten. For instance, a vertical stroke for 1, a hook for 10, a rope for 1,000, the pointing finger for 10,000, a tadpole for 100,000 (Rovenchak, 2012). These digits were written according to the direction of writing, such that higher ones preceded lower ones. Hieroglyphic inscriptions were bi-directional i.e., from left to right and from right to left with either human or animal figures prepended towards the beginning of the line to indicate how the text should be read. In Hieratic and demotic scripts, the right to left order was already fixed. However, if the symbols of lower power value were placed before higher ones, this depicted multiplication.

Fractions

In addition to multiplication, a special system of fraction was also developed with symbols availed for such fractions as 1/3, ⅔ and 3, 4, regrettably no sign existed for ½. The regular notation for fractions was used to write unit fractions with the numerator equivalent to unity. To this end, other fractions were decomposed as a sum of unit fractions; this was achieved by a lenticular symbol placed above the number symbol corresponding to the denominator. The other forms of Egyptian numeral notations were quite cursive and did not permit simple symbol decomposition. A case in point is the Hieratic script in which a dot was placed over a numeral to represent unit fractions. This is exemplified by the number $5^{5/75/7} = 5^{10/1410/14} = 5 + 1/2 + 1/7 + 1/145 + 1/2 + 1/7 + 1/14$. The Merotic notation represented fractions differently from the hieratic by using numbers $\square/10\square/10$ with n taking values from 1 to 9. It is posited in Gegg-Harrison (2001) that Egyptian fractions provide a representation of rational numbers that is anything but intuitive to most first-year Computer Science students. In addition to providing another example of a recursive algorithm, the conversion of a standard fraction into the sum of distinct unit fractions (i.e., fractions with a numerator of 1) provides an example of a greedy algorithm that uses linked lists. To this end, Egyptian fraction conversion makes an ideal programming project for Computer Science students.

In summarising, it is important to note that, in "modern" day society counting systems are at the core of how a computer system operates from both a hardware and software perspective. In the case of software, it is important to note that standard arithmetic is used in many functions of programming to the extent that, addition, subtraction, multiplication and division are used in almost every program that is written. Moreover, in the area of computer security, especially Cryptography or Cryptology which is concerned with the study of techniques for secure communication in the presence of third parties called adversaries, concepts derived from the Ishango and Lebombo bones are widely used.

African indigenous geometry

For many years, Africa has been in the mainstream of the history of mathematics. According to Powell and Frankenstein (1997), this history began with the first written numerals of ancient Egypt and has been reaffirmed by most written archaeological discoveries. Although all continents have played a role in the history of mathematics, the contributions of Africa are still not acknowledged by European and other historians. Gerdes (1997) indicates that the origins of mathematical thought lie in the concepts of number, magnitude, and form. Such concepts would have been part of everyday life in hunter-gatherer societies. The idea of the number concept evolving gradually over time is supported by the existence of languages which preserve the distinction between "one", "two", and "many", but not of numbers larger than two. Prehistoric artefacts discovered in Africa, dated 20,000 years old or more, suggest early attempts to quantify time. The following paragraphs prove that mathematics with particular interest in geometry has origins in Africa. Mastin (2010) states that the oldest undisputed mathematical documents are from Babylonian and dynastic Egyptian sources. The Moscow Papyrus, one of the oldest written mathematical texts from Egypt of old from around 2000 B.C and 1800 B.C, contains 25 solved mathematical problems. The Moscow Papyrus consists of what are today called *word problems* or *story problems*, which were apparently intended as entertainment. Because of age, some of the problems are unreadable to translate. According to Mastin, problem 14 shows an illustration to find the volume of a truncated pyramid, Mastin (2010) states that:

If you are told: A truncated pyramid of 6 for the vertical height by 4 on the base by 2 on the top. You are to square this 4, result 16. You are to double 4, result 8. You are to square 2, result 4. You are to add the 16, the 8, and the 4, result 28. You are to take one third of 6, result 2. You are to take 28 twice, result 56. See, it is 56. You will find it right.

However, the solution does not explain how the example in the problem worked, nor any reasoning behind the solution. This shows the brilliance of the ancient Egyptians.

One of the best examples of Egyptian mathematics, according to Mastin (2010), is the Rhind papyrus (sometimes also called the Ahmes Papyrus after its author), dated to c. 1650 BC but likely a copy of an older document from the Middle Kingdom of about 2000-1800 BC. The Rind papyrus is an instruction manual for students in arithmetic and geometry, which contains evidence of other mathematical knowledge, including composite and prime numbers and arithmetic. It shows how to solve first order linear equations as well as arithmetic and geometric series. The Berlin Papyrus 6619 (c. 1800 BC) shows that ancient Egyptians could solve a second-order algebraic equation. In Southern Africa, Mosimege (2015) investigated two cultural villages namely the Basotho and Lesedi cultural villages in South Africa. The study was carried out to help planners and implementers of the educational curriculum to incorporate indigenous knowledge systems aspects within the various learning areas of newly developed curricula. The investigation revealed use of innumerable mathematical concepts. Mathematical concepts like counting; estimation; straightness of lines; shapes and patterns; angles; etc., have been identified in the making of a grass container and beadwork. Educators need to play an important role of linking what happens at the cultural villages to various mathematics curricula requirements. Mosimege (2015) states:

As Graven (2000:159) correctly points out, current curriculum change demands that teachers (educators) use a learner centred approach and understand mathematics as a learning area which includes the following identity of mathematics as a school subject:

Maths as a useful subject for everyone, it is both relevant and practical and is applicable to everyday life.

According to Mosimege (2000:283), teachers are appropriately placed, due to their mathematical knowledge, to create linkages between various activities embedded within mathematical concepts to ensure that the experiences of learners are enriched through daily experiences of what they encounter outside the classroom. This helps ensure that students can relate to what they learn in class and see that it is not totally divorced from reality. In the traditional Nigerian society, before the introduction of colonial education, mathematics was used mainly in taking stock of daily farming and trading activities (Aguele and Usman, 2007). Most traditional societies used two number bases and had their own number systems which were either base five or base twenty. These number systems could be seen in their market days and counting systems. Aguele and Usman (2007) claim that the dawn of missionaries introduced the Western type of education to Nigeria where mathematics occupied a central position in the school curriculum. This has remained the position in the Nigerian education system up to today. The Yoruba people from present-day Nigeria created their own complex counting system based on units of 20 (instead of 10). According to Baiyelo (1987), mathematics is widely regarded as the language of science and technology. In agreement to Baiyelo's observation, Abiodun (1997) stated that while science is the bedrock that provides the springboard for the growth of technology, mathematics is the gate and key to the sciences. Also, Ukeje (1997: 293-296), in acknowledging the importance and contribution of mathematics to the modern culture of science and technology, stated that:

> without mathematics there is no science, without science there is no modern technology and without modern technology there is no modern society. In other words, mathematics is the precursor and the queen, of science and technology and the indispensable single element in modern societal development.

Mathematics education is therefore essential in nation-building. Since the introduction of colonial education in Nigeria, mathematics education has gone through several developments. These changes have always been necessitated by the realisation of the role mathematics should play in the nation's scientific and technological development as well as responses to societal needs and demands (Aguele, 2004). The world today is seen as a global village, characterised by computer and information technology which aids in global surveillance and control of indigenous people/societies. This age has brought with it lots of sophistication in mathematics to be able to sustain these developments. According to Gerdes (1999), rock paintings and engravings from all over Africa, some dating from several years ago (even thousands of years ago), have been reported. These often have a geometric structure. Other findings like stone tools and ceramics indicate geometric exploration by African hunters, artisans and farmers. Particularly exceptional are archaeological finds of perishable material like textiles, baskets and wooden objects which provide us with some idea of earlier geometrical explorations.

The archaeological findings from the caves in the Cliff of Bandiagara in the Republic of Mali show clear evidence of exploration of forms, shapes and symmetries (Gerdes, 1999). The earliest buildings in the caves are cylindrical granaries made of coils of mud, dating from the 3rd to 2nd century BC. In the 11th century, the now extinct people of the Tellem entered the area and buried their dead, with implements like hunting weapons and tunics, in the remaining old granaries made in the caves. Archaeologists and textile specialists who analysed the Tellem remains underscore that "..there is no other region in the world where such a great variety of linear and geometrical patterns has been obtained in cotton fabrics by means of a single colour, the only one available locally, i.e. Indigo.." (Bolland, 1991: 50). Examining some patterns found on preserved fragments of clothing, horizontal and vertical threads cross each other one over, one under. The average width of the threads is 1mm. The weavers alternated groups of natural white cotton threads with groups of blue, indigo-dyed threads. Six vertical white threads are followed by four blue threads; three horizontal white threads are followed by three blue threads, leading to the plane pattern. In general, the dimensions are (m+n)x(p+q), where m, n, p, and q are natural numbers. The Tellem weavers experimented with dimensions and discovered relationships between the dimensions and the symmetry properties of the resulting patterns. Gerdes (2013) reflects the use of geometry in Africa. The main objective of the book is to call attention to some mathematical aspects and ideas incorporated in patterns invented by women in southern Africa. Njock (1985: 4) characterises the relationship between African art and mathematics as follows: "Pure mathematics is the art of creating and imagination. In this sense black art is mathematics". Mathematicians have analysed mostly symmetries in African art. Symmetries of repeated patterns may be classified based on the 24 different possible types of patterns which can be used to cover a plane surface (cf. the so-called 24 plane groups due to Federov, 1891). Of these, seven admit translations in only one direction and are called strip patterns. The remaining 17 that admit two independent translations are called plane patterns. Crowe (in Zaslavsky, 1973), applies this classification to decorative patterns that appear on the raffia pile cloths of the Bakuba (Zaire) (Cf. Crowe, 1971), on Benin bronzes, and Yoruba admire cloths (Nigeria), showing that all seven strip patterns occur and many of the plane patterns. Crowe continued this research and published a catalogue of Benin patterns (Crowe, 1975) and a symmetry analysis of smoking pipes of Begho (Ghana) (Crowe, 1982a; cf. also Crowe, 1982b). In Washburn and Crowe (1988) several patterns from African contexts are classified in the same way. Washburn (1990) showed how a symmetry analysis of the raffia patterns can differentiate patterns produced by the different Bakuba groups. Although the use of the crystallographic groups in the analysis of symmetries in African art attests and underlines the creative imagination of the artists and artisans involved and their capacity for abstraction (cf. Meurant, 1987), these studies do not focus on how the artists and artisans themselves classify and analyse their symmetries. This is a field open for further research. Zaslavsky (1979) gives some examples of strip and plane patterns, and of bilateral and rotational symmetries, occurring in African art, architecture and design. Why do symmetries appear in human culture in general, and in African craftwork and art, in particular? This question is addressed by Gerdes in a series of studies. He analyses the origin of axial, double axial, and rotational symmetry of order 4 in African basketry (Gerdes, 1985a; 1987; 1989a; 1990c; 1991c). In Gerdes (1991b) it is shown how fivefold symmetry emerged quite "naturally" when artisans were solving some problems in (basket) weaving. The examples chosen from Mozambican cultures range from the weaving of handbags, hats, and baskets to the fabrication of brooms. Langdon (1989; 1990) describes the symmetries of 'adinkra' cloths (Ghana) and explores possibilities for using them in the classroom. In a similar perspective, Harris (1988) describes and explores not only the printing designs on plain woven cloths from Ghana, but also symmetries on baskets from Botswana and 'buba' blouses from the Yoruba (Nigeria). The development of geometrical thinking started in early African history as hunter-gatherers of the Kalahari Desert in southern Africa learned to track animals by getting to know the shape of their poop to learn which animal passed by, how long ago, if it was hungry or not, etc. Geometry and symmetry in repeated patterns can be seen throughout the area south of the Sahara, in forms of artistic designs on houses, gourd, baskets, pipes, and other everyday items. Throughout the area south of the Sahara, all adult members of a community had the mathematical understanding, design sense, and construction skills to build his/her own house. By analysing the variation of symmetry in geometric patterns shown on a piece of cloth and other cultural items, it is possible to identify which group of people made it.

In contemporary real-life situations, geometry has numerous practical applications ranging from the most basic to the most advanced phenomena in life. A basic application is in the concept of area when it comes to how one can do their daily business, for instance space is an important issue when dealing with construction projects. Furthermore, in designing and manufacture of domestic and industrial appliances, the size or area can greatly affect how a specific tool or appliance can fit in a home or workspace. In engineering projects, geometry is largely important in that by using the notion of perimeter, it is possible to compute the amount of materials needed for a project e.g. fencing, paint etc. In the fields of design such as interior design and architecture three dimensional figures can be used to demonstrate that a good knowledge of geometry is important in determining the proper style of a specific house, building, or vehicle.

In contemporary applied mathematics curriculum, specifically the area of operations research, it is important to note that concepts such as the space allocation problem are inspired by pre-colonial African cultural practices. The space allocation problem (SAP) is a process in architecture, or in any kind of space planning (SP) technique, of determining the position and size of several elements according to the input-specified design program requirements. In advanced phenomena perspective it is noted herein that, in Artificial Intelligence and computer programming, state space planning is deployed in designing programs to search for data or solutions to problems. In data structures and algorithms, a computer algorithm that searches a data structure for a piece of data, uses a program that looks up words in a computer dictionary, the state space is a collective term for all data to be searched.

Games and puzzles

In general, mathematical recreations are constituted by games and puzzles that range from naive amusements to sophisticated problems. Pre-colonial African recreations covered wide areas in mathematics such as algebra, geometry, theory of numbers, topology, combinatorics, graph theory, set theory symbolic logic as well as probability theory (Gerdes, 1994). To this end, there is evidence, from Egypt and the rest of Africa, of mathematical games dating back as far as 2000 BC.

Games

Games are related to mathematics. Pre-colonial games of chance lead to notions of probability, expectation and fairness. A player may be keen to know what the chances of winning are, what one can expect to win on average in the long run and whether each player has a chance of winning. Games of strategy lead to logical thinking about the best course of action in a competitive setting and how different actions may lead to different responses on the part of the opponent.

In this subsection we subsequently consider games of chance and games of strategy from an African setting.

(i) Mancala game

Mancala game has its origins dating back to the Empire Age of ancient Egypt (Broline and Loeb, 2018). According to Donkers, Uiterwijk and de Voogt (n.d), Mancala games are board games that are played almost all over the world in many variations and are characterised as follows:

a) The games are played on a board with several pits, usually arranged in two or more rows. Sometimes additional pits are used that we will call stores.

b) The games are played with a collection of equal counters (stones, seeds, coins, or shells).

c) Players own pits, not counters. Often, a player owns all the pits on one side of the board.

d) Moves are made by sowing, which is a form of counting.

e) After (or during) sowing, counters can be captured. (Hence Mancala games are also called count-and-capture games.)

f) The goal of the game in general is to capture most of the counters.

From a mathematical point of view, Mancala is a deterministic game with perfect information. Practically, there are not many choices per move, commonly not more than the number of pits on one row. However, the fact that a single move can influence the contents of all pits on the board, makes it difficult to foresee the consequences of even a few moves ahead, let alone the outcome of the game. An analysis of the various versions of the Mancala game reveals the existence of several contemporary mathematical concepts such as Combinatorial Game Theory, search algorithms, logical thinking, counting as well as empirical and mental calculation. The family of Mancala games offers opportunities for new research in both mathematics and Artificial Intelligence.

(ii) **Nine Men's Morris**

This is one of the oldest board games. Boards have been found carved on a roofing slab from an Egyptian temple (c. 140 BC) and on a stone from a Bronze Age burial site in Ireland.

(iii) **Morabaraba**

The Morabaraba game has its roots in the southern part of Africa; it has different names depending on the region where it is played. In South Africa, it is called Morabaraba in Sesotho language, Muravarava among the Xhosa and Ronga in Mozambique. It belongs to the class of three-in-a-row board games (Mogege and Ismael, 2004). The Morabaraba board game was historically used to share cattle herding strategies in parts of southern Africa (for example South Africa, Botswana and Lesotho) and discuss information related to war strategies. And legend has it that Oware was used in 1700s Ghana by Ashanti King Katakyie Opoku Ware I to resolve issues between married couples. Today, board games remain equally popular and culturally significant (Bayek, 2018). According to Mosimege and Ismael (2004) Morabaraba game is played by two players over three stages as follows:

- First stage each player starts with 12 tokens, and the players take turns placing the tokens on the board. Every time a three-in-a-row is made, the token belonging to the opponent is taken.
- Second stage when all the tokens have been placed on the board, they are then moved from one junction to another with the aim of making a row of three.
- Third stage when all but three tokens are lost, the player concerned may "fly" a token to any vacant junction on the board with each move. The game is won when the opponent cannot move any of the tokens, or when an opponent has lost all but two tokens. Nkopodi (2009) reveals the following mathematical concepts found in the analysis of Morabaraba:
  - Identification of various quadrilaterals (squares) and the similarities and differences between them;

Ratio and proportion between the lines and the squares making the complete Morabaraba board; • Symmetry: Symmetry is observed in at least three different instances, namely, (1) the various sides of the board; (2) within each side of the board; (3) the placement of tokens and repetitive movements of the tokens on the board;

• Logical deductions in the execution of the various steps of the game;

• Counting of the tokens;

• Addition and subtraction of the tokens until a game is won based on the remaining number of tokens.

Table 2: Mathematical concepts in African games

Game	Mathematical Concepts
Morabaraba	• Geometrical shapes • Algebra • Ratio and Proportion • Symmetry • Logical reasoning • Counting
Mancala	• Combinatorial game theory • Search algorithms • Logical thinking • Counting • Empirical and mental calculation

Games have been part of the social fabric of many African societies for hundreds of years. And a summary of the mathematical concepts from the popular games are shown in Table 2. Board games such as Morabaraba have been known to be useful in the teaching and learning of simplified concepts like perimeter and area of squares (Moloi, 2013).

Puzzles

(a) **A river crossing problem**

A man had to take a Leopard, a goat and a bunch of cassava leaves across a river. The only boat he could find could only take two of

141

them at a time. But he had been ordered to transfer all of these to the other side in good condition. (Zaslavsky, 1973). If he leaves the goat with the Leopard, the goat will soon be eaten. He cannot leave the goat with the cassava leaves because the goat will soon eat them. How this could be done. What is the fewest number of trips that the man can make across the river?

(b) **The jealous husbands**

This dilemma tale is about three women and three men who want to cross a river in order to attend a dance on the other side. With the river between them there is a boat with the capacity for taking only two people at one time. However, each of the men wishes to marry all the three women himself alone. Regarding the crossing, they would like to cross in pairs, each man with his female partner, but failing that any of the other men could claim all the women for himself (Gerdes, 1994).

(c) **Calabash puzzle**

This is a puzzle which is topological, meaning it is premised on geometric properties that are not affected by size and shape. The puzzle poses a challenge wherein two pieces of a calabash and a string are joined together. The challenge to the player is that he/she should separate one of the calabash pieces without necessarily cutting or untying the string (Gerdes, 1994).

From "ethnomathematics" to "ethnocomputing"

"Ethnocomputing" is the study of the cultural aspects of computing, and the computational aspects of culture. It inherits a great deal from the "ethnomathematics" research programs that preceded it (Babbitt, 2014).

Babbitt *et al.,* (2012) investigated Navajo weaving. This type of weaving shows a common re-occurring angle in the weaving patterns, of about 30 degrees. When asked about this particular angle, the weaver said it is created by an "up one over one" pattern (up one weft over one warp). The weaver also said she could do lots of other patterns (up one over 2, up two over 3, etc.) but explained that other angles gave a more jagged edge. In other words, they were concerned about the aliasing problem, a common feature in early computer graphics (and still a concern in certain situations such as bitmap images). This implies a host of new questions: Do some weavers use anti-aliasing techniques like those strategies used in computer graphics, such as using an in-between colour at the edges? What are the iterative algorithms for more complex shapes?

Thus the "ethnocomputing" approach offers two advantages. First, some pattern generation systems are better conceptualised through the disciplinary idioms of computer science. Second, the conceptual framework of computing - the idea of information processing, algorithms, graphical user interface, etc. - allows new insight into the artisans' own perspective in cases in which there is an analogous process.

Examples of "ethnocomputing"

Indigenous computing, a social category of "ethnocomputing" "translates" from indigenous culture to high tech frameworks: for example, analysing the African board game Owari as a one-dimensional cellular automaton. Oware is an abstract strategy game among the Mancala family of board games (pit and pebble games) played worldwide with slight variations as to the layout of the game, number of players and strategy of play. Its origin is uncertain but it is widely believed to be of Ashanti origin (Camberlin, 2017: 7). The game is played in the Ashanti Region of Ghana and throughout the Caribbean, and has many variant names.

Eglash (1999: 223) presents a few interesting points of view to recursion in ethnomathematics. He states that in addition to the apparent benefits of utilising indigenous knowledge for development and education in Africa, African fractals can also serve in education in the United States. It is his opinion that fractal design tools should be applied in the curriculum of especially African American students, since the African connection can spark the interest to the study of recursion among them. The Bamana sand divination (Eglash, 1997a) works as an indigenous example of recursion. The Bamana diviners pass the outputs of an operation back to it as the new input and iterate the process until certain criteria are met. Eglash (1999) also suggests developing the African continent by interconnecting African fractals (indigenous design) and modern computing. He mentions a few existing applications such as a Ghanaian national television broadcast test pattern and projects in Burkina Faso that combine traditional fractal architecture with modern techniques. Eglash's vision is further still in the future. He sees "grass roots" rather than top-down approach as the tool for putting African fractals to work for sustainable development. As examples of promising targets for development, Eglash mentions organising production and vending, decentralised electronic voting (decision making in many African cultures is traditionally decentralised) and neural-net style decision making. Eglash admits that neither the African fractals framework nor dissemination of information technologies offers panaceas. Rather, he suggests, the shift in perspective does not need to be a conservative return to the past, nor the epistemological equivalent of an alien invasion. African fractals offer a framework that is both rooted in indigenous cultures, and cross-pollinates with new hybrids (Tedre, 2002).

Conclusion

The markings on the Ishango and Lebombo bones point to the existence and use of mathematical concepts and principles such as counting, mathematical modelling in the case of the lunar calendar. Furthermore, numerical systems such as those found in ancient Egypt and Mali are important shreds of evidence that dispel the Eurocentric view that mathematics was non-existent in precolonial Africa. From a geometric point of view, the existence of a Rind papyrus instruction manual for students in arithmetic and geometry, contains evidence of other mathematical knowledge, including composite and prime numbers and arithmetic. It shows how to solve first order linear equations as well as arithmetic and geometric series. Recreational mathematics was also an important aspect of life to the extent that puzzles and games such as Mancala and Morabaraba have been found to encompass important modern day mathematical concepts such as geometrical shapes, algebra, ratio and proportion, symmetry, logical reasoning, counting, combinatorial game theory, search algorithms, empirical and mental calculation. The family of Mancala games offers opportunities for new research in both mathematics and Artificial Intelligence. Prior work in "ethnomathematics" and "ethnocomputing" found in traditional practices (e.g., weaving, beading, sculpture, tattoo, drumming, and graffiti) show mathematical concepts such as Cartesian and polar coordinates and transformational geometry, and computational practices such as iteration and conditionals. Just like computer science is nowadays considered to be a field of research distinct from mathematics, "ethnocomputing" is considered to be a research topic distinct from "ethnomathematics". Some aspects of "ethnocomputing" that have their roots in "ethnomathematics" include: counting and sorting, locating, measuring, designing, playing and explaining.

References

Aguele, L. I. & Usman, K. O. (2007). Mathematics education for dynamic economy in Nigeria in the 21st century. *Soc. Sci.,* vol 15(3): 293-296.

Apostolou, N. & Crumbley, D. L. (2008). The Tally Stick: The First Internal Control? The Forensic Examiner Spring 2008, www.acfei.com

Babbitt, B., Lyles, D. & Eglash, R. (2012). From ethnomathematics to ethnocomputing: indigenous algorithms in traditional context and contemporary simulation. 205-220 in Alternative forms of knowing in mathematics: Celebrations of Diversity of Mathematical Practices, edSwapnaMukhopadhyay and Wolff-Michael Roth, Rotterdam: Sense Publishers.

Babbitt, W. E. (2014). Ethnocomputing: The design and assessment of culture-based learning software for math and computing education, Doctoral dissertation, Rensselaer Polytechnic Institute

Bangura, A. K. (2014). Domesticating mathematics in the African mother tongue. *The Journal of Pan African Studies,* vol.6, (7)

Bhatia, A. (2015). Mathematical modelling: From times being. *IJSR - International Journal of Scientific Research* vol: 4 (1): 242-243.

Bolland, R. (1991). *Tellem textiles: Archaeological finds from burial caves in Mali's Bandiagara Cliff*. Leiden: Rijksmuseum voorVolkenkunde.

Broline, D. M. & Loeb, D. E. (2018). The Combinatorics of Mancala-Type Games: Ayo, Tchoukaillon, and $1/\pi$, https://arxiv.org/pdf/math/9502225.pdf,%20http://wiredspace.wits.ac.za/handle/10539/18749.pdf

Brooks, A. S. & Smith, C. C. (1978). Ishango revisited: new age determinations and cultural interpretations. *The African Archaeological Review*, vol 5: 65-7.

Camberlin, D. B. (2017). How to Play Warri: The Caribbean Oware Mancala Game (2nd ed.). Columbia, Missouri: Purple Squirrel Productions. p. 7. ISBN978-0-9994889-0-4.

Cornelius, M. 1. (1986). An historical background to some mathematical games, mathematics in school. *The Mathematical Association* vol. 15, (1): 47-49.

Crane, L. (1982). African games of strategy, a teaching manual, African Outreach Series, No.2, University of Illinois, Urbana-Champaign.

Crowe, D. (1971). The geometry of African art I. Bakuba art. *Journal of Geometry, München (FRG)*, Vol.1: 169-182.

Crowe, D. (1973). Geometric symmetries in African art. *Zaslavsky, Claudia* 190-196

Crowe, D. (1975). The geometry of African art II. A catalogue of Benin patterns. *Historia Mathematica*, Vol.2: 253-271.

Crowe, D. (1982b). Symmetry in African art, in *Ba Shiru, Journal of African Languages* and Literature. University of Wisconsin.

Crowe, D. (1982a). The geometry of African art III. The smoking pipes of Begho. *C and Literature* vol.3, (1): 57-71.

Crowe, D. (1987). Review of 'Mancala games' (Russ) and 'Code of the Quipu' (Ascher & Ascher). *The Mathematical Intelligener* vol.9, (2): 68-70

Davis, B. Grunbaum, F. Sherk (ed.) (1981) *The geometric vein, the Coxeter Festschrift*. New York: Springer Verlag.

De Heinzelin De Braucourt, J. (1962). Ishango. *Scientific American*, vol 206, (6): 105–116

De Voogt, A., Rougetet, L. & Epstein, N. (2018). Using Mancala in the mathematics classroom. September 2018 Mathematics Teacher vol 112 (1):14

Donkers J., Uiterwijk, J. & de Voog, A. (n.d). Mancala games - Topics in mathematics and artificial intelligence, http://citeseerx.ist.psu.edu/viewdoc/download?doi=10.1.1.502. 1565&rep=rep1&type=pdf

Eglash, R. (1997a). Bamana sand divination: Recursion in ethnomathematics. *American Anthropologist* vol 99(1): 112-122.

Eglash, R. (1999). *African fractals: Modern computing and indigenous design.* Rutgers University Press.

Friberg, J. (1981). Methods and traditions of Babylonian mathematics. Plimpton 322, Pythagorean triples, and the Babylonian triangle parameter equations. *Historia Mathematica,* vol 8: 277—318.

Gegg-Harrison, T. S. (2001). Ancient Egyptian numbers: a CS-complete example. *ACM SIGCSE Bulletin* vol. 33, (1): 268-272).

Gerdes, P. (1994). On mathematics in the history of Sub-Saharan Africa. *Historia Mathematica* vol 21: 345-376.

Gerdes, P. (2013). Decoration and ornament. Women, Culture and Geometry in Southern Africa. Lulu.com

Ghevarughese, G. J. (1987). Foundations of Eurocentrism in mathematics

First Published January 1, 1987 Research Article, https://doi.org/10.1177/030639688702800302

Gheverghese, J. G. (1987). Foundations of Eurocentrism in mathematics. *Race and Class.* Vol 28 (3): 13-28.

Gerdes, P. (1999). Geometry from Africa: Mathematical and educational explorations, Volume 10 of Classroom Resource Materials

Hadley, J. & Singmaster, D. (1992). Problems to sharpen the young. The Mathematical Gazette. Vol. 76, No. 475. The Use of the History of Mathematics in the Teaching of Mathematics (Mar., 1992), pp. 102-126, The Mathematical Association Stable URL: https://www.jstor.org/stable/3620384

Heath, T. L. (1963). A Manual of Greek mathematics, Dover, 1963, p. 1: "In the case of mathematics, it is the Greek contribution which it is most essential to know, for it was the Greeks who first made mathematics a science."

Hill, B. L. (1984). *Hungarian translation: Africa Szamo.* Gondalet. Budapest.

Ya Kama, L. (2018). Africa, Cradle of civilisation, http://en.lisapoyakama.org/africa-cradle-of-civilization/

Langdon, N. (1989). Cultural starting points for mathematics: a view of Ghana, Science Education Newsletter, British Council

Langdon, N. (1990). Cultural starting points paper presented at SEAMME 5, Brunei

Lelliott, A. (2016). Visitors' views of human origins after visiting the Cradle of Humankind World Heritage Site, *S. Afr. j. sci.* vol.112 (1-2) http://dx.doi.org/10.17159/sajs.2016/20150210

Mastin, L. (2010). "Egyptian Mathematics" The story of mathematics.
https://www.storyofmathematics.com/egyptian.html

Moloi, T. (2013). The teaching of mathematics in rural learning ecology using Morabaraba game (board game) as an example of indigenous games. *International Proceedings of Economics Development and Research*, vol 60, (124)

Mosimege M. & Ismael A. (2004). Ethnomathematical studies on indigenous games: Examples from Southern Africa, pg 199-137, Proceedings of the 10th International Congress of Mathematics Education Copenhagen

Neugebauer, O. (1969). *The exact sciences in antiquity* (2 ed.). Dover Publications.

Njock, G. E. (1985). Mathématiques et environment socio-culturelen Afrique Noire, in: *Présence Africaine, New Bilingual Series*, Vol 135, (3): 3-21.

Nkopodi, N., & Mosimege, M. (2009). Incorporating the indigenous game of morabaraba in the learning of mathematics. *South African Journal of Education*, 29(3).

Peter, U. T. (2015). The evolution of African indigenous science and technology, Historical Research Letter www.iiste.org (Online) Vol.16

Pletser, V. & Huylebrouck, D. (1999). The Ishango artefact: The missing base 12 link, in *Forma,* vol 14: 339–346.

Pletser, V. (n.d). Does the Ishango bone indicate knowledge of the base 12? An interpretation of a prehistoric discovery. The first mathematical tool of humankind.
https://arxiv.org/ftp/arxiv/papers/1204/1204.1019.pdf

Powell, A. B. & Frankenstein, M. (1997). *Ethnomathematics: Challenging Eurocentrism in mathematics education.* Sunny Press.

Rovenchak, A. (2012). Numerical notation in Africa. *Afrikanistik online* vol (9).

Tedre, M., Kommers, P. A. M., & Sutinen, E. (2002). Ethnocomputing: Towards ethnically fairer computer science, in Wyness, W & Richardson A. (eds.), *Exploring Cultural Perspectives.* Edmonton: ICRN Press.

Tedre, M. (2002). Ethnocomputing a multicultural view on computer science, Paper presented at IEEE conference ICALT, Kazan, Russia September 9-12, 2002

Van Sertima, I. (1983). The lost sciences of Africa: An overview. Blacks in Science: Ancient and Modern. 7 – 26.

Washburn, D. & Crowe, D. (1988). *Symmetries of culture, theory and practice of plane pattern analysis.* Washington: University of Washington Press.

Washburn, D. (1990). *Style, classification and ethnicity: design categories on Bakuba raffia cloth.* Philadelphia: American Philosophical Society.

Williams, S. W. (2005). An old mathematical object. Mathematicians of the African diaspora.
http://www.math.buffalo.edu/mad/Ancient-Africa/index.html

Woods, G. (1998). *Science in ancient Egypt.* Children's Press.

Zaslavsky, C. (1973). *Africa counts: Numbers and pattern in African culture.* Boston: Prindle, Weber & Schmidt.

Zaslavsky, C. (1973a). *Africa counts: Number and pattern in African culture.* Boston: Prindle, Weber and Schmidt.

Zaslavsky, C. (1973b). Mathematics in the study of African culture. *Arithmetic Teacher,* vol 20: 532-535.

Zomahoun, T. (2017). Africa: The Cradle of Mathematical Sciences. WCSJ San Francisco. http://wcsj2017.org/session/africa-cradle-mathematical-sciences/

Chapter Five

African Indigenous Knowledge Systems of Mathematics and Science: Insights from the Faculties of *Ifá* among the Yorùbá of Nigeria

Olúwolé Tẹ́wọgbóyè Òkéwándé

Introduction

Ifá is believed to be the foundation of Yorùbá culture. *Ifá's* scope of knowledge can broadly be categorised into religion and science. However, till today, within and outside the Yorùbá communities, *Ifá* is generally believed to be associated more with one of the major divinities than with any other human aspects of life. As a result, many people are uninformed, uneducated and ignorant about the faculties of *Ifá's* mathematical and scientific knowledge. Therefore, this study attempts to critically review available works on *Ifá* mathematics and science and then relate these to contemporary mathematics, computer science and biology. The aim in this study is to promote the development and sustainability of African mathematical and scientific knowledge systems: this is done through an evaluation of the African indigenous knowledge systems before the advent of colonialism. It is hoped that this chapter will go a long way to bring African indigenous knowledge systems of mathematics and science into limelight. The chapter demonstrates that colonial mathematics, science and technology were preceded by African indigenous science, mathematics and technology. The chapter urges Africanist researchers, authors and scholars - particularly, mathematicians and scientists - to delve more into African indigenous knowledge systems such as *Ifá's* mathematics and science. It concludes that, *Ifá* is more than a religion because; it encapsulates indigenous knowledge systems of mathematics and science that can be equated to contemporary mathematics, science and technology in other places of the world.

Indigenous scientific confluence with *Ifá* religion

There is no known human society where religion does not exist. Africans had their own indigenous religions before the incursions of foreign religions. It has been established that religion is as old as humanity itself (Dọpamu, 2009: 36). The divine or sacredness of the *Ifá* epistle makes its knowledge to be unchallengeable. The mathematical, scientific and technological knowledge evinced from *Ifá* are also encoded in the sacred *Ifá* epistles. Meaning that, "despite the grip of modern science and technology on all people…the main, magic, medicine, religion and science have continued to co-exist" (Dọpamu, 2009: 29).

It cannot be contested that, without yesterday there cannot be today, as today gives birth to tomorrow. This is to say that, African indigenous mathematics, scientific and technological knowledge have existed before the advent of the colonial/imperial system, since it is a fact that something cannot be built on nothing and what existed before the new serves as pillars that hold the new. The old is the foundation for the new systems of living (Dopamu, 2009).

Even though, findings revealed that there is a relationship between science and religion, not many thinkers believe that African religions possess indigenous mathematics, scientific and technological knowledge and values. Dopamu (2009: 39) notes thus:

> today, scientists and religious intellectuals are discovering anew the relationship between science and religion, and are now recognizing the inadequacies and the simplicity of the dichotomies and alleged warfare between them. It is now being argued that when science and religion are properly understood, they can be in perfect harmony. Consequently, the science and religion dialogue has been advocated in recent times, and this has attracted discussions at many levels of sophistication…Today, scholarship allows inter-disciplinary study of subjects.

The opinion above is a challenge for the scientists in various aspects or disciplines to investigate into the ingenuous scientific knowledge to demonstrate the precedence of the Africanist scientific ways of life before the incursions of colonial science.

Ifa cannot be confined to religion alone. Many authors and scholars cannot see *Ifa* beyond religious limitations. In fact, some scholars such as Akintọla (1999) and Òkéwándé (2017) demonstrate *Ifa* as a philosophy and *Ọ̀rúnmìlà*, the *Ifa* progenitor as a philosopher. Morakinyọ (1983) shows the influence of *Ifa's* knowledge of mental health care, not only among the Yorùbá people, but, in West Africa more broadly. *Ọ̀rúnmìlà* can also be described as *ònpìtàn*, the great historian. This is evidenced by the series of Yorùbá histories that are referenced from *Ifa*. History of the heroes, divinities and ancestors is grounded in *Ifa*. These are some aspects of Yorùbá life beyond religion.

The gamut of *Ifa* relates to the past (the memory), the present (contemporary) and the future (the unborn). This is why Akìwọwọ describes *Ifa* as *amọ̀ìmọ̀tán*, the one whose knowledge cannot be fully grasped:

> The central theme of the *Oríkì of Ọ̀rúnmìlà* which I shall label *phenomenological amọ̀ìmọ̀tán*. The term *amọ̀ìmọ̀tán* can be translated into English to mean 'that which is incapable of being completely known'. Hence, the term *phenomenological amọ̀ìmọ̀tán* means the belief and perspective of mind which holds that the perceptible presence of an objects as well as its substance are incapable of being fully or completely known or recognized. Judging from the content of oríkì of this being, the Babaláwo's classification of him is open ended because it makes room for some 'yet-to-be discovered' characteristics of the given group of existent' (A. R. p.87) belonging to his personality. It is for this reason, I believe, that Babalawo also refer to Ọ̀rúnmìlà as *ẹni amọ̀ìmọ̀tán*; one capable of generating infinite knowledge about himself, or one about whom there are infinite things to be known by those of Ọ̀rúnmìlà. If one applies this guiding principle to the analysis of the *oríkì of Ọ̀rúnmìlà*, **then it should be stated that this originating Ifa scientists most probably reason thus: 'We know there exists such an entity as Ọ̀rúnmìlà. We know many of his attributes; but he possesses others which we do not yet know and must struggle to**

153

discover for the rest of the period of our human existence.' For he is àmòìmọ̀tán' (1983: 143 & 48-9) (Bold mine).

The quotation above supports my earlier suggestion not to give a narrow definition to the *Ifa* knowledge that cannot be fully comprehended by ordinary humans. The assertions by Akìwọwọ̀, above, also evince the scientific knowledge of *Ifá* and *Ọ̀rúnmìlà* as elastic or unlimited. Also, "Embedded in the poems is celestial knowledge that can never be exhausted" (Salami, 2002: xvi).

I need to reiterate here that, even though *Ifá* belongs to the Yorùbá but,

> *Ifá* divination is not unique to the Yorùbá people; it has in fact diffused all over the Yorùbá diasporas. It is found among the *Fon* of the Benin Republic. There, it is referred to as *fa* (Bascom 1969, p. 10). The practice of ifa was also taken to the Americas during the mid to late eighteenth century by slaves from West Africa. Brenner records that the casting of sixteen palm nuts or cowry shells (ifa divination) is widely practiced today by Africans of West African descent in the diaspora. He observed that it is the most popular **of all the Africa's divination systems**. Pemberton (2007) corroborated this by noting that ifa divination is the best known in Africa (Pogosone and Akande, 2011: 5).

The above observation shows that *Ifá's* nomenclature has cut-across nations of the world.

In 2005, the United Nations Educational, Scientific and Cultural Organisation (UNESCO) proclaimed *Ifá* as one of the 86 traditions of the world to be recognised as masterpiece of oral and intangible heritage of humanity (Robinson, 2008: 1). By this proclamation, *Ifá* joined the league of heritages threatened by extinction and therefore requiring urgent preservation. *Ifá*, as a religion, science or literary text, has over time been of great interest to scholars in different areas of human endeavour, like medicine, philosophy, religion, art, mathematics, science, technology and culture. For example, all Yorùbá medical specialisations - pharmacy, ophthalmology, gynaecology, orthopaedics, pathology, general medicine and others are derived from *Ifá*.

Medicine, however, is the science or art of prevention, treatment, and cure of disease. The art of medicine is important because man recognizes that health can be lost and medicine helps the body return to its normal state…This is why medicine **men, known as traditional doctors, abound in Africa.** They regard their power as a gift from God through the divinities. They claim they are given the art of medicine by divinities (Aderibigbe, 2016: 201-2).

In Yorùbá religious belief, *Ifá/Òrúnmìlà* and *Òsanyìn* are the divinities that are associated with medicine and related knowledge. However, *Òsanyìn* possessed his knowledge of medical practice from *Ifá/Òrúnmìlà*. The intimacy of *Ifá/Òrúnmìlà* and *Òsanyìn* on one hand was of servant-master from heaven. "*Òsanyìn* was "Ọmọ ọdọ Òrúnmìlà lọrun." Meaning that, *Òsanyìn* was the house maid of *Òrúnmìlà* in heaven (Adéoyè, 1985: 214). On another hand, the relationship between the two divinities was described as "a brother, friend, partner or servant of Òrúnmìlà" (Simpson, 1980: 7). This association between *Òrúnmìlà* and *Òsanyìn* extends to the earthly world. This means, *Ifá* is the custodian of medicine in Yorùbá belief.

In Yorùbá communities, all the medical knowledge evolves from Yorùbá indigenous medical profession- *Ifá*. Ilésanmí succinctly put it that,

> Ọwọ́ Ifá ni gbogbo oògùn ti wà.
> Ọwọ́ Ifá nìkan ni gbogbo oògùn ti wà pátápátá poro-n-godo…
> Òòṣà ni Ifá, nnkan àálò ni
> Oògùn tún lò jẹ fún aráyé (1998: 10-11),
> All medicine came from *Ifá*.
> All the medicine related things only came from *Ifá* in its entirety.
> *Ifá* is a divinity; it is equally an instrument being used
> It is equally medicine for the world.

This aspect of *Ifá* (medical) specialisation is so important, that no *Ifá* practitioner can have a successful practice if he does not know anything about the medicine.

In the traditional Yorùbá society, Ifá priests were the physicians, psychiatrists, historians, and philosophers of the communities to which they belonged…even before initiation. The would-be priest must learn something about medicine so that he could cure his clients of minor ailments. No Ifá priest can have a successful practice if he does not know anything about medicine since many people go to Ifá priest to seek help in curing their ailments (Abimbọlá, 1977a: 13).

Therefore, in this study; I will not rely on any single definition about *Ifá*. However, in order to expand the horizon of *Ifá*, I will point to some authors and scholars that described *Ifá* as indigenous knowledge containing mathematics, science and technology.

Because *Ifá* is important to indigenous knowledge of science, I shall confine my review to authors and scholars that see *Ifá* as science. As far back as 1973, Yemiitan and Ogundele (1973) noted that, *Ifá* is a doyen of science and urged researchers, authors and scholars to focus more on the scientific knowledge of *Ifá*. In the opinion of Yemiitan and Ogundele:

> *Bí a bá wo ọ̀rọ̀ Ifá dáadáa, a ò rí i pé ọ̀nà méjì ni a lè pín in sí: ekinni, ó jẹ́ ìmọ̀ ìjìnlẹ̀ lọ́tọ̀-lọ́tọ̀ ara rẹ̀; ohun tí a le pè ní ẹka ìmọ̀ 'science' kan. Èkejì, ó jẹ́ oríṣi ẹ̀sìn ìṣẹ̀dálẹ̀ ilẹ̀ Yorùbá kan. **Kò sí eyí tí kò yẹ fún ìwádi nínú ẹka méjèèjì tí a pín Ifá sí yi. Ó yẹ k'á túbọ̀ ní ìmọ̀ nípa irú ìmọ̀ ìjìnlẹ̀ tiwa t'ó ti wa tipẹ́ yi…** (1973: ix).*

If we look at the word, *Ifá* properly, we will see that it can be divided into two major parts: first, it is a separate knowledge on its own, what can be referred to as a branch of science. Second, it is an indigenous Yorùbá religion. **None of these aspects of *Ifá*'s knowledge should be exempted from being researched. We need to have in-depth findings on our own ancient knowledge that has existed long ago** (bold mine).

The observations by Yemiitan and Ogundele (1973) above are a challenge for African researchers, scholars and authors. It was after this "clarion call" (about fifty years ago) that some authors, researchers and scholars focused on the inherent mathematical, scientific and technological knowledge of *Ifá*. As noted earlier,

156

Akiwọwọ (1983) and Yemiitan and Ogundele (1973), argue that one can group the knowledge within *Ifá* into two broad categories. Meaning that, researchers, scholars and authors on *Ifa's* knowledge can be grouped into *Ifá* scientists and religious scholars. For this reason, the works of a computer scientists like Longẹ (1983) and mathematicians such as McGee (1983) concentrated on indigenous mathematics and scientific knowledge of *Ifá*.

Ifá's indigenous knowledge of mathematics

The works of Ajayi (2009), Lijadu (1908), Longẹ (1983) and McGee (1983) established some mathematical principles in *Ifá*. One of the principles is the binary system. In the words of Lijadu (1908),

> Ifá is a divination system created by the Yorùbá people of South Western Nigeria some 2000 years ago. In the course of succeeding centuries, The Ifá priests (Babalawo) have developed the original form bequeathed them by **ỌRUNMILA**, the reforming prophet of the **ODUDUWA ERA** of Yorùbá history (5000B.C. – 500A.D.) in many ways but have kept its canons essentially unchanged to this very day. The divinatory process is based on the principle of **BINARY ARITHMETIC**, where if two dissimilar terms (0, 00 or 1, 11 in Ifa) are arranged in a fixed number of times (n), the total (s) is given by the formula: $S = 2^n$ since Ifá units are mixed 8times (i.e. n=8) the total number of arrangements possible is 256 (i.e. S=256). In the Yorùbá language each one of these 256 arrangements has a specific name (Lijadu 1908 as translated into English by Emanuel 2010: ix) (with authors bold).

The time of Lijadu's observations about *Ifá* was 1908. At that time *Ifá* had already been projected to have been in existence 2000 years earlier. It is by the occurrence of two and its multiples (2^n) that we can identify some values of *Ifá* corpus. The occurrence of two (2) in *Ifá* also symbolises some values in the *Ifá* divination system. For example, the value of two (2) in *Ifá Ọ̀kànràn Méjì* as contained in Abímbọ́lá

òòlù mẹ́jì di mẹ́rin
kò ṣẹ
òòlù mẹ́rin di mẹ́jọ
kò ṣẹ
òòlù mẹ́jọ di mẹ́rìndínlógún kò ṣẹ
(1968: 86).
Two gimlet turns four
to be executed
four gimlet turns eight
to be executed
eight gimlet turns sixteen
to be executed.

It is symbol two (2) that is used in generating further important *Ifá* symbols' four (4), eighth (8) and sixteen (16), which are symbols postulated by scholars on numbers of *Ifá* verses to be learnt by a prospective *Ifá* priest. McGee notes that, "some claim that there are 512, 1024, 2048 or 4096.

If he learns $2 = 2 \times 256 = 512/2^9$
If he learns $4 = 4 \times 256 = 1024/2^{10}$
If he learns $8 = 8 \times 256 = 2048/2^{11}$
If he learns $16 = 16 \times 256 = 4096/2^{12}$" (1983: 112).

Through the principle of duality and arithmetic progression, we are able to establish that for an *Ifá* priest to be initiated, he must be able to recite, mark, read and interpret sixteen verses of two hundred and fifty-six *Odù* present in *Ifá* corpus, $16 \times 256 = 4096$ or 2^{12}.

A continuous recurrence of two to the power of two (2^2), and two to the power of sixteen (2^{16}) are very important *Ifá* symbols. In other words, the 2, 4, 8 and 16 numbers are symbols of *Ifá* authority. This is why *Ifá* sanction or authority is applied to these figures in the *Ọ̀kànràn Mẹ́jì* quoted above. 'Àṣẹ' means 'authority'.

The use of binary represented in two (2) and its multiples has been associated with the Yorùbá ways and manner of life. McGee (1983: 97) opines that, "of course, all of these numbers except zero are even and multiples of two. As a people's belief system greatly influences their mannerisms and customs". In other words, all the occurrences of two (2) and its multiples as shown above are expressed in even numbers (number divisible by two (2). These figures have cultural and religious values. "The main point of interest here is that there are two gods working together. The number two is even. Its prime factors are two…Therefore, it can be expressed as two raised to an integral power, n, including zero. That is, $2 = 2 \times 1 = 2^{n\dots}$" (McGee, 1983: 97). Some prime factors of important *Ifá* symbols were given. For example, McGee (1983: 98) says, "The number four is of interest here. It is even. Its prime factors are all twos, thus it can be expressed as $4 = 2 \times 2 = 2^{2}\dots$ I wish to look at number eight. It can be expressed as $8 = 2 \times 2 \times 2 = 2^{3}$. The children of Ọ̀rúnmìlà are eight, the number of *ọpẹlẹ* seeds (Ifá divination chain) contains eight and so on".

The total number of *ikin*, *Ifá* sacred divination palm-nuts are sixteen in number. "The prime factors of 16 are all in twos, hence, we can write $16 = 2 \times 2 \times 2 \times 2 = 2^{4}$" (p. 28). The major *Ifá* corpuses are sixteen. The minor *odù* are 240. "The number 240 is even, its prime factors are $240 = 2 \times 2 \times 2 \times 2 \times 2 \times 3 \times 5$. Hence, we see that all the prime factors are not twos" (McGee, 1983: 100).

The total number of the sixteen major *odù Ifá* and the two hundred and forty minor *odù* is 265. "The number 256 is even. Its prime factors are all twos, thus, it can be expressed as $256 = 2^{8}$" (McGee, 1983: 100). Some authors have given some mathematical expressions of *odù Ifá* in different forms. McGee opines that,

other authors have used the expression, 2^{n}, in discussing some of the numbers in the Ifá Systems. W. Bascom (1969: 41) referred to it in explaining the markings of the Ifa Figures. E. M. McClelland (1966: 421- 430) referred to it in giving the different numbers in the Odù. In fact, he writes the expressions, 2^{2}, 2^{3}, 2^{4}, 2^{8}, 2^{12}, which give the numbers 4, 8, 16, 256 and 4096. His basis for using this expression or geometric progression is the concept of the principal of duality of the gods" (1983: 100).

The work of McGee also accounts for the mathematical expressions of the total number of *odù Ifá* a trainee must learn at each stage of *Ifá* training or apprenticeship. For instance, suppose the trainee or priest learns, say two, Ẹsẹ Ifá in each Odù, then he will know a total of, $2 \times 256 = 512 = 2^9$,…If he learn four, he will know, $4 \times 256 = 1024 = 2^{10}$,…If he learns eight, the he will know, $8 \times 256 = 2048 = 2^{11}$,…For the one who learn 16, he will know, $16 \times 256 = 4096 = 2^{12}$, the number given in E. M. McClelland's expression and for the one who learn 32, he will know, $32 \times 256 = 8192 = 2^{13}$. Therefore, it becomes obvious that the number of Ẹsẹ Ifá could become unlimited (McGee, 1983: 102).

Another mathematical expression of *odù Ifá* by McGee is in the visitation of *odù* to the surface of the earth. This is also coded in twos. *Èjì Ogbè* corpus testifies to this opinion as translated by the author that,

> *Èjèejì ni mo gbè,*
> *N ò gbẹnikan ṣoṣo mọ́.*
> It is in pairs that I support
> I no longer support one person alone (Ọlatunji, 2005: 137).

The visitation of *odù Ifá* and the implication of the two (2) as even number favoured by *Ifá* is shown in the table provided by McGee (1983: 104-108).

30 =	2c (15, 1)	=	2p (15, 1)	Èjì Ogbè
28 =	2c (14, 1)	=	2p (14, 1)	Ọyẹku Méjì
26 =	2c (13, 1)	=	2p (13, 1)	Ìwòrì Méjì
24 =	2c (12, 1)	=	2p (12, 1)	Òdí Méjì
22 =	2c (11, 1)	=	2p (11,1)	Ìrosùn Méjì
20 =	2c (10, 1)	=	2p (10, 1)	Ọwọnrín Méjì
18 =	2c (9, 1) =		2p (9, 1)	Ọbàrà Méjì
16 =	2c (8, 1) =		2p (8, 1)	Ọkanran Méjì
14 =	2c (7, 1) =		2p (7, 1)	Ogúndá Méjì
12 =	2c (6, 1) =		2p (6, 1)	Ọsá Méjì
10 =	2c (5, 1) =		2p (5, 1)	Ìká Méjì
8 =	2c (4, 1) =		2p (4, 1)	Òtúrupọn Méjì

6 =	2c (3, 1) =	2p (3, 1)	Òtúá Méjì
4 =	2c (2, 1) =	2p (2, 1)	Ìrẹtẹ̀ Méjì
2 =	2c (1, 1) =	2p (1, 1)	Ọsẹ́ Méjì
0 =	2c (0, 1) =	2p (0, 1)	Ọfún Méjì

(McGee, 1983: 104)

Table showing the visitations of *odù ifá*

In the above table, the table showing the arrangement of these *Àpólà* in *ẹsẹ Ifá*, starting with the second deity to the sixteen is helpful here to demonstrate the arrangement of the visitations of the *Odù* to the surface of the earth from heaven. It is demonstrated in the table that, the arrangement is in a decreasing geometric progression, by two from 30 to 0. Since the last deity cannot visit himself, it is marked by C (0, 1), which indicates that the last deity visits himself once. Abímbọ́lá (1976: 28) also observes that: "each *Àpólà* consist thirty *Odù* while the second section contains twenty-eight. The number of *Odù* in each section decreases in an irregular pattern, giving a total of two hundred and forty." The implication of the geometrical progression demonstrated in *odù-Ifá* above is that this principle of mathematics is implied in *Ifá*.

Referring to *Ifá*, Ọlátúnjí (2005: 127) says, "the 16 major *odù* are conceived as kings paying visits to those next below and having their visits returned. This, thus, gives *ÈjìOgbè* thirty visits altogether, *Ọ̀yẹ̀kú Méjì* twenty-eight and so on until we come to *Ọ̀fún Méjì* who has none to visit. A total of 240 visits, the number of the minor odù is made" *ÈjìOgbè* has the highest number of *Àpólà*; indicated with 15(2) that is, thirty (30) *Àpólà*. *Ọ̀yẹ̀kú Méjì* is the next, represented by 14(2) that is, twenty-eight *àpólà*. These number decreases by two to *Ọ̀fún Méjì* with 2(0) that is, zero (0), the *Odù* cannot visit itself. McGee (1983: 103) quoting McClelland (1966: 421-430) says "the arrangement is a decreasing geometric progression by two, from thirty to zero (30-0)."

Adéẹ̀kọ́ quoting Ilésanmí (2004) presented the *Ifá* inscriptions of the *odù* symbols in mathematical signs of plus (+)- positive/yes and minus (–)- negative/no. This concept has earlier been discussed as a principle of complementarity and not opposition as generally believed. These mathematical signs are based on binary principle rendered in the sixteen principal *odù Ifá*.

Àwọn odù méjì yìí ló tako ara wọn jù nínú àbùdá oníbejì bẹ́ẹ̀-ni-bẹ́ẹ̀-kọ́. Ọ̀kan kò ní bẹ́ẹ̀-kọ́ rárá, èkejì kò sì ni bẹ́ẹ̀-ni olóòkan. Kò sí ìgbà tí àwọn méjèejì jọ wá ohun kan náà. Gbogbo àwọn odù yóòkù ló ní bẹ́ẹ̀-ni díẹ̀, bẹ́ẹ̀-kọ́ díẹ̀ nínú. Nínú ọ̀kan ire lè pọ̀ ju ibi lọ, nínú òmíràn ibi lè pọ̀ ju ire lọ. Wàyí ò, ipò tí ibi àti ire wà tako ara wọn. Iye ire àti ibi kan náà ni Èdí àti Ìwòrì ní, ṣùgbọ́n wọ́n fi ipò tako ara wọn (2010: 290).

These two odu are polar opposite in the positive and negative binary structure. One has no negative at all, the other has not one positive. At no point do the two odu express the same attributes. All the other odu signs express a little of positives and negatives, in other words, negatives outnumber positives. The positioning of the attributes might oppose each other. Èdí and Ìwòrì express equal number of positives and negatives but in different positions.

The mathematical signs of the sixteen major odù are rendered with the charts below:

++++	Ogbè	1
————	Ọ̀yẹ̀kú	2
–++–	Ìwòrì	3
+——+	Èdì	4
——+	Ọ̀bàrà	5
+——	Ọ̀kànràn	6
——++	Ìrosùn	7
++——	Ọ̀wọ́nrín	8
–+++	Ògúndá	9
+++–	Ọ̀sá	10
+–++	Ìrẹtẹ̀	11
++–+	Òtúrá	12
–+——	Òtúúrúpọ̀n	13
——+–	Ìká	14
–+——	Òsé	15
+–+–	Ọ̀fún	16

Adéẹ̀kọ́ (2010: 290) as adapted from Ilésanmí (2004: 135)

Some of the mathematical expressions of some *Ifá* figures are equally integrated into the computer science as noted in this study.

Odù Ifá code in relation to computer coding

A code is "a means of conveying messages, a vehicle of communication" (Geoffery and Short, 1981: 122). The linkage of signs and their meanings are made known by code. Code helps to simplify phenomena in order to make it easier to communicate experience. Interpretation of the code **is important in understanding the meaning of a sign**, symbol or text.

Odù is a code of *Ifá*. Messages of *Ifá* are coded and interpreted by an initiated or professional *Ifá* priest. Meaning that, there are different codes left behind by *Òrúnmìlà*, through which we can read meaning to a particular situation. Adéẹkọ says, "However, life continues in the exchanges of traces of the instituted codes that bear fragments of *Òrúnmìlà's* record. *Òrúnmìlà's* permanent disappearance signifies that meaning in itself, is gone. The search for recovery launched by the *Ifá* left behind in the material world shows that continued existence revolves around the anxiety of contingency" (2010: 297). As it will be demonstrated in this chapter, the binary code in *Ifá* is foundational to the binary code in computer science.

The two major *Ifá* divination objects are *ọpẹlẹ* (divination chain with ọpẹlẹ seeds) and *ikin* (Ifá sacred palm-nuts). "The foundation of analysis in Ifá is a systematised graphic translation of the results of the random presentation of the divination objects, among which the chain (ọpẹlẹ) and palm nuts (ikin) are the most prestigious" (Adeẹkọ, 2003: 286). Fádípẹ gives the structural description of *Ọpẹlẹ* thus "As there are eight 'draws' and two possibilities to each 'draw', there are at least 256 combinations. It is also widely held that there are sixteen possibilities to each of the 256 combinations" (1970: 272). Àjàyí is also of the opinion that, the maximum number of *ẹsẹ* in an *Odù* signature is eight which has a link with numbers 1 to 8 as numerical count in the *Ifá* corpus above "bí wọn bá sọ ọ sílẹ tẹsẹ mẹjẹẹọ pé" (2002: 83). Meaning that, when *ọpẹlẹ* is spread on the ground, it gives the complete eight verses.

The inaugural lecture of Longe (1983) entitled "Ifá divination and computer science" gives a comprehensive knowledge on the indigenous *Ifá* as foundational to the contemporary computer knowledge. He introduced the concepts of computer in the earlier part of the lecture. "In an earlier section of this lecture, I discussed eight of the basic concepts of Computer Science. I now proceed to illustrate the presence of these concepts in the ancient system of Ifá Divination" (Longe, 1983: 22). I will briefly discuss the eight computer science concepts he demonstrated in his lecture.

The binary digit in *Ifá* is important to computer science. This is described around *ọpẹlẹ* (divination chain) each comprising of eight half-nuts in the process of divination. The reading of the symbols "is read as binary digit. A concave face denotes binary 0 and a convex face denotes binary 1. Similarly, each marking in the powder on the ọpọn-ifá is a binary digit. The names of the major odu of Ifá, such as Eji-Ogbe, Ọyẹku-Meji, Iwori-Meji, etc, have a pairing or binary connotation" (Longe, 1983: 22). It will be recalled that, the binary arithmetic is one of the basic elements in *Ifá*. The mathematical concept is well known in computer science.

There is representation of numeric values in *Ifá* and Longe says; "the most convenient Ifá number base is 2. Numeric values to be used in divination are expressed initially in binary. The more convenient hexadecimal (base 16) number system is more widely used in Ifá" (Longe, 1983: 23). McGee's (1983) observation on the mathematical principles in *Ifá*, earlier examined in this chapter, also emphasises on the numerical values of *Ifá*. The total number of principal *odù Ifá*, which is the square of 16 (sixteen raised to power 2): $16^2 = 256$, is the total number of the *odù Ifá*.

Modulo Arithmetic in *Ifá* is the third concept discussed by Longe (1983). This is demonstrated by the use of *ikin* (sacred palm-nuts) in divination.

> Divination by Ikin was modulo-2 arithmetic. When an attempt is made to scoop, at one try, the nuts in the left hand with the right hand, a number, x, of nuts remain in the left hand. The marking on the ọpọn-Ifá is determined using modulo-2 arithmetic as follows:
> If x = 0, marking is a two-stroke, 11, which represents binary 0, i.e.

0 modulo 2 = 0

If x = 1, marking of a one-stroke, 1, which represents binary 1, i.e.

1 modulo 2 = 1

If x = 2, marking is a two-stroke, 11, which represents binary 0, i.e.

2 modulo 2 = 0

Longẹ says,

it is necessary to use 'no-stroke' for 'blank!' Every computer scientist knows that it is very essential to be able to distinguish zero from blank" (1983: 23).

The analysis above is interesting because, the foundation of *Ifá* divination marking is implied in computer science knowledge: we therefore observe some mathematical and scientific rules in it. For example, *Ifá* symbolises and marks differences between zero and blank. Only the interdisciplinary knowledge such as that of Longẹ (1983) can unmask this veil.

The fourth concept of *Ifá* in relation to computer science is what Longẹ (1983) described under "permutation in Ifá." This is rendered according to the sixteen major *odù Ifá* in relation to the sixteen sacred *Ifá* divination palm-nuts. The 240 minor divinities derived their names from the sixteen major *odù Ifá*. "The number and the names of the minor divinities are thus based on permutations. There should be a total of 16P2 = 16/14! = 16x15 = 240 minor divinities. Indeed, there are exactly 240 ọmọ-odù (minor divinities). Together with the 16 *odù* (major divinities), there are altogether 16+ 240 = 256 divinities in Ifá" (Longe, 1983: 25).

The fifth concept of *Ifá* in relation to computer science is what Longẹ (1983) described as the "coding in Ifá." As earlier explained under code,

the convenient method of identification of the Ifá divinities is by coding. Since there are a total of 256 divinities and $256 = 2^8$, then, 8 binary digits, i.e. 8 bits are required for the identification code. Since each minor divinity bears the names of the two patron major divinities, the code corresponding to a major divinity consists of two 4-bit halves, each half corresponding to the code of a patron. Since a major odu cannot have a patron, he is, in theory, his own patron and his code must consist of two identical 4-bits, each 4-bit half being his own code within the major divinities. Indeed, the signature of each major divinity (odu) consists of two identical halves and this is why the name of each odu has the word 'meji' in it, e.g. Èjì-Ogbè (two identical Ogbè), Òyèkú-méjì (two identical òyèkú), etc. Thus, there is a sound theoretical reason why divination is always performed in two 4-bit halves....A certain 4-bit code is known as the hexadecimal code in Computer Science. Thus the signature of a divinity in Ifá consists of two hexadecimal digits. There is an order of seniority among the 16 major divinities. The following are the names, in order of seniority, of the major divinities, their divination codes or signatures and the corresponding standard hexadecimal digits (Longe, 1983: 26).

Rank of Seniority	Name of Odu	Divination Code or Signature	Standard Hexadecimal
1	Èjì-Ogbè	0000 0000	00
2	Òyèkú Méjì	1111 1111	FF
3	Ìwòrì Méjì	1001 1001	99
4	Òdí Méjì	0110 0110	66
5	Ìrosùn Méjì	0011 0011	33
6	Òwónrí Méjì	1100 1100	CC
7	Òbàrà Méjì	0111 0111	77
8	Òkànràn Méjì	1110 1110	EE
9	Ògúndá Méjì	0001 0001	11
10	Òsá Méjì	1000 1000	88
11	Ìká Méjì	1011 1011	BB
12	Òtúúrúpòn Méjì	1101 1101	DD
13	Òtúá Méjì	0100 0100	44
14	Ìrètè Méjì	0010 0010	22
15	Òsé Méjì	0101 0101	55
16	Òfún Méjì	1010 1010	AA

The 4-bit Ifá code is hereby designated the Ifá-Hex code. Therefore, the Ifá-Hex characters are, in order: Ogbè, Òyèkú, Ìwòrì,

Odí, Ìrosùn, Ọbàrà, Ọkànràn, Ogúndá, Ọsá, Ìká, Òtúúrúpọn, Òtúá, Ìrẹtẹ̀, Ọsẹ́ and Ọfún.

It is obvious that the collating sequence (seniority) of Ifá-hex code differs from that of standard hex code.

If the divination code words are regarded as standard hex code words, then, the collating sequence (or seniority) of the odu would be Ogbè, Ogúndá, Ìrẹtẹ̀, Ìrosùn, Òtúá, Ọsẹ́, Òdí, Ọbàrà, Ọsá, Ìwòrì, Ọfún, Ìká, Ọwọ́nrín, Òtúúrúpọn, Ọkànràn, Ọyẹkú (Longe, 1983: 27-8).

The sixth *Ifá* concept discussed by Longe in relation to computer science is the "Boolean Algebra and Logic in Ifá". Under this concept he sub-divided it into: "Complementarity of Adjacent Ifá-hex Code words, reflexity and groupings" (1983: 28-36). The principle of complementarity was addressed by Ilesanmi even though he did not relate the concept in *Ifá* to computer science. However, he observed that the concept is based on how nature works.

While the world sees the binary system as being opposition, the

Yorùbá see it as being complementary; contrary to the 'world', the Yorùbá would not conceive an idea that binary opposition would ever yield positive results, they believe that complementarity rather than opposition yield the visible positive results.

It is in the complementarity of the binary system that we can fully appreciate the interdependence and the interrelationship of all the aspects of our being (Ilesanmi, 2004: 108-9).

The view of the Yorùbá that binaries are complementary rather than oppositional is one of the foundational elements in computer science.

According to Longe (1983: 37), the seventh concept relating *Ifá* to computer science is "Basic Unit of Data and Addressing in *Ifá*". It will be recalled that, the 2^8 gives the total number of *odù Ifá*. That is, two to the power of eighth (2^8). Computer science also adopts or works with this concept.

It was not until 1964 that the 8-bit 'byte' was adopted as the standard unit of computer data and since then, the smallest addressable area of computer memory has been the 8-bit byte. The 8-bit byte had been the standard unit of the data in Ifá, centuries before 1964" (Longe, 1983: 37).

Longẹ gives the eighth concept of *Ifá* in relation to computer science as *"Ifá* matrix" subdivided into "Subscription" (1983: 37). He discussed this concept around the family interaction between the major and minor *odù Ifá*, whereby "each son in the family enjoys the patronage of an uncle who is one of the 15 other major odù" (Longe, 1983: 37). This interaction brings the derivation of the compound names of minor *odù* as *Ògbèyẹ̀kú* (Ògbè + Ọ̀yẹ̀kú), realised in 240 forms. The first name serves as the father and the other son. However, in *Ọ̀yẹ̀kúlógbè*, where *Ọ̀yẹ̀kú* is assumed to be father, *Ògbè* is the farther because, "Ògbè is senior to Ọ̀yẹ̀kú" (Longe, 1983: 37).

As shown earlier, there are 16P2 = 240 ọmọ-odù. Each omọ-Odù is a minor divinity. Therefore, the 16 major odù together with the 240 ọmọ-odù make a total of 256 divinities in the Ifá divination pantheon. The farther-son patron relationships of these divinities can be presented as a 16-square matrix. The main diagonal elements of the matrix represent the major divinities (odù) and the other elements represent the minor divinities, (ọmọ-odù) (Longe, 1983: 37).

In the concluding analysis of Longẹ's (1983: 41) lecture, he challenged his audience that, "You will probably now agree with me that *Ifá* Divination, as an ancient Yorùbá knowledge system reveals to us the coherence, logicality, precision and profundity of the thoughts, philosophy, mathematics and computer science as known and practiced by our forefathers (and mothers) before the 11th Century A. D., well before the same ideas were rediscovered in the West in later centuries". Lóngẹ́ essentially states that there is inherent scientific knowledge of *Ifá* and African scientific knowledge pre-date more recent scientific and technological developments in Africa that are often used to position science itself as a "modern" knowledge to the continent. Lóngẹ́'s work concludes that, the African indigenous knowledge still thrives despite the hegemony of "imported or foreign knowledge."

The work of Àjàyí (2009) addresses "The *Ifá* 6 A Bits Paper Computer Model N" as another point of convergence between knowledge within *Ifá* and in computer science. He adopts the use of *Ifá* divination by cowry shell, instead of the popular *ikin* and *ọpẹlẹ* by Lóngẹ. Cowry plays a vital role in the *Ifá* divination called *ibo* (lot cast).

> At a divination session several Ibo (instrument for casting lot) may be used to find detail information about a client's problem. The commonest and simplest form of ibo consists of a pair of Cowry Shells tied together representing "yes" (1) and piece of animal bone representing "no" (0).
>
> This relates to computer language since today we need prediction (which is scientific and reliable) more than divination (which is religious and uncertain). Considering the loci on the arms of the ọpẹlẹ, the "F" pairs could be punched (1) and the "b" pairs not punched (0). Using this code a paper model of Ifá 6 A Bits computer model N has been developed (Ajayi 2009: 12).

The output of Ajayi's model is not too different from the one presented by Longẹ. The area of difference is in the *Ifá* divination objects used. The marking of yes/positive and no/negative in Ajayi's model and Longẹ's models are marked by (1) for positive or yes and (0) is marked by negative or no. All these elements of computer science have existed in *Ifá* before the colonisation of Africa. Thus, contemporary elements of computer science are not new to the Africans; it is on the African indigenous computer systems that the "modern" ones are built.

Ifá's indigenous knowledge of biology

Ajayi (2009: 21) represented human skeleton by "X representing the minor Odù showing a geometrical progression in decreasing order from 30-2". One could note the veracity of this within the knowledge of *Ifá* that covers all human life (visible and invisible). In explaining and demonstrating "The Autonomic Nervous System and *Ifá* Narrative Concept", Ajayi (2009: 22-3) says:

> The autonomic nervous system of the human skeleton derived from the arrangement of the 16 major and 240 minor Odù can be further explained using Ifá narrative concept (Ajayi, 1997: 68-73)…The Ifá narratives can be further explained scientifically using the nerves' pathways of the sympathetic and para-sympathetic nervous system…
>
> Therefore, the listed organs of the body 1-10 below represent the head as all nerves attached to them originated from the neck region of the head:
>
> 1. Eye, 2. Nose, 3. Salway glands, 4. Heart, 5. Lung, 6. Esophagus, 7. Stomach, 8. Liver, 9. Pancrease, 10. Kidney. Similarly, the 11-14 (11, Small intestine, 12. Large intestine, 13. Bladder, 14. Uterus) represent the tail as all the nerves attached to them originated from the tail part of the body.

The general human body and bodily care are not left out in *Ifá*. As earlier pointed out in this chapter, all aspects of medicine and related disciplines are encapsulated in *Ifá*. *Ọ̀rúnmìlà* is also a witness to human creation as earlier explained.

Some *Ifá* Corpus are based on the knowledge of biology for their proper understanding. For example, there is indigenous science projected in *Ifá* corpus, *Ògúndá Ìwòrì*, the human body is examined and shown to be composed of nine different entry points. This is an indigenous knowledge that calls for the "modern" scientists to research and establish the *Ifá* projection. The *Ifá* epistle (in author's translation) says,

Ògúndá ni ò lápó/It is Ògúndá that has no Knapsack
Ìwòrì ni ò lọfà/Ìwòrì has no arrow
   Agbàrà ni ò lámọ̀nà/Runoff water has no lead
   Awo ilé Alágbàmákin ló díá fún/The prince of Alágbàmákin's house cast divination for Alágbàmákin
   Wọ́n ni ó rúbọ ọ̀nà mẹ́sẹ̀ẹsàn tó wọ inú ara ẹ̀/He was asked to perform sacrifice for the nine ways providing entries to his body.
   Kọ́kọ̀ọkan ó mọ̀ ṣe dí/That none would become blocked.

Ọ̀nà mẹ́sàán ni ń bẹ tó wọnú ara/There are nine ways providing entry into the body.

Imú méjì ni/Two nostrils.

Etí méjì/Two ears,

Ẹnu, ọ̀kan/One mouth,

Ojú méjì/Two eyes,

Méje ni ń bẹ lọ́dọ̀ orí/There are seven openings with the head.

Níbi a`á tíi tọ̀/The opening from where we urinate

Ojú kan ni/Is one opening.

Ọ̀nà mẹ́sẹ̀ẹ̀sán tó wọ inú ara nùu.../Those are the nine ways providing entrance into the body... (Salami, 2002: 459).

The *Ifá* corpus above shows the indigenous science on the entry points on human body. There are nine entries divided into two human body parts. Seven points of entries on the head and two others on the middle of human being. Proper care must be taken on these entry points as any blockage will lead to a major health deficiency. Alágbàlákin was the first *Ifá* supplicant/client that brought about this indigenous *Ifá's* biological science.

As explained earlier, medicine is a basic *Ifá* knowledge that all *Ifá* priests must learn and be proficient in. *Ifá* is also believed to be a witness in creation. This is why he is referred to as *elẹ́ríi ìpín*, meaning that, a witness of destiny allocation to mankind. Therefore, there is no part (visible and invisible) of any human being - the bone, flesh, brain and abdomen among others that is strange or unknown to *Ifá*.

Conclusion

This chapter recommends that collaborative research should be encouraged and carried out between the various academic disciplines especially, those in the African culture related fields with scholars, researchers and authors in the fields of mathematics, science and technology disciplines. The product of such works will be interdisciplinary, which will account for the discovery, development and sustainability of the African indigenous knowledge of mathematics, science and technology. Such works will also demonstrate or account for confluences or interfaces between the "modern" and African indigenous knowledge of mathematics, science and technology; which will pave ways for the development and sustainability of African indigenous knowledge of mathematics, science and technology that have been consistently pirated and plundered by the "modern" or foreign systems.

This study concludes that African indigenous knowledge of mathematics, science and technology is the foundation on which the "modern" system of mathematics, science and technology is built. Africans are naturally endowed with their indigenous knowledge of mathematics, science and technology, which is as viable as any other in the world.

References

Abímbọlá, W. (1968). *Ìjìnlẹ̀ ohùn ẹnu Ifá. Apá kìíní.* Ọ̀yọ́: Aims Press & Publishers.

_____ (1976). *IFÁ: An exposition of Ifá literary corpus.* Ìbàdàn: Oxford University Press.

_____ (1977a). *Ifá divination poetry.* New York: Nok Publishers.

Adéẹ̀kọ́, A. (2010). "Writing" and "Reference" in Ifá divination chants. *Oral tradition* Vol 25(2): 283-303. Retrieved from Journal oraltradition.org/files/articles/2511/03-25.2.pdf.

Adéoyè, C. L. (1985). *Ìgbàgbọ́ àti ẹ̀sìn Yorùbá.* Ìbàdàn: Evans Brothers Nigeria Publishers.

Adéríbigbé, I. (2016). *Contextualizing religion study and practice.* Ilọrin: University of Ilọrin Press.

Ajayi, B. (2002). *Ifá Divination: Its Practice Among the Yorùbá of Nigeria.* Ìjẹ̀bú-òde: Shebiotimọ Publications.

_____ (2009). *Yoruba cosmology and aesthetics: The cultural confluence of divination, incantation and drum-talking.* An inaugural lecture delivered at University of Ilorin, *Ilọrin*, Nigeria on 19 March.

Akíntọlá, A. (1999). *Yorùbá ethics and metaphysics.* Ògbómọ̀ṣọ́: YALOYN Publishing Ventures Limited.

Akìwọwọ, A. (1983). Understanding interpretative sociology in the light of the oriki Ọ̀rúnmìlà. *Journal of culture and ideas.* vol 1(1): 139-157.

Dọpamu, A. (2009). *In the service of humanity.* Ilọrin: Library and Publication Committee.

Fádípẹ̀, N. A. (1970). *The sociology of the Yorùbá.* Ìbadan: University Press.

Geoffery, L. & Short, M. (1981). *Style in fiction: Linguistic introduction to English fiction prose.* New York: Longman.

Ilésanmí, T. M. (1998). *Aroko létí ọpọ́n-Ifá.* Ilé-Ifẹ̀: Amat Printing and Publishing Ltd.

_____. (2004). *Yorùbá orature and literature: A cultural analysis.* Ilé-Ifẹ̀: Ọbáfẹ́mi Awólọ́wọ̀ University Press Ltd..

Lijadu, E. M. (1908). As translated into English by Emanuel, B. (2010). *A prophet called Ọ̀rúnmìlà.* Lagos: West African Book Publishers Limited.

Longẹ, O. (1983). *Ifá divination and computer science.* An Inaugural lecture delivered at the University of Ibadan on 22 December 1983.

McGee, A. (1983). Some mathematical observations on the Ifá belief system practiced by the Yorùbá people of Nigeria. *Journal of culture and ideas,* vol 1: 95–114.

Morakinyọ, O. (1983). The Yorùbá àyànmọ́ myth and mental health care in West Africa. *Journal of culture and ideas.* vol 1(1): 61-92.

Òkéwándé, O. T. (2017). A semiotic investigation of philosophical relations between *Ifá* and *ayò ọlọ́pọ́n* among the Yorùbá people of Nigeria. *Nokoko: Journal of Pan-African wisdom.* Vol 6: 317-346. Ottawa: Canada. Available online at https://carletoca./africanstudies/research/nokoko-6

Ọlátúnjí, O. (2005). *Features of Yorùbá oral poetry.* Ìbàdàn: University Press.

Pogosone, O. I. & Akande, A.O. (2011). *Ifá* divination trays from isalẹ-Ọ̀yọ̀. *Cadernos de Estudos Africanos.* Retrieved from Cea.reVues.org/196, 15-41.

Robinson, B. A. (2008). *Ifá: the religion of the Yoruba people.* Retrieved from http://www.religioustolerance.org/ Ifa.htm.

Salami, A. (2002). *IFÁ: A complete divination.* Lagos: NIDD Limited (Publishers).

Simpson, G. (1980). *Yorùbá religion and medicine in Ibadan.* Ìbàdàn: University Press.

Yemitan, O. & Ogundele, O. (1970). *Ojú òṣùpá. Apá kìnní.* Ibadan: Oxford University Press.

Chapter Six

'We Know Our Africans': Missionaries as Torchbearers of the Colonisation in Zimbabwe

Robert Matikiti

Introduction

Colonial era missionaries were like the contemporary missionaries of Eurocentric science and technology described in chapter two of this book. In both instances their objective is to erect surveillance mechanism to get to know the indigenous people who are targeted for colonisation. Besides, both paint a gloomy picture of what Africans are in their socio-cultural, political, economic and religious outlook – this then serves as a justification for the colonial mission to civilise the supposedly backward, savage and barbaric Africans. Colonial era missionaries were paid by the transnational corporations that are also sponsoring the contemporary missionaries of Eurocentric science and technology engaged in present-day technocolonialism.

The initial perception of Africans by colonialists and missionaries alike negated the possibility of tolerance towards African humanity, religion, and culture. Missionaries preached the duty of the representatives of the Christian civilisation to overthrow "animism" and "barbarism" which were assumed to exist among Africans. Some contemporary Eurocentric scholars are trying to revive colonial depictions of Africans as "animists". Depictions of Africans as "animists" legitimised the colonial project; the genocide, exploitation and dispossession of Africans were premised on the presupposition that Africans were indistinct from animals and had no knowledge of the God of Creation *ex nihilo* and that, therefore, the Africans had no morals, ethics, natural laws, science, rationality, hierarchy and did not belong to humanity. However, pre-colonial Africans had notions of morals (*unhu/hunhu*), laws (*mirawu*), the Heavens (*denga*) and even about *mhondoro dzedenga* (spirit mediums from Heaven) – like

European Heavenly saints. For many scholars of religion, the close interaction between the Church and imperialism in Zimbabwe can be traced back to the presence of Christian ministers of religion in the 1890 Pioneer Column that spearheaded the colonisation of Zimbabwe. Imperialism was viewed as the result of "racist" ideas of European cultural supremacy where people like Cecil John Rhodes saw colonisation as a vehicle for spreading British culture, Christianity and civilisation. Many missionaries were, in fact, torchbearers of colonisation, and hence many of them had the same goals as the colonisers. It is interesting to note that in the present unwrapping of the history of colonisation in Africa, the missionary who carried the Bible was not a spiritual appendix but an intrinsic part of the colonisation team of colonial robbers, exploiters, traders and explorers.

In the words of Muzorewa (1998: 24), the important point to bear in mind is that "the planting of Christianity occurred simultaneously with colonisation. Consequently, there is a thin line between the missionary intention and the intent of the colonizers." The European colonial powers saw the missionaries as partners in a campaign to civilise the 'native'. Van der Merwe (1982: 1) did acknowledge that in Zimbabwe, the establishment of a colony under a European flag facilitated missionary activity. Therefore, there was an obvious allegiance on the part of the missionary enterprise to the colonial government. Moreover, missionary enterprises sometimes became so closely associated with the colonial government that they were largely identified with them. This chapter will argue that the impulsive promulgation of Christianity and the colonial agenda in Africa gave impetus and strength to the establishment of Christianity as the dominant religion. Thus, linked to evangelisation was the attempt by missionaries to make Christianity an arbiter of morality and religious values among the colonised peoples that the missionaries ironically robbed while fronting the Bible. Missionaries destroyed, "collected", or more accurately stole African artefacts/skulls and skeletons which are still lodged in Euro-American museums and private "collections" even as indigenous people around the world are demanding their artefacts, skulls and skeletons back.

We know our Africans

The phrase 'We Know Our Africans' is not my own innovation, it is borrowed from a little booklet published by the Rhodesian Ministry of Information entitled "The Man and his Ways." The booklet was billed as an aid to understanding the mentality and customs of 'the African' (Frederikse, 1982: 16). The catchphrase in the booklet was 'We Know the African' (Frederikse, 1982: 16). 'We know the African' was the central belief, chorussed throughout the 20th century, but White Rhodesians did not know African people. They never consulted the Africans. Sociologist Rev M.F.C. Bourdillon was so exasperated with this text that he attempted to counter its inaccuracies and stereotypes with his own booklet called "Myths about Africans: Mythmaking in Rhodesia" (Frederikse, 1982: 16). Bourdillon's booklet pointed out that they knew the 'girl' (scullery maid), who cooked and cleaned and looked after their children, and the 'boy' (groundsman), who gardened on their lawns and laboured in their fields. White Rhodesians clung to their myths for their myths resolved the contradiction that was White Rhodesian. Through their mythology they coped. They read their mythology in newspapers and novels. They heard their mythology on the radio and from their neighbours. This little booklet is published as an introduction to the man whom you are - the African- and sets out to tell you a little of the customs and beliefs of his people.

For almost one hundred years, from the age of Rev J. S. Moffatt and Rev C. D. Helm to the age of Bishop D. R. Lamont and Father A. S. Cripps, Rhodesia was a classic example of the relationship of the colonial church and state in the perpetration of cultural and epistemological destruction and plunder. Cecil John Rhodes, the British agent, was a racist, looter and plunderer imperialist. He believed that British "civilisation" was the best in the world and that the British people had a duty to spread that "civilisation" partly for the benefit of the world and partly to enhance British prestige. According to Hastings (1985: 26), "Mr Rhodes was an atheist, but he understood better the uses of organised religion and by numerous land grants and other little forms of assistance he tied the missionaries of many churches and societies to the juggernaut with

177

remarkable effectiveness." In the Christian understanding of society and human relations there is no place for robbery, looting, plunder, exploitation and discrimination against persons based on race, religion, ideology, economic or social condition, since all people are equal before God. Many societies are caught up in tensions arising out of discrimination/plunder based upon differences in race, religion, culture and the like. All have the problem of "the stranger in our midst." It is often based not only upon fear or resentment of people of another colour or tradition, but also upon economic self-interest. In the colonial Zimbabwean situation, the policy of racial plunder, dispossession, destruction and assertions of supremacy was prevalent. There was a conflict between missionaries' willingness to be partners in the so-called civilising mission on the natives, on the one hand, and, on the other hand, their allegiance to the demands of the Christian faith that all people are equal before God. In the words of Banana (1985: 15):

> Through its development and history, Christianity has tended to be domesticated by the western cultures, and presented in the western mould – and anything familiar to the west has been termed pagan and unchristian. Christianity in Africa has not been permitted to discover its own roots; we have not been given the faith in its original purity.

The perpetuation of the myth of racial superiority in Rhodesia (now Zimbabwe) found expression in social conditions and human behaviour as well as in laws and social structures. Whites in Rhodesia typically acted to protect their "privileged" positions. Though some individual missionaries engaged in the efforts to ameliorate the vagaries of imperialism, the general attitude was to hear and see no evil. Overall, the churches acquiesced with the colonial status quo.

Ideological models employed by missionaries, explorers and colonialists

It should be noted from the onset that several conceptual models have been used to describe the interaction between Europeans and Africans. According to Jennings (1983: 59), these models range from innate inferiority, Euroconformity, and melting pot, to cultural pluralism. Missionaries did not want to be committed to disciplined reflection on matters pertaining to the cross-cultural communication of the Christian faith. Instead they were interested in preaching an idealised version of their own cultural and epistemological values. Their evangelism denoted the "pious" and "virtuous" supremacist life of the Westerners who ironically were dispossessing, robbing and exploiting Africans. The idea was Africans would dissolve into the White community of Christians. Not quite. It was difficult for Africans to be assimilated socially. Those who converted to Christianity found themselves culturally hanging. They appeared confused, weak, ungenerous and denying the social obligations of African membership which is communitarian while accepting European individualism and selfishness. Followers of the new faith largely became apostates and laughingstock for being trapped on the margins of society – rejected socially by both Whites and fellow Africans engrossed in tradition. To the White community, they remained Blacks and, thus, socially inferior. Whites denied converted Africans the joy of oneness in faith. These conceptual models may be briefly summarised as follows.

The innate inferiority model

Missionaries, explorers and colonialists thought of Blacks as racially inferior beings to be subjected to plunder and dispossession. Newman (2012: 405) defines racism as the belief in the superiority of one race over another. It may also include discrimination, dispossession, exploitation, prejudice, or antagonism directed against someone because they are of a different race or ethnicity, or the belief that members of different races or ethnicities should be treated differently. Thus, racism can be broadly defined to encompass individual and group prejudices and acts of dispossession and discrimination that result in material and cultural advantages conferred on a majority or a dominant social group (Feagin, 2000: 2). The concept of race did not originate with science. On the contrary, science emerged in the late 18th century and helped validate existing racial ideas and "prove" a natural hierarchy of groups. Throughout our history, the search for racial differences has been fuelled by preconceived notions of inferiority and superiority. Even today, scientists are influenced by their social context. Ideas and definitions of race have changed over time, depending on social and political climate. Historically, racial categories were not neutral or objective. Groups were differentiated so they could be excluded or disadvantaged, often in explicit ways. Sociologists and behavioural scientists, in general, recognise "race" as a social construct. This means that, although the concepts of race and racism are based on observable biological characteristics, any conclusions drawn about race since those observations are heavily influenced by cultural ideologies. Racism, as an ideology, exists in a society at both the individual and institutional level. In colonialists' views, Blacks could be dispossessed, employed and exploited like domestic animals. Many of them doubted whether Africans possessed a soul that could experience salvation. For this reason, Blacks were subjected to dispossession, exploitation, segregation and racial abuse.

The Euroconformity Model

There were some missionaries who were opposed to the Innate Inferiority Model discussed above. They argued that Africans were human beings made in the image of God and endowed with an immortal soul. It was therefore the divine duty of missionaries to bring to Africans the gospel message and to instruct them in Christian ways. In fact, this was a pointer to the contextualisation of the Christian message in non-Western cultures. In this model, missionaries regarded Africans as inferior by their racial constitution but equal by their religious constitution. Whites forgot that Christianity was of Middle East origin and they had only enriched it by adding their own cultural ethos. In this model the missionaries assumed the role of teachers educating Africans. Thus, the Euroconformists embarked on missionising and educating Africans. In the case of Zimbabwe, missionaries established mission schools such as Gokomere and St Anthony (both Roman Catholic), St Augustine (Anglican), Sandringham and Waddilove (both Methodist Church in Zimbabwe), Mt Selinda (United Church of Christ in Zimbabwe), Morgenster (Reformed Church) and Hartzell (United Methodist Church). Blacks were not to be transferred into replicas of

180

Europeans but into Christian versions of African types distinct from standard European Christians. Africans were mandated to absorb many of the cultural traits brought by the missionaries. It was thought the African culture would gradually disappear as its various traits were replaced by the corresponding European traits. Even in churches, Africans adapted to a lower-class style of life.

The Melting Pot Model

This ideological thrust points to the dominant ingredient in Zimbabwe's melting pot, it translates into a practical argument concerning governmental policies towards the dispossessed, exploited and "conquered" Africans; the same practicality bears upon the mission enterprise. The logic here was that if the heritage of Zimbabweans was to belong to Europeans, then "civilisation" programs for Africans must be oriented towards euroconformism or assimilationism. Jennings (1983: 63) describes the melting pot as a monocultural metaphor for a heterogeneous society becoming more homogeneous, the different elements "melting together" with a common culture or vice versa, for a homogeneous society becoming more heterogeneous through the influx of foreign elements with different cultural backgrounds, possessing the potential to create disharmony within the previous culture.

The Cultural Pluralism Model

According to William and Madelon (1973: 13), cultural pluralism is a term used when smaller groups within a larger society maintain their unique cultural identities, and their values and practices are accepted by the wider dominant culture provided they are consistent with the laws and values of the wider society. It occurs when smaller groups within a larger society maintain their unique cultural identities, and their values and practices are accepted by the wider dominant culture provided they are consistent with the laws and values of the wider society. The concept of cultural pluralism first emerged in 1910 among intellectuals debating in the United States over how to approach issues of immigration and national identity (William and Madelon, 1973: 13). Cultural pluralism is an understanding and appreciation of the cultural differences that people have. It focuses on society, and the uniqueness of each part that makes up the diverse population. Cultural pluralism thrives in an integrated and not a segregated society. As a sociological term, the definition and description of cultural pluralism has evolved over time. It has been described as not only a fact but a societal goal. It was largely with the rise of the viewpoint of "cultural relativism" in anthropology and of cultural pluralism as a framework for dealing with human beings that the cultural uniqueness of Africans came to be recognised and respected. Missiologists adopted concepts of indigenisation and contextualisation. The idea here is that Africans continue to function provided they acknowledged the sovereignty of the European power. Africans would live in their own fashion. Some missionaries and anthropologists argued that distinctive African values that have remained intact must be accommodated. In a pluralist culture, groups not only co-exist side by side, but also consider qualities of other groups as traits worth having in the dominant culture.

A brief history of Christianity in Zimbabwe

The history of Christianity in Zimbabwe must be seen within the context of colonialism in Zimbabwe as a whole. According to Bevans (2010):

> The modern missionary era was in many ways the 'religious arm' of colonialism, whether Portuguese and Spanish colonialism in the sixteenth Century, or British, French, German, Belgian or American colonialism in the nineteenth. This was not all bad — oftentimes missionaries were heroic defenders of the rights of indigenous peoples.

This partnership between missionaries and colonialists continued right through into the twentieth century. The first missionaries had come into the country with the armed colonialists who dispossessed Africans of their land, minerals, epistemologies and livestock. Missionaries and colonialists are often closely associated because Christianity was the religion of the European colonial powers and acted in many ways as Siamese twin. Andrews (2010: 663) is of the view that Christian missionaries were initially portrayed as "visible saints, exemplars of ideal piety in a sea of persistent savagery". By the time the colonial era ended in the last half of the twentieth century, missionaries became viewed as colonialism's "agent, scribe and moral alibi" (Comaroff and Comaroff, 2010: 32).

Roman Catholic missionaries were the first to arrive in southern Africa, and even to penetrate inland into present day Zimbabwe. The first attempt to introduce Christianity to Mashonaland was made by a Portuguese Jesuit missionary, Fr. Gonzalo da Silviera, at the court of the Monomotapa dynasty until he was murdered as a result of court intrigues in 1561 (Shaw, 1996: 129). Although many Roman Catholic churches were planted, they had all disappeared by the time Protestant missions arrived in the nineteenth century. Protestant missions to southern Africa effectively began with the Moravians in 1792. Right after them came a Dutchman, Johannes Van der Kemp, in 1799, who soon represented the newly formed London Missionary Society (LMS) in this newly claimed British colony.

The pioneers of Christian missions in Zimbabwe were members of the LMS who pioneered the missionary enterprise in Matabeleland. The LMS missionary who helped launch Protestant missions into Zimbabwe was Robert Moffat. He set out for Africa at the age of 21 and served primarily at the mission station of Kuruman for fifty years, as missionary to the Tswana peoples (Latourette, 1970: 345). His major work was the translation of the Bible into Tswana, but he was also famous for his son-in-law David Livingstone, whom he helped recruit to come to Kuruman in 1840 (Moffat, 1886:156). Moffat's greatest accomplishment for missions in Zimbabwe was his remarkable friendship with Mzilikazi, King of the Ndebele people, which created an enabling environment for the planting of missions in Zimbabwe. Moffat's friendship with Mzilikazi resulted in the founding of the LMS's first mission station at Inyati in 1859 and a second mission station at Hope Fountain in 1870.

Mzilikazi had fled from Chaka, the Zulu leader, with his people and crossed from coastal Zululand into Transvaal on the central plateau. In 1835 Moffat spent two months with Mzilikazi. Soon after this visit, however, Mzilikazi fled from the Transvaal due to skirmishes with Dutch Boers and retreated into south-western Zimbabwe. Moffat again visited him there for three months in 1853 and asked Mzilikazi's assistance in locating his explorer son-in-law, Livingstone, who had disappeared into the depths of Africa beyond the Zambezi River (Moffat, 1886: 205).

Moffat himself also accompanied the missionary expedition to the Ndebele in July 1859. He was aware that Mzilikazi was wary of outsiders and would only accept missionaries if Moffat brought them. Mzilikazi and his people shared a deep conviction that the opening of the country to White men to come and settle would be the beginning of the end for Mzilikazi's Kingdom. They were "not far wrong there" (Moffat, 1886: 218). While the Ndebele King welcomed Moffat personally, he was reluctant to allocate a place for a permanent mission for the missionary families. According to Zvobgo (1991: 7), in his chapter "An Overview of the Methodist Church," after several attempts at establishing missions, in late December 1859, Mzilikazi finally decided that the missionaries could build a mission station at Inyati, but since he no longer tolerated new openings to the outside world, he flatly refused any attempt to communicate with the Makololo missionary group.

Christian missions stalled

In 1870, Lobengula succeeded his father, Mzilikazi, as King of the Ndebele. It should be noted that by 1884 the mission had as yet been without visible success. Bhebe (1979: 28) cited several reasons for this complete lack of conversions: the King was an absolute monarchy, and his military Kingdom was squarely based on traditional religion; the Ndebele saw no need for learning to read or for other Western ideas; they saw no moral superiority of monogamy over polygamy and could not see why missionaries denounced their customs; Christianity did not seem to offer practical answers to the daily problems of Ndebele people, but answers were provided by their traditional religion; a high God of love did not square with the droughts and disasters they were experiencing (Bhebe 1979: 28). Lobengula prevented the spread of Christianity to the Shona people, as Western missionaries increasingly clamoured to gain permission to enter his territory. For example, Francois Collard, of the Paris Missionary Society, was sent - by a nascent indigenous church which the society had planted in Lesotho - to establish a new mission among the Shona people of south-eastern Zimbabwe.

As European imperialists like Cecil John Rhodes began to increasingly covet Lobengula's realm, the LMS missionaries stationed there "had by the 1880's come to the conclusion that the Ndebele political system must be overthrown to pave the way for Christianity" (Bhebe, 1979: 82).

Lobengula used a LMS missionary, C. D. Helm, as an interpreter and adviser in the negotiations with Rhodes' men, and Mark Shaw claimed that Helm deliberately misinterpreted portions of the Rudd concession that gave Rhodes the right to enter Shona areas to search for gold (Shaw 1996: 264). Rhodes had a vested interest in the continued expansion of White settlements in the region, so now with the cover of a legal mandate; he used the Gomara and Bere incidents, when the Ndebele attacked the Shona near Fort Victoria (now Masvingo) in 1893 as a pretext for attacking the Kingdom of Lobengula. Lobengula first tried to rescind the agreement. This culminated in the outbreak of the Anglo-Ndebele war in 1893-4. Shaw (1996: 264) stated that the first decisive battle was fought on November 1, 1893 when a laager was attacked on open ground near the Bembesi River by Imbezu and Ingubu regiments. The Ndebele were "defeated", and this compelled Lobengula to flee northwards. Lobengula died in January 1894, and within a few months the British South Africa Company controlled Matabeleland and White colonialists continued to arrive.

The establishment of mission stations in Zimbabwe

With the end of Lobengula's tenure, missionaries now saw an unprecedented opportunity for winning the Ndebele and Shona peoples of Zimbabwe to Christ. As the surviving leaders of the uprising were taken to the gallows, Jesuit priests persuaded many to accept baptism. Zvobgo (1991: 51), in his book *A History of Christian Missions in Zimbabwe*, pointed out that in Mashonaland, a female spirit medium named Nyakasikana of the Nehanda cult, however, remained defiant, refusing the Christian God. Significantly, after independence and majority rule in Zimbabwe in 1980, Nyakasikana

185

of the Nehanda cult became something of a cult figure. In fact, Black nationalist freedom fighters teamed up with a spirit medium, claiming to be possessed by Nehanda's spirit, in the guerrilla war that led up to independence (Lan, 1985: 7). To this day, she remains something of a patron saint of African traditional religion.

After the signing of the Rudd Concession (1888) between King Lobengula of the Ndebele state and Cecil Rhodes, a group of armed settlers, known as the Pioneer Column, began to invade Zimbabwe in 1890. Zvobgo (1991: 7) pointed out that the arrival of the Pioneer Column in Mashonaland and the subsequent raising of the British flag (the Union Jack) at Fort Salisbury (now Harare) on 12 September 1890 marked the end of indigenous African independence. For ninety years the indigenous people experienced the brutal and violent history of colonialism. In 1891 an Order-in-Council declared Matabeleland and Mashonaland British protectorates. Rhodes was an atheist, but he understood the uses of organised religion, and by numerous land grants and other incentives he tied the missionaries of many churches and societies to his Cape-to Cairo vision.

In the 1890s missionaries flooded Zimbabwe and lined up to ask Rhodes for huge tracts of stolen land on which to build mission stations. They expected a major turning to Christ. For example, the Roman Catholics returned in the wake of the occupation of Mashonaland by the British South African Company forces in 1890. In fact, Father Hartmann became chaplain to the "Pioneer Column" advancing on Mashonaland. In 1892 the Jesuits established a mission station at Chishawasha near Harare. In 1898 five missionaries from the Pennsylvania-based Brethren in Christ Church (BICC) obtained 3,000 acres in the Matopo Hills for their Matopo Mission, because Rhodes said, "Missionaries are better than policemen and cheaper" (Ndlovu, 1997: 74). Wesleyan Methodists had opened four stations by 1914. The American Methodist Episcopal Church, now United Methodist Church, under Bishop Hartwell's leadership, founded its first mission station at Old Mutare in 1898. The United Methodist Church received 13,000 acres at Old Mutare "free and clear" for their "great central mission" in 1898 (Goto, 1994: 16). The Berlin Missionary Society entered Zimbabwe in 1892 and built mission stations at Gutu, Zimuto, and Chivi, which were all taken over by the

South African Dutch Reformed Church in 1907 when the Berlin Society experienced financial difficulties (Daneel, 1971: 187). The pioneer of Dutch Reformed missions in Zimbabwe was Andrew A. Louw, who founded Morgenster Mission in 1894 next to the Great Zimbabwe Ruins.

Zvobgo (1991: 7) pointed out that in 1893 missionaries of the American Board of Commissioners for Foreign Missions (ABCFM), later named United Church of Christ in Zimbabwe, established their first mission station at Mount Selinda and the second at Chikore in 1895. In 1894 Cecil Rhodes "granted missionaries of the Seventh Day Adventist Church a farm of 12,000 acres at Solusi" (Zvobgo, 1991: 1). Bishop Knight-Bruce founded St. Augustine's Anglican mission near Penhalonga in 1891. The Salvation Army entered Zimbabwe in 1891 and received a farm of 3,000 acres in the Mazowe River valley. After 1898, several other missionary groups entered Zimbabwe.

Cultural captivity of the church

The military invasion was paralleled by a spiritual confrontation between Christianity and African traditional religion. Christianity's attitude to African indigenous religion was confrontational. The colonial church was taken captive to the prevailing colonial supremacist and criminocratic culture thereby leaving Christ out of the church. Christ was neither a criminal nor a racist. It is without doubt or question that it was a Christ-less Christianity premised as it was on colonial robbery, exploitation and criminality more broadly. This was a flaw that corroded and distorted Christianity. The centrality of Christ to vibrant Christian life and witness is critical. The church pandered to colonial racist and criminogenic ideas thereby corrupting confidence in biblical faith. Colonial Christianity had a deleterious effect on African culture and religion that created a spiritual vacuum. The church failed to engage and come into theological dialogue with African culture. There was no attempt to relate African thought to Christian faith. Banana (1991: 1) decried the lack of virtues of African life and culture:

It is pity that some of the virtues of African life and culture, moulded and developed before the coming of missionaries, were ignored, treated with contempt and sometimes totally dismissed and brushed aside as repugnant and savage by some zealous missionaries who were captives of their religious and cultural prejudice.

Since culture cannot be separated from religion in Africa, efforts by the missionaries to disparage African culture went a long way about damaging Africans. Upholding cultural values is a necessity for indigenous people's lives. The spread of Christianity was a serious threat to most indigenous cultures such as Ndebele, Zezuru, Karanga, Ndau, Venda, Varemba, Nambya, Korekore, Manyika and Tonga cultures. These ethnic groups were taught that many of their indigenous practices, epistemologies and values were evil. Westerners attacked African belief systems like death rituals, burial systems, marriage rituals and initiation ceremonies, and cultural practices such as music, dances and dressing. African culture provides identity, for Africans, without which there will be an identity crisis. If the Christian church in Africa is truly the church of Africa in Africa it must use African culture and epistemology as one of its important sources. The religio-cultural deposit of Africa can enrich Christianity. Early missionaries made no attempt to relate the Gospel to the African's life and thought.

Christianity came to Africa with Euro-American cultural elements which missionaries highly regarded. These elements were foisted on Africans as Gospel truth. Missionaries had misconceptions that Africans had no idea of God (*Mwari*). Pre-colonial Africans had notions of the Heavens (*denga*) and even about *mhondoro dzedenga* (spirit from heaven) – like European Heavenly saints (Mwandayi, 2016: 27). Missionaries prided themselves in the omnipotence of 'their' God. This is the kind of power described in the doctrine of *creation ex nihilo* (creation out of nothing) whereby divine power is not limited by or to any actuality. The missionaries did not realise that they also believed in a God who created the universe *ex nihilo* as well. For example, the Shona believe in a sacred being, *Mwari* (God), who created the cosmos out of nothing. They believe the universe or cosmos is the product of creation. It was created by the power of the

Supreme Being they call *Mwari*. The God of Christianity is the same God of African traditional religion. There is only one supreme God. Michael Gelfand acknowledged the fact that the Shona people of Zimbabwe can believe in their *Vadzimu* (ancestral spirits) and in their *mhondoro* (African saints) and in Christianity (Gelfand, 1981: 45). Gelfand's argument is that both Christianity and African Traditional Religions are mythical; therefore, the problem is not in the African converts but in the missionary agents who view the practice as syncretism.

Linked to evangelisation was the attempt by missionaries to make Christianity as an arbiter of morality and religious values (Gelfand, 1992: 180-182). Thus, African Traditional Religions were driven underground, and a new centre of authority was created by Western power structures (Monsma, 1979: 88-89; Mucherera, 2001: 5). The evangelisation of Zimbabwe did not happen on neutral, value-free and ideological innocence. The coming of Christianity happened simultaneously with colonisation, hence there is a thin line between the missionary intent and the intent of the colonisers (Muzorewa, 1985:24). The unsettling of traditional African institutions by the colonial regime created a collision course of ideologies and worldviews. Thus, legislation by the White colonial regime did not favour the Zimbabwean cultural values and epistemologies (Banana, 1989: 2).

There has been a growing misconception among many early missionaries to Africa that Christianity was going to obliterate other religions (Muzorewa, 1985: 25-26; Mwakabana, 1996: 17). The growing desecration of Africa in the past by the Western-European powers adversely affected the way Africans perceived Christianity. This gave rise to African nationalism.

Language distortions

Despite several decades of cultural and political oppression, however, the Black people have retained a spirit of independence and assertiveness. This is due in no small measure to the fact that the missionaries were disinclined to view the people they preached to, dispossessed and brutalised as real human beings. Their language and way of life were considered signs of inferiority. This was best demonstrated by the colonial language of the oppressor and dispossessor created to oppress and humiliate Africans. Language barrier made communication difficult. To enable communication Whites introduced a 'language' called *Chilapalapa* or *Fanakalo*. This language was imported from South Africa. It was the sort of language they developed in order to communicate with the local people. In fact, it was a language only meant to give orders to Africans. In line with this Frederiske (1982: 20) cited Aaron Hodza as saying:

> You cannot even tell a story successfully in *Chilapalapa* because it hasn't got much of a vocabulary. Most of the words are imperatives, given to an inferior, a servant. *Enza so* or *hamba so*, that's an order, an imperative. This is why we don't like it. If a white man speaks to me in that language, I will scold him.

There is no doubt *Chilapalapa* was the crudest colonial effort to overcome the language barrier. The language denigrated the significance of local languages such as Shona and Ndebele. It was an era of crazy racist jargon. The language was originally spoken in the mining sector in South Africa where many miners flocked from southern African countries for work. It became the *lingua franca* enabling different ethnic groups in the same country to communicate with each other. Thus, it was born out of necessity for a common language among ethnically diverse multitudes of economic migrants flocking to the gold and diamond mines seeking employment. *Chilapalapa* was a simplified language based primarily on Zulu, with English a small Afrikaans input. Unfortunately, for workers in Rhodesia, where a minority of Blacks speak a language with a Zulu root, this bastard tongue was not always successful in communicating the demands of the White boss or madam. It negatively added confusion and reinforced White stereotypes of Africans as "primitive" and "ignorant". *Chilapalapa* is a rare example of a pidgin based on an indigenous language rather than on the language of a colonising or trading power.

A valuable contribution of Christian missionaries in Zimbabwe was the development of literature in the local vernaculars; this included the translation of the Bible into some of the local languages. Missionaries and explorers learnt African languages by living in the villages where the languages were spoken. They lived the languages. These were mutually transformative encounters between European missionaries and African speakers of languages. Writing on the importance of learning African languages, Manyoba (1991: 59) has this to say:

> Unlike some catholic pioneer missionaries most Wesleyan missionaries did not learn the African languages until very late, even then only a few did. At first no language schools were set up by the churches. Later the catholic and American Methodist church (now known as the United Methodist Church) established language to prepare the newly arrived missionaries for the work. The language difficulty has remained a problem in the work of the Methodist church.

Many missionaries who encountered the natives of Africa found communication extremely difficult, so they had to use an interpreter. When converted Africans sent their children to missionary schools their African names were changed to Christian names. This was done partly because some of the missionary teachers who were often European did not want to learn the local language or how to pronounce the names. Often the missionaries taught that the African names were pagan. Missionaries who belonged to the cultural pluralism model have been sensitive to the cultural *milieu* in opposition to the *tabula rasa* ideologies that have been peddled by some missionaries in Africa. They hoped for a complete annihilation of other religions and cultures and in place establish a perceived God's kingdom ushered in by the preaching of the gospel of Jesus Christ.

Colonial freemasons and missionaries

Morris (2006), a Masonic historian and editor of the Scottish Rite Journal, describes freemasonry as not a Christian institution, though it has often been mistaken for such. Freemasonry contains many of the elements of religion; its teachings enjoin morality, charity, and obedience to the law of the land. There is no international administrative or controlling authority over freemasonry. Freemasonry is not a religion, nor is it a substitute for religion. It requires of its members a belief in God as part of the obligation of every responsible adult but advocates no sectarian faith or practice. Many freemasons appear to promote belief in God but there is not much known about their ideas about God. Masonic ceremonies include prayers, both traditional and *extempore*, to reaffirm everyone's dependence on God and to seek divine guidance. Freemasonry is open to men of any faith, but religion may not be discussed at Masonic meetings. An open volume of the Sacred Law, "the rule and guide of life," is an essential part of every Masonic meeting (Morris, 2006: 7). The Volume of the Sacred Law in the Judeo/Christian tradition is the Bible; to freemasons of other faiths, it is the book held holy by them. The obligations taken by freemasons are sworn on the Volume of the Sacred Law. They are undertakings to follow the principles of freemasonry and to keep confidential a freemason's means of recognition. There is no headquarters anyone can call to get the official, worldwide policy position on freemasons, because there is no such policy. Rich (1991: 14) states that freemasonry is the world's largest secret society, with a current membership of 6 million, but its leadership is divided amongst numerous autonomous organisations that cannot even agree as to its origins. The first Masonic lodge in Rhodesia was English and established in 1893 in Bulawayo. It was named Founders as the first of its kind in the country. The first Scottish lodge was also started in Bulawayo in 1897; the first Irish lodge was not launched until 1921. Just as Christian missionaries brought all kinds of religion to Zimbabwe, ranging from Seventh Day Adventism to Anglicanism, European and American freemasons introduced the division and schisms of their furtive brotherhood. That remains the case in Zimbabwe today. Zimbabwe had its own Grand Lodges of freemasons such as the Gatooma Lodge which changed its name to Kadoma Lodge at independence in 1980. A Masonic Grand Lodge or Grand Orient is the governing body that supervises and governs the individual lodges of freemasons in any geographical area. There are many freemasonic lodges

192

scattered throughout Zimbabwe. Freemasons helped towards the promotion of segregated settlements in Rhodesia.

Like Christianity, freemasonry was closely identified with the extension of colonialism and imperialism. It was arguably as much influenced by its contact with 'native' cultures as it was an influence upon them. It must be noted that because of the extreme secrecy which shrouded its activities, the subject is understudied. During the nineteenth and early twentieth centuries the various Masonic grand lodges of Europe established many subordinate lodges overseas. Freemasonry was free for Whites in racist Rhodesia. British lodges in the nineteenth century did not initiate Blacks. There was competition for membership and territorial influence among European freemasons patterned along the Scramble for Africa in the nineteenth century.

Freemasonry has, almost from its inception, encountered considerable opposition from organised religion, especially from Roman Catholic Church. It is the interpretation of a Masonic God that has led to debates about and condemnation of freemasonry by several religious groups. Masons believe that there is one God and that people employ many ways to seek, and to express what they know of God. Masonry primarily uses the appellation, "Grand Architect of the Universe," and other non-sectarian titles, to address the Deity (Rich, 1991: 3). Freemasonry lacks the basic elements of religion: (a) It has no dogma or theology, no wish or means to enforce religious orthodoxy. (b) It offers no sacraments. (c) It does not claim to lead to salvation by works, by secret knowledge, or by any other means. The secrets of freemasonry are concerned with modes of recognition, not with the means of salvation. In this way, persons of different faiths may join in prayer, concentrating on God, rather than differences among themselves. Masonry believes in religious freedom and that the relationship between the individual and God is personal, private, and sacred.

The Catholic Church prohibited Catholics from membership in Masonic organisations and other secret societies in 1738 (Hallissy, 2006). Masonic organisations were censured with automatic excommunication. Catholics viewed Masonic principles and rituals as irreconcilable with Catholic doctrines. Nevertheless, freemasons established schools such as Founders in Bulawayo, clubs such as the Italian Club in Strathaven suburb of Harare, temples such as the Grand Temple in Bishop Gaul Avenue in Harare and other notable lodges and clubs throughout the country. Freemasons were, however, not as impactful as missionaries in the education and health sectors. Critics of the freemasons say the organisation is secretive and serves the interests of its members over the interests of the public. The Masons deny this saying they uphold values in keeping with public service and high morals.

The rise of African nationalism in Zimbabwe

During the 1950's and 1960's, Africans gradually became more militant in their approach against colonialism. They recognised the need to cultivate African pride, assertiveness and self-reliance. The bones of contention were colonial dispossession, looting, robbery and plunder: Africans were the victims of racial oppression; accordingly, Africans united to wage their struggle against this dispossession and oppression. The rise of African nationalism in Zimbabwe can be traced largely from its association with the clergy. There was prophetic dissent against racism and against dispossession. There was a burst of prophetic dissent from clergymen such as John White of the Methodist Church and Shearly Cripps of the Anglican Church. Both clergymen challenged colonial authority in a way that no authoritative ecclesiastical voice had done in colonial Rhodesia. Dickson Mungazi notes with keen interest the life of Ralph Dogde a Methodist missionary from 1956 to 1968 who was instrumental in the social change in the then Rhodesia during the colonial rule of Ian Douglas Smith (Mungazi, 1991: ix). Dodge could not tolerate the social injustice in Rhodesia hence he criticised the existing social system which led to his deportation. Following Dodge's influence was Bishop Abel Muzorewa a well-known United Methodist clergyman who went into active politics that was instrumental to the liberation of Zimbabwe. We could mention quite a number of these African clergy who became active in politics. The Revd. Ndabaningi Sithole of the United Church of Christ is another example of the clergy who got into active politics. The essence of the matter is that any serious clergy/pastor or man of the cloth that claims to minister to people and fails to deal with the plight of the dispossessed, exploited, oppressed, disenfranchised and the voiceless masses has chosen a wrong vocation. Many clergymen found it hard not to turn prophetic in the criminocratic and racist Rhodesia.

Conclusion

There are many takeaways from this chapter. The spread of Christianity was a threat to African culture and epistemologies and explains why some Africans are no longer practising their indigenous customs, epistemologies and practices. The missionaries saw themselves as people created in a very superior and special way. The early missionaries were inclined to think that African practices, epistemologies and customs were unchristian. When missionaries introduced Christianity into Zimbabwe it brought with it an alien culture, which inevitably affected the psychological, sociological, cultural, epistemological and religious aspects of the natives. There is clear evidence that the missionaries viewed Africans as strange people whom the Europeans would easily consider subhuman, or at most would regard as worse than themselves. The Westerners that came to Africa saw the extraordinary everywhere. Their psyche misled them into seeing the opposite of the reality. Many early missionaries held that indigenous African religions and epistemologies were totally without merit. Colonialists, including missionaries commonly held that indigenous Africans were devoid of any culture and epistemologies. Such a prejudice on its own is uncalled for because Africans had a strong culture to reckon with as a people. Moreover, in the context of prejudices about Africans, we should bear in mind that the concept of Black inferiority reached its high point when the philosophers of the enlightenment era internationalised it. The description of the African by the colonialists and missionaries paints a gloomy picture of what an African was in the socio-cultural and religious outlook. The initial perception of Africans by colonialists and missionaries alike negates the possibility of tolerance towards their religion, epistemologies and culture. It is very important for Africans to guard their culture and epistemologies jealously as failure to do so creates an identity crisis since culture is the basis of African identity.

References

Andrews, E. (2010). Christian missions and colonial empires reconsidered: A black evangelist in West Africa, 1766–1816. *Journal of Church & State*. Vol 51 (4): 663–691.

Banana, C.S. (1996). *Politics of repression and resistance: Face to face with combat theology*. Gweru: Mambo Press.

Banana, C. S. (1991). *A century of Methodism in Zimbabwe 1891-1991*. Harare: The Methodist Church in Zimbabwe.

Banana, C.S. (1989). *Turmoil and tenacity, Zimbabwe 1980-1990*. Harare: The College Press (Pvt) Ltd.

Banana, C.S. (1985). The gospel of Christ and revolutionary transformation, in Verstraelen, F. J. (ed), *Christian Mission and Human Transformation*, Gweru: Mambo Press, pp.10-20.

Bevans, S. (n.d) Christian complicity in colonialism/ globalism (PDF). Retrieved 2010-11-17.

Bhebe, N. (1979). *Christianity and traditional religion in Western Zimbabwe. 1859-1923,* London: Longman Group Ltd.

Comaroff, J. & Comaroff, J. (2010). Africa observed: Discourses of the imperial imagination, in Grinker, R. R.; Lubkemann, S. C.; Steiner, C. B. (eds.) *Perspectives on Africa: A Reader in Culture, History and Representation* (2nd ed.). Oxford: Blackwell Publishing. pp.29-43.

Daneel, M. L. (1971). *Old and new in Southern Shona Independent Churches, background and rise of the major movements*. The Hague: Mouton.

Feagin, J. R. (2000). Racist America: Roots, current realities, and future reparations. Houston: Routledge.

Frederiske, J. (1982). *None but ourselves: Masses vs. media in the making of Zimbabwe*. Harare: Anvil Press.

Gelfand, M. (1981). *UKAMA-reflections on Shona and Western cultures in Zimbabwe*. Gweru: Mambo Press.

Gelfand, M. (1992). *The genuine Shona, survival values of an African culture*. Gweru: Mambo Press.

Goto, N. (1994) A Great Central Mission: The legacy of the United Methodist Church in Zimbabwe. *Methodist History*, Vol 33, (1).

Hallissy, M. (2006). *Reading Irish-American Fiction: The Hyphenated Self.* Springer.

Jennings, G.J. (1983). A Model for Christian Missions to the American Indians, in *Missiology*, Vol. XI (1).

Lan, D. (1985). *Guns & rain: Guerrillas and spirit mediums in Zimbabwe.* Harare: Zimbabwe Publishing House.

Latourette, K.S. (1970). A history of the expansion of Christianity, in Latourette, K.S. (ed) *The Great Century in the Americas, Australasia, and Africa, A.D. 1800-A.D. 1914.* Grand Rapids: Zondervan.

Manyoba, C. B. (1991). Methodist Church and its response to culture, in Banana, C.S. (ed), *A Century of Methodism in Zimbabwe 1891-1991,* Harare: The Methodist Church in Zimbabwe, pp.58-78.

Moffat, J. S. (1886). *The lives of Robert and Mary Moffat.* London: T. Fischer Unwin.

Monsma, T. (1979). *Urban strategy for Africa.* Pasadena: William Carey Library.

Morris, S. B. (2006). *The complete idiot's guide to freemasonry.* New York: Alpha Books

Mucherera, T. N. (2001). *Pastoral care from a Third World Perspective.* New York: Peter Lang Publishing.

Mungazi, D. (1991). *The honoured crusade.* Gweru: Mambo Press.

Mungazi, D. (1997). *The Mind of Black Africa.* London: Praeger.

Muzorewa, G. (1985). *The origins and developments of African theology.* New York: Orbis Books.

Mwakabana, H.A.O. (1996). *Theological perspectives on other faiths-Toward a Christian Theology of religions.* Geneva: Lutheran World Federation.

Mwandayi, C. (2016). *Death and after-life rituals in the eyes of the Shona: Dialogue with Shona Heavenly saints.* Bamberg: University of Bamberg Press.

Ndlovu, S. (1997). Historical brethren in Christ Missionary attitudes in Zimbabwe, in *The Conrad Grebel Review* 15, No. 12, pp.61-78.

Newman, D. M. (2012). *Sociology: Exploring the architecture of everyday life (9th ed.).* Los Angeles: SAGE.

Rich, P. (1991). *Freemasonry in colonial Africa: Competing allegiances of the Grand Orient of France and the Grand Lodge of England.* Sydney: The University of Western Australia.

Shaw, M. R. (1996). *The Kingdom of God in Africa: A short history of African Christianity.* Grand Rapids: Baker.

Van der Merwe, W. J. (1982). *The witness of the Church.* Cape Province: Lovedale Press.

William, R. H. & Madelon, S. (1973). Cultural pluralism and schooling: Some preliminary observations, in Madelon, S., William, H. R. and Harry, N. R. (eds). *Cultural Pluralism in Education: A Mandate for Change.* New York: Appleton-Century-Crofts, pp.1-19. Zvobgo, C. J. (1991). An overview of the Methodist Church, in Banana C. S. (ed), *A Century of Methodist in Zimbabwe 1891-1991.* Gweru: Mambo Press.

Chapter Seven

Algebra in African Indigenous History

Babarinsa Olayiwola

Introduction

The Etymology of algebra is from Arabic word *"al-jabr"* - restoration or the gathering of broken parts (Hoad, 1986). Literally, the term algebra referred to the surgical procedure of setting broken or dislocated bones (Katz, 1997). Although the word algebra was coined around 825 A.D, the concept as we have it now was different around 35,000 B.C. when it originated from Africa (Zaslavsky, 1994). Algebra can be traced back to ancient African countries such as Egypt, Eswatini (Swaziland), Democratic Republic of Congo (Zaire), Nigeria and Mali where applications of algebra involved astronomy, taxation, game, commerce and time recording. Algebra in ancient Africa was more of symbols, numbers and patterns using bones, stones, and papyrus – an ancient thick paper materials for writing (Zaslavsky, 1999). Thus, algebra has three stages of historical development: the rhetorical stage, the syncopated stage, and the symbolic stage (Katz & Barton, 2007). This chapter focuses on the origin of algebra in Africa. This chapter concludes that algebra originated from Africa and its people.

Algebra: The general history

Algebra is a broad part of mathematics where other major branches of mathematics sprung. Nowadays, algebra mainly studies the mathematical symbols and the rules for manipulating these objects. To manipulate the objects, basic arithmetic operations are required. Thus, Chinese mathematicians use the four basic algebraic operations which led Yang Hui, in the 12th century, to approximation methods with high accuracy: he worked with the help of Abacus machine (Huang, 1960). The "modern" algebra has roots from the two contributors, a Persian mathematician Mohammad ibn Musa Al-Khwarizmi and a Greek mathematician Diophantus of Alexandria. Thus, the definition of algebra in this century is different from what it was some centuries ago.

In 1748, a Scottish mathematician, Colin Maclaurin, gave the definition of algebra as a general method of computation by certain signs and symbols which have been contrived for this purpose, and found convenient with a universal arithmetic, operations and rules founded upon the same principles (Maclaurin, 1748). He gave the first published result on resultants on solving two, three and four simultaneous equations: the method is now called Cramer's rule (Tweedie, 1915). Hedman (1999) examined a manuscript that provides conclusive evidence that Maclaurin was teaching his students the rule over 20 years before Cramer published it. In fact, Boyer (1966) showed that Cramer's rule was published two years earlier. However, Kosinski (2001) argued that the rule he chose to appropriate sign for each summand was wrong, though his assertion of "opposite" coefficient was right, and this was corrected by Cramer by counting the number of transpositions in the permutation. Günther (1908) pointed out that, for lack of good notation, Maclaurin missed the general rule for solving linear equations. Then, in 1750, a Swiss mathematician called Gabriel Cramer hinted that resultants might be useful in analytical geometry (Cramer, 1750). The rule gave the method for solving n linear simultaneous equations in n unknowns. He further explained how to calculate the terms using his rule for determining the sign and for obtaining the numerator (Robinson, 1970). The Cramer's rule has many disadvantages as it fails when the determinant of the coefficient matrix is zero, it requires many calculations of determinants and also it is numerically unstable (Habgood & Arel, 2012; Higham, 2002; Vein & Dale, 1999). Regardless of its high computational cost, Cramer's rule for solving systems of linear equations is of historical and theoretical importance in algebra (Babarinsa & Kamarulhaili, 2019; Brunetti & Renato, 2014).

More so, in 1770 a Swiss mathematician, Leonhard Euler, defined algebra as the science which teaches how to determine unknown quantities by means of those that are known (Euler, 2012). However, a French mathematician, René Descartes, published *La Géométrie* and used the algebra to solve geometric problems - graphing algebraic equations, while Pierre de Fermat, a French mathematician, was interested in representing curves through algebra. But since Descartes and de Fermat showed how to represent a curve through algebra, analytic geometry gave mathematicians a mechanism for representing motion. Then an English mathematician and physicist, Isaac Newton, picked up on this and developed the calculus. In Greece, of course, mathematics was geometry but what we think of as algebraic notions were certainly present in the work of Euclid of Alexandria and Apollonius of Tyana (Heath, 1956).

Although several discoveries were made in algebra after al-Khwarizmi's work, those works were not well known for almost a millennium. Then, in the 16th century, an Italian mathematician, Gerolamo Cardano, provided a method to solve a system of linear equations which he termed *regula de modo*- mother of rules (Cardano, 1993). The rule is practically for solving 2×2 systems and larger ones were discussed by Leibniz (Eves, 1969). In the 17th century, algebra of matrices, especially on determinants, was developed by a British mathematician, Arthur Cayley. The idea of determinant appeared in Japan through Seki Takakasu (also called Kōwa) where he published his findings but without having a word which corresponded to determinant (Martzloff, 2008). On the other hand, a German mathematician, Leibniz Gottfried worked independently on determinant. Leibniz used the word *"resultant"* for certain combinatorial sums of terms of a determinant (Muir, 1906). Though Leibniz and Seki did not publish the findings, they are both aware that determinant could be expanded using any column with great insight to extend algebra (Debnath, 2013). In the 18th century, algebra dealt with determining unknowns by using signs and symbols and certain well-defined methods of manipulation of these. Within three centuries, algebra began to have branches such as algebra of vectors which was developed by American mathematician Josiah Gibbs, axiomatic thinking in algebra by English mathematician George Peacock (Macfarlane, 1916). In the 19th century, a French mathematician Augustin-Louis Cauchy computed the volume of several solid polyhedra and gave new results of his own minors and adjoints (Cauchy, 1812). He gave the context of quadratic forms in n variables, used the term "tableau" for the matrix of coefficients which led to eigenvalues and eigenvectors (Knobloch, 1994). Finally, in the 20th century, algebra touched every aspect of mathematics such as game theory, graph theory, operations research, statistics, and other aspect of natural sciences, applied sciences, engineering, medicine and agriculture.

Algebra: What they want Africans to accept

It was claimed that the earliest algebra started about 4000 years ago in Mesopotamia (Høyrup, 2016). The Mesopotamian mathematics or Babylonian mathematics were written in old-Babylonian clay tablets dating from 2,000–1,600 B.C. that contain extensive lists of specific examples (didactic problems) and shows, step by step, how to solve them (Neugebauer, Sachs, & Götze, 1945). The first true algebra text "*Kitab al-Jabr wa-l-Muqabala*" was written in Baghdad around 825 A.D. by a Persian mathematician Mohammad ibn Musa Al-Khwarizmi, who was appointed as the head of the library of the House of Wisdom in Baghdad (Mason, 1996). He described how to translate certain problems into the equations, especially inheritance problems, but the praise (father of algebra) was given to a Greek mathematician Diophantus of Alexandria in his *Arithmetica* (Al-Khwarizmi, 1831). Al-Khwarizmi's method can solve equations (linear and quadratic respectively) without negative numbers or zero while Diophantus of Alexandria associated letters to the geometric objects to solve determinate and indeterminate (Boyer & Merzbach, 2011; Meri, 2018). Thus, *Arithmetica* is syncopated algebra while *Kitab al-Jabr wa-l-Muqabala* is rhetorical algebra.

Struik (2012) notes that advanced arithmetic systems following certain algorithmic steps to solve equations (linear and quadratic) can be traced to Babylonians. But the Egyptians and Greeks used geometric approach to solve such similar equations (Heath, 1910). The well-known geometric approach can be attributed to Pythagoras of Samos, a Greek mathematician, who introduced proportion ratio and golden ratio around 490 B.C for geometrical magnitude (Boyer

& Merzbach, 2011). A Greek mathematician Euclid of Alexandria introduced natural number from the concept of arithmetic in which negative numbers and zero were not considered (Stakhov, 2009). In the 6th century, Indian mathematicians Brahmagupta and Bhaskara gave non-symbolic details for solving equations of degree one and two, and equations on more than one variable. This gave rise to decimal and numeral system with accurate and consistent sets of rules to handle negative and positive numbers respectively (Kieran, 2011). The Sumerians developed a counting system such as basic operations, multiplication, fractions and square roots. The Sumerians' system passed through the Akkadian Empire to the Babylonians around 300 B.C where the concept of zero was not properly developed (Gray & Parshall, 2011). It was Mohammad ibn Musa al-Khwarizmi who represented zero with little circle and termed it as "*sifr*" - empty. Due to suspicion, Italian government outlawed the use of zero from Arabic numbers in their commerce (Palgrave, 1866). Then, zero was later referred to cypher which does not only represent a numeric character, but also came to mean "code". Thus, the importance of zero came up when an Italian mathematician Leonardo Bonacci (also known as Fibonacci) used it for computational purpose, that led to Renaissance advances in algebra without an abacus, which was adopted by merchants to balance their transactions (Mohamed Aballagh, 1988; Gray & Parshall, 2011).

Sometimes when reference of algebra is made to Egypt, the Africanity of Egyptian mathematics is often denied (Adams, 1983). The fact that the Greeks stole Egyptian/African legacies in epistemology is noted by James (1993). For instance, Engels (2004) hypothesised how the Ancient Egyptian formula for the determination of the area of a circle could have been obtained before the Greek Mathematicians, Hippocrates of Chios and Archimedes of Syracuse's discovery.

Algebra: The African indigenous history

The history of mathematics, especially algebra, is both necessary and attractive with a valid case of Africa. This helps us not only to know the applications of the algebra in astronomy, physics and sciences but also to understand the cultural heritage (Struik, 2012). Algebra as a subject was not started in some parts of Africa but rather used as a means of carrying out daily or seasonal routine in the community. These activities were carried out as game, commerce, astronomy, taxation, and time recording. Since there was no algebra as a subject, in some parts of Africa, back in the ancient time, the south of the Sahara region used animal bones having carved notches or stones for geometric and symmetric patterns (Gerdes, 1994). Mathematics in ancient Africa, except perhaps Egypt, was more of "ethnomathematical" (D'Ambrosio, 1999).

The fibula of a baboon bone, unearthed at Ishango (Zaire), dated between 6,500 to 9,000 B.C. shows the early evidence of mathematical activity in Africa (De Heinzelin, 1962). The bone contains notches carved in three columns with tally marks (Zaslavsky, 1994). When Marshack (1991) reevaluated the Ishango bone, the dating was set to be about 8,000 to 20,000 B.C. and it was explained that the bone was used as an early lunar phase count or a tool for simple mathematical calculation such as multiplication, division and addition. For the lunar phase -astronomy, the Adam's calendar is a mysterious structure in southern Africa which was made up of stone circles dated 75,000 B.C. However, the Lebombo bone (a small piece of the fibula of a baboon) which was found in the Lebombo Mountains near Swaziland, now called Eswatini, is dated to be more than 35,000 years ago (Bogoshi, Naidoo, & Webb, 1987). The bone was marked with 29 notches (tally marks) which denote calendar sticks and the method was still being used by the indigenous people, in Namibia, in the 1970s (Townshend, 1977). This shows that ancient humans were using organised systems of mathematics to account for various quantities.

Furthermore, Gay and Cole (1967) revealed the extent to which mathematical ideas and techniques are built into the culture and language of the daily life of the Kpelle people in central Liberia. Gerdes (1990b) discussed the mathematical ideas of sand drawings (*sona*) of the Cokwe or Tsjokwe and Luchazi people in Angola, Congo and Zambia. These drawings (lusona ideographs – cingelyengelye or zinkhata) function as mnemonic devices and are best representative in our present algebra such as transformation geometry and abstract algebra (Rauff, 2010). African geometrical figures, especially from art of the Bakuba of Congo and in Benin, are appreciated in group theory such as Frieze (Crowe, 1975). The mat and basket weaving, pot making and house building are the early development of geometrical thinking in Africa (Gerdes, 1990a). The woven fabrics of Ashanti in Ghana, for example, shows geometrical drawing (Huylebrouck, 2006). In Guinea-Bissau, the Bijago used a purely decimal system. The common number system in Africa was on base two and twenty, though other base systems existed. For instance, Yoruba people in Nigeria used base twenty number system in their multiplication while South Africa used base two number system (Huylebrouck, 2006). For the Efik-Ibibio, counting words system is a mixture of both base five and base ten with the local concepts of lines and shapes. But in Tanzania, the Maasai rarely utter numbers without fingers' gesture (Zaslavsky, 1973) while Rwanda used animals such as elephant to represent large number (Kagame, 1960). Then, Fataki (1991) presents concrete examples for measurement, games and riddles adopted by Uganda and Congo (Zaire). Like Mancala game, the African board game (namely ayo, okweso, yoté, boa or igi) consists two to four rows and six to fifty holes in a row (Bell, 1979). In West Africa, the tendency to associate the numbers, such as three and four, with man and woman respectively is a profound practice usually attributed to the male domination and sexes. An analysis of Bisa society (Burkina Faso) shows how the meaning and function of this symbolism are directly related to representations of the person and his status (Fainzang, 1985).

In ancient Egypt, through the Recto of the Rhind's papyrus, there are algorithms in which rational numbers can be represented as sums of unit fractions (Sallán, 2001). The famous papyri (Rhind Mathematical Papyrus dated around 1,550 B.C and Moscow Mathematical Papyrus dated around 1,850 B.C) showed how ancient Egyptians used basic mathematical operations - multiplication, addition, subtraction and division, and how vast their knowledge was in arithmetic and geometry (Ritter, 2000; Spalinger, 1990). The largest precolonial library, library of Alexandria, was located in Egypt around

290 B.C with books on religion, science, agriculture and astronomy at its Mouseion institution of Alexandria (MacLeod, 2004). In the golden precolonial age, Sankoré University in Timbuktu of Mali was established in 989 A.D by Al-Qadi Aqib ibn Mahmud ibn Umar, and it had the largest collections and copies of books in Africa (Haidara & Taore, 2008). The Al-Azhar University at Cairo was established in 970 A.D in Egypt while the Al-Quarawiyyin University was established at Fez in Morocco in 859 A.D (Lulat, 2005). Another form of higher education in pre-colonial Africa is the 2,700 years old tradition of elite education of Ethiopia with an African script called Ge'ez (Woldegiorgis & Doevenspeck, 2013).

The beginning of African higher education is traceable back to the pyramids of Egypt, the obelisks of Ethiopia, and the Kingdom of Timbuktu (Goma & Johnson, 1997; Lulat, 2005). The book of *Kitâb al-kâmil* (Complete Treatise on the Art of Number) *written by* Abû Bakr Al-Hassâr in the 12th century shows mathematical activity in North Africa, especially Marrakech which is now called Morocco (Mohammed Aballagh & Djebbar, 1987). A Moroccan and Maghrebian scientist, Ibn al-Bannâ justifies certain definitions of the 'Science of Arithmetic' in his *Talkhîs* which contains the rule of signs and the justification of the algorithm (Mohamed Aballagh, 1988). Ibn al-Bannâ's mathematical papers allow for expression and resolution of problems of inheritances (Gerdes, 2007). In the 19th century, algebra comes as a subject taught in mathematics in Africa. In Tunisia, the teaching starts by introducing the historical context in the traditional school system at the Zitouna and the parallel development of a "modern" educational system embodied by the Military School of Bardo (1840-1864) and in 1875 by the Sadiki College (Ben Salem, 1994).

Conclusion

The history of algebra in Africa got relatively little awareness unlike other regions of the world. There are remarkable pre-colonial African achievements in mathematics. According to Ki-Zerbo (1990), it is forgotten, all too often, that Africa was the first continent to know literacy and to institute a school system. Thousands of years before the Greek letters or Arabic numerals were invented, and before the use of the Latin word "schola" school; the scribes of ancient Egypt wrote, read, administered, philosophised using papyrus (Brock-Utne, 1999). Although Mesopotamian mathematics is known from a great number of cuneiform texts, the Egyptian mathematics is known from only a small survived number of papyrus texts. Since, the Egyptian and Babylonian mathematical texts display great similarities, it is evident that algebra originated from Africa. Egypt existed long before Babylon and, anatomically, "modern" Homo sapiens and early civilisations (90,000 to 60,000 years ago) are traceable to the Great Rift valley in Africa (Ehret, 2002; Friberg, 2005).

References

Aballagh, M. (1988). " *Raf al-hijab*" *d'Ibn al-Banna: édition critique, traduction, étude philosophique et analyse mathématique.* Paris 1.

Aballagh, M., & Djebbar, A. (1987). Découverte d'un écrit mathématique d'al-Hassār (XIIe S.): Le livre I du Kāmil. *Historia Mathematica,* vol 14(2): 147-158.

Adams, H. H. (1983). African observers of the universe: The Sirius question. *Blacks in science: Ancient and modern:* 27-46.

Al-Khwarizmi, M. (1831). *The Algebra of Mohammed Ben Musa* (F. Rosen, Trans.). London: Oriental Translation Fund.

Babarinsa, O., & Kamarulhaili, H. (2019). Modified Cramer's Rule and its Application to Solve Linear Systems in WZ Factorization. *Matematika,* vol 35(1): 25-38.

Bell, R. C. (1979). *Board and table games from many civilizations* (Vol. 1): Courier Corporation.

Ben Salem, L. (1994). Les ingénieurs en Tunisie aux XIXe et XXe siècles. *Revue des mondes musulmans et de la Méditerranée,* vol 72(1): 60-74.

Bogoshi, J., Naidoo, K. & Webb, J. (1987). 71.36 The oldest mathematical artefact. *The Mathematical Gazette,* vol 71(458): 294-294.

Boyer, C. B. (1966). Colin Maclaurin and Cramer's rule. *Scripta Mathematica,* vol 27(4): 377-379.

Boyer, C. B., & Merzbach, U. C. (2011). *A history of mathematics:* John Wiley & Sons.

Brock-Utne, B. (1999). African universities and the African heritage. *International Review of Education,* vol 45(1): 87-104.

Brunetti, M., & Renato, A. (2014). Old and New Proofs of Cramer's Rule History , notations and tools. *Applied Mathematical Sciences,* vol 8(133): 6689-6697.

Cardano, G. (1993). *Ars Magna or The Rules of Algebra. Transl. and ed.* Retrieved from Dover: New York:

Cauchy, A. L. (1812). Mémoire sur les fonctions qui ne peuvent obtenir que deux valeurs égales et de signes contraires par suite des transpositions opérées entre les variables qu'elles renferment *lu à l'Institut le.*

Cramer, G. (1750). Introduction à l'analyse des lignes courbes algébriques. *Europeana:* 656-659.

Crowe, D. W. (1975). The geometry of African art II. A catalog of Benin patterns. *Historia Mathematica,* vol 2(3): 253-271.

D'Ambrosio, U. (1999). Literacy, matheracy, and technocracy: A trivium for today. *Mathematical thinking and learning,* vol 1(2): 131-153.

De Heinzelin, J. (1962). Ishango. *Scientific American,* vol 206(6): 105-118.

Debnath, L. (2013). A brief historical introduction to determinant with applications. *International Journal of Mathematical Education in Science and Technology,* vol 44(3): 388-407.

Ehret, C. (2002). *The civilizations of Africa: A history to 1800*: University Press of Virginia Charlottesville.

Engels, H. (2004). Quadrature of the circle in ancient Egypt *Pi: A Source Book* (pp. 3-6): Springer.

Euler, L. (2012). *Elements of algebra:* Springer Science & Business Media.

Eves, H. (1969). *An introduction to the history of mathematics.* New York: Holt, Rinehart and Winston.

Fainzang, S. (1985). Les Sexes et leurs nombres: sens et fonction du 3 et du 4 dans une société burkinabé. *L'homme:* 97-109.

Fataki, K. M. (1991). Mathematics in the daily lives of Afrikans, personal recollections. *Research Notes on Africa*, vol 3: 28-33.

Friberg, J. (2005). *Unexpected Links Between Egyptian and Ba*: World Scientific Publishing Company.

Gay, J., & Cole, M. (1967). *The new mathematics and an old culture: A study of learning among the Kpelle of Liberia*: Holt, Rinehart, and Winston.

George, G. (1993). Stolen Legacy: Greek Philosophy is Stolen Egyptian Philosophy: Trenton: Africa World Press.

Gerdes, P. (1990a). *Ethnogeometrie: Kulturanthropologische beiträge zur genese und didaktik der geometrie*: Franzbecker.

Gerdes, P. (1990b). Lusona: recreações geométricas de África. Maputo (Mozambique),: Instituto Superior Pedagógico.

Gerdes, P. (1994). On mathematics in the history of sub-Saharan Africa. *Historia Mathematica*, vol 21(3): 345-376.

Gerdes, P. (2007). *Mathematics in African history and cultures: An annotated bibliography*: Lulu. com.

Goma, L. K., & Johnson, A. G. (1997). *African Experience with Higher Education*: Ohio.

Gray, J. J., & Parshall, K. H. (2011). *Episodes in the history of modern algebra (1800-1950)* Vol. 32): American Mathematical Soc.

Günther, S. (1908). *Geschichte der Mathematik*. Leipzig: G.J. Göschen.

Habgood, K., & Arel, I. (2012). A condensation-based application of Cramer's rule for solving large-scale linear systems. *Journal of Discrete Algorithms*, vol 10: 98-109. doi:10.1016/j.jda.2011.06.007

Haidara, I. D., & Taore, H. (2008). The private libraries of Timbuktu. *The meanings of Timbuktu*: 271-275.

Heath, T. L. (1910). *Diophantus of Alexandria: A study in the history of Greek algebra*: CUP Archive.

Heath, T. L. (1956). *The thirteen books of Euclid's Elements*: Courier Corporation.

Hedman, B. A. (1999). An Earlier Date for "Cramer's Rule". *Historia Mathematica*, vol 26(4): 365-368.

Higham, N. J. (2002). *Accuracy and stability of numerical algorithms*: Siam.

Hoad, T. F. (1986). *The concise Oxford dictionary of English etymology*: Clarendon Press Oxford.

Høyrup, J. (2016). Mesopotamian Mathematics, Seen "from the Inside"(by Assyriologists) and "from the Outside"(by Historians of Mathematics) *Historiography of Mathematics in the 19th and 20th Centuries* (pp. 53-78): Springer.

Huang, S.-S. (1960). *Science and Civilisation in China.* (Vol. 3): Taipei: Caves Books, Ltd.

Huylebrouck, D. (2006). Mathematics in (central) Africa before colonisation. *Anthropologica et praehistorica,* vol 117: 135-162.

Kagame, A. (1960). *La langue du Rwanda et du Burundi expliquée aux autochtones.*

Katz, V. J. (1997). Algebra and its teaching: An historical survey. *The Journal of Mathematical Behavior,* vol 16(1): 25-38.

Katz, V. J., & Barton, B. (2007). Stages in the history of algebra with implications for teaching. *Educational Studies in Mathematics,* vol 66(2): 185-201.

Ki-Zerbo, J. (1990). *"Educate Or Perish": Africa's Impass and Prospects.* Unesco.

Kieran, C. (2011). Overall commentary on early algebraization: Perspectives for research and teaching *Early algebraization* (pp. 579-593): Springer.

Knobloch, E. (1994). From Gauss to Weierstrass: determinant theory and its historical evaluations *The intersection of history and mathematics* (pp. 51-66): Springer.

Kosinski, A. (2001). Cramer's rule is due to Cramer. *Mathematics Magazine,* vol 74(4): 310-312.

Lulat, Y.-M. (2005). *A history of African higher education from antiquity to the present: A critical synthesis.* Greenwood Publishing Group.

Macfarlane, A. (1916). *Lectures on ten British mathematicians of the nineteenth century* (Vol. 17): John Wiley & Sons, Incorporated.

Maclaurin, C. (1748). *A Treatise of Algebra in Three Parts.* London: A. Miller.

MacLeod, R. (2004). Introduction: Alexandria in history and myth. *The library of Alexandria: Centre of learning in the Ancient World:* 1-18.

Marshack, A. (1991). *The roots of civilization: The cognitive beginnings of man's first art, symbol and notation:* Moyer Bell Ltd.

Martzloff, J. C. (2008). Mathematics in Japan *Encyclopaedia of the History of Science, Technology, and Medicine in Non-Western Cultures* (pp. 1396-1400): Springer.

Mason, J. (1996). Expressing generality and roots of algebra *Approaches to algebra* (pp. 65-86): Springer.

Meri, J. (2018). *Medieval Islamic Civilization (2006): An Encyclopedia* (Vol. Volume I): Routledge.

Muir, T. (1906). *The theory of determinants in the historical order of development* (Vol. 1): Macmillan and Company, limited.

Neugebauer, O., Sachs, A. J., & Götze, A. (1945). *Mathematical cuneiform texts* (Vol. 29): American Oriental Society.

Palgrave, W. G. (1866). *Narrative of a year's journey through central and eastern Arabia (1862-1863)* (Vol. 1): Macmillan and Company.

Rauff, J. V. (2010). Sona geometry from Angola: mathematics of an African tradition. *Mathematics and Computer Education,* vol 44(1), 71.

Ritter, J. (2000). Egyptian mathematics *Mathematics Across Cultures* (pp. 115-136): Springer.

Robinson, S. M. (1970). A short proof of Cramer's rule (pp. 94-95): Mathematical Association of America.

Sallán, J. M. G. (2001). Una interpretación de las fracciones egipcias desde el recto del papiro de Rhind. *Llull: Revista de la Sociedad Española de Historia de las Ciencias y de las Técnicas,* vol 24(51): 649-684.

Spalinger, A. (1990). The Rhind mathematical Papyrus as a historical document. *Studien zur Altägyptischen Kultur:* 295-337.

Stakhov, A. (2009). *The mathematics of harmony: From Euclid to contemporary mathematics and computer science* (Vol. 22): World Scientific.

Struik, D. J. (2012). *A concise history of mathematics*: Courier Corporation.

Townshend, P. (1977). Les jeux de Mankala au Zaire, au Rwanda et au Burundi. *Les cahiers du CEDAF* vol 3: 1-76.

Tweedie, C. (1915). A study of the life and writings of Colin MacLaurin. *The mathematical gazette,* vol 8(119): 133-151.

Vein, R., & Dale, P. (1999). *Determinants and their applications in mathematical physics* (Vol. 134).

Woldegiorgis, E. T., & Doevenspeck, M. (2013). The Changing Role of Higher Education in Africa:" A Historical Reflection". *Higher Education Studies,* vol 3(6): 35-45.

Zaslavsky, C. (1973). Africa Counts. Prindle, Weber & Schmidt. *Inc., Boston, Mass.*

Zaslavsky, C. (1994). Mathematics in Africa: Explicit and implicit. *Companion Encyclopedia of the History and Philosophy of the Mathematical Sciences. London: Routledge. S: 85-92.*

Zaslavsky, C. (1999). *Africa counts: Number and pattern in African cultures.* Chicago Review Press.

Chapter Eight

Circularity in Msonge and Music: African Genius or Just "Primitivism"?

*David O. Akombo, Pearl S. Gray, George O. Griffin &
Baruti I. Katembo*

Introduction

The *msonge* symbolises part of Africa's architecture. Its image embeds concepts about African music, dress and community organisation – all of which will be discussed from that relational standpoint. Though Africa's thousand-plus languages all have words for such structures, the Kiswahili word for a round dwelling (*msonge*) is often used because of the language's pan-African flavour and appeal as a *lingua franca* (common language) within and across many African countries. The Western literature and "civilisation" movements have questioned the aesthetic qualities of Africa's architecture for many centuries without paying much attention to the beauty of African culture. The aim has been largely to equate the term 'rectilinear' with advancement, intelligence and civilisation as opposed to the 'African circular' which was/is erroneously viewed as "primitive" and "uncivilised" in many cases. European colonialism in Africa (1880s – 1960s) was a fundamental factor in Africa's underdevelopment because the colonial governments stole natural resources like gold, diamonds, and timber and in the process exploited African human labour. In turn, this pillaging greatly contributed towards Europe's economic and industrial development. The colonial educational systems for instance, with heavy reliance on unbalanced literature and

213

misuse of religious education, encouraged Africans to see themselves as inferior. The process and experience of colonialism had a negative impact on African efforts toward the use of indigenous resources and concepts to modernise indigenous societies. By and large, "modernisation" is usually linked with Westernisation. This chapter explores the ethnocentric aspects of European hegemony over the supposed African "primitivism". The chapter uses the metaphor of rectilinearity vs. circularity, specifically in reference to the constructs of architecture (and to some degree music). These constructs denote the use of geometry and eclectic images, respectively, to address and encourage Africa's peoples to utilise their indigenous, historical and cultural aspects, including technologies and architecture.

Primitivism in context

The Western view of living close to and in harmony with nature denotes being a "primitive." Primitivism constitutes the pursuit of ways of life against the backdrop of the technological development and its alienating antecedents (Filiss, 2001). For the African to be placed in an inferior position below everyone else, including those within a lower socio-economic status, two things had to be made to happen. First, everything made by the African was labelled as inferior and non-technological. After all, technology supposedly required higher order thinking and skill in critical analysis. Secondly, the African was made to believe that s/he was an inferior being. Instilling the inferiority complex was calculated to dampen the Africans' desire to compete with the Euro-American colonisers, who considered themselves to be civilised. Ethnocentrism provided an opportunity to further classify groups of people and then marginalise them. These groups became either the "brutal barbarian" or the "noble (but ignorant/uncivilised) savage". Cultural anthropologists' use of the concept of ethnology is intended to, among other things, reconstruct human history; ethnology is the branch of cultural anthropology dealing with the origin, distribution and characteristics of human societies ('Ethnology,' 2019). Use of ethnology also proves helpful in deconstructing and debunking human group information that is proven to be false. Ethnology encourages the politicisation of an academic discipline and it facilitates telling the truth untainted by racism, stereotypes and ethnocentric propaganda. Human groups can and do shape history in a variety of ways: increasing the body of knowledge; developing cultures which inspire the maximising of potential; conserving nature and the environment and respecting other humans. If one looks at human history through the lens of the human-shaped constructs, then we must acknowledge the contributions of the so-called "primitive" to human civilisation. The supposedly "non-industrialised" humans also have knowledge of what constitutes progress, growth, development and a sense of history. Indigenous people have a highly developed sense of history – a unique and intellectually stimulating concept of spirituality and profound memories - as evidenced by their ability to recite what the West calls epic poems. They also etch themselves in their history in terms of time and place. The history of primitivism lies within the contexts of sacred meanings whose timeline is cyclic as opposed to a lineal perception of time (Diamond, 1960). To divide the world into two opposing camps - one "primitive" and the other "civilised" - is to disavow the intellectual acumen of the so-called "primitive" and to give credence to the lie that Western civilisation brought order, stability, language and refinement to the world. A study of the West African oral tradition gives ample evidence that these people understood and commented on the human condition. These people had stable economies and a well-organised social structure.

The group philosophy is the most important, with each person having a place and a purpose within the unit. The individual's purpose is not divorced from the passionate notion of death and rebirth through ritual. These linkages are achieved through the spirit-world of the deceased, which in turn connect both the living and the unborn (Diamond, 1960). Their cosmos therefore is projected to the kinship of the society; the society subsequently shares a mutual existence with nature through creative associations and traditional subsistence techniques. These associations show that indigenous people use (and have used) physical, metaphysical, social and emotional attributes, just as Europeans have done. However, the thrusts and configurations were (and are) different. Balance is a fundamental construct in the world of the "primitive". Indigenous societies maintain themselves and exist in states of dynamic equilibrium and express human and natural rhythms in their daily lives.

The msonge

Msonge means 'round dwelling' in Kiswahili. Its linguistic use in this work, as a generic term denoting African round dwellings, stems from Kiswahili's pan-African flavour, appeal and wide use as a *lingua franca* (common language) within and across many African countries. Round (circular) dwellings have gained popularity as an African image, architectural pillar and symbol of heritage for many millennia as

Figure1: Kilalinda Luxury Lodge
Figure 2 (Insert): Interior View, Kilalinda Luxury Lodge
(*courtesy* Siyabona Africa)
Kilalinda Wildlife Conservancy
Tsavo East, Kenya
This msonge-inspired structure is a typical design found throughout ancient and contemporary Africa.

depicted in Figure 1: Kilalinda Luxury Lodge (Siyabona Africa Staffer, 2008) and Figure 2: (Insert): Interior View, Kilalinda Luxury Lodge (Siyabona Africa Staffer, 2008); however, similar round dwellings have been part of many ancient cultures throughout the world, for example, the Sioux in North America (Zaslavsky, 1989: 18-19). Most ancient cultures lived close to and in accordance with nature; see Baruti Katembo (*Mathematics, Circularity and the Msonge as African Heritages*), this volume, for a discussion of ancient perspectives on the intertwining of nature and geometry as a component of architectural design. From the aesthetic point of view, 18th-century French architect Marc-Antoine Laugier thought that the hut was the

216

epitome of nature, referencing that 'if architecture is to please through imitation, it must imitate nature (Hermitary Staffer, 2009).' Some scholars and theoreticians like Joseph Rykwert (as cited in Hermitary Staffer, 2009) have viewed and referenced the hut (i.e., thatched-roof dwelling) as imitative of trees with hanging branches - thus, an extension of the natural space and environment.

Africa and the stigma of colonialism

Apart from "tribe", no other word is as synonymous with colonialism as that of "native"; it is also coterminus with the connotations of "primitive" and has been used to define dark-skinned peoples (particularly Africans) as inferiors and underlings. The architects of colonialism invested considerable energy in creating and policing boundaries between "natives" and "Europeans." This intense effort sought to legitimise the subordination and granting of low status to the "colonised" in relation to the "coloniser", particularly regarding policies limiting rights, citizenship and access to wealth. To this end, each European colony in Africa (whether British, French, Portuguese or others) strategically defined "native" according to its own specific set of local circumstances and interests (Ray, 2006: 42). The goal of European colonialism in Africa (1880s-1960s) was mainly to steal natural resources (gold; diamonds; human labour; timber, etc.) for Europe's economic/industrial benefit. The control revolved largely around coercion of Africans so that they would view Caucasians as superior humans who have been endowed by the Creator with natural intelligence and divine blessings above those of Africans. The colonial educational systems, with heavy reliance on unbalanced literature and a misuse of religious education created by European missionaries and settlers, encouraged an inferior self-image amongst Africans. Edward B. Tylor, 19th century British anthropologist, (as cited in Zaslavsky, 1999: 9 and in Katembo, March 2008) received widespread coverage and notoriety for his book *Primitive Culture* which promoted the theory that a European person was the highest level of human and that the other races of non-European descent, particularly Africans, were incapable of advanced thinking. *Primitive Culture* became the leading reference work of its time for anthropologists, ethnologists and writers on the history of mathematics (as cited in Zaslavsky, 1999: 9; Katembo, March 2008).

The colonial regimes' aim of invading Africa was mainly for criminogenic and capitalistic ventures, sometimes cloaked in missionary initiatives and altruistic trappings. Colonialism helped to breakdown communal values and embedded bare capitalism as a future socioeconomic model to be continued once independence came to the 1960s African nations. In the contemporary era, the United States of America, the European Union and other players seek to use business sectors such as trade initiatives and commercial ventures to engage African nations for acquisition of raw materials (oil; platinum; coltan (aka tantalum); titanium, and other resources). However, these natural resources are also needed to facilitate Africa's own 21st century industrialisation, wealth, economic capital and developmental stability. Wise (prudent) economic colludings will mitigate against unfair quasi-trade wars, e.g., discouragement of countries like the Netherlands and Belgium from dumping chicken legs into Uganda, leaving the local poultry farmers economically non-competitive (Tandon, 2015). Such deterrence can lead to a continued industrialisation, geo-political power and global economic competitiveness depending upon the use of the raw materials.

An interesting paradox – Africa, the cradle of humanity, is blessed with the greatest natural resources and mineral wealth, yet its peoples, often hungry, ragged and economically destitute, languish on a continent decimated by war, famine, "tribalism" and the egregious abuse of human and natural resources (Katembo, February 2008). Since the 1960s, many African rulers have replaced the brutal exploits of the European colonial system with their own brand of tyranny, i.e., they have essentially become the new captured masters, in many cases creating more brutal regimes than the ones established by Europeans who have been supposedly gone nearly half a century; George Ayittey's book *Africa Betrayed* elucidates this fact and the contribution of Africa's captured ruling elite to the continent's continued underdevelopment (Ayittey, 1993). At the time of independence (1960s), physical freedom was achieved, but the minds of the people and their leaders were still shackled in terms of seeing themselves and their culture as inferior. Kenyan post-colonial literature theorist Ngugi wa Thiong'o (as cited in Zaslavsky, 1999:161-162) suggests in his novel *The River Between* that Africans who saw themselves as more Western believe that the geometry of circular houses, an indigenous concept, is "primitive" in comparison to rectangular designs which they associate with Europeans.

The msonge not only symbolises Africa's architecture, but all that is African from the mind's eye (particularly as a metaphoric depiction in movies, art, photographs, literature, and children's stories). Its image embeds concepts about African music, dress and community organisation. The Western literature and "civilisation" movement have questioned the aesthetic qualities of Africa's architecture for many centuries; thus, the term "primitive" denotes "savage", "crude" and/or "uncivilised" ('Primitive,' 2004). The aim has been largely to equate the term 'rectilinear' with advanced (innately intelligent and civilised) and "circular" with "primitive" (innately unintelligent and barbaric). By extension, media and literary socialisation psychologically shape thought to link hut (as a metaphor for Africa) with negative images (small; insignificant; poor; third world; non-Western) and house (as a metaphor for Europe) with positive images (large; important; rich; industrialised; modern; Western). Because of such thinking, "modernisation" is usually associated with Westernisation. In application, the process and experience of colonialism retarded African energy toward use of indigenous resources and concepts to "modernise" its nations in the post-independence era.

Scientific genius of the msonge and other round dwellings

In terms of scientific discovery, a circle maximises area over a square of the same perimeter measurement by an approximate margin slightly above 21% (Katembo, 2002: 70; see also Katembo *Mathematics, circularity and the msonge as African heritages*, this volume) for an illustration of the aforementioned circle area maximisation being verified by deductive reasoning. As a practical application, *misonge* (African circular dwellings) and other similarly-architectured residential structures featured amongst indigenous peoples of Asia,

Oceania, ancient Europe; and the Americas use round floor space to maximise internal area. Aside from concerns and considerations of aesthetic appeal and internal area maximisation, globally, people have for many millennia independently discovered the engineering practicality and functionality of constructing circular dwelling spaces. Thus, there exists the Convergent Evolution Theory - phenomenon when two distinct species with differing ancestries evolve to display similar physical features due to environmental circumstances requiring similar developmental or structural alterations ('Convergent Evolution Theory,' 2009; Parker *et al.*, 2013). A circle is a physically strong design structure for a building, with no building part bearing more load (supported weight) than another, i.e., it is the perfect shape for an even load distribution. The adoption of this shape meant that the builder could select small diamcter timbers and dispense with the need for exhaustive cutting, shaping and jointing of wood (Grampus Research Team Staffer, 2006).

The Crannog, *Europe's round hut*

The Celts, originating in what is now France and western Germany, migrated across and invaded many European lands, beginning in the Bronze Age (~1200 BCE). As a result, they extended their influence, traditions and culture that contemporarily remain as remnants from present-day Spain to the Black Sea's shores. Architecture being no exception, the Celts left their imprint on this area of culture in the lands which they voyaged, penetrated and later conquered - the crannog. This circular-shaped Celtic vernacular dwelling takes its name from the Irish word *crann,* meaning tree. Its superstructure was built entirely of wood and formed the ordinary living house for a family unit and, in some instances, livestock. Additionally, the crannog's size, like similar constructions in African settlements, was an indication of the status of the person living there (Grampus Research Team Staffer, 2006). Celtic architecture influenced many structures across Europe. However, round dwellings existed across Europe in the Neolithic period (~4000-2000 BCE), prior to Celtic dispersion; see Figure 3: Reconstructed *Round Thatch-Roof Celtic Hut* (Wagner, 2003). Archaeological excavations and research document this and verify the round structures' continued use into the 17th century in remoter parts of Ireland and Scotland. For the purpose of this work, the European round houses will be identified as crannogs in tribute to Celtic contributions to the popularity, visibility and use of this architectural style in ancient Europe. Remnants of these crannogs have been found throughout the regions of Celtic migration, e.g. Spain, UK, Italy, Greece, France, Portugal, Germany and Asia Minor (Balanck, 2009); see Figure 4: *Crannog* Reconstruction (Clark, 2006).

Figure 3: Reconstructed *Round Thatch-Roof Celtic "Hut"* (*courtesy* Art Wagner) Asturias, Spain @ Castro de Campa Torres This round dwelling is a replica of similar Asturian settlement dwellings dating to the 6th and 5th centuries BCE.

Theory on European abandonment of round dwelling construction

People's decisions, with reference to use of mathematics, technology and science, are influenced by societal needs (Zaslavsky, 1989); the design of dwelling spaces is also shaped in this way. Celtic societies of more than two millennia ago, like others of Europe, Africa, Oceania, Asia and the Americas, were primarily agrarian, i.e., organised around farming and livestock endeavours; thus, there were no true urban centres in the contemporary sense where a diversity of agricultural and non-agricultural trades like masonry and metalworking were functioning in the same congregational space (Balanck, 2009). The inhabitants' lives were governed by working on fields, tending crops or animals, and seasonal dependence on favourable soil fertility and weather conditions. As populations in medieval times grew exponentially across Europe with its vast areas of non-arable land due to harsh climates and cold weather, people moved near one another in areas where there were abundant arable land and fresh water. Therefore, vast numbers of Europeans were limited regarding food access, farming endeavours and livestock management: there were hazardous travel routes, non-arable land zones, climatic elements (snow; ice) and associated animal hibernations. Cities therefore sprung up near abundant arable land, fresh water and hunting game (Katembo, 2012: 121).

Figure 4: *Crannog* Reconstruction
(*courtesy* Martin Clark)
Connemara Heritage Centre
Galway, Ireland
Remnants of this Celtic-inspired round dwelling style have
been found throughout Europe, extending from
Spain to the Black Sea's shores.

In contrast, the majority of African areas have warm, subtropical climates suited for year-round fishing, hunting and growing seasons where fruits, vegetables, water, and game are in abundance over large territorial spaces; so, tight population packing was not needed as a means to provide food and water access to many (Katembo, 2012: 121-122). European societies, particularly in the Middle Ages, had mainly evolved into dirty, tightly packed and cramped settlements and environments (TimeMaps Staffer, 2019). These conditions contrasted immensely with those of African and other warm weather peoples where settlements mainly comprised widely spaced buildings. Accordingly, European ideas about architecture (in the transition from sparse-to-dense populations) may have leaned, out of environmental necessity and constraints, toward maximising space between buildings, i.e., external area maximisation, as opposed to the African concept of internal area maximisation for family and livestock sheltering.

Buildings can be squeezed closer together if they bear a rectilinear design (square/rectangular roof and body) rather than a circular one; essentially, the adjacency of round structures wastes external space.

223

The logical extension of this concept is that, as horizontal space became depleted due to continuous adjacent packing of rectilinear buildings, considerations were explored regarding the use of vertical space - hence, the concept of high-rise apartment buildings.

An irony: European disdain for African dwelling spaces

During the 15th century as Europeans began to explore African lands in search of valuable minerals, spices, new trade routes and eventually slaves (for colonial plantation labour), textbooks and propaganda were circulated across Europe to describe Africans as "primitive", i.e., "sub-human" (Akombo *et al.*, 2015: 8-9). The very notion of primitivism in reference to Africans had been largely misconstrued by Europeans. In his seminal work *Primitive Culture*, Edward Taylor (1871) regarded culture as a complex unit that includes knowledge, belief, art, morals, law, customs or any other socio-cultural attribute and habit acquired by man as a member of society (Taylor, 1871: 1). If the Europeans had understood the complex, esoteric and advanced aspects of the varied African cultures, the image of Africans as "primitive savages" would not have been used to justify African enslavement and colonisation. Additionally, the idea of 'civilising' process would not have been implemented. Over time, the colonial philosophy was imposed upon Africa and internalised by Africans themselves, i.e., the ideology that the European is innately intelligent and the African is an anthropological inferior. African architecture, like other components of culture, was promoted as inferior by Europeans who had gained economic and military control over large territories in Africa by the 17th century. Based on ignorance, racism and bigotry, Europeans, while ignoring their own circular architectural heritage, viewed Africans as living in isolated and unstructured bush communities supposedly with little or no understanding of architectural design or appreciation of aesthetics; they usually described the dwellings as monotonous, look-alike mud and thatch structures. They often ignored Africa's diverse architectural designs (beehive; rectangular; square-box with pyramidal roof; cone-cylinder; hump roof, etc.), e.g., rectangular Tanzanian tembe houses or aerodynamically shaped [i.e., loaf-designed], windowless Masai dwellings (Hull, 1976: 63). As mentioned, and discussed earlier, Europe's history is replete with documented evidence showing European construction of African-like, round dwellings during varying time periods.

African music and the concept of Afrology

The ideas of "primitivism" and "civilisation" draw controversial Afrocentric and Eurocentric considerations impinging upon the Age of Enlightenment. The term Eurocentric refers to "…European oriented western perspective in opposition to the term 'Afrocentric' that places African and Africa related issues at its center" (Okur, 1993: 92). Furthermore, Nilgun Okur defines Afrology as: "…the study of concepts, issues, behaviors with particular bases in the African world, either on the continent of Africa (continental), or on the other lands where other Africans are now settled (diasporan) (Okur, 1993: 89)."

The concepts of primitivism vs. civilisation and circular vs. linear structure go beyond architecture and can also be examined regarding music and dance using Okur's theoretical propositions of Afrology.

The Age of Enlightenment, spanning from the 17th century Scientific Revolution era to the turn of the 19th century, was supposedly characterised by a philosophical perspective centred upon epistemology and reason as opposed to emotion. It also was a period of scientific awakening centred on the attack upon metaphysical arguments by philosophers such as Rousseau and Descartes who developed their theories from the context and framework of geometrical forms. Reason, natural law, hope, and progress were catalytic to the thinkers of the Enlightenment. The very idea of "Return to Nature" and the exaltation of feelings, intuition and immediacy were advanced by Rousseau, who argued that humans are inherently good, but become corrupted by the evils of society. Rousseau saw that the power of passion could deflect human beings from knowledge of their true interests by inflaming their *amour-propre* (Mitchel, 1993: 648). These ideas led European composers such as Rameau to restructure his operas on the ideology of *returning to nature*. Rameau's best opera *Castor et Pollux* (1737) almost ruined his career as it was marked by controversies which led his contemporaries to criticise his "primitive" and old-fashioned French style (Rameau, 2008). This idea of "return to nature" had persisted for many years in the music of the "primitive" culture of North America.

Descartes thought there was great power in the single line, and therefore thought a straight line to be an equation of the first degree, whereas a conic section was an equation of the second degree (Bronowski & Mazliah, 1960: 217). Every human endeavour was approached from the perspective of "reason" because this was the primary source and legitimacy for authority. Humankind had the internal potential for happiness and to manifest it through reason. Eurocentric views reflected a disdain for the African past and an inclination towards utopian epistemological schemes while supposedly abandoning all emotion-based human activities to the "Dark Continent" (Africa).

These Aristotelian approaches were thought to be the preamble of "reason" by which emphasis rested upon processes which split (separated) reason from passion (James, 1997). However, 18th and 19th century Europeans interpreted these approaches as diametrically-opposed to the humanist idea of treating fellow humans with dignity – a concept expressed widely in pre-colonial Africa. Eurocentric musicians then began to compose their music based on a strict structure and linear formats reflective of Rococo architecture. Rococo (*rukō'kō, rō–*), an art of exquisite refinement and linearity, was utilised as an architectural style, especially in interiors and in the decorative arts (Kimball, 1943: 78); it originated in France and was widely used throughout 18th century Europe (Kimball, 1943: 78). The Eurocentric ideology on music during this time equated all musical forms with philosophy and reason.

Circular musical structures vs. linear musical structures

One of the basic criticisms of Afrocentricism rests on the prevalence of circular rather than linear qualities in terms of form, shape and structure in African art (Okur, 1993: 102). This premise is crucial in determining the aesthetic characteristics of African music.

226

Following the Age of Enlightenment, the Classical Era brought forth musical forms such as the Sonata which later became a touchstone for musical works keeping the *status quo*. At the onset of the Sonata form, the Italian predecessors like Stamitz, Samartini and Scarlatti all employed three-phrase binary forms in which the music was composed with some predetermined and reasoned formulae such as ABA, ABACA or ABACADA and many other forms that were aped on balanced and symmetrical aesthetics of the 18th century Eurocentric musical model.

The Sonata form, for instance, required that important musical statements made in a key other than the tonic or home key, be either restated in the tonic, or be brought into closer relationship with the tonic before the completion of the movement. If a piece of music began in a major key, it would modulate or change key to a relative key, and then make a recapitulation to finality. This was an antithesis to music of the "primitive" world where human emotions governed the composers with little regard to cognitive reasoning and numeric formulae. African music defied linearity and maintained curvilinear tendencies even during that same period. The cyclic nature of the music was embedded in the African cosmology where life was viewed as a cycle form creating the core of Afrocentricity. The significance of the curvilinear ideology in Africa is best expressed by Kariamu Welsh-Asante:

> Let the circle be unbroken or let us complete the circle is a creed in the African world. There is "power" in the circle, the curve, the round, supernatural power if you will....Curvilinear qualities of dance, art and music round, curve and carve out images that are similar and resemble aspects of African society and mythology, if only in essence (Welsh-Asante, 1985: 76).

Most African dances showed a curvilinear quality that appeared as the antithesis of Western dance, which has heavy reliance on symmetry, proportional, and profile-oriented form (Welsh-Asante, 1985: 90). According to Kariamu Welsh-Asante, Afrocentricity is a critical theory and method which serves as a generative concept where the African musician could be viewed as an Afrologist, thus conforming to his own musical lore (Welsh-Asante, 1985: 90). According to Okur, "...an Afrologist who is Afrocentric is first expected to know, recognise, and formulate the characteristics of his own culture, and later by virtue of his Afrocentric perspective, other cultures and viewpoints" (Okur, 1993: 89). Music based on emotion and an unstructured format was thereby only good for "third world" people, especially those in the "Dark Continent". After all, African thought was viewed to be non-scientific with spiritistic tendencies that supposedly distinguished it from Western peoples (Wiredu, 1976: 5). African culture, inclusive of religion, music, dance, festivals and martial arts, was achieved by divine inspiration as opposed to Western arts being formulated by human intelligence.

One of the compelling interpretations running through the African musical structure focuses on the ways in which Africans have embraced new ideologies such as conformism to exotic religions. The transfers of knowledge through the Eurocentric music education, sustenance of Africa's own music as a conduit for indigenous education and the use of African music to inculcate the young into adulthood are points of great interest. Music is used to disseminate knowledge and build the tripartite of the cognitive, affective and psychomotor domains of the children.

The four fundamental pillars of music are musical material, standardisation, presentation subjects and the impact on the listener (Adorno & Simpson, 1941). With these in mind, a clear judgment concerning the structure of African music from the Eurocentric musical structure can be arrived at only by strict attention to its fundamental characteristics.

African music is rhythmical; its melodies are cyclic with essentially timeless, repetitive patterns. This music may be characterised as polyphonic. In all African music, a predilection for the combination of melody and rhythm is apparent. All African melodic instruments can provide a percussive rhythmic accompaniment. The stylistic characteristic for which African music is widely known is its rhythm. Individual parts in some performances may be extremely rhythmically complex, but it is the way the simple rhythms of individual parts are combined that create the whole musical mosaic. This combination is often created by accentuating patterns of each part counter to one another, creating a tapestry of rhythm and melody. The instrumental music employs a short-repeated phrase (ostinato) as in Figure 5: *Ostinato* examples in selected musical instruments (Akombo, 2009). The rhythm is subjected to diminutive but continuous improvisations. Vocal lines can be very short but can also be extremely long and complex. African music utilises descending melodic structures that reflect the tonal nature of African languages. African musical anatomy has been circular from time immemorial. All African music and dance forms utilise some form of circular motions as an imbedded feature.

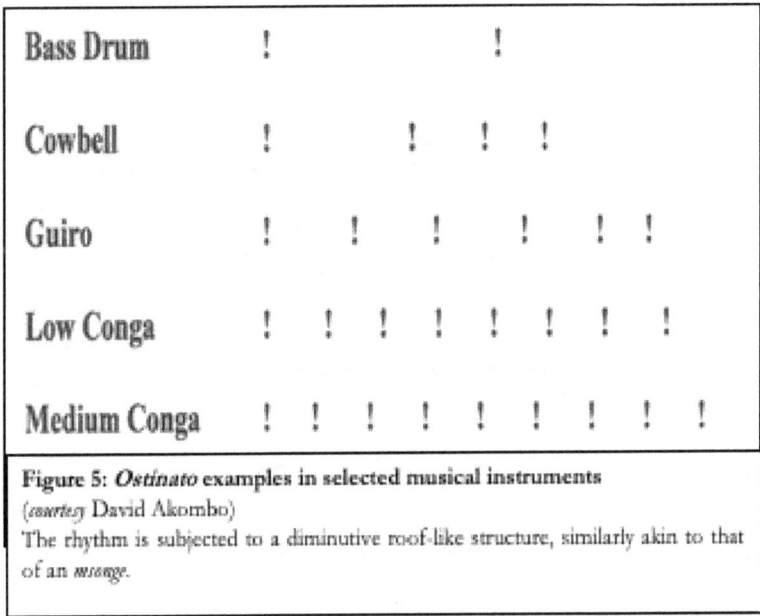

Bass Drum	!			!				
Cowbell	!		!	!	!			
Guiro	!	!	!	!	!	!		
Low Conga	!	!	!	!	!	!	!	!
Medium Conga	!	!	!	!	!	!	!	!	!

Figure 5: *Ostinato* examples in selected musical instruments
(*courtesy* David Akombo)
The rhythm is subjected to a diminutive roof-like structure, similarly akin to that of an *msonge*.

In African musical traditions, music and dance cannot be complete without circular movements. The Wataita (Bantu-speaking ethnic group of southeastern Kenya), in their brisk movements, sing repetitive songs such as *Ngelekele* (Figure 6: Opening measures of Ngelekele) (Akombo, 2006: 41). By shuffling their feet, small circular movements on the ground (as seen aerially), are created in the form of half-moons in space. For the Wataita dancers, leg movement may be important (vital) to their *mwazindika* healing dance (Akombo, 2006: 41).

Despite the revolutions that came with the Age of Enlightenment that codified the existing musical taxonomy, it is imperative to question the legitimacy of such criterion, and presumably view this as a two-way analysis based on the dichotomy of the artist's music and the people's music. While in a typical Eurocentric music-making domain, the artist is governed by a strict consideration to reason and philosophy, the African musician on the contrary is more preoccupied with the human emotions that bind his work to the African egalitarian principle of a people's music.

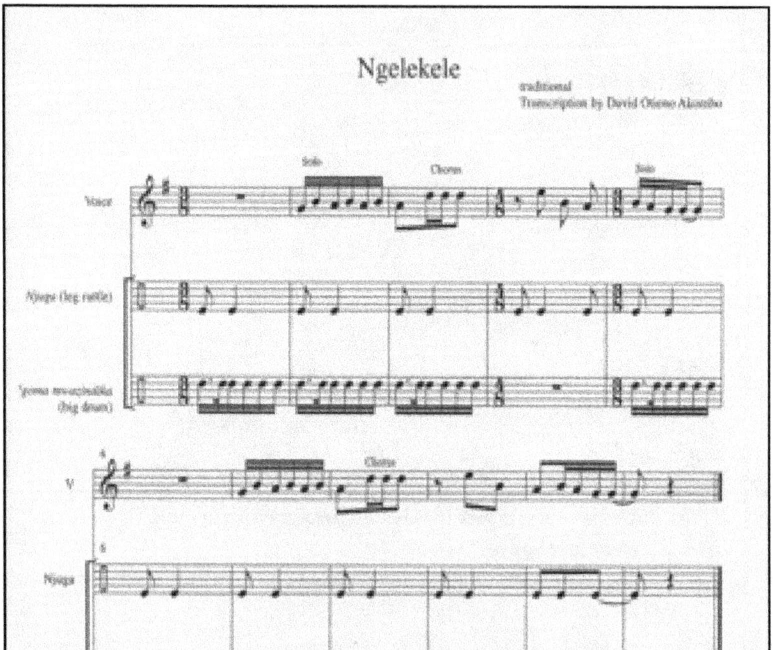

Figure 6: Opening measures of Ngelekele
(*courtesy* David Akombo)
Repetitive ostinato song used in the *maragindiku* healing dance.

Just as the fundamental aesthetics of music suddenly changed with the arrival of the European missionaries to Africa, so did the inspiration of African music's curvilinear nature. European missionary music had a profound effect on African music in terms of form and structure. Having been taught to sing European church hymns - many of which were based on the Wesleyan harmonic structure, even after independence – a significant number of African musicians began to compose music based on these hymns and other structural definitions of European music. The African musicians approached their art with linearity – an act in total disregard to their hitherto, civilised circular and emotional symbol. As Smith (1952: 14) noted, a symbol is a product of the imagination; furthermore, in order to understand a symbol, its appeal is to the feelings; its meaning is grasped by intuition. You can understand a people's symbols, only in so far as you enter sympathetically into their daily experience and see the world through their eyes (Smith, 1952: 14).

After the colonial impact, Africans saw their communities divided; therefore, destroying the pan-African ethos. They endeavoured to eliminate all artificial boundaries within the African continent, leading to the creation of a united African art. Inspired by the nationalistic movement that ruled post-independence Ghana as headed by the then President Kwame Nkrumah, Nana Danso Abiam (a leading ethnomusicologist and scholar) undertook a music project at the University of Ghana's Institute of African Studies. Nana Danso Abiam established a scholarship to attract students for the start-up and development of an Afrocentric orchestra, officially named Pan-African Orchestra (PAO). The PAO, formed by Abiam in 1988, travelled across Africa to perform music compositions adapted for modified traditional instruments (Adjahoe, 2017: 100). The associated scholarship was a useful tool and component in the restoration of African identity. The Orchestra became a conduit for re-examining African music from the perspectives of acoustics, melody, harmony and instrumentation. It is led by a conductor and uses solely African instruments, which are organised into symphonic-like sections (Lawrence, 2015).

In African belief systems, spiritual realities are timeless; they are not limited to categories of time and space (Richards, 1985: 207); hence, the essence of curvilinear, musical attributes. The African ideology on the curvilinear coherence and oneness in Afrology is best summarised by Okur: "The dead ones are not separate from the living; the babies represent the timeless regeneration of man. Spirit and matter are strongly intertwined, and their relationship completes the circle; the unity is thus achieved" (Okur, 1993: 103).

Conclusion

The Eurocentric disdain for the supposed primitivism of Afrocentric culture can be detected and examined at many levels; however, as illustrated by the architectural examples cited earlier, this supposed European superiority may well be based on ignorance of cultural history. The inherently genius design of the msonge – mathematically, structurally and spatially – was also known to early Europeans. The central hypothesis here is that Europeans abandoned the natural advantages of circularity in favour of rectilinearity only as a pragmatic necessity due to the dense populations of emerging cities; the architectural shift was therefore an essential adaptation rather than an intellectual advancement. Similarly, the circularity of African music and dance is in direct reflection of the native cultural philosophy on life – not dissimilar from the European attempt to synchronise musical compositions rectilinearly with the emerging philosophies of reason. African "primitive" architecture and music hold no false pretence of sophistication; rather, they reflect a culture fully accepting and incorporative of their natural innate beauty, intelligence and genius.

References

Adjahoe, M.Q. (2017). From Ghanaian folk song to contemporary art music for Bb atɛntɛbɛn and piano. *Malaysian Music Journal,* vol 6 (2): 94-114.

Adorno, T. (1990 [1941]). On Popular Music, in Frith, S. & Godwin, A. (eds.), *On Record: Rock, Pop, and The Written Word.* New York: Pantheon Books.

Adorno, T & Simpson, G. (1941). On Popular Music. *Studies in Philosophy and Social Science,* vol IX: 17-48.

Akombo, D. O. (2006). *Music and Healing Across Cultures.* Ames, IA: Culicidae Press.

Akombo, D. O. (2009). (Image Creator). Figure 5: Ostinato examples in selected musical instruments. [image].

Akombo, D., Katembo, B. & Shockley, K. (2015). *UWENZI: The Pan-African Factor, A 21ˢᵗ Century View*. Bloomington, IN: AuthorHouse.

Ayittey, G. (1993). *Africa Betrayed*. New York, NY: Palgrave Macmillan.

Balanck, M. (2009). *The Celts*. AncientSpiral.Com. Retrieved February 15, 2009 from http://www.ancientspiral.com/Celt.htm

Bronowski, J. & Mazliah, B. (1960). *The Western Intellectual Tradition*. New York, NY: Harper & Row.

Clark, M. (Photographer). (2006). *Crannog* Reconstruction. [digital image]. Retrieved February 15, 2009 from http://www.grampusheritage.fsnet.co.uk/ticatec%20Crannog2.jpg

Convergent Evolution Theory. (2009). In *The American Heritage® Dictionary of the English Language, Fourth Edition*. Retrieved February 21, 2009 from http://science.jrank.org/pages/2608/Evolution-Convergent.html

Diamond, S. (1960). The Uses of the Primitive. *Primitivism*. Retrieved from https://theanarchistlibrary.org/library/stanley-diamond-the-uses-of-the-primitive.pdf

Driscoll, G. (2003, June 4). Nation's Legislators Ask, Do Clothes Make the Kenyan? *Los Angeles Times*. Retrieved September 19, 2008 from http://articles.latimes.com/2003/jun/04/world/fg-jammies4

Eagleton, T. (2000). *The Idea of Culture*. Oxford, England: Blackwell.

Ethnology. (2019). In *Dictionary.com*. Retrieved August 26, 2019 from https://www.dictionary.com/browse/ethnology

Filiss, J. (2001). What is Primitivism? *Primitivism*. Retrieved February 18, 2009 from http://www.primitivism.com/what-is-primitivism.htm

Fowale, T. (2008, February 18). Caught in the Crossfire: Africa in the oil battle between the great powers. *American Chronicle*. Retrieved February 7, 2009 from http://www.americanchronicle.com/articles/view/52790

Grampus Research Team Staffer. (2006). "To build a crannog!" *Grampus Heritage*. Retrieved February 15, 2009 from http://www.grampus.co.uk/parabow/projects/building/ireland/crannogie.htm

Hermitary Staffer. (2009). Joseph Rykwert's *On Adam's House in Paradise: The Idea of the Primitive Hut in Architectural History (2nd edition)*. Retrieved February 21, 2009 from http://www.hermitary.com/bookreviews/rykwert.html

Hull, R. W. (1976). *African Cities and Towns before the European Conquest*. New York, NY: W. W. Norton & Company, Inc.

Huntington, S. P. (1998). *The clash of civilizations and the remaking of world order*. London, England: Touchstone.

James, S. (1997). *Passion and Action: The Emotions in Seventeenth-Century Philosophy*. Oxford, UK: Oxford University Press.

Rameau. J. P., (2008). *The Columbia Encyclopedia, Sixth Edition*. Retrieved February 20, 2009 from http://www.encyclopedia.com/doc/1E1-Rameau-J.html

Katembo, B. (2002). *Elephants in a Bamboo Cage: The Black Condition, the American Psyche, and the Next Step Forward*. Raleigh, NC: Mkuyu Books.

Katembo, B. (2012). *Scattered Assets: How African Americans & Other Resources Can Shape 21st Century Pan-African Empowerment*. Bloomington, IN: AuthorHouse.

Kimball, F. (1943). *The Creation of the Rococo*. Philadelphia, PA (Philadelphia Museum of Art): W. W. Norton.

Hart, K. (1973). Informal Income Opportunities and Urban Employment in Ghana. *Journal of Modern African Studies,* vol.*11*, (1).

Lawrence, B. (2015, October 13). Nana Danso Abiam & The Pan African Orchestra. *Ghana Goods*. Retrieved July 20, 2019 from https://ghanagoods.co.uk/nana-danso-abiam-the-pan-african-orchestra/

Mitchel, H. (1993, October). Reclaiming the Self: The Pascal-Rousseau Connection. *Journal of the History of Ideas*, vol 54 (4): 637-658.

Okur, N. A. (1993, September). Afrocentricity as a Generative Idea in the Study of African American Drama, *Journal of Black Studies,* vol 24 (1): 88-108.

Parker, J., Tsagkogeorga, G, Cotton, J. A., Liu, Y., Provero, P., Stupka, E. & Rossiter, S. J. (2013). Genome-wide signatures of convergent evolution in echolocating mammals. *Nature*. Vol 502 (7470): 228–231.

Primitive. (2004). In *The American Heritage® Dictionary of the English Language, Fourth Edition*. Retrieved February 7, 2009 from http://dictionary.reference.com/browse/primitive

Primitivism. (2019). In *Dictionary.com*. Retrieved August 5, 2019 from https://www.dictionary.com/browse/primitivism?s=t

Ray, C. (2006, April). Are you a native? *New African*: 42-43.

Reynolds, J. (2007, July 3). China in Africa: Developing Ties. *BBC News*. Retrieved from http://www.news.bbc.co.uk/2/hi/asia-pacific/6264476.stm

Richards, D. (1985). The Implications of African American Spiritual in Asante, M. K. & Welsh-Asante, K. (eds.), *African Culture: The Rhythms of Unity*. Westport, CT: Greenwood.

Siyabona Africa Staffer. (Photographer). (2008). Kilalinda Luxury Lodge. [digital image]. Retrieved February 16, 2009 from http://lodges.safari.co.za/images/kilalinda-280-gen1.jpg

Siyabona Africa Staffer. (Photographer). (2008). Interior View, Kilalinda Luxury Lodge. [digital image]. Retrieved February 19, 2009 from http://www.kilalinda.com/html/lodge.htm

Smith, E. (1952). African Symbolism. *The Journal of the Royal Anthropological Institute of Great Britain and Ireland*, vol 82 (1): 13-37.

Tandon, Y. (2015). *Trade is War*. New York, NY: OR Books Press.

Taylor, E. B. (1871). *Primitive Culture: Researches into the Development of Mythology, Philosophy, Religion, Language, Art and Custom*. 2nd ed. London, UK: John Murray.

TimeMaps Staffer. (2019). Medieval Europe. *TimeMaps*. Retrieved July 23, 2019 from https://www.timemaps.com/civilizations/medieval-europe/

Wagner, A. (Photographer). (2003). Reconstructed *Round Thatch-Roof Celtic "Hut."* [digital image]. Retrieved February 18, 2009 from http://www.arteasturias.com/images/asturias/GijonAsturesHut B_300.jpg

Wainaina, B. (2005, Winter). How to write about Africa. *Granta 92: The View from Africa*.

Welsh-Asante, K. (1985). *Commonalities in African Dance: An Aesthetic Foundation*, in Asante, M. K. & Welsh-Asante, K. (eds.), *African Culture: The Rhythms of Unity*. Westport, CT: Greenwood.

Weru, G. (2007, November 10-16). Dr. Watson says all Africans are daft. *The Arusha Times*. Retrieved February 14, 2009 from http://www.arushatimes.co.tz/2007/44/Prejudice.htm

Wiredu, K. (1976, July-December). How not to compare African Traditional Thought with Western Philosophy. *Ch'Indaba*, vol (2): 4-8.

Zaslavsky, C. (1999). *Africa Counts: Number and Pattern in African Cultures*. Chicago, IL: Lawrence Hill Books.

Zaslavsky, C. (1989, September). People Who Live in Round Houses. Reston, VA: *Arithmetic Teacher*. 18-21.

Chapter Nine

Liberating African Theology from Misfooted Eurocentric Theologisation

Martin Mujinga

Introduction

The history of Christianity has taught us that Africa is the home of theology and the past five centuries succinctly espouse how Africa shaped global Christianity. The exodus event, the coming of the baby Jesus to Africa, the formulations of the creeds, monasticism and the Christian doctrines are clear testimonies that Africa has always been the tabernacle of God, and Godly knowledge and wisdom. This honour was distorted in two ways. First, it was grabbed by the missionaries in the nineteenth century as they "brought" Christianity to Africa like a "potted flower". Instead of reintroducing the gospel of Christ to Africa, the missionaries engraved Africans into their western culture and epistemology taking advantage of the colonial environment that favoured them (Pobee, 1979). Similarly, contemporary Eurocentric scholars and thinkers would want to foist their colonial animistic and earthly theology about Gaia or Mother Earth onto Africans. This is being done so that Africans stop worshipping the God (*Mwari*) in Heaven (*kudenga*) who was known even in precolonial Africa. In this regard, the contemporary era has seen the emergence of **missionaries of Gaia** who are bent on persuading indigenous people that the Gaia is for them and is their traditional Goddess (Nhemachena *et al.*, 2018).

In their effort to "enlighten" Africa, missionaries never replanted Christianity in the African soil so that it would grow using the African conditions. This action had a detrimental effect to the Africans given that until the 1960s when African theology was officially reintroduced, Africans viewed the Western God as superior and African religion and spirituality as inferior. The Westerners were depicted as possessing saints whereas Africans were portrayed as possessing and possessed by evil spirits. Writing on Ghana's missionary experience White (2017) stresses that the Western missionaries encountered the Ghanaian traditional worldview and religion from a background of Christianity embedded in Enlightenment. They came with a perception and approach that presented them as superior and viewed the African traditional worldview and culture as paganism.

The second distortion of Africa's Christian pride was through African theologians themselves. The moment African theologians re-joined the theological discourse, they left the legacy that was started by African scholars like Origen, Athanasius, Augustine of Hippo, Tertullian, Clement of Alexandria and Cyprian during the Patristic Period (Cains, 1996), and concentrated on African culture and epistemologies that were demeaned by the missionaries. African theology came on fold at the same time African states were receiving independence from the Western world. In so doing, African theology rejoiced in spirituality more than it strove to rehumanise the African integrity that had been dehumanised by the Western world. This chapter argues that the approach taken by Africans also contributed to the process of misfooting African theology.

Although the focus of African theology was culture, it remained difficult to define African culture given the diversity of Africa. Moreover, the term culture remained ambiguous. Culture has many meanings and dimensions, and there is no one definition that is agreed by scholars because they differ in their understanding of the subject (Hewitt, 2012). Yankuzo (2013:3) contends: "that in the global world, cultural convergences have made the cultures of the world to be seen as growing increasingly similar at some degree and in some way". Yankuzo (2013:3) has a feeling that "there is a tendency to see global assimilation in culture in the direction of dominant groups and societies in the Western world. This domination is cultural imperialism, westernization and Americanization of the weaker societies". Africa is a case in point. By concentrating on the abstruse term- culture, African theologians misfooted the mandate of African theology as a tool of making Christ at home with Africans in their daily life of dispossession, exploitation and suffering. African theologians fed from the colonial plate in spiritualising a theology that should have been liberative to the Africans.

Understanding African theology

The existence of African theology is no longer a subject of debate (Gifford, 2008). Anglophone, Francophone and Lusophone scholars have researched intensively on this subject. The definitions of African theology by these scholars are spiced with African flavour oriented in African history, African ethos, language, culture and milieu. Of interest to note is that these definitions seem to point in the same direction. Selected definitions have been identified with the aim of emphasising how African theological patterns are related to each other in the decolonial emphasis of African culture and epistemologies. However, despite all the rigorous efforts by African scholars to inculturate, localise, contextualise or Africanise Christianity (Martey, 1993), theology in Africa remains engrossed in the Western philosophy and thought forms.

According to Nyamiti (1971:1) African theology, "is a discourse on God and what is related to God in accordance with the African needs and mentality". For Nyamiti (1971), African theology is the expression of Biblical Christian doctrine in African mentality and needs. Setiloane (1988:34) adds that "by African theology we mean a theology which is based on the Biblical faith and speaks to the African's soul". This theology is expressed in the categories of thought which arise out of the philosophy and worldview of Africans. Mbiti (1979a) further describes African theology as a theological reflection and expression by African Christians. The term as understood by Bowers (2002:109) also refers to "the lively conversations within the African Christian community that began early in the 1960 and increased unabated to the present and seeks to address the intellectual and theological issues which concern that community". Mugambi cited in Magezi and Igba (2018) prefers to take the definition further to the pre-classical Africa where he states that African theology could generally refer to such theological reflection and discourse as was carried out by Africans before the advent of both Christianity and Islam to the continent.

239

An analysis of these definitions brings to light several issues. First, African theology as a term implies that this theology is not universal but is Africa-oriented thereby making it contextual theology in Africa, by Africans and for Africans. Second, it is a theology brewed in an African calabash (Orobator, 2008). Third, it refers to the efforts by Africans to reflect on Christianity, utilising African concepts and categories (Chitando, 2009). Fourth, it is a theology that aims to liberate African culture although African culture is an equivocal term. Fifth, almost all definitions including those not cited in this chapter, highlight the fact that African theology is intentionally designed to present Biblical Christianity to Africa in an African perspective.

Meiring (2007:733) holds that, "the Bible is very much an African book, in which African Christians and theologians see themselves and their people reflected and in which they find a personal place of dignity and acceptance before God." In spite of all the vigour demonstrated by these scholars to define African theology, their efforts were short changed first by their ignorance of the heritage left by the African Patristic Fathers who nursed the church in the turmoil of heresy and by their quiet diplomacy to theologise issues of God's involvement in African affairs and third by globalisation which is now the "modern" culture (Obioha, 2010).

"Foot in the academia and head in the West"? The dilemma of African theology

Although debates on African theology entered the theological discourse around the 1960s (Muzorewa, 1985; Parratt, 1997; Pobee, 1979; Dickson, 1984; Bujo, 1992; Bowers, 2000), this theology has its foot in African academia and head in the Eurocentric world. African theology remained abstract to the realities of African experiences of oppression, poverty, slave trade and land grabbing by the Western governments. By oppression, I am referring to the state of being subjected to oppressive treatment of Africans by the Western world. African theology did not manage to address Africa's socio-political, economic and theological challenges fully. These challenges, according to Tutu (1997), were a seedbed for Black theology in South Africa because African theology had failed to answer South African problems of colonial oppression, dispossession, exploitation, sorrow, bitterness, anger and hatred in the hands of the colonialists/imperialists. In differentiating the two theologies, Tutu avers that African theology grew out of the joys and experiences of the Christian faith whereas Black Theology emerges from the pain of oppression (Tutu, 1997: 39). Ferm (1990) categorised theology in Africa into two, liberative theology in South Africa namely Black theology and a theology that seek to respond to indigenous African religions called African theology.

Mbiti (2016) agrees to the above point as he stresses that the Western Christianity that had principally mediated the African faith since the 19th century was largely foreign to African culture, worldview and lifestyle, thus African theology is the panacea to this theological crisis. Although Mbiti thinks that by the close of the twentieth century Christian faith had fallen in love with Africa and Africa falling in love with Christianity, unfortunately African theology remained an elitist and academic speculative discourse. Chitando (2009:7) maintains that "although from its inception African theology emphasised on contextual relevance as a theological task that entails grappling with local realities, it did not live according to its pretexts".

It was unfortunate that in the process of trying to position itself, African theology failed to redefine African experiences in the twenty-first century. Borrowing the sociological discourse on Africa by Warikandwa, Nhemachena and Mtapuri (2017: xvii), "in theology, there are some of the fundamental issues that African theology remained a spectator to. African theology failed to include the action and agency of African people in their struggle for restoration and independence from colonialism and being neglected in a world that is paradoxically increasingly focused on the significance of contextless agency and action". For the three scholars, it is therefore important to understand that in the interest of justice, real democracy, freedom, liberty, agency and action, Africans must be sensitive to the contextual realities of the continent. And yet African theology did not have a word on these fundamental issues.

One of the reasons that made African theology to remain domiciled in the Western soil and yet growing within the African continent has been stressed by Fashloré-Luke (1975). Fashlore-Luke states that theological articulation in Africa has been done in the West for a long time, and theological education in the developing world has traditionally assumed the inviolability of the theological insights emanating from the West. Fashloré-Luke (1975) stresses that it is not without a touch of exasperation that African theologians continue to mouth theological platitudes they have picked up in universities, seminaries and colleges abroad or parade their erudition by quoting the latest theological ideas in Europe and North America. In critiquing Fashloré-Luke's observations, Dickson (1984:3) states that "the net effect of theological education in Africa generally had the effect of producing theologians who seem to be more at home with western theological thought even if such thought patterns appeal only to a certain level of their conscience". A case in point is Mbiti cited in Ferm (1988:69) who argues that "the Church in Africa is a Church without theology and a Church without theological concerns". Mbiti's anti-liberative expression of African theology agrees with Fashloré-Luke although the two seem to be antagonists: Fashloré-Luke thinks that African theology should suite the tongue, style, genius, character and culture of African people (Ferm, 1988:71).

Sundkler (1961) maintains that, theology in Africa must interpret Christ in terms that are relevant and essential for African existence. Mbiti buttresses Sundkler's assertion by expressing how Christianity strived to match Africa's theological mandate in the 21st century. Mbiti (2016: xix) holds that:

> Africa contributed to millions of churches and places of worship of every size and shape. The worship cannot be adequately defined as it includes shouting to the Lord, dancing, to the Lord, speaking in tongues, healing the sick, casting unwanted spirits, clearing the defiled spirits soliciting in business, family, examinations, spirits soliciting protection against the unwelcome forces of evil like possession by unwanted spirits, sickness unclean thoughts, witchcraft, unresponsive love etc.

In analysing Mbiti's statement, it shows that what is "relevant existence" in Africa is spiritualising issues with the mentality that

242

Africa is haunted with evil given that black is evil and white is purity. Mbiti like many other African theologians such as Charles Nyamiti (1984); Koffia Appiah-Kubi (1986); and Alywald Shorter (1988) did not pay attention to the issues of the dehumanisation of Africans that includes neocolonial dispossession, robbery, looting, exploitation, forced migration, human rights abuses, torture, rape, killings, abductions and the impact of transnational companies. Warikandwa, Nhemachena and Mtapuri (2017) state that global empires are controlling Africa from a distance terming them 'via global ideologies' and media controlling education, political, religious and social systems. Sadly, African theology is quiet on these issues.

From these debates, it is evident that ignoring the role of God, who is above cultures in Africa, is misfooting theology. African theology that was championed by the pioneers was theoretical more than it was practical. It was a theology defined more by colonialism (Parratt, 1997) than the words of God to the suffering Africans. African theologians had an opportunity to rehumanise Africa in the postcolonial era. Missionaries had had their chance to dehumanise Africans during the colonial era. In the postcolonial era, two strands of theology arose, and both were fighting to be called African theology. One strand was militant and the other was passive. The militant theology arose in South Africa as a voice of protest Black oppression and was named Black Theology. The other was concerned about the relationship of theology and culture and this became African Theology (Parratt, 1997).

African theologians lost an opportunity to make Christ speak in the African colonial history of dehumanisation and instead allowed the nationalists like Kwame Nkrumah a seminarian, Kenneth Kaunda, a son of the clergy, and Julius Nyerere, a Catholic, to define the fate of theology. African nationalism as espoused by Muzorewa (1985) was concerned with preserving African cultural heritage, including the justice attendant to restitution of land and other resources. It was a search for a theology that is relevant to the African cultural belief systems.

The pioneer African theologians rode on this culturated theology instead of liberative theology that had a rehumanised agenda. Liberative theology has the force to set Africans free from being treated as savages by both the missionaries and the colonisers. This is probably the reason why the likes of Bolaji Idowu (1973), John Mbiti (1969), Charles Nyamiti (1971); and Kwesi Dickson (1984), among other pioneer African theologians, had an African body whose head was grafted in Western philosophy. Some of these scholars tended to forget that Africa has always been a dialectical centre of oppression with Egypt and a place of God's hospitality during the time of Jesus.

Theologically, the Exodus history which is the basis of Judaism and Christianity locate Africa as the starting point of their theology. This history starts by God's involvements in the suffering of his people and this should remain the proper business of African theology today (Exodus 3: 7). The oppression of the weak in the Ancient Near East was never history in Africa as such. Concentrating on culture and ignoring the rehumanisation agenda of the African people is a serious error by African theology.

It is also evident that Africa produced key theologians who defended the church and redefined theology in the face of heresies as argued earlier. Africa also left an indelible inscription of Latin Christianity that bears the marks of Tertullian and Augustine (Cains, 1996). The Christian doctrines of Trinity, Ecclesiology, Pneumatology, Soteriology and the Creeds were formulated in Africa by African theologians (1996). Historically, the pride of monasticism and associated universities also traces its roots from Africa. Characters like Antony and Pachomius whose names come first in the history of monasticism were Africans whose call was necessitated by the favourable warm temperatures of Egypt. From the points raised above, theology was born in Africa and it addressed the fundamental issues of that day. When Christianity was transported and transmitted to Africa at the close of the nineteenth century it was never transplanted to grow in Africa. Africans received the residues of secularised Western Christianity instead of the rich tradition of African theology that was born and nursed in Africa.

(De) culturation as a process of eroding the African pride

In the introduction, two issues were raised as impediments of African pride. We will start with the missionary efforts to deculturate Christianity in Africa. Instead of reviving theology that had been brewed in Africa, they introduced Western culture that induced self-hatred among Africans. These misdemeanours explain their use of terms like "Africa is a Dark continent." Such claims were expressed by Tienou (1997:93) who cites one missionary William Caley as saying:

> ...four hundred and twenty millions...are still in pagan darkness...they have no written language, consequently no Bible, and are led by the most childish customs and traditions.... They are in general poor, barbarous, naked pagans, as destitute of civilization as they are of true religion.

Such derogatory and belittling of African religion led the missionaries to embark on what they called "lighting the Dark Continent". This process was far from being an innocent endeavour. The Western missionary activities in Africa came with a lot of Western theological orientation and colonialism in terms of their mission, theology and praxis. They did not only see their theology as superior but also imposed their theological worldview on African converts. This theology involved several factors that introduced Africans to Western religion or "Western culture" instead of theology, which is, "the language about God." Cook (2009:671) stresses that, "I observed in Africa that the experience of the people has too often been one in which their history has been suppressed, their culture despised, their spirituality alienated, and their communal values of solidarity and co-operation devalued." These processes were done with the aim of pacifying Africans and sock them in the Western philosophy that dehumanise them in the guise of enlightening the indigenes.

When African theology came onto the scene, it neither paid attention to the dehumanised Africans nor fashion their theological discourse towards rehumanising the locals. Until today, African theology does not have answers to the problems of Africa like neocolonial dispossession, robbery, exploitation, looting, corruption and abject poverty, land grabbing and plundering of African resources. Academically, African theology addresses the experiences and worldview of the people of Africa but practically it is silent on issues that haunt Africans every day. Schreiter (1991), subscribe to the notion that, for too long, embarrassing Christ and his message meant rejection of African culture, epistemologies and values, Africans were taught that their ancient ways were defiant or even evil and had to be set aside if they hoped to be Christians. Missionary theology made African Christianity invisible and inaudible. This of course was a specific manifestation of the problem of Christianity's reluctance or in some instances refusal or inability to incarnate itself in Africa. Up to this day, African Christianity is burdened by European structures, European mind-set and European culture is regarded as the starting point of Christianity in Africa (Schreiter, 1991).

One myth of White superiority was their definition of the "otherness" of Africans in terms of religion and epistemology. Accounts written by travellers commonly stated that Africans "had no religion" (Idowu, 1973). Commenting on the Batswana religious beliefs, Nkomazana (2016:33) argues that, "these sources generally reveal the cultural bias of the Europeans. They were sometimes based on inaccurate information and cultural prejudice. They made Tswana religion to appear to be a morass of bizarre beliefs and practices of a people generally believed to be "savages" and "primitive". "Savages" and "primitives" were the opposite of the missionaries who represented "European civilisation" (Nkomazana, 2016:33). These attitudes angered African theologians and they have been at pains to demonstrate that Africans traditionally did indeed have a religion that was not merely magic, but that it had a Creator God who provided for the needs of humanity. On one hand, Mbiti (1991: 1) began his book *African Religions and Philosophy* with the words: "Africans are notoriously religious". On the other hand, Idowu (1973) wrote that Africans are incurably religious in all things.

European travellers, anthropologists and missionaries also described African religion derogatively as fetishism, animism, ancestor worship, naturism, tribalism, paganism, primitive religion etc. Missionaries claimed that Africans were subhuman (Idowu, 1973). African theologians however castigated such terms as misguided but without attempting to rehumanise Africans using the Word of God as was done by South African Black Theology. For example, to say Africans had fetish, it entails that they used charm. Such terms were used to emphasise the supposed difference between Africans and Europeans: when an African performs a certain action, it is called "fetish-worship", but when a European does exactly the same thing, it is called "owning an amulet" (Evans-Pritchard, 1965). While the tendency had been to regard indigenous religions as 'fetishistic' and 'polytheistic', African Christian scholars emphasised the centrality of God in African indigenous religions (Chitando, 2000). Europeans also regarded Africans as having been adherents of "primitive" religions such as "animism". Evans-Pritchard (1965: 6) states that "animism meant "primitive" culture whose audience believe all things are animated with spirit or breath". Missionaries also used terms like naturism to suggest that Africans worship nature which was a theological distortion of African theological heritage.

In Africa, God has always been the foundation of life and so nothing happens without God. God lives and does not die. The way Africans experience God is portrayed in the language used about God, especially the names by which God is known. These names are not mere labels, but they are descriptive characters that depict Africans' experience of God. God has been with Africans from the beginning and features in prayers and greetings, blessings and curses. Africans always worshipped God called *Mwari* among the Shona, *Olodumare* in Yoruba, *Chukwu* in Nigeria, *Modimo* in Batswana, Katonda in Baganda and *Leza* in Zambia among other contextual African names of God.

Nkomazana (2016) accounts that the religion of the Batswana was from time immemorial monotheistic. This God is believed to be the Creator, Maker, Originator and Source of all things, including life and one too great to be directly approached by mortals. Idowu (1979:79) espouses that, there is no place, age, or generation which did not receive at some point in history some form of revelation from God and Africans are not an exception. For Healey and Syberts

(1996:295), "as people everywhere see one sun, so they all have one God suggesting that God was never brought to Africa but was always part of the African historical religion". Missionaries condemned local practices without proper evaluation of African religious beliefs and practices and authenticated them with their cultural and religious practices. In Africa, life is an endless act of worship. Indeed, from birth to death, this attitude to daily worship and the concept of personhood are pivotal (Parratt, 1997). In the missionaries' understanding, becoming a Christian also meant becoming 'White'. This in their view implies that conversion of Africans meant total denunciation of African culture and epistemology. Converts were thus expected to learn to behave, dress and act like the missionaries and the mission station was the centre of deculturality. The mission centres were meant to demean the African culture as spiritually evil and uncivilised thereby embracing the Euro-centric missionary cultures as spiritually life giving and humanely civilising (Mujinga, 2017).

Some missionaries that came to Africa were ill equipped for the task. They claimed to liberate the continent from darkness and yet they were bringing darkness and leaving Christ dressed in their Western regalia and did not allow him to speak with the Africans in the ghetto (see also Banana, 1990). Setiloane (1988) feels that African theology must liberate itself from these very foundations of Western theology because the widespread incidence of this practice attests to the fact that imported traditional theology from the West is inadequate for Africa.

Cook (2009) argues that Christ has been presented as the answer to the question a White man would ask and a curse to African questions. Udoh (1988) also mentions that Christ entered the African scene as a forceful, impatient and unfriendly tyrant. He was presented as invalidating the history and institutions of a people in order to impose his rule upon them. Many have experienced Jesus as an alien, a stranger who comes from elsewhere or, at best, a "guest" but one who has "no home" in Africa (Udo, 1988). We can go on and on arguing how Africa was despised. However, for Kealotswe (2016:51) it is not fruitful at this stage to keep pointing out the mistakes made by the missionaries and colonial powers in planting Christianity in

Africa. This point takes us to ask how African theology contributed in misfooting itself.

Decolonising African theology

Decolonisation is the meaningful and active reversal of processes and forces of colonialism that perpetuate the dispossession, biopiracy, robbery, exploitation, subjugation and the exploitation of African minds, bodies, and land. Its ultimate purpose is to overturn the colonial structure and realise indigenous liberation, including restitution and reparations (Waziyatawin & Yellow Bird, 2012). Whereas missionary theology made African theology to stand on the shaky ground, however, African theology also contributed to its own collapsing. First, African theology majored on culture without liberating the people from Western culture. The theme of liberation theology was common in Latin America, Asia and South Africa but rare in Africa in general. Segundo (2002:3) underscores that liberation of theology means a point of no return. Writing from a South African perspective, Boesak (1976:3) argues that, "behind the reality of the theology of liberation and the challenge it possesses for the Christian church are realities hitherto anxiously ignored by the theology of the western world - the realities of the rich and the poor, the oppressors and the oppressed or oppression and liberation from oppression". Boesak was at pains to explain that the Christian church has chosen to move through history with a bland kind of innocence, hiding these painful truths behind a façade of myths (Boesak, 1976: 5). It is this decision by African theologians that I would prefer to call "the quiet diplomacy of the beneficiaries". This diplomacy of majoring on the minor (liberal freedoms) and minoring on the major (colonial dispossession, suffering and exploitation) is no longer relevant. Theology in Africa must allow the dispossessed and oppressed who believe in God to move from believing in the myths of colonial/imperial superiority. Boesak holds that "it is no longer possible to innocently accept history as it happens silently hoping that God would take the responsibility for human failure".

The liberation of theology in Africa is an irreversible thrust in the Christian process of creating a new vista of consciousness and maturity in faith. This type of definition was not applicable to Africa where colonial/imperial culture was the letter and spirit of theologisation. It is sad that in anchoring theology on imperial/colonial culture, African scholars did not imagine that such a culture legitimises colonial dispossession, robbery, biopiracy and exploitation.

For African theology to be liberated from Eurocentric theologisation, first the prejudice that Europeans brought "civilisation" to uncivilised "primitives" who had no history, no culture, no epistemologies, no laws, no morality and no religion should be dispelled. Second, African theology should reinterpret the Bible in the context of the dispossessed, exploited and impoverished Africans. Adamo (2005), proposed a form of hermeneutics which amounts to a reaction against the Western and European Biblical interpretation. He argues that missionaries established Bible colleges and seminaries in Africa in which: theological studies were taught from a Eurocentric perspective. A typical example is at United Theological College in Zimbabwe where students of theology can articulate Western theologies with zest because the institution does not offer African theology as an important component to study (UTC Handbook, 2016). Theological students find it difficult to remember the theologies of some prominent theologians like John Mbiti (1969), Kwame Bediako (1997; 1999; 2000), Canaan Banana (1977; 1991) and Ezra Chitando (2000; 2009), among other African scholars. One of the reasons was well articulated by Katongole (2002) that African theology has been circulating in the theological seminaries without making sense to those who still view the Eurocentric theology as the starting point of theology. African theological teachers must abate their enthusiasm to teach students how to communicate the gospel of the Lord Jesus Christ in the Western thought forms and culture. This was overdone by missionaries who taught all students to learn how to interpret the Christian scripture the way it was interpreted in the West. African culture and religion were relegated to the background and therefore were not really taught to the students (Adamo, 2005).

Third, African theologians should take the Africans back to the crossroads and start rebuilding African Christianity where Jesus left

(Kealotswe, 2016). Theology in Africa must go back to the intersections, reread the Bible, reinterpret the teachings of Jesus and re-establish the church in Africa. Fourth, African theologians must have their total body in Africa where the head that is in Europe should join the feet that are in Africa and see how culture and suffering can join in addressing the situations using liberation theology tools of praxis and hermeneutics of suspicion.

Fifth, African theology should address real life experiences of Africans like colonial/imperial dispossession, biopiracy, exploitation and oppression of the Africans. African theology must also fight neo-colonisation by the Chinese. This theology must be the tool to liberate people from all forms of falsehood by politicians and neo-colonisers. Sixth, African theology must realise that decolonisation of culture and epistemology are no longer its enemy but the recolonisation of culture by globalization and the new empire. Ritzer (2008: 573) defines "globalization as the spread of worldwide practices, relations, consciousness, and organization of social life … that transforms people around the world with some transformation being dramatic". This cultural transformation for Ritzer affects the cultural identity of people that are being transformed. The key effect of globalisation is that African societies are forced into accepting uniform moral principles of what is right and wrong within the global cultures.

According to Obioha (2010:2) "globalization is not a value free, innocent, self-determining process, but is an international, socio-politico-economic and cultural permeation process facilitated by policies of government, private corporations, international agencies and civil society organizations". Giddens, cited in Yankuzo (2013:1) further defines globalisation as the intensification of world-wide social relations, which link distant localities in such a way that local happenings are shaped by events occurring many miles away and vice-versa. Yankuzo (2013: 2) stresses that globalisation is the coalescence of varied transnational processes and domestic structures, allowing the economy, politics, culture and ideology of one country to penetrate another. In this process, the chain of causality runs from the spatial reorganisation of production to international trade and to the integration of financial markets.

Globalisation, therefore, is a multi-dimensional process whereby cultural, economic and political relations increasingly take a global basis. Culture is the dominant perspective in Africa. This makes African (Cultural) theology to lose its identity in the global world of multiculturalism.

Obioha (2010) warns that no nation is an island to itself. In the process of international interactions, there is an interface of cultures and thus, a borrowing and diffusion of cultures amongst nations. Unfortunately, there is the plunder of one culture by the other. In the rise of a global culture, Western norms and practices are gradually being transported across the globe as the standard and acceptable way of behaviour. Africa is the hardest hit in this regard. The hitherto rich, cherished and dynamic African culture has been diluted if not totally eclipsed.

Conclusion

Jesus addressed the contemporary issues of oppression of his day. African theologians and Christians should address issues of colonial/imperial dispossession, biopiracy, looting, plunder, robbery, exploitation and impoverishment on the continent of Africa. African theology is also challenged to expose the dehumanisation of Africans, colonial/imperial dispossession, robbery and oppression all of which are haunting African peoples. In the light of the fact that colonialism and imperialism destroyed African cultures and epistemologies, it is imperative for decolonial scholars and thinkers to ensure that African cultures and epistemologies are revived and recentred.

References

Adamo, D. T. (2005). *Decolonizing teaching of Old Testament in Africa*. Abraka : Delta State University.

Appiah-Kubi. K (1986). *The ecumenical importance of African theology. Voices from the Third World*. New York: Orbis Books.

Banana, C. S. (1990). *The gospel according to the ghetto*. Gweru: Mambo Press.

Bediako, K. (1997). *Christianity in Africa: The renewal of a non-western religion*. Edinburgh: Edinburgh University Press.

Bediako, K. (1999). *Theology and identity: The impact of culture upon Christian thought in the second century and in modern Africa*. Carlisle: Regnum Books in Association with Lynx Communications.

Bediako, K. (2000). *Jesus and the gospel in Africa: History and experience*. Nashville: Orbis Books.

Boesak, A. A. (1976). *Farewell to innocence: A Socio-ethical study on Black Theology and Black power*. New York: Orbis Books.

Bowers, P. (2002). African theology: Its history, dynamics, scope and future. *African Journal of Evangelical Theology, vol* 21(2. 109-125.

Bujo, B.(1992). *African theology in its social context*. Maryknoll, NY: Orbis Books.

Cains , E. E. (1996). *Christianity through theh Centuries: A History of the Christian Church*. Zondervan: Grands Rapids.

Chitando , E. (2009). *Troubled but not Destroyed: African Theology in Dialogue with HIV and AIDS*. Geneva: World Council of Churches.

Chitando, E. (2000). African Christian scholars and the study of African Traditional Religions: A Re-evaluation. *Journal of Religion in Africa vol* 30(4). 391-397.

Cook , J. S. (2009). The African experience of Jesus. *Theological Studies* Vol 70. 678-691.

Dickson, K. (1984). *Theology in Africa*. London : Longman and Todd.

Evans-Pritchard, E. E. (1965). *Nuer religion*. London: Oxford University Press.

Fashlore-Luke , E. W. (1975). The quest for an African Christian Theology. *Ecumenical Review*. *https://doi.org/10.1111/j.1758-6623.1975.tb01173.x.*

Ferm, D. W. (1984). *Third World theologians: An introductory survey*. Maryknoll: Orbis Books.

Gifford, P. (2008). Africa's inculturation: Observation of an outside. *Hekima Review* Vol 38. 18-34.

Healey, J. & Sybertz, D. (1996). *Towards an African narrative theology*. Maryknoll: Orbis Books.

Idowu, E. (1962). *Oludumare : God in Yoruba belief*. London: Oxford University Press.

Idowu, E. (1973). *African Traditional Religion : A definition*. London: SCM Press.

Katongole, E. (2002). *African Theology Today*. Eugene, Oregon: Wipf and Stock.

Kealotswe, O. (2016). African Christianity in colonial times, in Phiri, I. A. *et al.*, (eds). *Anthology of African Christianity*. Pietermaritzburg: Cluster Publications.

Magezi, C. & Igba, J. T. (2018). African Theology and African Christology: Difficulty and complexity in contemporary definitions and methodological frameworks. *HTS Teologiese Studies/Theological Studies* 74(1), 4590. https://doi.org/10.4102/hts.v74i1.4590

Martey, E. (1993). *African theology*. Maryknoll Orbis Books.

Mbiti, J. S. (1979a). "The Biblical bais for the present trends in African t heology". In *African Theology en route*. Maryknoll: Orbis Books, pp. 83-94.

Mbiti, J. S. (1991). *African religion and philosophy*. New York: Doubleday.

Mbiti, J. S. (2016). Foreword, in Phiri, I. A. *et al.*, (eds). *Anthology of African Christianity*. Pietermaritzburg: Cluster Publications.

Meiring, A. (2007). As below, so above: A perspective on African theology. *HTS Theological Studies / Teologiese Studies* Vol 63(2). 733-750.

Mujinga, M. (2017). *Historical development of Methodism: A North-South paradigm*. Harare: Connexional Bookshop.

Muzorewa, G. H.(1985). *The origins and development of African Theology*. Eugene, Oregon: Wipf and Sock Publishers.

Nhemachena, A. *et al.*, (2018) Identity, originality and hybridity in jurisprudence and social theory: An Introduction, in Nhemachena, A., Warikandwa, T. V. & Amoo, S. K. (eds) *Social and Legal Theory in the Age of Decoloniality: (Re-)Envisioning Pan-African Jurisprudence in the 21st Century*. Bamenda: Langaa RPCIG.

Nkomazana, F. & Senzokuhle , D. S. (2016). Missionary colonial mentality and the expansion of Christianity in Bechuanaland Protectorate, 1800 to 1900. *Journal for the Study of Religion* Vol 29(2). 29 - 55.

Nyamiti, C. (1971). *African theology: Its nature, problems and methods.* Kampala: Gaba Publications.

Nyamiti, C. (1984). Christ as our ancestor: Christology from an African perspective. Gweru: Mambo Press.

Obioha, U. P. (2010). Globalization and the future of African culture. *Philosophical Papers and Reviews* Vol 2(1). 1-8.

Orobator, A. E. (2008). *Theology brewed in an African pot.* Maryknoll, New York: Orbis Books.

Parratt, J. (1997). *A reader in African theology.* London : SPCK.

Pobee, J. S. (1979). *Toward an African theology.* Nashville: Abingdon Press .

Ritzer, G. (2008). *Sociological theory.* New York, NY: McGraw-Hill

Setiloane, G. M. (1988). *African theology: An introduction.* Johannesburg: Skotaville Publishers.

Shreiter, R. J. (1991). *Faces of Jesus in Africa.* Maryknoll: Orbis Books.

Sundkler, B. (1961). *Bantu prophets in South Africa.* London : Lutterworth.

Tienou, T. (1997). *Authentic African Christianity: A Reader in African theology.* London: SPCK, pp. 91-98.

Tutu, D. (1997). Black theology and African theology: Soulmates or anatagonist?, in Parratt, J. (ed) *A Reader in African Theology.* London: SPCK, 36-44.

Udoh, E. B. (1988). *Guest Christology: An interpretative view of the Christological problem in Africa: Studies in the intercultural history of Christianity.* Frankfurt : Peter Lang .

United Theological College. *Handbook* (2016).

Warikandwa, T. V., Nhemachena, A. & Mtapuri, O. (2017). *Transnational land grabbing and the restitution in an age of the (de) militarized new scamble for Africa. A pan-African socio-legal pespecctive.* Bamenda: Langaa RPCIG.

Waziyatawin, T & Yellow Bird, M. (2012). *For indigenous minds Only: Santa Fe. A decolonization handbook,* School of American Research Press.

White, P. (2017). Decolonising Western missionaries' mission theology and practice in Ghanaian Church history: A Pentecostal approach. ', In die Skriflig 51(1), a2233. https://doi.org/ 10.4102/ids.v51i1.2233

Yankuzo, K. I. (2013). Impact of globalization on the traditional African cultures. *International Letters of Social and Humanistic Sciences* 15 . 1-8.

Chapter Ten

Pentecostalism and the Suppression of African Indigenous Religion: The Rejection of African Spiritism in the Apostolic Faith Mission (AFM) in Zimbabwe

Collins Nhengu

Introduction

The AFM missionaries who arrived in Zimbabwe in 1915 exuded colonial superiority over African indigenous beliefs and epistemologies to the extent of excluding African beliefs and epistemologies in their churches. In this regard, the missionaries demonised African ancestors that could have been sources of indigenous epistemologies much in the same was European philosophers, mystics and scientists like Rene Descartes relied on their dreams to establish science (see introductory chapter to this book). The missionaries were bent on erasing and editing African originality, history and spirituality and so they adopted an exclusivist model in engaging indigenous cultures and epistemologies. They arrogantly and scornfully depicted the African indigenous religions as animistic, primitive, magic, fetish, barbaric and witchcraft. These colonial missionary descriptions of the African Indigenous Religions (AIR) are misleading because they were only meant to justify the colonial enterprise and, in the process, legitimise the colonial plunder of the African resources and heritage. The intention of the missionaries was to paint Africa black and inferior to Western religiosity. The missionaries treated African cultures and religions with suspicion. Strictly speaking, the missionaries espoused mono-cultural make up with superiority inclinations. Consequently, Christianity was seen as inerrant and invincible. The idea of mono-culturalism is in contrast to religious pluralism which believes that all religions provide valid premises to the existence of God (Chad, 2008:31). The missionaries asserted that they alone represent the one true church to which Jesus gave his authority for the great commission. The great commission is the gist of evangelism that saw the spreading of Christianity from Jerusalem to the ends of the world. The great commission is the mother of such movements like the AFM in Zimbabwe. The AFM church has remained cast in Western theology which is oppressive of African Indigenous Religions. Spiritism in African Indigenous Religions is viewed by the AFM church as demonic even though like Christianity African Traditional Religion possessed its own African saints. For this reason, the concept of spiritism was suppressed in the church. Hence the rejection of African spiritism by the AFM church. Critically interrogating the position of the church, this chapter is based on interviews with members of the AFM.

The concept of spiritism[1] in African Indigenous Religions has been vehemently rejected by the Pentecostal movements in Zimbabwe, and in Africa. However, it must be noted that this phenomenon permeates the African Indigenous Religion and its operations and activities so much that it is at the core of African beliefs and culture. To take away this prodigy is to extirpate the lifeblood of the African Indigenous Religion. There remains a surety to the effect that the concept of spiritism is as important to African indigenous religion as it is to the Pentecostal movements when they experience the Holy Spirit and speaking in tongues. In addition, the Christian concept of sainthood can be equated to the concept of ancestorship in African Indigenous Religion. The process of making one a saint has similarities with how one becomes an ancestor in African Indigenous Religions. There are qualifications required for one to acquire that status. By dismissing African spiritism, Christianity fails to penetrate the heart of the African soul. What Pentecostalism has done is to demonise the phenomenon in so far as it relates to the African indigenous Religions. The demonisation rests on the premise that the African Indigenous Religion itself has been trashed to the dustbin by those movements that have been sired by Western Religiosity of which AFM is the product. Machingura, (2010) asserts that spiritism as understood in African Indigenous Religions is taken as wholly other and as evil spirits. Missionaries and the AFM church suppress African ancestors who are summarily described as pagan. The AFM adherents believe that for someone who has been born again it is unchristian to apotheosise the ancestors because it represents an old life of which when one becomes a Christian that old life is left behind, and one has a new life in Christ Jesus. According to Anderson (1993), Pentecostals are more forthright in their rejection of these traditional practices which they see as incompatible with their Christianity.

Apostolic Faith Mission theology and culture

Clark and Lederie (1989:8) avow that providing an account of the rise of the Pentecostal movement is no straightforward task. This assertion is also true of the Zimbabwean scenario. It is important to highlight that there is a dearth of written sources and what constituted early preaching and practices of the founding fathers of the Apostolic Faith Mission in Zimbabwe. John G Lake, the founder of AFM, had his work published long after his exodus.[2] The works were published in the South African monthly magazine called Comforter and Messenger of Hope. When the first publication was printed in 1948, the AFM church was already well established and fully operational in Zimbabwe. According to Synan (1997), many of the early Pentecostal movements can be traced back to the Holiness movement and to this day, many classical Pentecostals maintain much of the Holiness doctrine and many of its devotional practices. There is no doubt, however, that the AFM grew out of the Holiness movement in the United States of America. However, one wonders why the holiness factor could not inform these missionaries about the evil of colonising, dispossessing and exploiting indigenous Africans. Colonisation was day light robbery, plundering and looting of African resources including land and livestock. Darkness was at work here and indeed this was not in sync with the Bible they read which says light and darkness have nothing in common: "....... for what fellowship hath righteousness with unrighteousness? And what communion hath light with darkness?" (2 Cor. 6:14)

Surely holiness cannot co-habit with colonial plunder, theft and robbery of which the missionaries were accomplices. While they preached the gospel, they were looting in the name of religion. Gish,

(2004:101) quotes Desmond Tutu thus: "When the missionaries came to Africa they had the bible and we had the land they said, "let us pray." we closed our eyes. When we opened them, we had the Bible and they had the land."

Latourette (1975: 1167) points out that the holiness movement stressed baptism with power and Holy Spirit with immediate occurrence of supernatural intervention. The Holiness movement involves a set of beliefs and practices which emerged chiefly within 19th-century Methodism. The movement is Wesleyan-Arminian in theology (Olson, 2009:25). The movement denied the validity of the religious worldview of potential converts. As the AFM missionaries went out to evangelise in Zimbabwe [from South Africa], they demanded cultural change for converts. There was no constructive dialogue between Pentecostal Christianity and African social and cultural traditions. Many Africans began to challenge AFM Christology as biased and superficial. AFM spread by eroding African beliefs, epistemologies and practices.

The history of the holiness movement is important in that it has a bearing on the theology of the AFM in Zimbabwe. Holiness movement was strictly pivoted on Jesus as the only way to heaven. Vinson (1997:6) asserts that characteristic feature of the holiness movement is its emphasis on the second work of grace leading to Christian perfection. The AFM church in Zimbabwe emphasizes this doctrine as central to its belief system. The Holiness movement's absolute dependence on Jesus and baptism in the Holy Spirit with the evidence of speaking in tongues impacted negatively on culture and indigenous knowledge systems. The cardinal ingredient of the Holiness movement is that the individual is cleansed of the tendency to commit sin. It is referred to as entire sanctification which enables the believer to live a holy life without wilful sin. It is of paramount significance to note that the Holiness movement emphasised the 'Wesleyan-Armenian doctrine of outward holiness which includes the wearing of modest clothing and not using profanity in speech as well as nonconformity to the world' (Headley, 2014). Holiness groups believe the moral aspects of the law of God are pertinent for today, and so expect their adherents to obey behavioural rules for example, many groups have statements prohibiting the consumption of alcohol, participation in any form of gambling, and other such forms of entertainment. The motto of the Holiness people comes from the book of 1 Peter 1:16 which says *'Be ye holy as I am holy.'* They believe that the holy actions must replace the unholy ones. This is the basis of the AFM theology.

The AFM heritage is derived from the Holiness movement which anchors its teaching on the fact that African culture and epistemologies are patterned according to the mould of this world. Thus, African culture and epistemologies supposedly reflect unholy actions and must be replaced with the holy actions of missionary teachings. Another central feature of the Holiness movement is that the Methodist church played a pivotal role in the spreading of the gospel in Zimbabwe. Matikiti (2018) opines that while some may dispute this fact, it must be noted that the most anointed and effective evangelists in Zimbabwe came out of the Methodist Church. These are the Apostles of the 1930s, 1940s and the 1950s and they became the key figures and spiritual leaders of the Apostolic Faith Mission in Zimbabwe. It was through the outreach activities of the Methodist Church that many people came to know the gospel of Jesus Christ. However, most of these evangelists left the Methodist church because of the problem of doctrine. Some of them began to pray for the sick while others began to cast out demons from the people; others spoke in tongues. The demons that were cast out of the people include what the African indigenous adherents referred to as ancestral spirits. While others left the church voluntarily to start their own movements, there are others who were expelled from the church and those who were expelled were the likes of Paul Mwazha who formed his own church known as the African Apostolic Church (AAC). Whether they were expelled, or they left voluntarily, the bottom line is that these people have a belief system that is traced to the Holiness movement.

History of the Apostolic Faith Mission

In tracing the history of the AFM, it is necessary to note that scholarly work concerning this church is very scarce. However, of late there are some scholars that are coming up with literature in relation to this church. In this regard, the works of Hwata, (2005), Maxwell (2006) Togarasei, (2016), Musariri (2018), Ndlovu (2018), Matikiti, (2018), and others shall be used in this chapter. Togarasei (2006) points out that while it is confirmed that AFM is the largest and the earliest Pentecostal movement in Zimbabwe, very little has been written about this church. For him, some of the reasons why the church has very little information about its history is because firstly, it was not recognised by the government. Secondly, the church was started by people who were illiterate hence they did not keep proper records as was the case with mainline churches. Thirdly, the church did not engage social services such as health and education hence it did not attract much attention from the public. Probably, the reason why such social services as health were not engaged is because they did not believe in people going to hospital, but they believed in praying for the sick and getting them healed. Going to hospital was regarded as a sin which must be confessed if it was discovered that a congregant consulted a doctor.

The history of the AFM in Zimbabwe can be traced back to South Africa where it was given birth to by John G. Lake and Thomas Hezmalhach. They were the products of the Azusa street revival that was started by a group of the Pentecostal charismatics led by Charles Fox Parham and William Seymour in 1906. Seymour gave assent to John G. Lake and Thomas Hezmalhach in 1908 to start a mission in Africa. They left for South Africa in April 1908 and they arrived on 14 May 1908 (Maxwell, 2006). With the arrival of Lake and his fellow preachers, the Dutch Reformed Church was greatly weakened in its stability. The team took advantage of this and rode on the wings of the already established Zion Pentecostal movement in South Africa. That led to the formation of a very solid Pentecostal movement that became a force to reckon with. South Africa was a good breeding ground for AFM because there were so many people moving from surrounding countries into South Africa in search of greener pastures particularly in mining towns. Togarasei (2016:3), states that the church began to spread to those neighbouring countries through these migrant workers who would be travelling back to their home countries. These migrant workers adopted the Pentecostal religion which they would then carry with them back home. Such was the case with the spread of AFM to Zimbabwe. These workers went back to their native lands and began to spread the gospel which they adopted during their stay in South Africa. What it means is that even before the recorded case of the famous Zacharias Manamela, who is said to have set ablaze the area of Gwanda with the Pentecostal gospel in 1915/16, one can say that the Pentecostal gospel under the banner of AFM was already in full swing in some parts of Zimbabwe. It was spread by migrants from Johannesburg; often called *vana Mujubheki* which is an appellation for the returning migrant workers. The reasons raised by Togarasei (2016) which are; lack of education, failure to engage social services and that it was not a recognised movement, made the church's history to remain veiled in obscurity. However, the little information available shows that Zacharias Manamela is the pioneer of the AFM church in Zimbabwe and that he laid the foundation for this church. Scholars such as Hwata (2005); Maxwell (2006) and Togarasei (2016) have also added their voices in this regard. But in addition to these scholars, there are other popular church historians who echo the same sentiments. Togarasei (2016:3) cites the AFM in Zimbabwe New Life Assembly Church of Chitungwiza website which says the following on the history of the church: "The work of the AFM in Zimbabwe is said to have begun in 1915 in Gwanda through the preaching of Zacharias Manamela, a convert of the AFM of South Africa."

This is confirmation that AFM was pioneered by Manamela although it cannot be dismissed that other migrant workers from South Africa could also have contributed to the spreading of AFM. Maxwell (2000), opines that as early as 1917, there were already about four hundred AFM adherents within Gwanda, in Southern Rhodesia, or present-day Zimbabwe. When Manamela visited Zimbabwe, his visit was not official. But it should be noted that although his visit was unofficial, the church officials in Johannesburg saw the work that he did when he came into Zimbabwe and they recognised this as very significant in the spreading of the gospel. These officials are said to have sent Rev. G. J. Booysen from Louis Trichard (Makhado) in order to facilitate the registration of the church with the Rhodesian authorities. When Manamela came into Zimbabwe, it is not clear how long he stayed and the extent of the work that he did. History seems to indicate that he did not stay long in Gwanda as is shown by the fact that he was succeeded by Mr Kgobe who worked under the leadership of Rev. Booysen. Ncube (2018), is of the opinion that Manamela was deported by the Rhodesian authorities to South Africa in 1916 because his church was not registered and there was suspicion in his miracle working powers. Kgobe's stint revolved around the working of miracles that is faith healing practices. Unfortunately, the working of miracles by Kgobe received heavy criticism from the government for the same reasons that made Manamela to be deported. Chandomba, (2007) avows that this criticism led to the church failing to receive official acceptance, which dampened its spirit of evangelism. Nonetheless, even though the government did not officially recognise the church, this did not deter the movement which soldiered on with the work of the preaching of the gospel. Amid all these hurdles, the church acquired a farm in 1919 in Gobatema, south of Gwanda. It was this farm that the evangelists used as their base from which they operated. The church tried frantically to operate a school which they wanted to build on this farm, but their efforts were hampered by the colonial government which closed the school on the ground that the church had not been officially registered by the government.

Later, about four years after the arrival of Manamela, the church was introduced in Kadoma by Luttig. His work in Kadoma was so successful that several people gave their lives to Jesus. According to Dillon-Malone (1978), Luttig, who was a South African based European, was working with a preacher whose name was John Wesley Dingiswayo. Dillon-Malone is of the opinion that the church was introduced by Luttig in 1918. However, the evidence that the church was already operational in Gwanda from 1915 was so widespread that attributing the work to Luttig constituted a clear contradiction of historical facts. Some of the people that were converted by Luttig were the ones who became the early leaders of the church in Zimbabwe. From the works of Hallencreutz (1999) and Togarasei (2010) it is shown that Luttig and some of the preachers that he travelled with, that is, Bodenhorst and Dingesaku, introduced Pentecostalism in Harare. But Togarasei notes that much of the work in Harare is attributed to Enock Gwanzura. Despite these efforts, the

Pentecostal features of the church (especially glossolalia and faith healing) led it to be denied official status. The authorities were not happy with the way the church operated.

In the 1920s the overseer of the AFM in Johannesburg, Bosman, resettled to Gobatema in Gwanda to work on church recognition but he was not successful. Kruger did the same but this time operating from Harare following the South African AFM's decision to make Southern Rhodesia a mission field independent from South Africa. Still the church could not be officially recognised. Maxwell (2006) gives a number of reasons why the church was not recognised, but as Togarasei (2010: 21) argues, the more likely explanation is that the AFM missionaries caused political uneasiness by freely roaming through the reserves without observing the missionary boundaries that the colonial government seems to have instituted. Ndlovu (2018), is of the opinion that the entrance of AFM into Rhodesia was viewed with great suspicion by the Rhodesian government due to the developments that had taken place in Nyasaland (Malawi) as a result of the John Chilembwe uprising. Ruzivo (2014) similarly argues that the missionary outreach of the AFM came to Zimbabwe (Rhodesia) in 1915 and unfortunately coincided with the John Chilembwe uprising in Malawi. Duncan (2015), points out that the John Chilembwe uprising was a rebellion against British colonial rule in Nyasaland in January 1915 led by John Chilembwe, an American-educated black millenarian Christian. Therefore, the uprising hardened Rhodesian authorities' response to Pentecostalism. Related to this was also the fact that the AFM missionary work was not clearly organised and coordinated. The faith healing practices and glossolalia (speaking in tongues) made people very uncomfortable because they were only used to the kind of worship that was practiced by the mainline churches.

Ndlovu (2018), points out that Kruger was appointed the overseer of the church that was based in Harare (formerly Salisbury). But even if that was the case, the *laissez faire* attitude of Pentecostal evangelists continued to damage the image of the church. Hwata (2005: 28) made a very interesting observation when he asserts that parallels could be drawn between the speaking in tongues of the AFM church and the spirit possession of the African Indigenous Religion, as well as witchcraft. For Hwata, AFM's glossolalia and faith healing; and traditional spirit possession and witchcraft eradication practices, made the local chiefs and native commissioners to be suspicious of the Christianity preached by the AFM missionaries. This led to a drawback in relation to the registration of the church that had been achieved by Kruger in 1934. Togarasei (2010: 21), posits that the official recognition by the government that Kruger had achieved in early 1931 was withdrawn in 1934. However, the fire of the Pentecostal gospel could not be doused, as such, the lack of official recognition did not hog-tie the escalation of the Pentecostal gospel in Zimbabwe. By the 1930s one can say the Pentecostal storm was blowing through the country, sending vibrations and shock waves disturbing established mainline churches. Though this was the case the state eventually recognised the church and it was given an official status through state registration in 1943 under the leadership of Enoch Gwanzura. As has been noted by many scholars (Hallencreutz, 1999; Maxwell, 2006; Togarasei, 2010), this 'pentecostalisation' of Zimbabwean Christianity through the AFM gave birth to several African Initiated Churches (AICs). The AFM is a product of its own environment. The philosophies that surrounded it are those of the superiority of the White people. It was born in racist America when racism was still very rife. Matikiti (2017) points out that often the gospel has been transported garbed in the paraphernalia of Western culture. Pentecostalism was to transmigrate from America then South Africa and eventually landed in Zimbabwe. The idea was that the church was invading the darkness that was enveloping the "Dark Continent". It should be noted that AFM was not part of the pioneer column that occupied Zimbabwe: it was a late comer and land was not parcelled to the church as it was with Roman Catholic and other mainline churches.

The Kerygma of the early AFM Missionaries

The message of the early missionaries was based strictly on Jesus Christ giving no room for any ideas from other cultural beliefs. Copeland (1995) in Pavari (2011:82), quotes a snippet of Lake's (1914) message:

When the conception of a Christian has been established within our spirits as the New Testament establishes the ideal of Christian, we understand then how it is that men have been ready to abandon all else in the world in order to attain Christ, in order to become the possessor of His Spirit.

A closer look at the words of Lake shows that this means abandoning traditional cultural practices to follow the culture of the Bible. But what is interesting is the fact that, as Matikiti (2017) points out, William J. Seymour's Azusa Street revival, of which AFM is connected, formed the most prominent and significant centre of Pentecostalism. Such Pentecostalism was predominantly Black and had its leadership rooted in the African culture of the nineteenth century. Nevertheless, notwithstanding the cultural connection, when AFM arrived in Zimbabwe, it was against the cultural practices of the people of Zimbabwe. One is made to think that this was the reason why the missionaries were at loggerheads with the indigenous people for they were accused of being in the same boat with the colonialists. Machingura, (2010) is of the view that the missionaries were fronting the Bible in order to clear the way for the colonialists. They were accused of preaching the gospel to pacify the natives while they were squandering their resources. The Early missionaries therefore adopted the exclusivist mode of preaching.

Key to the AFM kerygma is the concept of demonology. Demonology is the study of demons, especially the methods used to summon and control them. Demons when regarded as spirits may belong to either of the classes of spirits recognised by primitive animism. This is captured clearly in the sermon of John G Lake as stated in Pavari:

> Every student of the primitive church discerns at once the distinction between the soul of the primitive Christian and the soul of the modern Christian. It lies in the spirit of Christ's dominion. The Holy Spirit came into the primitive Christian soul to elevate his consciousness in Christ, to make him a master. He smote sin and it disappeared he cast out devils (demons); a divine flash from his nature overpowered and cast out the demon. He laid his hands on the sick and

the mighty Spirit of Jesus Christ flamed into the body and the disease was annihilated (Pavari, 2011:62)

In the eyes of Lake, African culture was characterised by demonology. He equated primitiveness to the work of the devil. African culture was supposedly primitive culture. In Lake's view, deities of other religions are interpreted or created as demons. These deities have evil qualities. His ideas developed from a simple acceptance of the existence of demons. Christianity is regarded as the only true religion in spiritual warfare with African traditional religion. African supernatural entities were considered malevolent or even evil. Christians detached themselves from the culture of their surrounding world. They never borrowed principles of managing the church of God from the systems of the world. According to Bosch (1991:455) Western missionaries domesticated the gospel in their own culture while making it unnecessarily foreign to other cultures.

The gospel preached by Lake was transported to Zimbabwe by the first AFM missionary to Zimbabwe, Zacharias Manamela. He was a convert of AFM in South Africa. His triumphalist gospel found resonance with people of Gwanda in the southern part of Zimbabwe. His preaching was characterised by the manifestation of demons which is a key feature of Pentecostalism. Manamela emphasised the invincibility of Jesus in the manner of Thomas Hazmalhalch and John G. Lake of AFM in South Africa. The AFM became a church of choice in Gwanda. The speaking of tongues and healing were draw cards for the AFM within the Gwanda area particularly those who were affected spiritually found refuge in a new church that emphasised the power of healing in Jesus alone. In his preaching of Jesus Christ Manamela emphasised that there is no salvation in any other name except the name of Jesus. Thus, the worshipping of ancestors was regarded as devilish and unacceptable to those who have received Jesus. AFM, like all other members of the Pentecostal movements, follows Manamela's gospel. They are unanimous in their rejection of the ancestral spirits and all the rituals that are associated with them. According to Anderson (1993), the ancestors are believed to exist, but the Christians do not have anything to do with them or make ritual killings for them. However, colonialists, missionaries and other churches 'ritually' killed the Africans by 'ritually' dispossessing them and robbing them of their heritage. They took their land, livestock and artefacts which make up the African culture, yet they demonised the same culture. This is tantamount to hypocrisy. Matikiti (2018) decried the European supervision of African missionaries as tantamount to superiority complex. This led to African rejection of Eurocompliance or Americancompliance in Christian faith. In the same manner Manamela was being supervised by Rev. G.J. Booysen. White Superiority saw African leaders being supervised by Whites to make sure that they conformed to the gospel that was preached back in South Africa. There was no room for accommodating African culture.

According to Matikiti (2018), another revered missionary is Paul Kruger. He was a towering figure in AFM so much that the church was referred to as the church of Kruger. This shows that Kruger was a missionary connoisseur who penetrated the tightly knit culture of Zimbabwe and brought the gospel to the people. According to Rev. Shumbambiri in one of his sermons at the AFM quarterly conference, it was during the time of Kruger that a lot of Africans stopped respecting ancestors: they started destroying ancestral regalia and artefacts. This is reminiscent of the preaching of the Apostles in the book of Acts of the Apostles (Acts 19:19). Mujeyi (2006) asserts that Kruger is famous for converting and nurturing outstanding leaders of the AFM such as Mashavave, Mugodhi, Chiumbu, Masembe, the Gwanzura brothers, Mutemererwa and Kupara. These became African leaders of the blossoming AFM church.

Among these leaders Langton Kupara became the first A.F.M.Z.'s Black Superintendent in 1983. He took over from Pastor Gashwend who gave him a golden watch. The watch was a symbol of passing on the baton to the African leadership. According to Madziyire and Risinamhodzi (2016:73), Pastor Gashwend officially handed over AFM. to African leadership in 1983. Ruzivo (2014) is of the opinion that the handing over of the church to the Blacks was necessitated by the Zimbabwean attainment of independence in 1980. The Whites were not very comfortable with the government of Robert Mugabe whom they suspected would not allow the Whites to remain in the country because of his Marxist policies. So, the handing over of the church to the Blacks was a way of safeguarding the church and ensuring its continuity by the Black government would respect the African leadership.

When Langton Kupara died in 1988, his deputy Jeffries Mvenge took over as the next President. Ndlovu (2018) argues that Mvenge trained as a pastor in Kasupe Bible College in Zambia and on his return, was assigned to be a pastor of the AFMZ in Manicaland Province. He established leadership structures, which enabled elders to be sole authorities of their assemblies during that time. Mvenge was the first to be given the substantive title of President. Madziyire and Risinamhodzi (2016) state that Mvenge retired in 1996 and his Deputy President Rev. Stephen Mutemererwa was elected the President. Reverend Enos Manyika was Stephen Mutemererwa's Deputy President and was elected his successor in the year 2000 after Mutemererwa's retirement. According to Madziyire and Risinamhodzi (2016:95) professionally, Manyika was an upholsterer but he found a high-paying job as a bookkeeper at the then Founders' Building Society Bank in 1970s. Aspher Madziire took over from Manyika. Ndlovu (2018) states that the presidency of Madziyire was prophesied by Prophetess Mashamba who prophesied that he was going to be a great servant of God. The gospel that was preached by all these leaders was not different from that which was sown by the pioneers of AFM. They stood unequivocally on the idea that those that are in Christ are new creatures, the old things (of the world, following the ancestral worship) have passed away now in Christ all things have become new.

The African Christians murmur because of the inability of the Pentecostal Christians to recognise the value of African culture as a world treasure. The Early missionary enterprise to Zimbabwe has always looked at the African culture as something that is "primitive" and has no capacity to add value to human existence. This provides us with a very important lesson in that the missionaries have never wanted to recognise the African culture as valuable. The African culture was demonised to the extent that Africans themselves began to see the Western culture as superior to the African culture. The missionaries have treated the culture as barbaric simply because it was practiced by a people who were targeted for colonisation.

Matikiti (2018) observed that in pursuit of ideological thinking, the language of missiology was characterised by what has been termed as the "theology of the curse." For him, Missionaries who came later did not change course. The theology of the curse is based on the Western myth that Africa is "the land of the deepest, darkest, heathen night." It should be noted that African culture cannot be divorced from African religion and epistemology. In practicing culture, the Africans will simultaneously be practicing religion. It is these practices that were referred to as "magic" simply because they were not understood by the White missionaries. So, the White missionaries imposed their understanding of God on the Africans. Those that got converted to Christianity were made to renounce their allegiance to the African culture. Machingura (2011) points out that the AFM, just like other Pentecostal churches in Zimbabwe, exhibits an aggressive assault and intolerance towards certain aspects of the African culture which they label as tradition. This includes such aspects as paying homage to the ancestral spirits, *kurova guva* (that is the bringing back of the spirit of the dead to look after the family), and marriage customs. These aspects are painted as "primitive" and "demonic". The young generations who did not want to hear anything about these traditional practices flocked to the AFM church. Martin (1996), asserts that the movement has managed to rid itself of the dominance of the male adults and the floodgates were opened to young men and women, who are supposedly the victims of traditional "patriarchy".

In their quest for saving souls, the missionaries regarded anything that did not sound Western and not in the Bible as unchristian and pagan. In fact, the African religion which is interwoven with the African culture is not classified under world religions. While the Europeans do not classify African Indigenous Religion as a world religion, they ironically want to usurp African Heritage sites as world heritage sites. James (2018) asserts that a World Heritage site is a natural or cultural site that the world community regards as having immense universal value. Ironically, these sites are not divorced from the African religion. Bishau (2018) argues that they are places where African Indigenous Religion is practiced. Matikiti (2018) points out that the reason why they value heritage sites and not African Indigenous Religion is because the sites are a source of tourist funds.

They ironically demonised the religion while grabbing the sites associated with the same religion. One reason why it is not included in the class of world religions is the fact that it does not have written scriptures. The culture of the Africans therefore does not fit to be classified as worth of recognition because it does not have any point of reference. It should be noted that AFM whose roots are deeply pithed in Western Pentecostalism painted black the African culture and its activities. Matikiti (2018) calls this an "implicit psychological violence". The objective of the Western Pentecostalism is to turn the Africans wholly from following their culture and epistemologies. The idea is of glorifying the Western culture while demonising the African culture and epistemologies. This became the crux of the preaching of the early AFM missionaries and the same button was passed on to those who came after them. It is aimed at turning the minds and hearts of people away from their culture and epistemologies. They taught indigenous people to hate their culture and epistemologies, to be generally unsympathetic and hostile to their own heritages. This is noticed in the claims by one parent who got so concerned about the behaviour of her children who unequivocally refused to follow her advice regarding the African values simply because their church does not teach anything of that nature.

> Every time I try to sit down with my children and teach them traditional values they are quick to dismiss me saying their church teaching does not say so. They even disobey me telling me openly that they have the blessing from the church. (Angela Matambo, quoted in News Day 04-01-15).

In this regard, the Africans are encouraged to have a kind of thinking that is inclined towards dependence mentality, while submitting themselves under the standards and cardinals of the West. When the gospel came to Africa, one can see that it was not in its original form, but it was enveloped in the Western way of doing things. AFM like any other Pentecostals in Zimbabwe emphasised on the salvation of the soul. The church emphasised on the gifts of the Holy Spirit, divine healing, and living a holy life at the expense of cultural and epistemological accommodation. The missionaries believed that to become a Christian, the African people in Zimbabwe must totally abandon their indigenous cultures and epistemologies. Senzokuhle and Setume (2016) argue that the missionaries treated African religions as evil and did everything possible to ensure that it was ousted. The Western missionaries believed that traditional religious beliefs, epistemologies and practices were inferior - and together with the traditional customs - had to be thrown away at conversion to Christianity.

The concept of exclusivism

Pratt (2007) states that 'Exclusivism is more than simply a conviction about the transformative power of the particular vision one has; it is a conviction about its finality and its absolute priority over competing views. It must be noted that most of the Pentecostal Christians advocated for the idea of exclusivism in their preaching. They believed that among the people that they evangelised, the only way to win them to Christianity is to adhere to strict exclusivism. The most fundamental concept in exclusivism is that Christians should not be unequally yoked with unbelievers. At the heart of exclusivism is the scripture in 2 Corinthians 6:14 which states that:

> Be ye not unequally yoked together with unbelievers: for what fellowship hath righteousness with unrighteousness? And what communion hath light with darkness? And what concord hath Christ with Belial? Or what part hath he that believeth with an infidel?

This scripture points to the fact that anyone who is not a Christian is an unbeliever, unrighteous, darkness, belongs to Belial, and is an infidel. Matikiti (2017), adds to this by raising the fact that the exclusivists stick to their guns with the idea that 'Jesus is the way, the truth and the life' (John 14:6). Consequently, according to the exclusivists apart from Christ there is no salvation that can be attained, and Christianity is the only true religion and it totally replaces all others. Those who die without Christ will perish eternally. This is the gospel that the early missionaries in AFM preached when they came into Zimbabwe.

The idea of exclusivism in AFM became so deeply ingrained in the church that it extended to other areas of life. They even did not want to seek medical attention in hospitals because they believed exclusively in the healing power of God. It was a taboo to go to hospital such that in the past if a church member is known to have visited the hospital, the first time he or she came to the service he or she was supposed to confess. This is because according to the AFM standards, seeking medical treatment from hospitals and traditional healers was deemed sinful. This is further supported by Ruzivo (2014:18), who declares that in 1927 the Director of Education in the Rhodesian government, L. M. Floggin, wrote to the Inspector of schools:

> The colonial secretary sees these activities of this mission (A.F.M.) as mischievous and is anxious that anything which can be done to restrict them should be done…the Government has good reasons for disapproving of the mission in question. For your own information, I may state that the main ground of this view is the fact that this mission is urging natives to abstain from consulting medical authorities or using drugs in the event of ulcers and they endeavour to persuade the natives that taking of any such action is sinful.

From the above contents of the letter, Ndlovu (2018) asserts that it is therefore evident from the above letter that it was the official teachings of the A.F.M. to make its believers to rely purely on Jesus Christ for their healing.

According to Machingura (2011), in rural areas people with various kinds of sicknesses would not go to hospital. Those who used to go to the traditional healers as was their custom and tradition ceased doing so. They relied purely on the healing powers of their leaders who preached to them that visiting traditional healers was dinning with demons and would attract the wrath of God upon an individual. These people would now crowd around the residences of a man or a woman of God who could either be a prophet or church leader where they were prayed for until they received their deliverance from various ailments. In addition to this, even pregnant mothers were helped to deliver by local women in the church who were believed to have a special gift in the area. Machingura (2011) recounts the women in the church who were very popular in this regard and they include those like prophetess Kerina Murape and Ambuya Mugadza.

Missionaries and religious artefacts

The people of Africa do not take for granted their heritage especially the heritage that was passed from generation to generation. The heritage carries with it the spiritual connection which affects their day to day lives spiritually, economically, politically, religiously and even socially. It is this heritage that the missionaries demonised and called all sorts of names in a bid to show how supposedly evil the African heritage was. However, what is interesting is the fact that while the missionaries demonised the African indigenous religion, part of the resources that they smuggled out of Africa were the artefacts that were used in rituals and ceremonies in African Indigenous Religion. According to Siamonga (2018) during some colonial wars in Africa, the White soldiers took everything they could lay their hands on and stashed these cultural artefacts in private galleries and homes for resale or for souvenirs. He argues that the Curators of museums say these pieces of art are worth millions of dollars on the black market. The missionaries therefore deliberately and conveniently decided to treat African Religion as demonic even as the same missionaries looted the African artefacts. They separated religion from culture yet from an African perspective, religion and culture are interwoven. By demonising the religion, they pacified the adherents while taking away from them their cultural heritage.

There has been a battle in returning some of the artefacts back to some African states where they belong. Interestingly, some missionaries took possession of these artefacts. For example, the Zimbabwe birds that were taken from Zimbabwe. Ebrahim (2016) states that in 1907, a German missionary had in his possession the pedestal of one bird from Zimbabwe, which he sold to the Ethnological Museum in Berlin. When Russian forces occupied Germany at the end of World War II, the bird was taken from Berlin to Leningrad, where it remained until after the Cold War when it was returned to Germany. In 2003, the German museum returned it to Zimbabwe. There was joy for the people of Zimbabwe when this pedestal was returned because their understanding is that in these artefacts lie the power of the fortunes of the nation. These birds were eight but only seven have been returned. Ebrahim (2016) further asserts that many Zimbabweans believe that their country will never experience good fortune or return to its former glory until its eight mythical soapstone birds are reunited. One wonders why it took so long to have these artefacts returned if they were demonic and unholy. It took almost one hundred years to return them. The Zimbabwe Herald quoted Mugabe welcoming the pedestal that was returned to Zimbabwe after having been in exile for almost a hundred years. The former President said: "The fraction of the bird that we are officially welcoming back today has had a very eventful if not troubled existence during its almost 100 years in exile" (Herald 14 May 2003). Mugabe described the taking away of the artefacts as "ruthless cultural plunder." It is ruthless because the missionaries did not want the African owners to realise the value in these artefacts: therefore, the missionaries described the artefacts as demonic.

AFM and language

African culture is expressed in language. Culture is deeply integrated with its language, so to truly experience it one must speak that language. It is a highly enriching experience. The coming of the White missionaries into Zimbabwe made English normative. This set up showed a colonial mind-set. Local languages were not given the importance that they deserve in the AFM church. Instead of learning local languages, the missionaries were spreading their culture through the English language. A language gives a capacity for spreading ideas about a great variety of things. For the local people, expressing themselves in English or South African languages such as Zulu posed a great difficulty. Local languages simplify the conveyance of ideas, smoothen social contacts, conserves culture and transmit it to future generation. A westernised African influenced by European culture and Christianity would deny African traditional culture and epistemologies. Disparaging African culture led to increase in African nationalism as a way of recovering a culture lost. Cultural regeneration became a slogan for nationalists and what was happening in the political front was replicated in the ecclesiastical circles. Local languages such as Shona, Ndebele and Kalanga increasingly became the languages of communication in most AFM assemblies in the country. In an interview that this researcher had with Rev. Arnold Muringisi at Living Waters Theological College on the 25th of July 2019, he had this to say:

> Language has been a source of problems in AFM from the beginning. The church fathers from South Africa largely used Zulu as a mode of communication. English was also prevalent in sermons. As time went on believers started to use local language. You must understand that the mother church in South Africa would regularly come to supervise the way the gospel was preached and communicated and foreign languages were emphasised as true tools for the gospel.

Spoken languages are a large part of our innate ability to form lasting bonds with one another. Language integrates the church community. Language instils values and importance of one's culture. It also provides the foundation for one's communication abilities for the future.

AFM and birth, marriage and death rites

Bishau (2018), states that there are many rites that are performed in African Indigenous Religion. The traditional practices are performed by most Africans in their day-to-day lives. Africans believe that all rituals pertaining to human life especially birth, funeral and burial are to be performed. The rituals begin from the time a person is born to the time a person dies. AFM suppresses all these traditional customs. According to Machingura (2011), these customs include paying homage to ancestral spirits, *kurova Guva* (bringing back the spirit of the dead ceremony), and *barika* (polygamy), *masungiro* (sanctification of the first-born ritual) and *nyaradzo* (the consolation ceremony). He further attests to the fact that some ritual practices in the Roman Catholic Church and liberal churches correspond to those that are found in African Traditional Religion, for example, the consolation ceremony (*nyaradzo*) is similar in some respects to the *kurova guva* ceremony in Traditional Religion. While interviewing Pastor Shirichena at his church in Warren Park on the 16th of August 2019 this researcher discovered that Christians who practice *Nyaradzo* (consolation ceremonies) are not different from those who practice the traditional *kurova guva* ceremony and this is not acceptable in AFM. According to him:

> *Kana vanhu vachiita nyaradzo, havana kusiyana nevanhu vanoita zvekurova guva. Musiyano wavo ndewekuti vanoita nyaradzo vanoverenga bhaibheri. Asi zvakangofanana. Saka isu hatiite izvozvo.* (If people are practicing the consolation ceremony, they are no different from those who practice *kurova guva.* The only difference is that those who practice the consolation ceremony they hide behind reading the bible but it is the same thing. So we do not do that.

Should Christians participate in family cultural practices such as '*kurova guva*' so as to comply with cultural obligations or expectations? Participation can be in two forms which can either be in form of providing resources for the rituals or to be physically present taking part in the rituals. Most African Christians placed much importance on the *kurova guva* ceremony while on the other hand the missionaries taught that to take part in the ceremony was sin, however behind the scene *kurova guva* ceremonies went on. However, in an interview that was carried out with Rev. Machote an AFM pastor, at his home in Mabelreign Harare on the 9th of August 2019, he had this to say:

> It does not matter you are not present physically, if you send your money to these functions, your money is going to represent you. So in the eyes of God you are as good as you are there because your money has your name on it. If you send your money, you are also participating in those activities and it means you are there.

Ndlovu (2018), declares that this ceremony inaugurates a new status for the deceased, ensures entry into the spiritual world so they can take up the role of ancestor or guardian for the family. It is believed that the deceased can only become an ancestral spirit after a *kurova guva* ceremony has been performed for him. This ceremony gives legitimacy to the relationship between the living and the departed. The AFM vehemently opposed this cultural practice as demonic and evil. An interview that this researcher had on the 8th of August 2019, with Francis Deredzai an elder for AFM Shiloh Assembly in Harare CBD, revealed that all these practices are primitive, and they were done before people knew God:

> Before we knew God we encouraged people to do those things because there was no other way to seek guidance and protection. We believed that ancestors were our protection. *Ndozvatakadzidziswa nana VaKupara vakatanga ne Chipostori. Mudzimu haigoni kutichengeta vanhu vakafa* (This is what we were taught by the pioneers of the Apostolic Faith Mission like Pastor Kupara. The Ancestors cannot protect us because these are dead people.

The Catholic Church has played a great role in incorporating the *kurova guva* ceremony in their liturgy. There is a heavy Christianisation of African practices in the Roman Catholic Church. But this is not the case in AFM which considers this as "worshipping" the dead who know nothing concerning the living. They are forgotten because they cannot contribute anything in the world of the living.

While tombstone-unveiling is done among other religions and other churches in Zimbabwe, the AFM church looks at that as unacceptable. According to Matikiti (2018), there is a popular saying in Harare: "*ukaona makuva ese asina kugadzirwa ndeevanhu veAFM*" (there is no tombstone unveiling for the dead members of the AFM). Central to their belief is: "For the living know they shall die, but the dead know not a thing neither do they reward amongst the living for the memory of them is forgotten." (Eccl 9 verse 5).

It should be noted that failure to perform such practices among the indigenous people is tantamount to cutting ties with the departed and they will not bless the family. In addition to this, there is family disintegration and sharp disagreements because of these traditional activities especially if the other family members do not belong to these Pentecostal movements. Those that do not want to participate

279

in these traditional activities are seen as betrayers. AFM regards the birth ceremonies, death rites and burial rites as the work of the devil. They are regarded as heathen practices and they are not acceptable in the church.

Conclusion

In conclusion, the chapter has shown that the Apostolic Faith Mission in Zimbabwe despised and rejected African spiritism. There was no attempt to accommodate positive aspects of African Indigenous Religion. The AFM shared similarities with the colonialists in that they regarded the Africans as inferior and their religion as demonic, primitive, fetish, magic, barbaric and witchcraft. These terms were used to justify the colonial enterprise, to pave way for the colonisers. That is, the same attitude that the early missionaries portrayed as they facilitated the colonial projects. The suppression of African spiritism is a confirmation that the AFM remains cast in the Western mould of worship. Any attempt to show respect for African ancestors was seen as sinful. AFM is a church whose principles rest squarely on exclusivism and hypocrisy.

End notes

1.   This is a belief that the spirits of the dead are able to communicate with the living by the agency of the medium who could be the relative of the deceased. It could be the spirit of an alien who died away from home and is coming to seek accommodation in a family that would accept the spirit.

2.   The term exodus generally means going out like in the case of the children of Israel going out of Egypt. It means going out from one place to another. But in this case, it is used with reference to death. So, Lake's works were published long after his death.

References

Anderson, A. (1993). African Pentecostalism and the ancestors: Confrontation or compromise? Paper read at the Annual Conference of the Southern African Missiological Society. Published in Missionalia 21:1.

Bishau, D. (2018). *Family and religious studies*. Harare. CPS Books.

Clark, M. S. & Lederie, H. I. (1989). *What is distinctive about Pentecostal theology?* Pretoria: University of South Africa.

Dillon-Malone, C. M. (1978). *The korsten basketmakers, Lusaka*. The Institute for African Studies.

Douglas, P. (2007). Exclusivism and exclusivity: A contemporary theological challenge. *Pacifica* vol 20 (3).

Duncan, G. A. (2015). *Ethiopianism in pan-African perspective, 1880-1920*. Studia Historiae Ecclesiasticae Headley, A. J. (2013). *Getting it right: Christian perfection and Wesley's purposeful list*. Seedbed. Retrieved 21 August 2018.

Gish, S. (2004). *Desmond Tutu: A biography*. London: Greenwood Press.

James, E. M. (2018). Gaps and opportunities for the World Heritage Convention to contribute to global wilderness conservation. *Conservation Biology.* Vol 32 (1):116-126. doi; 10.1111/cobi.12976.PMID 28664996. Accessed 18 September 2019.

Machingura, F. (2011). *The significance of glossolalia in the Apostolic Faith Mission in Zimbabwe*. Edinburgh University Press.

Madziyire, A. & Risinamhodzi, T. (2016). *Pentecostal dawn: the history and tenets of A.F.M in Zimbabwe*. Harare. www.pentecostaldawninzimbabwe.com accessed 29 August 2019.

Matikiti, R. (2017). *Moratorium to preserve cultures: A challenge to the Apostolic Faith Mission in Zimbabwe?* Studia Historiae Ecclesiasticae, Church History Society of Southern Africa and Unisa Press.

Martin, D. (1996). *Forbidden revolutions: Pentecostalism in Latin America and Catholicism in Eastern Europe*, London: SPCK.

Maxwell, D. (2000). Catch the cockerel before Dawn': Pentecostalism and politics in post-colonial Zimbabwe. *Africa* vol 70 (2).

Maxwell, D. (2006). *African gifts of the spirit: Pentecostalism and the rise of a Zimbabwean transnational religious movement*. Harare: Weaver Press.

Mujeyi. S. M. (2006). *Apostolic Faith Mission's magazine*. Harare: Living Waters Bible College.

Ndlovu, C. (2018). *The management of the Apostolic Faith Mission in Zimbabwe: A model founded in the Apostolic vision*. Doctor of Philosophy thesis. North-West University.

Olson, R. E. (2009). *Arminian theology: Myths and realities*. InterVarsity Press.

Pavari, N. (2011). *The historical background of the Apostolic Faith Mission*. Harare. Pavari Publishers.

Ruzivo, M. (2014). *A history of the Apostolic Faith Mission in Zimbabwe 1908-1980*. Pretoria: UNISA. (Thesis- DTh).

Siamonga, E. (2018). *Cultural artefacts piracy and our stolen heritage*. Harare: The Patriot.

Synan, V. (1997). *The holiness-pentecostal tradition: Charismatic movements in the twentieth century*. Grand Rapids, Michigan: William B. Eerdmans Publishing Company

Togarasei, L. (2016). Historicising Pentecostal Christianity in Zimbabwe. *Studia Historiae Ecclesiasticae* vol 42 (2) http://dx.doi.org/10.17159/2412-4265/2016/103

Vinson, S. (1997). *The holiness-pentecostal tradition: Charismatic movements in the twentieth century*. Wm. B. Eerdmans Publishing. pp. 6–7. ISBN 978-0-8028-4103-2. Retrieved 27 August 2019

Newspapers

News Day, Harare. 04-01-15. Angela Matambo, quoted in *"The Pentecostal Churches Blamed for Divorces."*

The Star independent News Paper: (2016 April 1). *Bring Back The Zimbabwe Bird*. Story by Shanon Ebrahim.

Interviews

Shirichena, C. Living Waters Theological College. (2019 August 16)

Deredzai, F. AFM Shiloh Assembly Mabelreign. (2019 August 8)

Machote, S. Mabelreign (2019 August 9)

Muringisi, A. Living Waters Theological College (2019 July 25)

Chapter Eleven

Mathematics, Circularity and the Msonge as African Heritages

Baruti I. Katembo

Introduction

Mathematics facilitates the explanation of any subject's numerical aspects and thus functions as the conduit through which the relationship(s) amongst any system's components are measured. Its use and applications, in many instances, have usually arisen as a function of societal needs, views and values. The design of round dwelling spaces is one such mathematical application which shares a common ancestral presence in many distinct cultures, particularly in reference to Africa, Asia, Europe, Oceania and the Americas; hence, the emergence and validity of the Convergent Evolution Theory. This chapter showcases the msonge ('round, pointed-thatched-roof dwelling' in Kiswahili) as a medium to discuss the cultural relevance of circular design in space optimisation, in engineering efficiency and as a link to socioenvironmental perception and understanding.

Mathematics and cultural circularity

The definition and scope of mathematics has often been debated; however, most theoreticians agree that mathematics facilitates the explanation of any subject's numerical aspects. It is the technique of discovering and conveying, in the most economical possible way, useful rules of reliable reasoning about calculation, measurement and shape (Zaslavsky, 1999: 6).

Mathematics is the conduit through which to measure the quantitative relationship amongst components within any system. Thus, social science (the study of communities through multiple aspects) and natural science (the study of physical environment through multiple aspects) such as geography and chemistry, respectively, use mathematics as a common thread of connection and interface. For this reason, mathematics is both a tool and component of all science (Katembo, 2008). Historically, mathematics and its usage and applications arose out of the need for humans to understand interactions with their environment; therefore, it facilitated that comprehension (and does so, today, as well). For example, calculate, meaning "to compute", is derived from calculus, the Latin word for *pebble*; often in ancient eras, such items as stones, shells, nuts and beads were used as media of counting (Zaslavsky, 1999: 7). Subsequently, mathematics aids our ability to explain the world in which we live.

Historically, the development of crafts, pottery, building boats and shelter have all been useful entities in advancing and maintaining a society; today (as was the case in times past) mathematics has to be looked upon as a tool for the erection, maintenance and/or advancement of a society or civilisation. By extension, it opens doors to new ideas which are crystallised by technology (improvement upon existing systems and concepts). For example, architecture, an extension of geometry, evolved from an interface of needs (shelter; security, etc.) and means (skill; material, etc.) while accounting, an extension of numeration and counting, arose with the need to maintain records of quantity, particularly regarding agricultural products ('Architecture,' 2009; 'Accounting,' 2009); consequently, these subjects are examples of applied mathematics, i.e., the insertion of quantification and problem-solving computation into the analysis of a system or endeavour. The evolution and emergence of architecture and accounting denote the epitome and use of applied mathematics in advancing human development; hence, the term sociomathematics. The teaching of mathematics from the 'society' slant and perspective will help to ease mathematics-phobia and encourage a viewpoint that it is not abstract nor disconnected from practicality.

Figure1: Kilalinda Luxury Lodge
(*courtesy* Siyabona Africa)
Kilalinda Wildlife Conservancy
Tsavo East, Kenya
This msonge-inspired structure is a typical design found throughout ancient and contemporary Africa.

The msonge (*mmm-sohn-gay*) is one such entity whose circular essence and design can be studied as a mathematical concept and as a link to culture, ethos and socioenvironmental understanding. It is a KiSwahili word for a round, pointed-thatched-roof structure, particularly a dwelling. Charles M. Bwenge, African languages professor and researcher, (personal communication, January 13, 2018) posits that the word msonge is derived from part of 'enju ya mshonge', a phrase in KiHaya (a Tanzanian language), where mshonge specifically references a pointed-tip and enju is a house; hence, 'enju ya mshonge' (literally, house of pointed-tip) is a round dwelling with a thatched, pointed-tip roof. There are many, African (Bantu) language words which denote such circular spaces (Katembo,

2012). The round, thatched-roof structure is symbolic of Africa and is a hallmark of a definitive architectural ingenuity.

In this work, the msonge's linguistic use as a generic term for an African round dwelling stems from Kiswahili's pan-African flavour, appeal and wide use as a *lingua franca* (common language) within and across many African countries, particularly those in the east and central regions of the continent. Routinely, round (circular) dwellings have gained popularity as an enduring African image, architectural pillar and symbol of heritage for many millennia (Akombo *et al.*, 2009); however, similar round dwellings have been part of the ancestral, architectural tapestry of Europe, Asia, Oceania and the Americas (Zaslavsky, 1989). Many ancient cultures lived close to and in accordance with nature, i.e., they constructed circular living spaces (in many instances) as an extension of their view that roundness reflected nature's geometry and cyclical aspects, e.g., rotation of the Earth; oval trajectory of the rising and setting of the sun; roundness of leaves and tree trunks. Additionally, nature is the primary source for life's necessities including food, water, shelter, clothing and medicine. Some modern-day structures such as the Kalilinda Luxury Lodge (Tsavo East, Kenya) mimic the ancient, geometric design ideas concerning roundness; see Figure 1: Kilalinda Luxury Lodge (Siyabona Africa Staffer, 2008).

Geometry is the branch of mathematics that deals with the measurement, properties and relationships of points, lines, angles, surfaces (2D spaces) and solids (3D spaces) ('Geometry,' 2019); thus, architecture as a geometry-based application and discipline explores the theory, rationale and methods for designing indoor and outdoor spaces. Architecture reflects the culture and distinct civilisation elements of a given society (Katembo, 2002: 64). Some scholars like Joseph Rykwert (as cited in Hermitary Staffer, 2009) have viewed and referenced the "hut" (i.e., thatched-roof dwelling) as imitative of trees with hanging branches - thus, an extension of the natural space and environment.

Ingeniousness of the msonge

Misonge (plural of msonge) were constructed for sound (valid) reasons. A circle is a physically strong structure for a building, with no part of the building bearing more load (supported weight) than another, i.e., it is the perfect shape for an even load distribution. The adoption of this shape meant that the builder could select small diameter timbers and dispense with the need for exhaustive cutting, shaping and jointing of wood. Traditionally, msonge builders realised that these structures were comparatively easy to build (erect) from a circular foundation with use of cheap, readily available raw materials: mud, clay and tree branches, primarily. The oldest forms of indigenous shelter were often round because the ovoid shape — eggs, tree trunks, stones and the Earth — is what ancient peoples saw reflected in the surrounding natural environment. These early architects and artisans understood that the design and quality of a round domicile or shelter were the synthesis of intelligent energy-use and clever space allocation coupled with the powerful, natural movement of air and sound.

Writer and home-builder Rachel Ross points out that there is some fascinating natural science which makes round buildings more comfortable, energy-efficient, space-efficient and safer than other design configurations - especially if the circular shape is combined with "modern" materials (Ross, 2017):

a. Wind and tsunami waves move naturally around a round building rather than getting caught at (and potentially ripping off) corners. A rounded roof avoids 'air-planning' - a situation where a strong wind lifts the roof structure up and off the building.

b. There are dozens of interconnected points in a round dwelling. These are sites where builders can connect parts of the building together. Historically, the connecting materials were rope, vine and hides. Modern materials are engineered components - like a centre radial steel ring, steel brackets, ties (seismic; hurricane), bolts and steel cables. These connect the structural pieces and give the building a unique combination of flexibility and strength - qualities which cause them to be significantly safer than other component

287

designs, given severe weather conditions like earthquakes, extreme winds and heavy snowfall.

c.   Circles are closed planes consisting of all points equidistant from a centre point, i.e., ringlike formations or arrangements ('Circle,' 2018). In terms of scientific discovery, they maximise area over squares of the same perimeter measurement by an approximate margin slightly above 21%, as illustrated in Figure 2: Circumscribed Square (Katembo, 2002: 70), The aforementioned fact can be verified via deductive reasoning – thought process which draws specific conclusions from general principles ('Deductive Reasoning,' 2007):

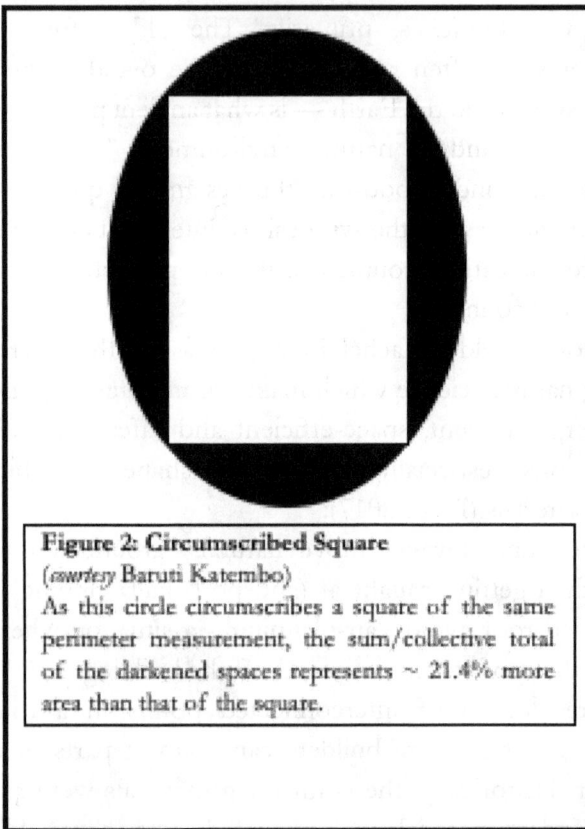

Figure 2: Circumscribed Square
(*courtesy* Baruti Katembo)
As this circle circumscribes a square of the same perimeter measurement, the sum/collective total of the darkened spaces represents ~ 21.4% more area than that of the square.

Suppose that a square and a circle both have the same perimeter p. Using the common perimeter measurement, i.e., in terms of p, each side of the square is p/4 and the circle's radius (obtained from solving $p = 2\pi r$ for r) is $p/(2\pi)$. Now, let's find the areas of the square and the circle in terms of p; area of a square = s^2, where s =

measurement of a side, and the area of a circle $= \pi r^2$, where $\pi = pi = 22/7 \sim 3.14$ and $r =$ radius. Consequently, the square area $= (p/4)^2 = p^2/16$ and the circle area $= \pi(p/(2\pi))^2 = p^2/(4\pi)$. In finding the square's percentage area of the circle (x), $x(p^2/(4\pi)) = p^2/16$ such that $x = \pi/4 \sim .7857143 = 78.6\%$.

As illustrated in Figure 2, any circle constitutes approximately 21.4% more area than a square of the same perimeter distance. In addition to Africa (as noted earlier), misonge and other similarly-architectured residential structures have been featured in varying eras amongst indigenous peoples of Asia, Oceania, ancient Europe and the Americas; these ethno-cultural communities have used (and some instances, still use) round floor space as a practical utility, medium and extension of msonge geometry to maximize internal area. Round buildings use less wall, floor and roof materials to enclose the same square footage as a rectangular structure. The same square foot circular building compared to a rectangular design is created with 15%-to-20% less material, thus facilitating the possibility for a smaller eco-footprint and more living space for less cost. Also, there is less surface area in contact with adverse weather conditions, thus improving the overall durability and energy efficiency of the home.

d.   The acoustics of round space are incredible. The associated curve softens the sounds inside the building, making it the perfect place for rest, reflection, and socialising as well as listening to and playing music. The shape also prevents outside noise from pen-etrating inwardly (inside). Sound waves dissipate as they wrap around the building, shielding the interior from loud outside noise.

In 2016, Ugandan architect Sadam Kakande told *THIS IS AFRICA* that the re-emergence of the [msonge] stems from the increasing temperature in Africa due to global warming (Taremwa, 2016). In order to attract clients, hotels and luxury pubs have often adopted a grass-thatched style for their cottages and bars. Traditional round houses are very comfortable, mainly due to the building materials used. Clay and grass are both good insulators, but additionally are porous and allow a free flow of air. "It is often very hot during the afternoons in Africa. The hut remains cool and is a welcome resting place. At night, when temperatures fall, the hut retains its daytime temperature, keeping the inhabitants warm," Kakande explained. The construction rationale was more than just architectural, but also was steeped in communalism and the complementary nature of society. Traditionally, social gatherings and councils took place in circles around a focal point. Within an msonge, a family would eat together and sit together in the same way (circular configuration), while telling stories to the exclusion of no one. Due to their benefits, like natural air conditioning, serenity and tranquillity, the msonge has found its way into the "modern" age (Taremwa, 2016).

Round dwellings, an example of Convergent Evolution Theory

Aside from concerns and considerations of aesthetic appeal and internal area maximisation, people all over the world have independently discovered the engineering practicality and functionality of constructing circular dwelling spaces; thus, an example of the Convergent Evolution Theory, i.e., phenomenon where distinct species with differing ancestries evolve to display similar physical features due to environmental circumstances requiring similar developmental or structural alterations ('Convergent Evolution Theory,' 2009). The comparison of Africa's msonge and Europe's crannog gives proof, validity and support to the Convergent Evolution Theory. Crannog (from the Irish *crann*, meaning tree) is a common name given to the Celtic-inspired round dwellings dating back to pre-Medieval Europe that stretched from Spain to the Black Sea's shores; see Figure 3: *Crannog* Reconstruction (Clark, 2006). Its superstructure was built entirely of wood and formed the ordinary living house for a family unit and, in some instances, livestock (Grampus Research Team Staffer, 2006).

Figure 3: *Crannog*
Reconstruction (*courtesy* Martin Clark)
Connemara Heritage Centre
Galway, Ireland
Remnants of this Celtic-inspired round dwelling style have been found throughout Europe, extending from Spain to the Black Sea's shores.

Environment as a factor of architectured-space

In reflection, the ancient societies of Africa, Asia, Oceania, Europe and the Americas were primarily agrarian, i.e., organised around farming and livestock endeavours; thus, there were no true urban centres in the contemporary sense where a diversity of agricultural and non-agricultural trades such as masonry and metalworking were functioning in the same congregational space (Balanck, 2009). The inhabitants' lives were governed by working on fields, tending crops or animals, and dependence on favourable soil fertility and weather conditions throughout the seasons.

As populations in medieval times grew exponentially across Europe with its vast areas of non-arable land due to harsh climates and cold weather, people moved in close proximity to one another in areas where there were abundant arable land and fresh water; therefore, vast numbers of Europeans were most likely limited regarding food access, farming endeavours and livestock management by hazardous travel routes, non-arable land zones, climatic elements (snow; ice) and associated animal hibernations. Cities therefore sprung up near abundant arable land, fresh water, and hunting game (Katembo, 2012: 121).

In contrast, the majority of African areas have warm, subtropical climates suited for year-round fishing, hunting and growing seasons such that fruits, vegetables, water and game are in abundance over large territorial spaces; as a result, tight population packing/density was not needed as a strategic measure to provide food and water access to many (Katembo, 2012: 121-122). On the other hand, European societies, particularly in the Middle Ages, had mainly evolved into dirty, cramped, tightly packed settlements and environments (TimeMaps Staffer, 2019). These conditions contrasted immensely with those of African and other warm weather peoples who commonly resided in widely spaced domiciles. So, European ideas about architecture (in the transition from sparse-to-dense populations) may have leaned (out of environmental necessity and constraints) toward maximising space between buildings, i.e., external area maximisation, as opposed to the African concept of internal area maximisation for family and livestock sheltering.

Buildings can be squeezed closer together if they bear a rectilinear design (square/rectangular roof and body) rather than a circular one; essentially, the adjacency of round structures wastes external space. The logical extension of this concept is that, as horizontal space became depleted due to continuous adjacent packing of rectilinear buildings, considerations were explored regarding the use of vertical space — hence, the concept of high-rise apartment buildings. Accordingly, people's decisions, with use of mathematics, technology and understanding, are influenced by societal needs (Zaslavsky, 1989); subsequently, the design and associated geometric parameters of dwelling spaces are also shaped and influenced in this way.

Conclusion

The msonge as discussed in this chapter is much more than a shape or dwelling. It encapsulates heritage aspects of Africa's art, technology and nature-based worldview through a geometric aesthetic – circularity. Round dwelling structures are iconically African but are found in the ancestral architecture of most global societies; it is something that most human cultures share – a connector. Ancient treasures should be preserved in the present, i.e., "modernity" can be enriched with the past. In the case of Africa, msonge-inspired applications should be incorporated into societal architecture – schools; hospitals; office buildings; churches; residences and other structures.

References

Accounting. (2009). In *Dictionary.com*. Retrieved January 5, 2009 from http://dictionary.reference.com/browse/accounting

Akombo, D., Gray, P., Griffin, G. & Katembo, B. (2009, March). Msonge (The Circular "Hut"), symbolic of Africa's genius and Europe's idea of primitivism. Paper presented at the

University of Texas Africa Conference, themed 'Science, Technology and Environment in Africa', Austin, TX.

Architecture. (2009). In *Dictionary.com*. Retrieved January 25, 2009 from http://dictionary.reference.com/browse/architecture

Balanck, M. (2009). The Celts. *AncientSpiral.Com*. Retrieved from http://www.ancientspiral.com/Celt.htm

Circle. (2017). In *Dictionary.com*. Retrieved March 17, 2018 from http://www.dictionary.com/browse/circle?s=t

Clark, M. (Photographer). (2006). *Crannog* reconstruction. [digital image]. Retrieved from http://www.grampusheritage.fsnet.co.uk/ticatec%20Crannog2.jpg

Convergent Evolution Theory. (2009). In *The American Heritage Dictionary of the English Language, Fourth Edition*. Retrieved February

21, 2009 from http://science.jrank.org/pages/2608/Evolution-Convergent.html

Deductive Reasoning. (2007). In *The sourcebook for teaching science*. Retrieved July 29, 2019 from https://www.csun.edu/science/ref/reasoning/deductive_reasoning/index.html

Geometry. (2019). In *Merriam-Webster.com*. Retrieved May 2, 2019 from https://www.merriam-webster.com/dictionary/geometry

Grampus Research Team Staffer. (2006). "To build a crannog!" *Grampus Heritage*. Retrieved February 15, 2009 from http://www.grampus.co.uk/parabow/projects/building/ireland/crannogie.htm

Hermitary Staffer. (2009). Joseph Rykwert's *On Adam's house in paradise: The idea of the primitive hut in architectural history (2nd edition)*. Retrieved February 21, 2009 from
http://www.hermitary.com/bookreviews/rykwert.html

Katembo, B. (2002). *Elephants in a bamboo cage*. Raleigh, NC: Mkuyu Books.

Katembo, B. (2008, April). Mathematics, the all-purpose glue in the village of learning and discovering science. Paper presented on a panel ('The Relevance of Mathematics in the 21st Century') at the Edward Waters College First Annual Mathematics, Science and Engineering Workshop, Jacksonville, FL.

Katembo, B. (2012). Mathematics, circularity and the msonge. *Scattered Assets: How African Americans & Other Resources Can Shape 21st Century Pan-African Empowerment* (112- 125). Bloomington, IN: AuthorHouse.

Mathematics. (2009). In *Dictionary.com*. Retrieved February 20, 2009 from http://dictionary.reference.com/browse/mathematics

Ross, R. (2017). Why our ancestors built round houses – and why it still makes sense to build round structures today. *Inhabitant*. Retrieved March 5, 2018 from https://inhabitat.com/why-our-ancestors-built-round-houses-and-why-it-still-makes-sense-to-build-round-structures-today

Siyabona Africa Staffer. (Photographer). (2008). Kilalinda Luxury Lodge. [digital image]. Retrieved February 16, 2009 from http://lodges.safari.co.za/images/kilalinda-280-gen1.jpg

Taremwa, A. (2016). The wisdom of the African hut. *THIS IS AFRICA*. Retrieved March 10, 2018 from
https://thisisafrica.me/lifestyle/wisdom-african-hut/

TimeMaps Staffer. (2019). Medieval Europe. *TimeMaps*. Retrieved July 23, 2019 from
https://www.timemaps.com/civilizations/medieval-europe/

Zaslavsky, C. (1999). *Africa counts: Number and pattern in African cultures.* Chicago, IL: Lawrence Hill Books.

Zaslavsky, C. (1989). People who live in round houses. *Arithmetic Teacher.* 18-21.

Chapter Twelve

African Indigenous Science as a Solution for Students' Underachievement in Science Education: Insights from Nigeria

Okewande Esther Oyeniwe

Introduction

The contemporary challenge of underachievement being experienced by science students in Nigeria and many other African countries necessitates research on ways of improving students' achievement in sciences. Underachievement can be alleviated by tailoring the delivery of classroom instructions with indigenous science. The development of science depends largely on the scientific and technological literacy possessed by the citizens of Africa. Students learn scientific principles, facts, values and norms through subjects like chemistry, physics, biology and agriculture among others.

The significant role that science plays in provision of basic needs and improving quality of human life in the "modern" day world cannot be overemphasised, thus students should be taught in a way that will enhance creative thinking by making use of indigenous science. This chapter, therefore, examines the need for the pendulum of science teaching, in Nigeria and Africa at large, to swing into the direction of indigenous science. Indigenous science is the system of knowledge that is embedded in indigenous culture. It gives meaning to how the contemporary world works through cultural perspectives.

The chapter discusses the goals of science education, the concept of African indigenous science and the challenges and prospects of adoption of indigenous science in Nigerian schools. The argument in the chapter is that indigenous science helps to ensure that science reflects the values and aspirations of African communities. On the same note, it makes students not to experience science as a foreign culture. The chapter recommends the centring of indigenous science in science curricula in Nigeria and Africa as a whole. Responsive science teachers should culturally be raised through seminars, workshops and conferences that will produce students with richer understanding of science.

The goals of science education

British Christian Missionaries were responsible for the emergency of Western science in Nigeria in the 1840s. Science was not their major focus initially, because they were only interested in training clerks and evangelists that would help in the propagation of Christianity among Nigerians. However, the missionaries eventually introduced science subjects such as biology, chemistry and physics.

The National Curriculum Conference held in Lagos in 1969 gave room for the development of science education in Nigeria (Abimbola & Omosewo, 2006). The National Policy on Education (NPE) was a product borne out of the conference. The latest edition of NPE was published in 2013, this edition recognises the importance of science in the development of a nation. Thus, it recommended that the ratio of science students to non-science students' admission to the university should be 30: 70.

It is against this background that the number of students for science education in Nigeria has increased tremendously. It is as a result of the realisation of the importance of science in nation-building that the Federal Republic of Nigeria categorically stated in its National Policy on Education that "Government shall popularize the study of the sciences and production of adequate numbers of scientists to inspire and support national development"(FRN, 2004: 29). This shows the stretch of government expectation and dependence on science education for attaining developmental goals. Odo (2013) opines that the science education is the authentic instrument for the transmission of science to emerging generations in any culture and nation.

Science education can be seen as the field of study that consists of education in science: science education brings about the learning and application of science to solving everyday life problems (Okeke, 2012). Similarly, Ekanem and Obodom (2014) note that science education is the mother of all sciences that can help learners to acquire requisite knowledge in science related courses. Science education can also be regarded as the application of educational theories to search for knowledge which gives room for the development of the cognitive, affective and psychomotor domains through processes such as observation, deduction and testing (Igbaji, Miswaru & Sadiyya, 2017).

The goals of science education in Nigeria according to the National Policy on Education (FRN, 2004:29) are to;

i. cultivate inquiring, knowing and rational mind for the conduct of a good life and democracy;

ii. produce scientists for national development;

iii. service studies in technology and the cause of technological development;

iv. Provide knowledge and understanding of the complexity of the physical world, the forms and the conduct of life.

Despite the laudable goals of science education, it is obvious that students' underachievement in sciences at all levels of institutions in Nigeria has been an obstacle in achieving these goals. The secondary school science education according to the National Policy on Education (FRN, 2013) includes core subjects like physics, chemistry, biology, agricultural science and mathematics. The role of these subjects in national development is indisputable. However, the underachievement by Nigerian students is inimical to national development. The reason being that, science education at secondary school level, which is the gateway for national development, has become a citadel for breeding scientific illiterates who only read and memorise scientific facts rather than applying them. Igbaji, Miswaru and Sadiyya (2017) observe that, students with poor background in sciences at secondary level tend to be mere 'scientific historians' in the universities.

Several researchers have attributed rote learning in science to many factors such as students' negative attitude toward sciences (Obomanu & Adaramola, 2011); lack of reading habit (Olatunji, Aghimien & Oke, 2016); students' anxiety (Jegede, 2007); poor teaching strategies (Omiko, 2017) and the abstract nature of science

(Samba & Eriba, 2012; Otor, 2013). To adequately address the aforementioned factors, there is need to recentre indigenous science in teaching and learning of science in order to facilitate learners' understanding of science phenomena in connection with their cultural background. This calls for reformation of delivery of contents of science curriculum that will restructure classroom instructions towards culturally and environmentally pertinent topics and strategies.

Concept of indigenous science

Indigenous science is also referred to as "ethnoscience". "Ethnoscience" according to Abonyi (2012) is the knowledge that deals with perceptions, practices, skills and ideas in a local way with their underlying cosmologies in the context of processes of socioeconomic development. This implies that it is a concept that allows articulation of a culture into a knowledge obtained through systematic investigation which helps to find solutions to problems bedevilling humans. Harding (1998) argues that all knowledge is local and rooted in a precise physical, social and historical context. The author further explains that each culture brings its own resources to bear on the construction of its knowledge system. The term "ethnoscience" is a broad concept that comprises of subsets such as "ethnochemistry", "ethnobotany", "ethnoecology", "ethnobiology", "ethnomathematics", and "ethnophysics", to mention a few.

In Africa, especially Nigeria, there is possession of a form of science which is utilised in indigenous practices that is aimed at satisfying the basic needs of the people. These practices had been in existence prior to the advent of Western education. Magirosa (2014) opines that Timbuktu as a pre-colonial great centre of learning makes Africa the world' oldest record of human technological achievement. The author further states that subjects like mathematics, chemistry, physics, optics and medicine were studied in the African University of Timbuktu (the oldest university in the world) long before the Europeans came to Africa. Slavery, colonialism and racism striped away self-respect, pride, honour and dignity from Black Africans.

Odo (2013) ascertains that the use of herbs in curing ailment and application of physical principles in invoking certain forces of nature are indigenous sciences that are relevant to contemporary university science curricula. Unfortunately, these practices have been rendered obsolete because of attrition with colonial science. Similarly, Waldstreicher (2004) notes that the knowledge of inoculating against smallpox was known to West Africans since the 18th century. Bone-setting was also practised by many groups of West Africans. Indigenous practices could be polished and integrated to enrich teaching and learning of science because they involve direct experiences with the immediate environment and with the natural world.

Anderson (2011) opines that the neglection of indigenous science in Nigeria, and Africa as a whole, has increased the relative advantage of Western countries over the developing ones; this is due to the fact that the science currently being taught and practiced in schools and universities is the "ethnoscience" of Western nations. Although, there is universality of concepts, skills and attitudes in science, learning becomes meaningful when examples are drawn from learners' immediate environments. "Ethnoscience" advocates for blending of different sciences for the betterment of understanding of science concepts. This would enable learners to perceive science as an activity operationalised daily in their environments. Odo (2013) states that countries such as Japan, India, Kenya, Bolivia, Sri Lanka and Australia are giants in scientific development because they have triumphantly blended Western science with their indigenous sciences, experiences and practices.

Table 1 shows some of the indigenous science practices that can be articulated with formal sciences in order to enrich classroom learning experiences.

Table 1: Science Concepts that can be Blended with Indigenous Activities

Science Concepts	Indigenous Activities
Separation Techniques, Colour, Chemical Reactions & Solvent	Tie and dye
Nutrition, Food, Preservation, Evaporation and Microorganisms	Addition of salt and smoking for preservation
Saponification, Soap and Hardness of Water	Local soap production
Fermentation, Distillation, Fractional Distillation and Hydrocarbon	Local gin production
Separation Techniques, Fermentation, Acidity and Alkalinity, Food and Cash Crops, Carbohydrates, Monocotyledon and Dicotyledon.	Production of cassava flakes (*'gari'*) and production of pap (*'Ogi'*) from maize
Soil Fertility	Application of manure
Crop Pests and Diseases, Hygiene and Food Preservation	The use of ashes and gun powder to prevent crop diseases and pests
Oxidation, Exothermic Reaction and Heat of Combustion.	The use of palm kernel shell for source of heat during blacksmithing.
Tensile Strength	Compression of hot metal for reshaping
Air, Oxygen and Combustion	Fanning of fire when cooking using firewood

Source: Adapted from Alebiosu (2006); Erinosho (2013)

The centring of indigenous science at all levels of education in Africa is imperative because it provides learners with the suitable circumstance to learn appropriate community attitudes and values for sustainable development. Hassan and Yonah (2013) argue that the centring of African indigenous knowledge in teaching and learning enhances the relevance and effectiveness of education by providing an education system that adheres to students' own inherent perspectives, experiences, languages, and customs. Ugwu and Diovu (2016) concluded that the centring of indigenous knowledge and practices into chemistry teaching enhances the understanding of chemistry concepts and hence, enhances students' academic achievement in the subject. If students' achievement in chemistry could be enhanced through indigenous science, other science subjects would not be exceptions. Therefore, it is imperative to centre African indigenous science in science education in Nigeria and Africa as a whole.

The problems of centring African indigenous science in science education in Nigeria

Despite the enormous importance of African indigenous science, there is a myriad of challenges in recentring it in African countries, especially Nigeria. These problems range from dissension between indigenous science and Western science, lack of cooperation of the custodians of indigenous science, lack of documented experiments and lack of indigenous science instructional methods.

Dissension between indigenous science and Western science
The centring of indigenous science into science education might be unassailable because it involves merging with Western culture that appears to conflict with the traditional views. Diwu and Ogunniyi (2012) contend that indigenising the science curriculum is difficult because the indigenous science and Western knowledge have different epistemological assumptions. It is noted that indigenous science is erroneously regarded as unscientific and superstitious.

Lack of cooperation of the custodians of indigenous science
People may want to protect their knowledge and resources. They may think that those harvesting the indigenous science might be minded on looting and commercialising the indigenous science.

Although, science has roots in alchemy that has to do with transmutation of matter, Olawepo and Ayinde (2016) lament the fact that African indigenous scientists are often demonised as witches. Witches are believed to cause poverty, diseases, accidents, business failure, famine, earthquake, infertility and difficulties in childbirth. Therefore, the so-called witches are persecuted or even killed. African teachers of science are made to believe that indigenous science is inferior and tantamount to witchcraft.

Lack of documented experiments

Scientific experimentation as one of the criteria that supposedly defines true science is deemed by some thinkers to be lacking in indigenous knowledge. Thus, teachers have the fear that integration of indigenous knowledge is tantamount to teaching pseudoscience (De Beer & Whitlock, 2009). It is believed that indigenous science does not emphasise empirical evaluation that can give room for testing explanations or hypotheses. Most textbooks do not make enough provision or at all for indigenous science.

Lack of indigenous science instructional method

There is no systematic approach that allows flow of information between teachers and students when adopting indigenous science during classroom instructions. Teachers' lack of pedagogical content in indigenous science contributes to inability to determine the appropriate and suitable strategies to employ in recentring indigenous science in teaching science. Erinosho (2013) opines that despite the effectiveness of indigenous science as a pedagogical tool, there is no systematic effort to develop an effective framework for centring indigenous science into school science curricula and instruction process in Nigerian schools. The designers of curriculum are Western oriented, therefore recentring of indigenous science is very difficult.

Cultural diversity

Nigerian classrooms are multicultural. Teachers may find themselves in a classroom setting where learners are from the three major nations (Igbo, Hausa and Yoruba) in Nigeria. These three categories of learners have different backgrounds and different indigenous science. Thus, teachers can be in a state of dilemma as regards whose indigenous sciences to be used during instructions. Kurtz (2000) contends that there are no dilemmas when teaching Western science because it has been hegemonic for centuries already and its domination has come to be accepted widely. However, this chapter argues that there is a dilemma in that Western science is imposed on African indigenous science and technology.

Prospects of African indigenous science in science teaching in Nigeria

African indigenous science has so many prospects if the right attitudes are adequately channelled towards their actualisations. Some of the prospects include the following:

Sustainable development

Education systems of a nation are pivotal to sustainable development. Sustainable development is a consolidated theme that helps learners to make sense of the world and their place in it (Lozano & Watson, 2013). Learning about farming, fishing, hunting, and preparation of food, building and running a home from an African indigenous science could provide the basic needs for sustainability in African societies. African indigenous science can meet the needs of the present without harming the environmental resources needed for future generations. Thus, if topics to be featured in science subjects reflect the use of local cultural knowledge which is an important base for acquisition of knowledge production, education for sustainable development would be achievable.

Provision of education for living

The major focus of African indigenous science is to equip youths for adulthood in the society. This fosters lifelong education despite the variations in African indigenous science systems from one society to another. Eze and Ike (2013) contend that African indigenous science provides education for living because of its emphasis on normative and expressive goals that are concerned with accepted standards, beliefs governing appropriate behaviour, unity and consensus. Hence, the centring of African indigenous science in science teaching could curb social vices and promote unity across the continent.

Motivating tool

When concepts of science are taught based on what learners have known before from their communities, they might be thrilled to see the relevance of natural phenomena to the science lessons and thus improve students' interest and achievements. Abbah, Mashebe and Denuga (2015) opine that the centring of indigenous science into classroom activities takes learners understanding beyond simple memorisation of facts since critical concepts will be presented in terms of indigenous meanings. This is because meaningful learning does not take place in isolation from the belief held by the learners. Mawere (2015) notes that indigenous science is a powerful tool that makes Western science accessible. It involves moving from the known to unknown. The author further stated that teaching indigenous knowledge connects learners with their culture that is relevant for learners' daily lives and brings back the roles of parents, and elders into education.

Collaborative learning

Collaborative learning is defined as a teaching arrangement in which small heterogenous groups of students work together to achieve a common goal (Sabiru, 2014). Students construct new knowledge not only by their involvement in handling objects physically and mentally but also by interacting with their colleagues. Learner- learner and teacher-learner discourses during lessons that involve indigenous science knowledge give room for cognitive growth and collaborative learning. The flexible interaction involved paves the way for inquiry-oriented discussion and open-ended questions.

Conclusion

The chapter contended that indigenous science, when recentred, can support the teaching of science in Africa, and Nigeria in particular. Western science does not have a monopoly on experimentation, positivism and truth: indigenous people in Africa also had their own sciences which were positivistic, rational, logical, and which were realised through experimentation in the field and not necessarily always in enclosed laboratories. Indigenous science is not necessarily about the supernatural, the irrational, the mystical, magical or esoteric. Indigenous knowledge included the esoteric and supernatural but indigenous science is irreducible to such mysticism and esotericism. In much the same way Westerners have their science as well as their esoteric and mystical religions, indigenous Africans have their own science as well as religions including the esoteric and mystical. African indigenous knowledge is not all about the mystical, esoteric and spiritual – there is more to these aspects.

References

Abbah, J., Mashebe, P. & Denuga, D. D. (2015). Prospect of integrating African indigenous knowledge systems into the teaching of sciences in Africa. *American Journal Educational Research*, vol 3(6): 668-673.

Abimbola, I. O., & Omosewo, E. O. (2006). *History of science for degree students*. Ilorin: Authors

Abonyi, O. S. (2012). Effective approaches of science education delivery: A roadmap to Vision 20:20. *Journal of Science Education*, vol 1 (1): 8-12.

Alebiosu, K. E. (2006). Indigenous science practices among Nigerian women. *Journal of New Horizon for Learning*. Retrieved from http://archive.education.jhu.edu/PD/newhorizons/Transformi ng%20Education/international/alebiosu.htm

Anderson, E. A. (2011). *Science and ethnoscience*. Retrieved from http://www.krazykioto.com/articles/science-and-ethnoscience-part-2-european-biology-as-et

Diwu, C. & Ogunniyi, M. B. (2012). Dialogical argumentation instruction as catalytic agent for the integration of school science with indigenous knowledge systems. *African Journal of Research in Mathematics, Science and Technology Education*, vol 16 (3): 333-347.

Ekanem, N. U., & Obodom, M. I. (2014). Education for all: Problems and prospects of science education in Nigerian schools. *Journal of Resourcefulness and Distinction,* vol *8* (1): 1-4.

Erinosho, S. Y. (2013). Integrating indigenous science with school science for enhanced learning: A Nigerian example. *International Journal for Cross-Disciplinary Subjects in Education (IJCDSE),* vol *4* (2): 1137-1143. Retrieved from https://pdfs.semanticscholar.org/01ae/4e63b7e14faf36968746d 1f7cd499eb395d2.pdf

Eze, U. T. & Ike, E. M. (2013). Integrating African indigenous knowledge in Nigeria' formal education system: It's potential for sustainable development. *Journal of Education and Practice,* vol *4* (6): 77-82.

Federal Republic of Nigeria (2004). *National Policy on Education (4th ed).* Lagos: NERDC Press.

Federal Republic of Nigeria (2013). *National Policy on Education (6th ed).* Lagos: NERDC Press.

Harding, S. (1998). *Is science multicultural? Postcolonialism, feminisms, epistemologies.* Bloomington: Indiana University Press.

Hassan, O. K. & Yonah, N. S. (2013). African indigenous knowledge systems and relevance of higher education in South Africa. *The International Education Journal: Comparative Perspectives,* vol *12*(1): 30–44.

Igbaji, C., Miswaru, B. & Sadiyya, A. S. (2017). Science education and Nigeria national development effort: The missing link. *International Journal of Education and Evaluation,* vol 3 (5): 46-56. Retrieved from https://iiardpub.org/get/IJEE/vol%20320NO,%205%202017/ SCIENCE%20EDUCATION.pdf

Jegede, S. A. (2007). Students' anxiety towards learning of chemistry in some Nigerian secondary schools. *Educational Research and Review,* vol 2(7): 193-197. Retrieved from http://www.academicjournal.org/ERR

Kurtz, P. (2000). Humanist manifesto: *A call for a new planetary humanism.* Amherst, N Y: Prometheus Book.

Lozano, R., & Watson, M. K. (2013). Chemistry education for sustainability: Assessing the chemistry curricula at Cardiff University, *Education Quimica,* vol *24*(2): 184-192.

308

Magirosa, M. (2014). *The legacy of Timbuktu, Africa's oldest university.* Retrieved from https://www.the patriot.co;zw/old_posts/the legacy-of-timbbuktu-africas-oldest-university/

Mawere, M. (2015). Indigenous knowledge and public education in Sub-Saharan Africa. *Africa Spectrum,* vol *50* (2): 57-71.

Obomaru, B. J., & Adaramola, M. O. (2011). Factors related to under achievement in science, technology and mathematics education (STME) in secondary schools in Rivers State, Nigeria. *World Journal of Education,* vol 1(1).

Odo, E. E. (2013). Integration of ethnochemistry into chemistry curriculum in Nigeria: Option for sustainable development. *53rd Annual Conference Proceedings of Science Teachers Association of Nigeria:* 260-266.

Okeke, E. A. C. (2012). Effective approach to science delivery: Concept, analysis and challenges. *Journal of Science Education* vol 1 (1): 1-21.

Olatunji, S. O., Aghimen, D. O., & Oke, A. E. (2016). Factors affecting performance of undergraduate students in construction related disciplines. *Journal of Education and Practice,* vol 7 (13).

Olawepo, E. T., & Ayinde, A. A. (2016). African worldview and science education: Implication for meaningful science learning. *57th Annual Conference Proceedings of Science Teachers Association of Nigeria:* 302 - 311.

Omiko, A. (2017). Identification of the areas of students' difficulties in chemistry curriculum at the secondary school level. *International Journal of Emerging Trends in Science and Technology,* vol 4(4): 5071-5077. Retrieved from http://ijets.in/article/v4-14/4%/20ijets.pdf

Otor, E. E. (2013). Effects of concept mapping strategy on students' attitude and achievement in difficult chemistry concepts. *Educational Research,* vol 4(2): 182.

Sabiru, D. Y. (2014). Effects of collaborative learning on chemistry students' academic achievement and anxiety level in balancing chemical equations in secondary schools in Kastina metropolis, Nigeria. *Journal of Education and Vocational Research,* vol 5 (2): 43-48.

Samba, R. M. O., & Eriba J. O. (2012). Background information on teaching difficult science concept in Samba R. M. O. and Eriba J.

O. (Eds). *Innovative approaches in teaching difficult science concepts,* 1-5. Makurdi, Nigeria: Destiny Ventures.

Ugwu, A. N., & Diovu, C. I. (2016). Integration of indigenous knowledge and practices into chemistry teaching and students' academic achievement. *International Journal of Academic Research and Reflection,* vol 4 (4): 22-30.

Waldstreicher, D. (2004). *Runaway America Benjamin Franklin, slavery, and the American revolution. Macmillan, 40. ISBN 978-0-8090-8314-5.*

Chapter Thirteen

Decolonising Mathematics in Africa

Sibongile Nyoni

Introduction

When reflecting on the learning and teaching of mathematics, it is important to consider how the learners identify themselves with what has been taught and the extent to which the mathematics is meaningful to them. Brodie (2016) acknowledges that all over the world, Black people and women mathematicians remain rare as compared to their White counterparts and males. Several scholars have argued that all people regardless of sex or colour are capable of learning mathematic to higher levels. Mathematics has long been an area that held back indigenous students because of dominance of Eurocentrism (Plevitz, 2007). In this regard the protests for the decolonisation of the university curricula by South African students in 2015 is an eye-opener to the education institutions. There is a need to consider reclaiming indigenous cultures and values and to build the capacity of a quality workforce that matches with the national needs and goals through the teaching and learning of mathematics.

D'Ambrosio (2007) says mathematics is the basis of many significant developments in technology, industry, economy and politics. D'Ambrosia (2007) goes on to describe mathematics education as a lever for the development of the individual, national and global well-being. The importance given to mathematics and mathematics education shows that they are valuable tools in solving problems related to socio-economic and political developments. To yield the positive fruits from mathematics and its education, mathematics teaching should be meaningful to the learners and should be connected to their environment. D'Ambrosio (2002), Bishop (1988) and Cherinda (1994) note that in different regions of the world, situations gave rise to different mathematical practices, mathematical concepts, mathematical problems and their solutions.

The Africans also have their indigenous mathematical practices and applications that need to be attended to. Cherinda (1994) observes that before colonisation, the indigenous people developed mathematics to deal with their local problems and their daily tasks. Joseph (1991) also notes that precolonial indigenous people had a scientific base that was innovative and self-sufficient, but this was destroyed by the intrusion of the Europeans. In this regard, the mathematical experiences that the learners are exposed to in contemporary education institutions do not contextualise pedagogies with the indigenous culture and perceptions and therefore cannot produce productive citizens who can resuscitate the economies of their nations.

Africa is busy promoting colonial ideas by uncritically adopting and perpetuating Western epistemologies. The fact that indigenous people could invent and innovate their own mathematical solutions to their problems means that even today indigenous Africans can recentre their indigenous mathematics to solve their problems. If colonialism had not destroyed indigenous knowledge systems, Africans could be at a more advanced stage and they could be better able to solve their problems. Thus, Ocheni and Nwankwo (2012) recommended that, for the African states to overcome their woes, Africans must recreate their own identity, culture and technology. This chapter argues that indigenous mathematics education can contribute to the creation of this identity, culture and technology - and this begins with the decolonisation of the teacher education curricula.

Harris and Sass (2011) observe that teachers are the key to the quality of an education system. High quality teacher workforce for nations does not happen by chance. Teacher education training should empower the teachers with knowledge and skills to produce productive citizens. Teacher training curricula should produce teachers who promote indigenous contextual learning. D'Ambrosio (2001) states that the important principle of the curriculum is valuing indigenous knowledge systems. This chapter appraises teacher education in relation to the implementation of a Eurocentric mathematics education in African schools. The mathematics curricula in the teacher education institutions are perpetuating the colonial ideas about mathematics resulting in the poor achievement and negative attitudes towards mathematics by the African learners.

This chapter adds to the arguments for the decolonisation of the mathematics curricula in Africa so that mathematics can be used to find solutions to African problems. Wenger in his social learning theory believes that learning is inherently a social process and that it cannot be separated from the social context in which it happens (Smith, Stuart and Lerman, 2003). Learning according to Wenger (1998) must be placed in the context of the learners' day to day life experiences of participation yet this is not the case in our classrooms in the learning and teaching of mathematics. Scholars, according to Gay (2000) and Tate (2005), view cultural bias in mathematics instruction as a major factor affecting the learners' performances in mathematics. This chapter draws its theoretical framework from the culturally responsive pedagogy in which researchers are calling for more appropriate and more responsive learning and teaching practices.

Mathematics teaching and learning is a cultural product and it depends on the culture of those in power. Failure to put the African culture and epistemology at the centre in mathematics curricula contributes to the low performance in the subject. The way mathematics is taught by the teachers shows that though the European colonisers have come and gone, their dominance still lives on through education systems.

The concept curricula of colonisation

Basu (1989) describes colonialism as the establishment of a colony in one territory by a political power from another territory. Enwo-Irem (2013) describes colonisation as the annexation and subsequent dispossession, plunder, exploitation and domination of one country by another. The term colonialism is also used to describe looting, dispossession and unequal relationship between the coloniser and the colonised. In Africa most states were colonised by Western European countries such as Britain, Germany, Italy, Portugal and France. Ochen and Nwanko (2012) note that the first objective in colonialism is dispossession, plunder, looting and political dominance and the second is to make possible the exploitation of the colonised country. To force the Africans to accept and submit to colonial rule, the colonialists employed several strategies and, according to Masaka (2016), the colonial education system was one way that was used successfully for this purpose. This chapter contends that colonialism was essentially about dispossession, robbery, looting, plunder and exploitation of the colonised whose indigenous knowledge was also subjected to biopiracy for centuries.

Baylies and Bujira (1990) argue that the nature of the content of a given curriculum used in each state is primarily a reflection of the culture and ideology of its designers and in the case of the colonised African states the designers where the colonialists. The curriculum in the schools was used as a tool to oppress the indigenous people through content that was meant to make them submit themselves to the colonisers (Ochen and Nwankwo, 2012). The introduction of colonial education led to the abandonment of indigenous technological skills and education systems. This means the Africans were not only colonised politically but also their education systems were colonised. For the purpose of this chapter the curriculum inherited by schools perpetuates the interests of the former colonisers and the mathematics curriculum will be specifically considered. This curriculum is implemented by the teachers who are also a product of a teacher education curricula that perpetuates the colonial perceptions of the mathematics education that considers mathematics as a Eurocentric subject. Gerdes (1988) says the mathematics education in colonial Africa was structured in the interest of the colonisers. D'Ambrosio (1998) supports this notion by acknowledging that mathematics was used as a barrier to social access and describes it as the most effective education filter. The content and the methods used in the teaching and learning of mathematics did not make sense to the indigenous learners since it was divorced from their environment and epistemologies. Most learners viewed mathematics as useless and mathematics anxiety is widespread among the indigenous learners (Gerdes, 1998). Cherinda (2012) notes that mathematics is viewed as something far away from the African culture.

The teachers are entrusted by the society with the transmission of the society's beliefs, attitudes and behaviours needed to be active in society and the economy. Swennen (2008) states that in order to model what the teachers are going to teach, teacher educators need to link the theories and practice to the intended curriculum. This implies that the training of teachers during colonialism perpetuated the interest of the colonial regime. Shizha (2006) argues that, in post-colonial states, the promotion of Eurocentric knowledge and the superiority of Western knowledge is still perpetuated by the education systems. Similarly, Nyamber (1997) contends that curricula in African countries is failing to prepare its graduates for the realities of Africa and its future. Indirectly the failure of the school curricula is, by extension, failure of the teacher training curricula - which needs to be decolonised.

The concept of curricula decolonisation

An education system which derives its content from the epistemological paradigm of the colonisers, in independent African states, is valueless and this is qualified by Bishop (1988) who says mathematical practice is a cultural product. During colonialism the Africans were denied what was termed "quality education" because the few who were privileged to access this education lived a materially better life compared to those who did not. At attaining independence, the African states pushed for Education for All policy without changing the school curricula. According to Shizha (2006) the colonial curricula were extended to all the African people in the independent states. Shizha (2006) further argues that the fundamental problem with colonial education was not access but the irrelevance of the education system to the indigenous people. Today most African states face problems of low attainments in mathematics because the goals, contents and methods of mathematics education are not sufficiently adapted to the cultures and needs of African people (Gerdes, 1994).

To decolonise the mathematics curricula is to invert and reverse the colonial curricula so that it provides answers to the African problems. For Stevens (2008), every culture despite its level of civilisation should have an education system that ensures that it is transmitted, perpetuated and changed in line with prevailing conditions within a given social group. Betrand Russel and Albert Einstein cited in D'Ambrosio (2007:26) opine that a new thinking in mathematics education is needed.

In this chapter, to decolonise the mathematics curricula is to come up with an indigenous culturally centred curricula for training teachers so that all Africans can access mathematics and appreciate the beauty in it. This is in line with Gerdes' (1994) and Gumbo's (2009) arguments that it is necessary to develop culturally based and relevant curricula.

To overcome the obstacles faced in mathematics education, Gerdes (1994) suggests that the mathematical heritage of Africans must be valued and embedded in curricula. Equally, Bertrand Russell and Albert Einstein (cited in D'Ambrosio, 2007:26) support curricula premised on African heritages. For a long time, most Africans have been excluded from the learning of mathematics and African mathematics has been conceived as inferior because of the Eurocentric scholarships and the colonial mind-set which narrowly defined what constituted mathematics literacy. To narrowly interpret mathematics in a Eurocentric way is a great disservice to Africans.

The power of a heritage-based curricula

Moodley (1991) urges Africans to look at the world through cultured eyes and according to him people of Africa can progress if they discover their soul which lies in their heritage or patrimony. Education can be used as a medium of resistance against the foreign cultural dominance. Kelly (2006) (cited by Gumbo, 2006) asserts that education can be used to protect the oppressed cultures. Averil, Anderson Easton, Smith and Hynds (2002) advise that one of the strengths that the learners bring into the classroom is their cultural capital. Similarly, Anderson (2007) acknowledges that identity is an important element in learning therefore the mathematics curriculum should be based on the cultures of the learners for it to be meaningful. It is the aim of this section to expose the power of a heritage/culturally based mathematics curricula.

316

Banks (2008) defines culture as the beliefs, values, attitudes, customs, social relations, art and literature that define an ethnic group of people. Banks (2008) goes on to say many teachers of the subjects such as mathematics and other science subjects tend to have an impression that mathematics is a non-cultural subject. This impression is a result of the way these teachers themselves experienced mathematics both as learners and as teacher trainees. The wildly held negative attitudes towards mathematics and bad performance in mathematics as compared to other subjects in Africa is a result of the discontinuity between school mathematics and the learners' cultures. Presmeg (2007) contends that mathematical learning activities must promote cultural integrity of learners at the same time assuring academic success. Cultural heritage plays an important role in the creation of a curriculum which aims at connecting mathematics and the personal experiences of the learners.

Mathematical concepts based on cultural perspectives, according to d' Entremont (2014), allow learners to reflect and appreciate their cultures as well as the cultures and traditions of other people. In the same vein, Rosa (2010) argues that educators need to understand their own cultures and how cultural biases influence the teaching styles which in turn influence the student academic performance. To maximise the learning opportunities of the learners, teachers should have knowledge of the cultures represented in their classrooms so that they can translate this knowledge in the preparation of meaningful instructional practices. Thus, a culturally responsive teacher recognises, respects and uses students' identities and backgrounds as meaningful sources for creating optimal learning environments (Nieto, 2002).

If learners are exposed to a culturally based mathematics curriculum, they can learn mathematics in a more meaningful and relevant context rather than relying on memorised algorithms. This would motivate learners because mathematics would be brought closer home than being treated as an external subject that has no connection with the learners' life. The teachers need to possess knowledge of the everyday social and cultural contexts of the learners so that they can discover the hidden mathematical knowledge in their everyday experiences.

Mathematics as a subject becomes meaningful to the learners if it is treated as a cultural product. Learners are empowered intellectually, socially, economically and politically by a heritage or patrimony-based curriculum as it improves the understanding of the subject. The learners' attitudes and beliefs about mathematics and their perceptions about their ability to do mathematics are reinforced by the mathematical experiences and behaviours. A heritage-based mathematics curriculum has higher chances of yielding positive reinforcement because mathematics would cease to be a foreign incomprehensible subject.

The bullying nature of western scholarship

According to Pearce (2002) the extreme Eurocentric model asserts that all mathematics is a European product and gives no credit to non-European contribution. The history of human civilisation is presented by the European scholarship as a product of Europe not Africa or any other place. This model represents some of the bullying nature of the European scholarship which pictures Africans as inferior in reason when compared to their White counterparts. Western knowledge based on scientific model was the standard knowledge such that the superiority of Western knowledge was internalised. Knowledge from the indigenous people was classified by the European scholars as folk stories of rituals and beliefs of myths which according to the Western epistemology is not knowledge. They regarded the Africans as incapable of knowing (Shiva, 1998).

Francois and Van (2010) argue that the story of any mathematical practices that did not contribute to the development of Western mathematics gets little or no mention in the classical books. The European scholars exclude the mathematical knowledge and experiences outside of Europe. The history of mathematics in these Non-Western states begins after their encounter with the Europeans as if these people had no mathematical knowledge before this encounter. Wane (2006) acknowledges that the Africans had meaningful and organised ways of living, educating and governing their societies. This counters the notion that knowledge in Africa was

318

brought by the Europeans. When the colonisers set up schools based on the Western models, they deliberately emptied the African content because, to them, that was not knowledge worth to peruse. They destroyed the African sensibilities toward education.

The ideology of European superiority made the indigenous people to associate scientific progress with Eurocentrism. However, case studies by Teresi (2002) indicate the existence of scientific creativity and technological achievement in African and other states long before the incursion of Europeans into these areas. Every society, through the pressures and demand of its environment, has come up with necessary scientific bases to cater for its material requirements. Precolonial Africans had mathematics education, they had inventions that enabled them to deal with their problems; for instance, youths were taught to make rectangular bases for huts (Cherinda, 1981; Gerdes and Cherinda, 1993). Similarly, Bishop (1997) describes some of the mathematical competences that every culture should possess - to be able to respond to problems arising from their environment - which are measuring, counting, designing, playing and explaining.

The irony is that the Greeks are acknowledged as founders of mathematics even though they stole the mathematical knowledge from Egyptians (Joseph, 2016). Developments of mathematics in Egypt and other nations outside Europe are dismissed by Eurocentrists, who sadly assume that they are universal judges.

This chapter advocates for fair treatment of cultures and acknowledgements of their contributions to the body of mathematical knowledge. Learners should be exposed to the truth of the history of the development of mathematics knowledge through multicultural activities. Superiority is not in the race or colour, so for one race to go about bullying the other races and claiming to be superior is not acceptable (D'Ambrosio, 2007). The ideology set by the colonisers that mathematics education is a non-African cultural product has been internalised by some Africans and has blocked some from advancing in mathematics at higher levels of learning; hence the need to decolonise mathematics in Africa.

The bullying nature of the Western scholarship does not end in claiming to be the sole pioneers in the development of mathematical knowledge but is also extended to the philosophies and theories that shape the academic practices. According to Dei (2000), Western colonisation brought with it the Western theories which Africans are not allowed to question but to just apply. Mabeer (2018) says the non-Western theories and curricula ideologies are not recognised and where non-Western philosophy does appear, it is considered as theoretically and methodologically flawed and unreliable. For this reason, Mbembe (2015) notes that the Eurocentric way of doing things is considered as the norm and it is difficult to think outside this frame.

Mental colonisation

The visible political colonisation has come and gone in Africa but there are invisible consequences of colonisation in which the colonised Africans participate wittingly and unwittingly. Apart from the necessity of mental decolonisation, Fanon (cited by d' Errico, 2011:1) wrote: "For colonised people the most essential value, because it is the most concrete, is first and foremost the land: the land which will bring them bread and above all dignity".

One of the invisible colonial consequences is mental colonisation. Most Africans have attained political independence, but mental and material independence are yet to be attained. Freire (2004) says apart from politics and economics, colonialism also encompasses consciousness. Colonial political and economic control could not be successfully attained without the colonisation of the minds of the dispossessed. In this regard, Wane (2006) argues that Western education left spiritual and mental scars that are still mentally and physically harmful to the Africans. It is the aim of this chapter to attempt to decolonise this type of colonisation. Before the discussion on the effects of mental colonisation, the concept of mental colonisation is discussed.

Dascal (2004) defines mental colonisation as the coloniser's interference with the mental faculties of the colonised. For Freire (2004), mental colonisation involves inducing a set of beliefs in the colonised people through a process that is cognitive in nature. Fanon (2004) adds to this view by saying that it is in the habit of the colonised to perpetuate their oppressed condition by striving to emulate the culture and ideas of those that oppress them. The colonisers go out of their way to make the colonised persons to admit that their cultures are inferior and uncivilised. One of the first scholars to study African American history, Dr Carter Woodson (1933) in his very old book "Miseducation of the Negro" says that when one controls a man's thinking, one needs not to worry about his actions because he will find his proper place and will stay in it. This is an indication that the colonisation of the African mind is all that the colonisers needed to control the Africans, and this had a serious impact because this colonisation is still extant in the African schools.

This chapter adopts the above conceptions of mental colonisation where the colonisers are the Western countries and the colonised are the Africans. Colonisation of the mind may take place through transmission of mental habits and contents by means of different social systems (Dackal, 2004). The vehicle used by the colonisers to mentally colonise the Africans is the school, particularly in mathematics education where the teachers are the main drivers of the system. The teachers and the teacher educators are perpetuating mental colonisation in the name of abiding with the school mathematics curriculum or the teacher education curriculum. The colonisers are no longer there to monitor the education system they imposed on Africans, but their education system is still practised.

During the teaching and learning of mathematics, teachers use methods and curricula that intentionally omit and trivialise the role and contribution of the Africans in developing mathematics; they promote the superiority of the European culture. Parry (2007) and Ofori-Attah (2006) describe the colonial teaching methodologies as authoritarian in nature were learners are inhibited from critical thinking. Most learners are made to hate mathematics, they are made to believe that they cannot do mathematics because of the fear instilled in them as a result of the pedagogical strategies by the mathematics teachers in their classrooms. All attention, according to D'Ambrosio (2007), is given to skill and drill which is very much supported by the examination systems in Africa. Efforts and learning resources are aimed at improving scores in the tests and the examinations which are used as a yardstick for mathematics literacy brought about by the colonialists to create the Black elites whom they used to oppress the rest of the Africans. Ralston (2002) argues that raising the scores in tests and examinations is not a sign for mathematics literacy but hide serious learning deficiencies in the mathematical learning of the child as they thwart creativity.

Mignolo (2011) acknowledges that mental colonisation is still alive in most of the African states. The establishment of Western forms of colonial education displaced the indigenous and traditional schools and promoted mental colonisation. Those who completed the colonial schooling system were employed by the colonisers and accorded privileged social statuses and this improved their way of living such that they were emulated by other societal members. In this regard, Hendricks and Leibowitz (2016) state that the few Africans where kept out of higher education or pushed into institutions that were reserved for non-whites, where they were indoctrinated. This is supported by Gerdes (1988) who observes that the colonial education provided to Africans was for indoctrination purposes or to prepare them for jobs in Western styled economy to lure the fellow Africans to give in to mental colonisation.

Education in the minds of the Africans is meant to prepare learners for white collar jobs and this has resulted in high unemployment rates in Africa. We are preparing learners for the jobs that we do not have instead of preparing job creators. Thus, Mbembe (2015) laments that colonialism robbed Africans of ideas, skills, creativity, originality, talent and knowledge. The colonial education system that we inherited as Africans is continuing to produce job seekers.

Residual effects of mental colonisation in the 21st century Africa

Education, according to Freire (1968), is either used as an instrument of integrating the oppressed persons into the logic of the oppressors or as a practice of freedom. The teaching and learning of mathematics during colonialism was used as a tool of promoting inequity in the education system and this still exists in our politically liberated African states. Aguire (2016) describes mathematics learning as a struggle for just outcomes, a struggle for just experiences and equitable treatment and a struggle against limited opportunities. This struggle has been precipitated by the colonisers because according to them the goal of education is to adapt the colonised to their oppressive situation and to plant the ideology that mathematics is difficulty and is meant for few individuals. Freire (2004) gave an analysis of a mind colonising education which he termed the 'The Banking model'. In this model knowledge is deposited by teachers in the minds of the learners. It treats the learner as a passive recipient of knowledge whose duty is to receive, memorise and repeat: learners do not become producers of knowledge.

The Banking system of education, according to Freire (2004), removes the learners from their context. In this vein, Ochen and Nwankwo (2012) acknowledge that before fully embracing colonial education, the Africans were great scientists and technologists. The Africans, before colonialism, were cloth weavers, sculptors, carvers, miners and they practised many other different sorts of arts to provide and satisfy the technological needs to fellow Africans. This technological ability was robbed off from them by the colonial education. According to Ochen *et al.*, (2012) this colonial education was not deeply rooted in African culture and environment which made it to be unsuitable and meaningless in terms of bringing about technological advancement.

Aguire (2016) describes the mathematics education established in the African states as a White institutional space in terms of its demography, ideology and policy. For Akyeampong (2002), school mathematics is viewed as vocational experiences coupled with the examination culture that filters learners towards better paying jobs in the labour market. The prestige associated to occupations that are science and mathematics-based is a residual effect of mental colonisation. Mathematics is viewed as a high-status knowledge subject entitled to be done by a few individuals. As a way of justifying the assumption that mathematics was not for Africans, most schools attended by Africans did not teach the subject in Ghana (Chitumba, 2013). Black learners, according to Thesee (2003), are associated with interest and success in sports, music and dance but not in the sciences. The underrepresentation of Africans in the sciences is a manifestation of the mental colonisation that inculcates inferiority complex among them. The analysis by Ocheni and Nwako (2012) revealed that the dominant role of the African states in the international world as sources of raw materials and consumers of manufactured goods is a result of the long years of colonialism. African states find it difficult to establish industries and to be full manufacturers because in their minds their role is to consume goods that have been manufactured by the superior race. This position is perpetuated by the underrepresentation of Africans in sciences and technology: the pure mathematics they experience in the schools does not promote indigenous development.

Though African states appear to be moving towards technological development, the process is hampered by lack of inventive and innovative African scientists, engineers and technologists. According to Amuche and Musa (2013), the cause of the lack of scientists, engineers and technologists is that the African learners are not equipped with meaningful mathematics. Most studies in Africa have found the causes of poor performance to be associated with the negative attitudes towards the subject, lack of interest, anxiety in mathematics and ineffective teaching methods. For d' Entremont (2015), after learning mathematics in schools all learners should be able to realise the relevance of mathematics in their personal lives and to their communities. According to the National Council of Teachers of Mathematics (2000), this is not possible because the school mathematics exist separate and apart from the cultural contexts in which it is practised. This makes mathematics to be meaningless and detached from the learners' lives thereby making them to lose interest in doing it and finding it difficult to comprehend. Furthermore, Oguniyi (2007) argues that despite concerted efforts by South African government and other African states to encourage teachers to incorporate indigenous knowledge in the teaching of mathematics, teachers continue to resist. Teachers continue using the Western pedagogies because of the pressure to achieve high test scores and good examination results. The downside is, as noted by Nardia and Steward (2003), that these mathematics classrooms characterised by factual recall and procedural understanding lead to the alienation and dissatisfaction of learners. The teachers continue to ignore the cultural profile of the learners because they are not trained to connect mathematics education with African culture. According to Stinson (2012), learning of mathematics presents a traumatic and unfair learning experience yet if connected to the learners' culture it can be enjoyable. For this reason, Parry (2007) observes that colonial teaching emphasised authoritarian teaching styles and rote learning and these methods of teaching are still prevalent in the classrooms thereby facilitating dependence of learners on the teacher: this inhibits critical thinking. Teachers are merely concerned with the mathematical procedures and ignore the fact that the mathematical ideas are developed by people and that these ideas are connected to their cultures.

Considering the foregoing, Noltemeyer, Mujic and Mcloghin (2012), note that the power of the few educated elite served as a mechanism of sustaining disparities in educational access. The most disadvantaged are the economically poor. Learners from such backgrounds are the least likely to benefit from quality education. This class division still exists in the present African states with the elite schools charging exorbitant tuition fees to prevent the economically challenged to enrol in these schools.

Need for decolonisation of mathematics teacher education

The first indigenous leader of the Republic of Congo Patrice Lumumba in his speech in 1960 said: "...we have to rediscover our most intimate selves and rid ourselves of mental attitudes and complexities and habits that colonisation trapped us in for centuries." (D' Errico, 2011:1).

This appeal by Patrice Lumumba indicates that though mental decolonisation is not an easy process, something can be done to decolonise African minds. Kelly (1986) cited in Gumbo (2009) asserts that the function of education can be understood in the light of protecting the oppressed cultures. Mathematics education among African learners, if appropriately planned, can be used as a tool of the decolonisation of minds in Africa. For this reason, Carruthers (1999) opines that the intellectual warfare must begin within the minds of the young warriors who are learners in schools. To achieve decolonisation of the young minds, the minds of the teachers who are the main drivers of the learning process need to be decolonised first. For Hurel (2013), effective learning is a result of effective teaching. In the same vein, Forzani (2009) notes that the improvements in the learning of mathematics depends on how the teachers are prepared in terms of the mathematics content knowledge and pedagogical knowledge. Shizha (2007) suggests that to address the hidden cultural biases in mathematics, teachers must first address their own personal attitudes, and this can only be done during the process of learning to be a teacher.

The teacher education curricula should aim at improving the teachers' situational understanding of mathematics in the African context rather than promoting the exclusion of Africans in the fruitful and meaningful learning of mathematics. Learners' underachievement in school mathematics is attributed to the cultural gaps between the expectations of school curriculum and the environment in which the learners are socialised (Thaman, 2009). For this reason, Akyeampong (2002) notes that in African contexts, no concerted efforts are made to evolve systems of teacher education that are culturally sensitive and relevant to local needs. On the other hand, Akyeampong (2002) blames lack of research in African contexts. The researches relied on by the teacher education curriculum that have been tested and validated in European contexts might not be applicable. In line with the foregoing, Chiromo (1999) revealed that student teachers in Zimbabwe indicated that some of the ideas in the theory of education were not useful during their teaching practice. This could be a result of certain assumptions and issues made in the Western theories that might not be applicable in the African contexts.

According to Lewin and Stuart (2001), studies show that teachers in Africa might be aware of and might appreciate the value of more progressive approaches to teaching in the African context but fail to implement them in their practice. This is due to the teachers' lack of faith in the Africanised mathematics since everything labelled as indigenous is looked down upon and viewed as inadequate (Mwenda 2006). The more these teachers view indigenous knowledge in mathematics education as inadequate and inferior, the more they accept that mathematics education is not for the African child and is of no value in addressing their socio-economic needs. Ukipokodu (2011) researched on why teachers do not engage learners in culturally responsive teaching, and he got the following responses:

- Mathematics is culture free
- Classroom instruction is dominated by the textbook approaches and these do emphasise this approach
- There is a lack of culturally responsive models to emulate
- There is pressure for high scores as determinants of mathematics literacy.

The teachers do not attach their teaching of mathematics to deep understanding of concepts, but they merely drill the learners. The way mathematics is taught in the African schools forces the learners to absorb the mathematics they do not understand thereby inhibiting critical thinking needed to lay foundations for national development. For Sayed and Novelli (2017), the current curriculum in teacher education limits the student teachers' ability to expand their imaginations beyond the conceptual boundaries that colonialism has normalised. The student teachers' capacity to connect the classroom mathematics to the lived experiences of the African learners, is in turn, limited.

The absence of connections between classroom and the African context is explained by Sayed, Motala and Hoffman (2017) who found out that most texts used in South Africa were written by White authors. These texts do not mention anything on African heritage but mere perpetuation of Eurocentric supremacy. Sayed *et al.* (2017) also found out that some White authors appear to place themselves in the positions of Africans. The sad thing is that such authors are not able to communicate from an African perspective because they lack hands-on experience of African realities. The point, as Mikman, Akinola and Chaugh (2012) note, is that there is evidence that the rules of scholarstic excellence are biased along the lines of race and gender. This is supported by Fletcher (2015) who states that most textbooks reviewed in his study perpetuated colonial legacies.

Towards the decolonised teacher education curricula

Teacher education curricula can be used as a mechanism for producing the type of teachers that the society needs. According to Akeye (2002), if the teacher education of any society is poorly conceptualised and structured it can serve as a weak link between a student teacher and the society's expectations. Jadhav and Pantankar (2013) assert that the quality of teachers produced in an institution depends on the curriculum offered to them during their training program. Thus, UNESCO (2005:2) suggests that teacher education addresses environmental, social and economic contexts to create locally relevant and culturally appropriate teacher education curricula. The African conditions, discourses and experiences in education curriculum planning for Africans should inform the curriculum designers so that they stop relying on foreign discourses and policies. Culturally responsive teacher education curriculum is the key to decolonisation of the mathematics curriculum. This is supported by Muniz (2019:7) when he says: "Building a diverse pool of educators who are prepared to demonstrate culturally responsive teaching or relevant teaching...is critical to reversing underachievement and unlocking the potential of students ...."

Muniz (2019) came up with eight competencies that the teacher education programmes should instil among its grandaunts. Below is a summary of these competencies.

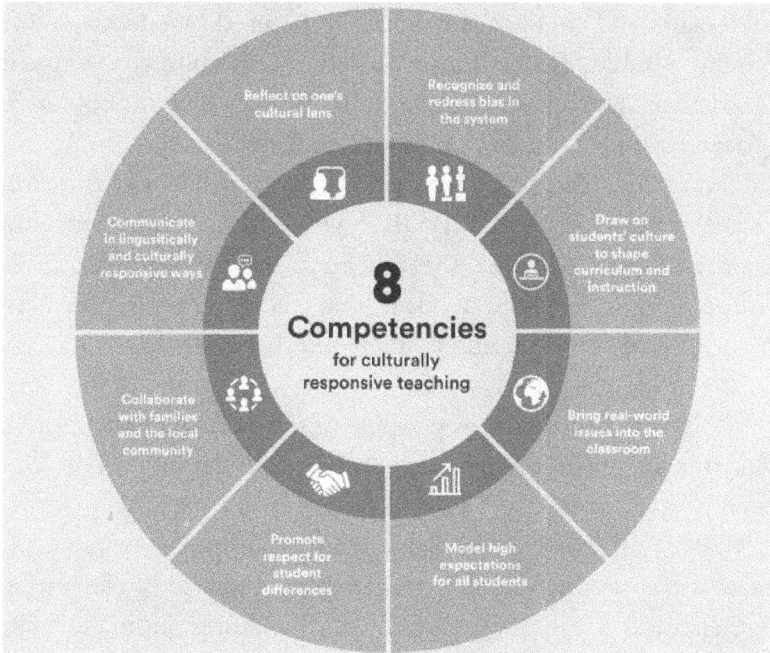

Competencies for culturally responsive teaching adapted from Muniz (2019)

Considering defamiliarisation as a pedagogical technique, Zayd and Waghid (2018) suggest that students should be engaged in particular heightened critical and inclusive participation in the study of social issues, and for this chapter the social issue is making classroom mathematics relevant to the society. Defamiliarisation will enable the student teachers to recognise and redress the biases in the teaching and learning of mathematics. For Kaomesia (2014), defamiliarisation in higher education institutions may assist the educators in looking at familiar objects or texts with an exceptionally high level of awareness. New perceptions can emerge through teaching and guiding the student teachers to resist the existing colonial education practices in mathematics.

To enable teachers to resist colonial practices, Bishop (1991) says one of the important tasks for teacher educators is to help prospective teachers to effectively assume their roles. The prospective teachers should be educated about the cultural aspects of mathematics, African values in mathematics and different histories of mathematics. For this to happen, the pre-service teacher education should provide appropriate experiences. The literature for referencing and sources of material to be used by educators during training should foster the acquisition of culturally embedded knowledge. The libraries should be furnished with books from African authors and researches done in Africa.

The teacher should understand the cultural diversity of learners. According to Scott (2001) this knowledge creates favourable communication between the teacher and the learners. Besides, Bishop (1997: 7) suggests ideas that can be injected into every mathematical course during training and these are:

- Keeping as much as possible of the cultural context involved with the activity as the meaning and significance of each activity is given by its context.
- Including locally available material resources or pictures for those objects that cannot be brought into the classes since mathematical ideas are represented in cultures in many cultural artefacts.

According to Gerdes (1988), cultural mathematics reaffirmation plays an important part in cultural rebirth. Mathematics education should include inventing and discovering of mathematical knowledge hidden in the African cultural artefacts/technologies. During training the prospective teachers must be encouraged to investigate mathematics embedded in the socio-cultural environment (Bishop, 1999). The research outcomes should be made accessible to schools and teacher training institutions. In addition, Gerdes (1999) suggests that teachers on training should be encouraged to produce local materials for the teaching and learning of mathematics. The accessibility of locally available teaching resources will also reduce the domination of Eurocentric textbook approaches in the mathematics classroom and learners will find meaning in mathematics problems. Textbooks have presented mathematics as a series of meaningless procedures with no relation to African lives (Nyamukye, 2010).

Conclusion

Schools are supposed to be viewed as privileged centres for transmission and perpetuation of cultural heritage or patrimony of all learners rather than hero worshipping the supremacy of a particular race. The mathematical heritage of the Africans must be valued, and African cultures must be embedded into the mathematics teacher education curriculum. Mathematics education promotes the learners' understanding of their lives and the world if there is connection with their everyday experiences.

Teacher education is linked with the preparation of future citizens therefore it should reflect what is currently important to the nations which they serve. Africa presently needs youths that are creative and innovative. The teacher education programs for training mathematics teachers should equip the teachers with skills and knowledge of centring indigenous mathematics.

References

Aguirre J. M. (2015). Enhancing the Common Core with Culturally Responsive Mathematics Teaching: Key Principles and Strategies. National Council of Teachers of Mathematics Grades 3-8 Summer Institute Anaheiim, C A.

Akyeampong, A. K (2002). Reconceptualising teacher education in the Sub-Sahara Africa context. *Journal of International Co-operation in Education*, vol 5 (1):11-50.

Australian Education Council (1991). A National Statement on Mathematics for Australian Schools. Carlton Curriculum Co-operation.

Banks, J. A. (2008). *An introduction to multicultural education*. Pearson Education.

Basu, A. (1989). Indian higher education colonialism and beyond, in Altibach, P.G., Salvaralnam, V. (eds) *From Dependence to Autonomy*. Springler. Dordrecht. https// doi.org/10.1007/978-94-009-2563-2-7

Bernstein, B. (2000). *Pedagogy, symbol control and identity. Theory, research and critique.* Lahan: Rowman and Littlefield.

Bishop, A. (1997). The relationship between mathematics education and culture, opening address delivered at the Iranian Mathematics Education conference in Kermanshah, Iran

Bishop, A. J. (1988). *Mathematical enculturation: a cultural perspective on mathematics education.* Dordrecht: Kluwer.

Bishop, A. J. (1991). *Mathematical enculturation: A cultural perspective on maths education.* Dordrecht: Kluwer.

Brodie, K. (2000). Mathematics teacher development in under resourced contexts: A case study, in Mahlomaholo, S. (ed) Proceedings of the eighth meeting of the Southern Africa Association for Research in Mathematics and Science Education

Brodie, K (2016). Yes, Mathematics can be decolonise. Here's how to begin The Conversation. https://theconversation.com/yes-mathematics-can-be-decolonised-heres-how

Cherinda, M. (1994). Children's mathematic activities stimulated by an analysis of African cultural elements, in Julie, C. *et al.,* (eds). Proceedings of the 2nd International conference on the Political Dimensions of Mathematics Education. Curriculum reconstruction for society and transition. Cape Town: Maslew Miller Longman, 142-148

Chiromo, A, S. (1999). Teacher education courses in relation to preparation for teaching practice: view from student teachers in Zimbabwe. *Journal of Education Research* vol 11(1): 58-69.

Chitumba, W. (2013). University education for personhood through Ubuntu. *Journal of Asian Social Sciences* vol 3(5): 1268-1776.

D'Ambrosio, U. (2006). Ethno mathematically link between traditions and Modernity. *ZDM* vol40: 1033-1034.

D'Ambrosio, U. (1997) Ethno mathematics and its place in the history and pedagogy of mathematics, in Powel, A. B. & Frankenstein, M. (eds) *Ethno Mathematics. Challenging Eurocentrism in Mathematics Educations.* Albany: State University of New York Press.

D'Errico, P. (2011). What is a colonised mind? Academia edu retrieved from https:www. Academia.edu.

Darling-Hammond, L. (2000). Teacher quality and student achievement: A review of state policy evidence. *Education Policy Analysis Archives* vol 8(1) Retrieved from http://epaa.asu.edu/epaa/V8n1

Dascal, M. (2007). *Colonising and decolonising minds.* New York Times.

Dei, G. J. S. (2004). *Schooling and education in Africa: the case Ghana.* Trenton NJ: Africa world Press.

Del, G. J. S. (2000). Rethinking the role of indigenous knowledge in the academy. *International Journal for inclusive Education* vol 4(2):111-132.

Del, S. G. J. (2002). African development: The relevance and implications of indigenous, in G.J.S Del, G. J. S. & Rosenberg D. G. (ed) *Indigenous knowledge, in global contexts: multiple readings of our world.* Toronto: University of Toronto Press.

Department of Basic Education. (2011). Report on the National Annual Assessment of 2011

Enwo-Irem, I. N. (2013). *Colonialism and Education: The challenges for Sustainable Development* in Nigeria. Mediterranean Journal of social sciences vol 4, No

Freire, P. (2004). *Pedagogy of the indignation.* Boulder, Co: Paradigm publishers.

Gay, G. (2000). *Culturally responsive teaching theory research and practice.* New York.

Gay, G. (2010). *Culturally responsive.* New York: Teachers College Press.

Gerdes, P. (1998). *Ethnomathematics and education in Africa.* Sweden: Institute of International Education, Stockholm University.

Gerdes, P. (1985). Conditions strategies for emancipatory mathematics education\\n in undeveloped Countries. *For the Learning of Maths* vol 5(1): 15-21.

Gerdes, P. (1988). On cultures, geometrical thinking and mathematics education. *Educational Studies in Mathematics,* vol 12 (2): 137-162.

Gerdes, P. (1995). *Ethnomathematics and education in Africa.* Sweden: Stockholm University.

Heleta, S. (2016). Dismantling epistemic Decolonization of higher education violence and Eurocentrism in South Africa. *Transformation in Higher Education* vol 1: 1-8.

Harris, D. N. and Sass, T. R. (2011). Teacher training, teacher quality and student achievement. *Journal of Public Economics*, vol 95(7-8): 798-812.

Joseph, D. (2005). Localising indigenous knowledge systems down under, sharing my different worlds with one voice, indenting. *African Journal of Indigenous Knowledge Systems*, vol 4(1): 295-305.

Joseph, G. G. (2016). Foundations of eurocentrism in mathematics, downloaded from rac. Sagepub.com at Pennsylvania State University

Kaomesi, J. (2014). Reading erasures and making strange: Defamiliarisation methods for research in formally colonised and historically oppressed communities. *Education Researcher*, vol 32(2): 14-25.

Lerman, S. (2000). The social turn in mathematics education research in Boaler, J. (ed) *Multiple Perspectives on Mathematics Teaching and Learning*. Westport: C T Albex Publishing.

Lerman, S. (2001). A review of research perspectives on mathematics teacher education, in Lin, F. L. and Cooney, T. (eds) *Making Sense of Mathematics Teacher Education*. Dordrecht: Kluwer.

Mahabeer, P. (2018). Curriculum decision makers on decolonising the teacher education Curriculum. *South African Journal of Education* vol 38 .4 Pretoria retrieved from https://dx.dol.org/10.15700/Saje.v 38n4a 1705

Mbembe, A. (2015). *Rhodes must fall* in conservation with Achille Mbembe, Part 1 Filmed by Wandile Kasibe, Accessed at: Http://wwwyoutube.com/watch?v=giu4BCsL8w feature YouTube g data player

Mbembe, A. (2016). Decolonizing the University: New directions, Arts and Humanities. *Higher Education* vol 15(1): 29-45.

Mignolo, W. (2007). Introduction. *Cultural studies*, vol 21(2-3): 155-167.

Milkman, K., Akindala, M. & Chaugh, D. (2012). Temporal distance and discrimination: Audit study in academia. *Psychological Science,* vol 23(7): 710-17.

Moodley, K. (1991). The Continued impact of Black consciousness in South Africa. *The Journal of Modern African Studies* vol 29 (2): 237-251.

Muday, V. (2004). Modelling of real-world problems is often the starting point for proof. *Pythagoras* vol 60: 36-43.

Mulenga, T. M. and Luangala, J. R. (2015). Curriculum design in contemporary teacher education: What makes job analysis a vital preliminary Ingredients? *International Journal of Humanities Social Sciences and Education* vol 2 (1): 39 – 51.

Muni, Z. J. (2019). *Culturally responsive teaching:* a 50-State Survey of Teaching Standards newamerica.org/education/policy/culturally-responsive teaching.

Mwenda, A. (2003). The challenges of education and development in post-colonial Kenya. *Africa Development*: 28-34.

NCTM. (2000). *Principles and standards for school mathematics.* Reslon 2VA:

Nieto, S. (2010*). Language, culture and teaching critical perspectives.* New York: Taylor and Francis.

Nieto, S. (2002). Equity and opportunity: Profoundly multicultural questions. *Educational Leadership* vol 60(4): 6-10.

Nkomo, M. (2000). Educational research in the African development context, in Higgs, P.(ed). *Africa Voices in Education.* Cape Town: Juta.

Noltemeyer, A. L., Mujic, J. & McLoughin, C. S. (2012). *Dispropriatinally in education and special education.* Springfield: Charles C. Thomal Publishers Ltd.

Ochen, S., Nwankwo, B. C. (2012). Analysis of colonialism and its impact in Africa. *Cross Cultural Communication* vol 18, (3): 46-54.

Phillips, J. & Whatman, S. (2007*). Decolonising preservice teacher education, Reform many cultural interfaces Dater presented at the American* educational research association meeting Chicago, USA, retrieved from http;//eprints.co.qut.edu.qu/7333/

Pillay, S. (2015). Decolonising the University. Azawa House Branma Building. University of Cape Town. http://africacountry.com

Plevitz, L. (2007). Systematic racism: The hidden barrier to educational success for indigenous school students. *Australia Journal of Education*. Vol 51(1): 54-71.

Presmeg, N. (2007). The role of culture in teaching and learning mathematics, in Lester, F. Jr (ed), *Second Handbook of Research on Mathematics Teaching and Learning*. Reston: VA; NCTM.

Sayed, Y., Motala, S. & Hoffman, N. (2017). Decolonising initial teacher education in South Africa Universities: *More than on event Journal of Education* vol 68 http://joe.ukzn.ac.za

Shiva, V. (2002). Cultural diversity and the politics of knowledge, in Dei, G. J. S. *et al.,* (eds) *Indigenous Knowledges in Global Contexts: Multiple Readings of Our World*. Toronto: University of Toronto Press.

Shizha, E. (2006). Legitimizing indigenous knowledge in Zimbabwe: A theoretical analysis of post-colonial school knowledge and its colonial legacy. *Journal Contemporary Education* vol 1(1): 21-35.

Swennen, A. (2008). Preach what you teach! *Teacher Educators and congruent teaching* vol 14: 531-542. retrieved from https://doi.org./10.1080/1354600802571387

Tate, W. F. (2005). Race, retrenchment and the reform of school mathematics, in Gustein, E. and Peterson, B. (eds). *Rethinking Mathematics Teaching for Social Justice by Members*. Milwaukee: WI Rethinking Schools Publications.

Tato, M.T., Lerman, S., & Novotna, J. (2010). The organisation of the mathematics preparation and development of teachers: a report from ICME study. *Journal Maths Teacher Education*. Vol 13: 313-324 Doi 10.1007/s 10857-009-9139-7.

Ukipokodu, O. N. (2011). How do l teach mathematics in a cultural responsive way identifying empowering teaching practices. *Journal of Praxis in Multicultural Education*, vol 8(2): 1-21.

UNESCO. (2015). *Incheon Declaration Education 2030. Towards inclusive and equitable Quality Education and Lifelong Learning for All UNESCO*. Paris

Wane, N. N. (2006). African women and spirituality: connection between thought and education, in O'Sullivan, E. *et al.,* (eds) *Expanding the Boundaries of Transformative Learning*. New York: Palgrave Macmillan.

Wenger, E. (1998). *Communities of practice; learning, meaning and identity.*
New York: Cambridge University Press.

www.ingramcontent.com/pod-product-compliance
Lightning Source LLC
Chambersburg PA
CBHW060024030426

42334CB00019B/2173